# BUDDH

## THERAVADA BUDDHISM AND MODERNIST REFORM IN THAILAND

SILKWORM BOOKS

ISBN 974-7551-91-8

This edition first published by Silkworm Books in 2003

Silkworm Books
104/5 Chiang Mai–Hot Road, M. 7, T. Suthep, Muang,
Chiang Mai 50200, Thailand
E-mail address: silkworm@loxinfo.co.th
Website: http://www.silkwormbooks.info

Typeset by Silk Type in Garamond 11 pt.
Cover photograph: Buddhadāsa at Suan Mokh © by Feature Magazine
Printed in Thailand by O. S. Printing House, Bangkok

# CONTENTS

# FOREWORD TO THE FIRST EDITION

THE TEST of greatness for any philosophy or religious system is the success with which it enunciates principles of such universality that their validity persists through the change and flux of human life across the ages. The comprehensive reinterpretation of the Theravada Buddhist doctrine to which the Venerable Buddhadāsa devoted more than half a century reaffirms the rich vitality of that canon as a source of guidance to humankind even two and a half millennia after the Buddha promulgated his teachings.

Buddhadāsa's life work was to demonstrate the compatibility of Theravada tenets with modern scientific rationalism, the accessibility to ordinary persons of the highest goals of Buddhist teachings, and the integral relationship within a religious context between ultimate human salvation and the development of a more just and equitable socioeconomic order in the world of here and now. Theravada Buddhism is shown to be the edifying refuge both of mystics whose sight is fixed on the ultramundane and of workaday people in the street or field striving for a better condition of life.

Buddhadāsa's attainments won him high praise and a dedicated following. Conversely, the originality of his perceptions and the boldness of his insights have raised questions among those of traditionalist inclination, while certain of his methods of analysis and the broad philosophical spectrum from which he bolsters his arguments have stimulated a variety of comment. Peter Jackson, the author of this comprehensive and profound study of Buddhadāsa's thought, thus approaches his task with what he felicitously describes as "sympathetic engagement," giving full credit to the vigour, humanitarianism, and depth of Buddhadāsa's theses, while bringing a scholar's constructive criticism to bear where he feels it warranted.

Dr. Jackson is a philosopher by intellectual bent and disciplined training. He is also a lucid writer who, while making no facile concessions to oversimplification, presents the substance of his analysis with such clarity and logic that it is assimilable by the interested layman while amply satisfying the demands of rigourous scholarship. His work in making Buddhadāsa's distinguished reinterpretive contributions more widely available to an international readership is timely, commendable, and important. I am most happy to take the opportunity to introduce it to the public as the latest in the series of publications issued by the Siam Society under Royal Patronage.

Professor Sanya Dharmasakdi
President of the World Fellowship of Buddhists
Bangkok, 10 May 2531 B.E. (1988)

# PREFACE TO THE SECOND EDITION

THE FIRST edition of this book, published by the Siam Society in Bangkok in 1988 under the title *Buddhadāsa: A Buddhist Thinker for the Modern World*, has been out of print for almost a decade. However, Buddhadāsa Bhikkhu's reinterpretations of Theravada Buddhist teachings in Thailand remain as intellectually and socially important at the beginning of the twenty-first century as they were when the research for this book was begun almost two decades ago. It is especially gratifying for an author when his first book can retain a degree of current relevance even after such a number of years and I wish to thank both the Siam Society and Silkworm Books for giving me the opportunity to emend and expand upon the first edition.

This book is an edited version my doctoral dissertation, "Buddhadāsa and Doctrinal Modernisation in Contemporary Thai Buddhism," completed in the Australian National University's Department of Philosophy at the beginning of 1986. It is based on two years of field research conducted in Thailand. The first research period was from 1982 to 1983, when I was attached to Silpakorn University at Nakhon Pathom. My second period of research was undertaken from 1984 to 1985, when as a recipient of a Royal Thai Government UNESCO Fellowship I was attached to the Philosophy Department of Chulalongkorn University in Bangkok.

The studies detailed here to a large extent reflect the political, economic, and social situation in Thailand in the first half of the 1980s, when my fieldwork was conducted. While the Cold War was soon to end and Thailand was about to embark upon its decade-long economic boom, internationally and in Southeast Asia the first half of the 1980s was still dominated by the titanic clash between capitalism and communism, liberal democracy and socialist autocracy. Debates over globalization, the economic crisis of the late 1990s, and the security issues posed since 11 September 2001 were challenges of the even more remote future. While a few errors in the first edition have been corrected and some minor stylistic matters have been addressed, I have not altered the main body of the text or attempted to reflect on Buddhadāsa's position and relevance in the rapidly changing situation of the new millennium.

This text presents a historical snapshot of Buddhadāsa's ideas and his intellectual, social, and political influence in the final decade of his life. It reflects on Buddhadāsa's lifetime of thought, writing, and teaching at a point in time when he was still a living presence in the religious, intellectual, and political life of Thailand. Sadly, Buddhadāsa left this world in 1993, some ten years after I met him at his forest monastery of Suan Mokh in southern Thailand's Suratthani Province. However, I have decided to keep the references to Buddhadāsa in the present tense and have not revised the text to write of him in the past tense. This is because to large numbers of Buddhadāsa's followers in Thailand indeed he remains a living presence. Buddhadāsa's ideas continue to resonate through the discourses that surround new social trends such as the NGO movement and the rise of Thailand's civil society, the on-going struggles against bureaucratic and political corruption, money politics and autocratic tendencies, and the intense debates about the challenges to national autonomy and cultural integrity posed by globalization.

A new epilogue summarizing the contentious issues surrounding Buddhadāsa's death in 1993 and reflecting on his relevance to Thailand in the era of globalization is also included here. This epilogue was written in 1994 at the suggestion of several members of the Publications Committee of the Siam Society, and it first appeared in the society's Journal. I wish to thank the Siam Society for permission to include this article here. However, even this "new" chapter is now something of an historical document, given that it was written at the height of the economic boom before the disastrous crash and the years of national soul-searching that enveloped Thailand after July 1997. Despite the fact that rapidly changing socioeconomic and political events have outpaced some of the issues raised in the epilogue, I hope that readers may nevertheless find it an interesting and useful document.

It is arguably better for an author to revisit his older texts by way of appending a new commentary rather than by attempting to revise the entirety of those texts in a vain attempt to reflect all the nuances of changed conditions and new understandings. There is value in remaining true to the historical moment in which an idea was first expressed and when a study was initially undertaken in order to record the way the world once was and the ways we once thought. Buddhadāsa's greatness emerges from the fact that his ideas were relevant in his own lifetime and have remained just as relevant after his passing. I hope that contemporary and future students of Buddhadāsa's thought may find this 1980s text and its 1990s epilogue useful in developing their own critical understandings of "Than Achan's" continuing contribution to Thailand's intellectual life and to Buddhism's place in the lives of people across the world.

I would also like to take the opportunity provided by this second edition to thank Dr. Tony Diller for his tremendous encouragement and support during my time as a doctoral student at the Australian National University. I did not thank Tony sufficiently in the acknowledgements included in the first edition. Without Tony's tuition and professional support this book would never have been written. I learnt Thai from Tony, who generously provided daily one-on-one language tuition over my first summer at ANU. And it was Tony who first brought Buddhadāsa's books to my attention when he pointed out the unusual ways that the monk used the Thai language to communicate his ideas on Buddhist doctrine. It was also Tony's sage advice that I relied upon in organizing my first tentative fieldwork visit to Thailand. Indeed, generations of Australian students have Tony to thank for opening their eyes and minds to "Amazing Thailand" and with his retirement from the ANU's Thai Language Department he will be a much-missed teacher and colleague.

Since the first edition of this book was published I have come to know many more wonderful scholars of Thai religion and Thai history whose ideas, comments, and wisdom I have drawn upon in my subsequent research. Those who have been especially helpful in the writing of the epilogue are Craig Reynolds, Grant Olson, Phra Santikaro Bhikkhu, Louis Gabaude, and Jim Taylor. My debt of gratitude to these scholars for their collegial support in the never-finished academic enterprise can be summed up in the following words of the French thinker, Georges Bataille.

> The foundation of one's thought is the thought of another; thought is like a brick cemented into a wall. It is a simulacrum of thought if, in his looking back on himself, the being who thinks sees a free brick and not the price this semblance of freedom costs him: he doesn't see the waste ground and the heaps of detritus to which a sensitive vanity consigns him with his brick.
>
> The work of the mason, who assembles, is the work that matters .... A philosophy is never a house; it is a construction site.
>
> —Georges Bataille, "Introduction" to *Theory of Religion*

Peter Jackson
Canberra
November 2001

# ACKNOWLEDGEMENTS IN THE FIRST EDITION

I WISH to thank the following people for their cooperation and assistance during the research and production of this work, both in Australia and in Thailand.

In Australia: Dr. Nerida Cook, Dr. Tony Diller, Mr. William Ginnane, Mr. Preecha Juntanamalaga, Dr. Barend Jan Terwiel, Dr. Gehan Wijeyewardene.

In Thailand: Achan Banyat Ruangsi, Achan Bamrung Torut, Achan Sa-ngiam Torut, Associate Professor Sunthorn Na Rangsi, Buddhadāsa Bhikkhu, Phra Thepwethi (Prayut Payutto).

# NOTE ON TRANSLITERATION AND REFERENCING

EXCEPT WHERE there is an established convention, such as where Thai authors have already decided on the spelling of their names in English, Thai terms are transcribed according to the Thai Royal Institute system and not in the Pali or Sanskritized forms sometimes used. Where in quotations from English language sources other authors have followed different transliteration systems, their slight variations are retained. What differences do result are few and minor and easily traceable. In keeping with their traditional canonical and literary languages, Theravada and Mahayana Buddhist technical terms are written in their Pali and Sanskrit forms, respectively. For example, the Pali term *nibbāna* is always used to refer to the Theravada notion of salvation, while the related Sanskrit term *nirvāṇa* is always used to refer to ultimate salvation as conceived within Mahayana Buddhism.

These linguistic differences are retained because such cognate terms often have different nuances in the two traditions, the most notable example in this work being the differences between the notion of "voidness" in Theravada Buddhism (Pali: *suññatā*) and in Mahayana Buddhism (Sanskrit: *śunyatā*) discussed in chapter 7. I do not follow the custom of many authors who give Theravada technical terms in artificial Sanskrit forms, but where in quotations and references other authors have used Sanskrit forms for Theravada terms those forms are kept for accuracy's sake.[1]

Below is a short list of some of the most common Pali terms used in this work and their cognate Sanskrit forms sometimes used as alternatives.

| PALI | SANSKRIT |
|---|---|
| *attā* | *atman* |
| *cakkavattin* | *cakravartin* |
| *dhamma* | *dharma* |
| *jhāna* | *dhyāna* |
| *kamma* | *karma* |
| *nibbāna* | *nirvāṇa* |
| *sutta* | *sutra* |
| *tipiṭaka* | *tripiṭaka* |

In keeping with the analytical focus on Thai Buddhism in this work, references to and quotations from the *Tipiṭaka,* the canonical Theravada scriptures, are wherever possible taken from the Thai version of the canon. Throughout this work all references to the *Tipiṭaka* are to the forty-five-volume *Phra Traipidok Phasa Thai Chabap Luang* (พระไตรปิฎกภาษาไทยฉบับหลวง – The official Thai language edition of the *Tipiṭaka*) published by the Thai Department of Religious Affairs in B.E. 2535 (A.D. 1982).[2] In referring to this Thai edition of the *Tipiṭaka,* I follow the Thai system of citing sections of the scriptures or *suttas* by: volume/verse/page.[3] In a very few places where it was deemed appropriate, the Pali Text Society's English translations of the *Tipiṭaka* have been referred to instead of the Thai version.

I follow the custom of using the first names of Thai nationals as the formal style of address, although in most cases both given and family names are provided for clarity's sake. For non-Thais I follow the Western custom of using surnames as the formal style of address. For example, the Thai author Sulak Sivaraksa is referred to as Sulak while the English author Trevor Ling is referred to as Ling.

Because of the varied nature of the Thai and English language sources referred to and because of the different bibliographical conventions used for describing works in the two languages I have had to use special footnoting and bibliographical systems capable of fully documenting my source materials. Two separate bibliographies are listed at the end of this book, the first for English language materials referred to in the text and the second for Thai language materials. References in the body of the text to Thai language materials as well as quotations translated from Thai sources are marked with a bracketed capital T, i.e. (T), indicating that the relevant bibliographical details are found in the Thai language bibliography. All Thai language bibliographical details are given in Thai script as well as being transliterated into Roman script. The translated titles of Thai works are also given in brackets. Following the Thai custom, materials in the Thai language bibliography are arranged in Thai alphabetical order according to the author's first name, not according to the author's surname.

Some Thai authors cited below have written books both in English and in Thai. For such authors, Thai language works are listed alphabetically according to their first name.

Many Thais prefer to spell their names in English according to the Thai spelling rather than according to the actual pronunciation. Because Thai names often include silent letters when written in Thai script such English versions often vary significantly from the actual pronunciation. For example, the monk referred to in this work as Buddhadāsa, which is that monk's own preferred spelling of his name in English, is in Thai referred to as Phutthathat, and the monk Rajavaramuni is referred to in Thai as Ratchaworamuni. Where a person has already decided on the English spelling of his or her name I respect that non-phonetic convention in the body of the text and in footnoting and bibliographical details for his or her English language works. However, to retain such non-phonetic conventions when detailing Thai language materials would introduce severe contradictions and breach the Thai alphabetical ordering of the Thai language bibliography. Consequently, in the bibliographical details given for the Thai language works of such authors in the Thai language bibliography all names are spelt phonetically. Some of the most common differences in the spelling of Thai names found in this text are listed below:

| ENGLISH CONVENTION | PHONETIC THAI SPELLING |
| --- | --- |
| Buddhadāsa | Phutthathat |
| Bodhirakśa | Phothirak |
| Kukrit Pramoj | Khukrit Pramot |
| Rajavaramuni | Ratchaworamuni |
| Sulak Sivaraksa | Sulak Siwarak |

# INTRODUCTION

SINCE THE early 1970s the thought of the Buddhist monk Buddhadāsa[1] has become a primary focus of debates about Theravada Buddhist doctrine in Thailand. Buddhadāsa began to systematically reappraise and reinterpret Theravada Buddhist teachings in 1932, and some of his sermons and articles were published in local Buddhist journals in the 1930s and 1940s. However, it was not until the late 1960s and early 1970s, in particular during the period of civilian government from 1973 until 1976, that Buddhadāsa's ideas found a broader national audience in Thailand. This is because it has only been during the last couple of decades, in response to the rapid socioeconomic development of the country, that considerable numbers of fellow Thais have come to share the modernist and reformist views on Buddhism that Buddhadāsa has been propounding for over fifty years.

Buddhadāsa has been hailed as a progressive reformer and even a genius by his supporters and followers. His critics, however, have labelled him a dangerous heretic whose work subverts both the teachings of the Buddha and the institution of Buddhism in Thailand. But whatever the status of such conflicting claims, it is nevertheless still the case that no serious study of the interpretation of Buddhist doctrine in contemporary Thailand can omit a consideration of Buddhadāsa's views without being left deficient and inadequate. This is true whether one's interests lie in the area of

Buddhist doctrine and accounts of salvation and spiritual practice, or whether one is concerned with issues such as the role of Buddhist monks and laypeople in modern Thai society, for Buddhadāsa's reinterpretative work covers all areas of Buddhist doctrine and practice. Indeed, Buddhadāsa's life work can be regarded as an attempt to develop a thorough reinterpretation of the entire body of Theravada doctrine, including both the soteriological and the social aspects of Buddhist teachings. Not since the *Visuddhimagga*, written by Buddhaghosa in Ceylon in the fifth century of the Christian era, has there been such a comprehensive attempt to systematically reinterpret the entirety of Theravada doctrine in the light of contemporary views and expectations.

I believe that both the theoretical and social implications of Buddhadāsa's work are of equal importance, and that it is necessary to consider both of these aspects when analysing the complex and multifaceted phenomenon of his six decades of scholarly activity. Consequently, I take the starting point of this study to be the total phenomenon of Buddhadāsa and his reinterpretative work, a phenomenon which at one and the same time has theoretical and doctrinal as well as social and political significance in contemporary Thailand. The goal of this work is, firstly, to systematically describe the details of Buddhadāsa's doctrinal reinterpretations and, secondly, to evaluate the import and significance of his views and theories in modern Thailand.

A major part of this study is devoted to the simple presentation of Buddhadāsa's views, because no systematic overview of the details of his various theories and reinterpretations has previously been published. In order to evaluate Buddhadāsa's theoretical and sociopolitical importance it is necessary to construct an overview of his arguments and to isolate the theoretical emphases of his work from his voluminous writings, which include pamphlets and theoretical tracts as well as reports of his many talks and sermons. Buddhadāsa himself has not presented a summary or guide to the total system of his views, which has developed organically over the decades. Consequently, the various theoretical foci chosen as the bases of the following chapters represent my own interpretation of what Buddhadāsa has said and argued.

The theoretical foci of Buddhadāsa's work which I have chosen as the bases of this analysis are:

(1) Buddhadāsa's theory of scriptural interpretation, called *phasa khon–phasa tham* (chapter 3);
(2) his criticisms of traditionally accepted canonical scriptures and commentaries, especially the *Abhidhammapiṭaka* and the *Visuddhimagga* (chapter 4);
(3) his reinterpreted theory of salvation based on the notion of *chit wang*, "voided mind" or "freed mind" (chapter 5);
(4) the system of practices presented as leading to the attainment of salvation or *nibbāna* by the development of *chit wang* (chapter 6);
(5) the influence of Zen and Mahayana Buddhist notions on his reinterpretations of Theravada doctrine (chapter 7);
(6) the social doctrine that emerges from Buddhadāsa's system of thought (chapter 8); and
(7) Buddhadāsa's comments on and criticisms of political activity and political involvement (chapter 9).

In reinterpreting the totality of Theravada doctrine, Buddhadāsa is fundamentally concerned to shift the focus of Thai Buddhism from the transcendent to this world, and to incorporate the hopes and aspirations of contemporary Thai laymen and laywomen into Buddhism by conferring religious value on action in the social world. However, to do this Buddhadāsa must move the entire theoretical structure of Buddhism, or to use another structural metaphor, he must rebuild Buddhist doctrine upon the new theoretical foundations that he lays. In this study I consider the entirety of this theoretical reconstruction of Buddhism, plotting the contours of the new vision of Buddhism revealed in Buddhadāsa's work, and also revealing the major weaknesses of this new edifice.

## METHOD OF ANALYSIS

While it is important to isolate the theoretical pivots upon which Buddhadāsa constructs his system (these pivots form the bases for the following chapters as briefly outlined above), a simple study of the explicit details of Buddhadāsa's thought would not reveal its full significance. It is important that any account of Buddhadāsa's system should reveal the underlying and often implicit themes which provide the framework of his broad and diverse body of thought. The significance of his theories and ideas can often only be comprehended when their relation to general underlying themes is made manifest, themes whose provenance lies outside of Buddhism in contemporary changes in Thai society.

Two broad themes underlie all of Buddhadāsa's reinterpretations of Buddhist doctrine. The first theme is Buddhadāsa's desire for Buddhist teachings to conform to rational and scientific standards of argumentation and analysis. This desire is demonstrated forcefully in his systematic demythologization of Buddhist doctrine and in his reduction of all supernatural conditions and non-empirical entities described in the Buddhist scriptures to psychological states. Buddhadāsa reinterprets the traditional cosmology of Theravada Buddhism, which describes successive rebirths over eons in an elaborately structured cosmos of heavens and hells, as occurring within the mental scope of human beings alive on earth here and now. The second and related theme informing Buddhadāsa's work is his wish for Buddhism to retain its social relevance in contemporary Thailand in the face of rapid socioeconomic development and cultural change. Buddhadāsa believes Buddhism should demonstrate its ongoing relevance to human life and aspirations by providing a moral and ideological basis for action in the social world which simultaneously promotes both the progressive development of society and the individual attainment of spiritual salvation. The theoretical development of each of these themes, the desire for rationalism and for contemporary social relevance, requires a radical departure from traditional Theravada teachings, and in order to develop and justify his views within the conservative Thai Buddhist context Buddhadāsa has been forced to take an equally radical approach to the interpretation of doctrine.

The sources of Buddhadāsa's concern with rationalism and the social relevance of the religion lie outside of Buddhist doctrine in the realm of contemporary social relations and social change. His ideas can be regarded as responding to the cultural and religious challenges presented by socioeconomic development and modernization in Thailand. Consequently, it is impossible to limit this study to a purely theoretical or philosophical analysis. The methodology of this analysis of Buddhadāsa's work matches the actual character of his work by integrating both a social and a philosophical or theoretical approach.

A combined social and philosophical study of Buddhadāsa's work is also necessary because of the character of Thai Buddhism as a living religious tradition. Buddhism is arguably the most important cultural institution in Thai society, and the teachings of the Buddha and the formal institution of the monkhood or Sangha remain the basis not only of everyday social relations in Thailand but also of the Thai political structure and of the related religio-political institution of the Thai monarchy. In developing a comprehensive analysis of Buddhism in Thailand it is necessary to recognize that the religion exists in a dynamic relation with Thai society, and has political, cultural, and ideological as well as religious significance.

This study, then, attempts to develop a socially informed evaluation of the totality of Buddhadāsa's reinterpretations of Buddhist doctrine. It is an analysis of doctrine which considers:

(1) the social context of Buddhadāsa's theoretical work;
(2) the relation of Buddhadāsa's doctrinal reinterpretations to the history of the theoretical tradition of Theravada Buddhism; and
(3) the views and reactions of Buddhadāsa's audience and readership; in other words, the social impact of, and response to, his ideas.

In evaluating Buddhadāsa's work it is also necessary to recognize that his doctrinal reinterpretations are part of a non-Western intellectual tradition. Buddhism is a religious tradition with a distinctive theoretical history in which notions of argumentation, methods of reasoning, and the place of reason in human knowledge differ markedly from the situation in the Western tradition. For these reasons it is not possible to evaluate Theravada Buddhism using precisely the same intellectual tools used to critically assess Western theoretical works. To uncritically apply Western analytical criteria to Buddhism may lead to the fundamental differences in the character of Buddhist thought being misperceived as theoretical weaknesses and logical deficiencies, a result which may unnecessarily and unjustifiably undervalue or devalue that system of thought.

To insist on applying a strict Western critical analysis to all theoretical systems, even those developed in non-Western societies, fails to recognize that significantly different discursive systems in fact operate upon different theoretical and epistemological principles. A strictly logical (Western) analysis of Buddhadāsa's thought would lead to an unwarranted concentration on the details and specific intellectual failings of his work. But such a strict logical analysis would fail to recognize that, when viewed in the context of the principles and intellectual history of Theravada Buddhist thought, Buddhadāsa's system cannot but be seen as an important theoretical development with profound implications.

But just as an unqualified Western-styled critique of Buddhadāsa's thought is unacceptable, so too a solely contextual or internal study which abandons or holds in abeyance criteria of discursive criticism would be an inadequate theoretical approach. To define Buddhism as a system to which one cannot apply Western notions of logical argumentation would be to deny the possibility of a Western student developing an evaluation or judgement of Buddhist thought which has theoretical significance within the context of Western discourse and intellectual history.

What is required in analyzing Buddhadāsa's work is a critical approach to Buddhism which at the same time appreciates the significance of Buddhism in its own historical and theoretical context. This involves maintaining a balance between a critical analysis or theoretical engagement of Buddhism and a sympathetic understanding and appreciation of the religion in its own terms. A sympathetic engagement with Buddhism would seek neither to devalue that theoretical system because of its culturally determined differences nor to demean it by patronizingly holding criticism in abeyance and avoiding evaluative comment. A sympathetic understanding or engagement with Buddhism implies neither agreement with its theoretical assumptions nor the development of an apologetic for Buddhist doctrines. Instead, sympathetic engagement represents a recognition of differences and, if necessary, an acknowledgement of the need to agree to disagree over fundamental values, but not to either disparage Buddhism or to refrain from further engagement because of these differences. Such an approach neither assumes that Buddhist doctrine is a perfectly consistent development of the religion's principles, nor does it refrain from making internal inconsistencies apparent where they in fact exist.

The approach of sympathetic engagement followed in this study is a two-pronged analysis. Engagement denotes analyzing and criticizing the details of arguments, the assumptions underpinning notions, and the particulars of logic and reasoning. On the other hand, a sympathetic or contextual understanding denotes looking more at generalities, the context of history, and broad theoretical principles which inform and pattern the details of doctrine and teaching. However, these two moments are not separate but occur in tandem, critical engagement being tempered by sympathetic or contextual awareness and, similarly, a cutting or critical edge to sympathetic understanding being maintained by critical engagement.

More specifically, the sympathetic engagement of Buddhadāsa's work means that it is evaluated both in terms of strictly Western criteria *and* in terms of its own internal Buddhist-derived principles. However, neither of these approaches dominates the other, the results of an external criticism always being weighed against a contextual appreciation of the issues at hand. No simple theoretical formula can be given for whether the external Western or internal Buddhist evaluation of Buddhadāsa's doctrinal reinterpretations should predominate or be the ultimate basis for making some single final judgement on the overall value and importance of his work. This is because any simple judgement is likely to represent the dominance of one discursive system's principles over the other, resulting in a loss of perspective. The method of sympathetic engagement does not and in fact cannot define any precise theoretical relation between Buddhism and Western thought. Rather, it is an ethical and political approach to the study of contemporary Thai Buddhism which aims towards a balance in theoretical evaluation. Sympathetic engagement can be likened to a methodology of diplomacy. Sympathetic engagement acknowledges that there are irreducible theoretical differences and so tensions between Buddhism and Western thought, but neither retreats into a pure, non-judgmental observationalism because of these theoretical tensions nor attempts the impossible task of resolving such tensions by appealing to some abstract or metaphysical unifying principle between cultures. Rather, like diplomats skilled in the political arts of international relations, this method seeks to engage the foreign party and arrive at a balanced judgement which gives value and weight to both Western and Buddhist analyses of Buddhadāsa's work.

The methodological approach of this study is then complex in two senses. Firstly, it involves appreciating Buddhadāsa's work both as a theoretical system and as a social phenomenon. And secondly, this social-philosophical analysis is undertaken in a way that sympathetically engages Buddhadāsa's work, evaluating it both in terms of the Buddhist tradition from which it is drawn and the Western intellectual tradition which has significantly influenced it.

However, before beginning the detailed description and criticism of Buddhadāsa's reinterpretations in chapter 3, the first two chapters of this study outline the historical and theoretical back-ground of Buddhist discourse and the social significance of Bud-dhism in Thai society. These introductory chapters provide the detail necessary to arrive at a balanced theoretical and sociopolitical appraisal of Buddhadāsa's work.

Throughout this study it is assumed that the reader will already be acquainted with the history and basic principles and doctrines of Buddhism. For those unfamiliar with the terminology and concepts of Buddhist thought a brief overview is presented in an appendix.

The remainder of this introductory section presents a brief biographical review of Buddhadāsa's life.

## BIOGRAPHICAL INFORMATION ON BUDDHADĀSA

Buddhadāsa was born on 27 May 1906 at Phumriang *tambon* (village) in what is today the *amphoe* (district) of Chaiya in Suratthani Province, Southern Thailand.[2] He was the first son of a Chinese store owner, Siang Phanit (เซียง พานิช), and his Thai wife, Khluean (เคลื่อน), and was given the name Ngueam (เงื่อม). Buddhadāsa is a Pali pen name which he later assumed and by which he later preferred to be known. Buddhadāsa's father was born in Thailand, his grandfather coming from Hokkien (Fujian) in China in the mid–nineteenth century. The Chinese family name was originally Sae Khwo (Hokkien/Fujian: โข่ว Taejiw/Chaozhou: โค้ว), Phanit being an officially conferred Thai surname given in the reign of King Rama VI. Buddhadāsa's mother was of a Thai family from the village of Tha Chang. He had a brother, Yikoei (ยี่เกย), and a sister, Kimsoi (กิมซ้อย).

The Phanit family was reasonably well off, Buddhadāsa's father, Siang, having established a general store at Phumriang which in the early years of the twentieth century functioned as a local meeting place and as the *amphoe* police station before the district centre was moved to Chaiya just before the Second World War. Buddhadāsa's education began when, at the age of eight, he became a temple boy at Wat Nok (also called Wat Ubon) in Phumriang, where he lived for three years. However, his formal schooling started in 1914 when he began attending Phothiphitthayakon School at Wat Photharam (also called Wat Nai) in Phumriang, where he studied for three years and completed the primary education grade of Prathom III. He then moved to Chaiya where his father worked and he began studying at the Chaiya District School, Saraphi-uthit School. Buddhadāsa completed the high school grade of Mathayom III but had to leave school to run the family business at Phumriang when his father died in 1922. He then took on the responsibility of supporting the education of his younger brother, Yikoei, who was studying at the prestigious Suan Kulap School in Bangkok. Yikoei subsequently began studying medicine at Chulalongkorn University but did not complete his course.

When Yikoei returned from studying in Bangkok in 1926 he took over the running of the family business. Buddhadāsa was then freed from his family responsibilities and was able to follow the Thai custom of being ordained into the monkhood at the customary age of twenty-one. He was ordained into the Mahanikai Order at Wat Nok (Wat Ubon), Phumriang, on 29 July 1926 by Phrakhru Sophanaceta-sikaram (Vimalo), who gave him the Pali clerical name of Indapañño (Thai: Inthapanyo). Phra Ngueam Indapañño then spent his first *phansa* or rainy season retreat at Wat Mai (also called Wat Phum-riang), where he passed his Naktham Tri (III) exam.[3]

Buddhadāsa was a bright and studious child, and as a high school student in Chaiya he was interested in reading about and discussing Buddhism. However, there is no indication that he felt any special inclination towards becoming a monk in his youth. Initially he had decided to remain in the monkhood only for the three or four months of the rainy season monastic retreat. However, he quickly developed a liking for the monk's life and soon showed promise both as a scholar and as a teacher; and Buddhadāsa never disrobed after that first ordination. Perhaps the young man's interest in remaining a monk was stimulated by the existence at nearby Wat Photharam, Chaiya, of a temple school for monks, which had been established in 1925 by monks of the Thammayut Order from Wat Rachathiwat in Bangkok. In the 1920s educational facilities in provincial Thailand were extremely poor and for an academically-minded youth temple schools often provided the only means for furthering intellectual interests.

Nevertheless, Buddhadāsa seems to have quickly developed more than a purely academic interest in Buddhism. In addition to doing well in his monastic examinations he also gained a reputation as a good preacher of the Dhamma, and as having an engaging style of presentation which was more than simply a recitation of the Pali scriptures. Buddhadāsa also developed a preference for monastic solitude and because his brother, Yikoei (who now uses the Pali name Dhammadāsa, in Thai: Thammathat), was managing the family business Buddhadāsa received his mother's blessing and encourage-ment to remain a monk.

At the instigation of an uncle, Buddhadāsa went to Bangkok in order to further his studies in July 1928, staying at Wat Pathum-khongkha. However, he did not find the sort of spiritual education he had expected and met no-one whom he regarded as an able teacher. Buddhadāsa was also dissatisfied with the clerical education of the time and complained that, "In studying the *pariyattidhamma*[4] in this period we don't truly study the *Tipiṭaka* itself, we study only the commentaries."(T)[5] This together with his disappointment with laxities in the practice of the *vinaya* among Mahanikai monks in Bangkok, made him disinterested in obtaining a theological degree. After only two months Buddhadāsa found his studies oppressive and boring and returned to Chaiya.

In 1929 one of Buddhadāsa's uncles, Nguan Setthaphakdi, of the neighboring town of Ban Don, donated 5,000 baht for the establish-ment of a school of scriptural studies at Wat Phrathat in Chaiya, and Buddhadāsa was invited to be the instructor. Buddhadāsa also wrote his first book in 1929, a cremation volume for Phrakhru Sophanacetasikaram, entitled, *Kan Tham Than* (การทำทาน) or "giving alms." When his students passed their Naktham III and Naktham II exams well, Buddhadāsa's family decided that he should not waste his obvious academic talents teaching novices and advised him to return to Bangkok and attempt higher study there once again.

The year 1930 found Buddhadāsa once more at Wat Pathum-khongkha in Bangkok, although this time he decided that he could study more efficiently by doing a significant part of the work by himself. His individualistic approach, so characteristic in the later style of his life and in the innovativeness of his ideas, paid off well and he topped his class in the Parian Sam Prayok (III) Pali exam-inations that year. However, his interests ranged far outside the scriptures and Pali studies and he followed courses in science, photography, and radio, as well as the traditional lectures on the exegesis of the *Tipiṭaka*.

The years Buddhadāsa spent in Bangkok in the early 1930s saw his ideas about Buddhism and the direction of his life crystallize. It was a period when a set of diverse influences prodded him to take a course of action he himself later described as daring. Gradually the issues of religious reform became Buddhadāsa's predominating concern and he began to neglect his formal studies, which he came to see as irrelevant to the crucial problems facing Buddhism. In 1931 he failed his *parian si prayok* (IV) Pali examination, something he had expected. After his private reading of the *Tipiṭaka*, Buddhadāsa felt that there were significant differences between the commentaries upon which his clerical examinations were based and the actual canonical scriptures. He realized that even if he gave the answers to questions on doctrine which he regarded as being correct, he would fail the Pali examinations, because his views differed radically from the orthodox interpretations taught in Bangkok. As a consequence, he regarded further formal education to be pointless. A letter written to his brother Dhammadāsa towards the end of his second stay in Bangkok shows how Buddhadāsa's reformist ideas had crystallized. He wrote that he intended to discontinue his studies, leave Bangkok, and that he had resolved to

> look for a quiet place free from internal and external vexations . . . in order to examine and research the Dhammic science which I have been studying.
>
> I have had a stroke of good luck . . . in that I have found a friend who has the same feelings about life . . . we each have the same intention in the future work. We have agreed that Bangkok certainly is not the place to find purity; blundering around studying the scriptures in a way polluted by concern for status. The benefit of this is that we realize we have been misdirected. We have followed the world from the minute we were born until the minute we gained this awareness. After this we will not follow the world, and will farewell the world in order to search for what is pure by following the path of the *ariyans* (saints) who searched until they found [*nibbāna*].(T)[6]

In fulfillment of his desire to follow the actual path of the Buddha, Buddhadāsa left Bangkok on 5 April 1932 and returned to Wat Mai at Phumriang. Other monks were to have accompanied him but because of family pressures they abandoned the idea, leaving

Buddhadāsa to carry on alone. But Dhammadāsa and a small party of his associates strongly supported Buddhadāsa, and together they decided that his spiritual retreat should be undertaken at a long-abandoned and overgrown monastery, Wat Traphangchik, near Phumriang. Buddhadāsa took up residence there on 12 May 1932 and renamed the monastery area Suan Mokkhaphalaram (สวนโมกขพลาราม), literally, "The garden to arouse the spirits to attain liberation". Today the monastery is usually simply called Suan Mokh, "The garden of liberation."

In the following month, June 1932, the democratic revolution overthrew the absolute monarchy, and Buddhadāsa's comments on this event reflect how he viewed his religious enterprise: "We take this event [the revolution] as an omen of changing to a new era, for rectifying and improving various things as much as we can."(T)[7] The intensity of the twenty-six-year-old monk's determination can be gauged from the following vow, written in a notebook on 28 August 1932:

> I commit this life and body as a dedication to the Lord Buddha. I am a servant of the Buddha, the Buddha is my lord. For this reason I am named "Buddhadāsa" [literally, "servant of the Buddha"].[8]

For the following two years Buddhadāsa lived alone at Suan Mokh, following the solitary life of a forest monk. In 1935 another monk, Phra Sasanapachoto, remained with him for the rainy season retreat and over the next few years the number of monks and novices residing at Suan Mokh grew to ten. Because of limited space at the Wat Traphangchik site, in 1943 Suan Mokh was moved to its present location on almost a hundred acres of hilly land at Wat Than Nam Lai, several kilometres Southeast of Chaiya.

Dhammadāsa was far from inactive during these formative years and was in constant contact with his brother. Together they developed a plan for propagating their ideas of the purer, original Buddhism. They agreed that their work needed to proceed gradually, starting with a few and only slowly building up numbers. They also felt it had to be a truly religious work, avoiding fame and honour. The first stage was for Dhammadāsa to establish a group of people interested in publishing books on the Dhamma, and the second stage was for this group to actively promote the Dhamma. Dhammadāsa established the Khana Thammathan (คณะธรรมทาน), "The Society of the Gift of Truth," and took the Pali motto, *sabbadanam dhammadanam jinati*, "The gift of truth excels all other gifts."

With the object of "propagating the correct principles of the Dhamma,"[9] Dhammadāsa in 1933 began publishing a magazine, *Phutthasatsana* (Buddhism), aiming at national distribution. And in the first heady years after the democratic revolution his small group was infused with a strong sense of destiny and of the possibility of effecting real progress in the character of Buddhism. As Buddhadāsa noted at the time,

> We have consequently reached the appropriate time for promoting the progress of the practice of Dhamma to obtain true fruits of the blessed religion. And we should do this by trying to find ways or means to help a large number of individuals understand correctly and more truly the dhammic principles of the blessed prophet, son of the Sakyas.(T)[10]

Just as the 1932 democratic revolution brought the promise of devolving political power, so too Buddhadāsa saw his and the Khana Thammathan's propagatory work as revealing the true core of Buddhism for all to know.

Since World War II other organizations have been established with the specific purpose of publishing and distributing Buddhadāsa's writings and sermons. In 1953 Dhammadāsa formally incorporated the Khana Thammathan as a foundation, the Thammathan Munnithi. In association with this Chaiya-based organization, which has its own library and press, is the Bangkok-based Thammabucha (ธรรมบูชา—honouring Dhamma) printing house, which in turn is operated by the Khana Phoeiphrae Withi Kan Damnoen Chiwit An Prasoet (คณะเผยแพร่วิธีการดำเนินชีวิตอันประเสริฐ—the group for promoting the method of leading one's life perfectly). Another organization dedicated to the publication of Buddhadāsa's work is the Ongkan Fuenfu Phra Phutthasatsana (องค์การฟื้นฟูพระพุทธ

ศาสนา—the organization for the revival of Buddhism), which was established by the late Pun Chongprasoet at Samut Prakan near Bangkok.

Gradually since 1932 Buddhadāsa's ideas have become more and more widely recognized. While not always being in agreement with them, Buddhadāsa enjoyed the company of two generations of liberal democratic politicians, indicated by his meetings with Pridi Banomyong and his sometimes stormy interactions with Kukrit Pramoj. During the Second World War a politician from Buddhadasa's home province of Suratthani, Wut Suwannarat, came to know of his ideas and gave some of Buddhadāsa's books to the democrat and former prime minister, Pridi Banomyong. Pridi invited Buddhadāsa to Bangkok and when the two met they spoke from 1 P.M. till 10 P.M. on three consecutive days. While the content of their conversations is not recorded, the mere length of time the cabinet minister took off from his duties indicates something of the importance Pridi placed on the discussion. Pridi was also inspired to consider arranging for a temple like Suan Mokh to be built in his home province of Ayutthaya, but his being forced into exile after the death of King Rama VIII in 1947 meant the plan was never realized.

At the same time, Buddhadāsa was also invited to give a series of addresses to the Phutthasamakhom (Buddhist Society of Thailand), the content of his talks and responses setting a pattern for his relations with the Sangha hierarchy which has by and large continued to the present day. He entitled one of his addresses, "The Mountainous Methods of Buddhist Dhamma—Things Which Obstruct People From Obtaining Buddhist Dhamma."[11] It was a criticism of the practice of Thai Buddhism which in turn drew vehement criticism both from lay and clerical members of the audience. One Phra Thipprinya accused Buddhadāsa of debasing the Theravada tradition by his views. Indeed, as Sulak Sivaraksa notes, "The work of Buddhadāsa has never received any encouragement from ecclesiastical circles."(T)[12]

However, while drawing severe criticism from some, even being labelled heretical, the Sangha has not been able to ignore Buddhadāsa, for as Sulak glowingly reports:

> At the present time, his impact is nation-wide. It is largely due to Buddhadāsa that the younger generation in Siam now turn to Buddhist values and take Buddhism seriously. He has written more books on Buddhism than any other scholar—past or present—and his thought continues to become even more profound.[13]

Recent years have seen Buddhadāsa receive increasing public recognition, being the first monk to be made an honorary member of the widely recognized academic body, The Siam Society. During the 1973–76 period Buddhadāsa received nationwide coverage when he debated the senior Thai politician Kukrit Pramoj on television and radio. In 1980 the Mahachulalongkorn Buddhist University[14] conferred on him an Honorary Doctorate of Buddhism, the first it had presented in its ninety-year existence. This degree was conferred by none other than the supreme patriarch of the Thai Sangha. Buddhadāsa was also awarded the honorary clerical title of Phra Ratchawisutthimethi (พระราชวิสุทธิเมธี).

The monastery site at Suan Mokh has grown considerably over the years and now there are often up to eighty monks and perhaps some hundreds of laymen and laywomen visiting or staying at the centre at any one time. A branch monastery of Suan Mokh is located at Wat Umong near Chiang Mai. Wat Chonprathan Rangsarit at Pak-kret in Nonthaburi also has close associations with Suan Mokh, its abbot, Phra Ratchananthamuni or Panyanantha Bhikkhu, being a former student of Buddhadāsa's.

# 1 THE SOCIAL AND THEORETICAL CONTEXTS OF BUDDHADĀSA'S WORK

## THE HISTORICAL CONSERVATISM OF THAI BUDDHISM

THE BUDDHIST intellectual tradition in Thailand and the other Theravada countries differs significantly from the Western intellectual tradition. For example, in Theravada Buddhism there is more emphasis on correct practice, or orthopraxy, as the basis of authoritative presentations of doctrine than on correct belief, or orthodoxy, which underpins the interpretation of religious doctrine in Western societies. In some respects this predominating emphasis on correct practice has led to a relatively free approach to doctrinal interpretation. For example, in contrast with the intellectual history of Christianity, the concern with heresy has been relatively unimportant in Buddhist countries. However, this relative freedom in the realm of doctrine (always associated with strict conservatism in religious practice) has not led to the development of a dynamic intellectual culture in Thailand. On the contrary, Buddhist intellectual culture in Thailand until the twentieth century can only be described as conservative and stagnant. At least two factors lie behind the historical stagnation of Buddhist scholarship in Thailand. Firstly, the unrestricted operation of reason, or free rational enquiry into Buddhist doctrine, has not been regarded as a "profitable" or appropriate intellectual activity. Secondly, Theravada Buddhism's historical function as the legitimating ideology of the Thai state has been associated with the imposition of political controls on the religion, which have in turn restricted and inhibited doctrinal innovation. In this chapter I detail these points, i.e. the emphasis on practice in Theravada Buddhism, the devaluation of reason, and the imposition of political controls on Thai Buddhism, which together constitute the most important features of the intellectual and sociopolitical context in which Buddhadāsa worked.

While Buddhadāsa's reworking of traditional Buddhist teachings is a theoretically complex phenomenon, I do not regard the most outstanding feature of his work to lie in any specific theory or reinterpretation of doctrine, but rather in the fact that he attempted such a radical and systematic review of Theravada Buddhism at all. Theoretical innovativeness in doctrinal interpretation has not been a historical feature of Thai intellectual life. The interpretation of Buddhist teachings has been a static field, the primary concern of Buddhist monks being with the conservation and faithful reproduction of holy texts and established commentarial interpretations from one generation to the next.

The conservatism of Buddhist teachings in Thailand in part results from historical factors. By the time the Thais formally adopted Theravada Buddhism, sometime around the twelfth or thirteenth century of the Christian era, the religion was already eighteen hundred years old. The scriptures had been determined and recorded, first in Ceylon; commentaries had been written and patterns of religious practice and organization had long been systematized. In a sense, all that was required of the relatively newly converted Thai Buddhists was to maintain and faithfully to reproduce the already laid down forms of practice and teaching, and preservation of the already fixed doctrines became the predominant concern of the official hierarchy of Buddhist monks in Thailand.

But this simple historical explanation cannot fully account for the intellectual conservatism of traditional Thai Theravada culture. Indeed, Buddhism as a whole can in no sense be called an inherently static intellectual system, for around the same time the Thais were adopting Theravada Buddhism in Southeast Asia, the schools of Chan and Zen were foci of religious and intellectual innovation in Buddhist China and Japan. Buddhism elsewhere and in other periods has been characterized by innovation and reform, and that

Buddhadāsa's work represents so radical an outbreak of reinterpretative activity within the Thai tradition indicates that Thai Buddhism's historical conservatism needs further explanation. As already suggested, the static character of traditional Thai Buddhist approaches to doctrine has multiple roots, which lie both in the intellectual tradition of Theravada Buddhism and in the history of Buddhism's institutional role in the Thai sociopolitical order.

## ORTHOPRAXY-ORTHODOXY

The distinction between the teachings and the practices of Buddhism provides a useful theoretical tool in accounting for the historical conservatism of studies of Theravada doctrine in Thailand. In the history of Theravada Buddhism disagreement over matters of practice rather than about doctrinal issues has been the main cause of religious disputes. As Thomas Kirsch observes, when the history of Theravada Buddhism is reviewed, one finds that

> disputes within the Theravada Buddhist tradition have rarely focused on doctrinal questions. More commonly, disputes have taken place within the Sangha [monkhood] and have centred on questions of monastic discipline.[1]

Kirsch notes that the main differences between the two *nikai* (นิกาย) or orders of Buddhism in Thailand, the traditional Mahanikai (มหานิกาย) Order and the reformist Thammayut (ธรรมยุต) Order established by King Mongkut (Rama IV, 1850–1868), are not based on conflicting interpretations of doctrine or teaching but on divergent interpretations of correct clerical practice. The differences between the *nikai* concern such matters as the proper format of initiation into the Sangha, the manner of accepting almsfood, methods of physically dealing with money, and the manner of wearing the monk's robes. The significance of issues of religious discipline and practice in Thai religious and political history can be gauged from the fact that King Rama III (1824–1851) did not sponsor Mongkut, his half brother, to be king after him because he felt Mongkut would cause religious dissension. Rama III was afraid that Mongkut would impose his Thammayut Order's practice of wearing the monk's robes so as to cover both shoulders on the Mahanikai monks, who had traditionally worn their robes so as to cover only one shoulder.

In the context of an analysis of Hinduism, Frits Staal has called a religious emphasis on correct practice "orthopraxy,"[2] as opposed to correct belief or orthodoxy. Staal argues that the orthopractic emphasis of Hinduism is related to the stress placed on the ritualistic aspect of the doctrine of *karma* or the belief that "only the correct performance of *karman*, 'ritual activity,' will lead to the desired result (for example, wealth, offspring, heaven, immortality)."[3] Theravada Buddhism in Thailand also has a distinct emphasis on orthopraxy and, like Hinduism, has also historically emphasized the theory of *kamma*. This has, as in Hinduism, led to a corresponding concern with "right action" in order to guarantee "right results." For example, the Thai academic philosopher, Sunthorn Na-Rangsi, says:

> It is to the credit of Buddhism that the law of *kamma* has been worked out in great detail until a specific *kamma* can be rationally related to a specific result.[4]

At least three factors have influenced Theravada Buddhism's emphasis on correct practice. These are the teachings of the canonical scriptures, the size and importance of the scriptures dealing with correct clerical practice, and the character of the Buddhist notion of salvation.

One of the sources of the orthopractic concern with *kamma* and "right action" in Thai Buddhism lies in the Buddhist scriptures. Sunthorn Na-Rangsi cites the *Culakammavibhaṅga Sutta* in the *Aṅguttara Nikāya* as isolating the following specific actions and their precise kammic results:

> The killing of living beings leads to a short life . . . the persecution of living beings leads to a sickly life . . . Irascibility, anger or hatred leads to an ugly figure or a bad complexion . . . Envy leads to

powerlessness. Non-envy leads to powerfulness . . . Miserliness or selfishness leads to poverty or pennilessness.[5]

A second source of Theravada Buddhism's concern with correct practice lies in the importance placed on the large amount of canonical literature dealing with correct clerical practice, the eight volumes of the *Vinayapiṭaka*. Because of the detail in which ascetic practices are laid down in the *Vinayapiṭaka*, the notion of conformity to the scriptures in Buddhism implies not only correct belief or understanding of the recorded doctrine, but also the correct practice of the path to salvation whose description occupies such a substantial part of the Theravada canon.

Practice also has an important place in the religion because, according to Buddhist doctrine, *nibbāna* or salvation depends on an insight which can be developed only through moral and meditative practice. *Nibbāna* is only attained as the result of an extraordinary insight into reality, which does not arise from mere faith or belief but from sustained mental practice or meditation. In Buddhism spiritual attainment or holiness is not simply manifested in acts of piety but is regarded as being generated and produced by ascetic practices. This equation of spiritual attainment with strict abidance by the clerical code of conduct blends in the popular, animistically influenced religion with magical beliefs in the supernatural efficacy of religious practice per se. Barend Terwiel makes the following observations of Central Thai farmers' beliefs:

> Many laymen believe that the monks who behave strictly according to the precepts [i. e. the *vinaya*] are generating more and stronger beneficial power than less strict *bhikkhu*s [monks] and such monks should be supported in preference to those who do not make these efforts.[6]

Because Buddhist salvation ultimately depends upon religious practice rather than belief, and because moral and immoral actions are regarded as having precise and specific consequences, the historical focus of the religion has been on correct clerical practice rather than on matters of doctrine. While not directly hindering the development of an analytical or questioning approach to doctrine, the key teachings of *kamma* and *nibbāna* have nevertheless contributed to the relative focus on practice in Theravada Buddhist history. However, the emphasis on practice has not been the only internal determinant of the historical lack of doctrinal innovation in Thailand. The secondary and subsidiary place accorded to reason and rational analysis in Buddhist thought has also hindered the development of philosophical enquiry.

## THE SECONDARY PLACE OF REASON IN BUDDHIST THOUGHT

Philosophical activity in the Western intellectual tradition has historically been characterized by the acceptance of the authority of reason. This has involved, at least in theory, a preparedness to accept the conclusions of logical analysis and reasoned argumentation, however personally unpleasant those conclusions may at times be. Buddhism, however, recognizes suprarational forms of knowledge as being superior to mere reason, and as a consequence does not regard rational enquiry as being of ultimate significance. As Robert Slater notes, in Buddhism,

> Intellectual activity is never regarded as a means sufficient in itself . . . it is always a means to an end, to that Ariyan intuition which is indispensable to nibbanic fulfilment.[7]

The intellectual activities of conceptual thought or reasoning are encompassed within the Buddhist notions of *vitakka*, "thought conception," and *vicāra*, "discursive thinking." In contrast, spiritual insight is regarded as developing through meditation, whose various levels are called *jhānas* or "absorptions." The rational and discursive thought processes of *vitakka* and *vicāra* are described as characterizing only the lower meditative states and are wholly transcended in the higher states, where they give way to suprarational wisdom or *paññā*, which in turn leads to the attainment of *nibbāna*. This *paññā* or insight into the fundamental conditions of reality (i.e., change, *anicca*, and non-self, *anattā*), which liberates one from suffering, *dukkha*, is not of a rational character and cannot be arrived at by any logical analysis. Because reason alone cannot lead to *paññā* or saving insight, Buddhism does not give it the pride of place that it has traditionally occupied in Western thought, and neither is intellectual speculation valued as highly as in Western philosophy.

Unrestrained rational enquiry is criticized by the Buddha as being without spiritual "benefit" in the effort to attain salvation from suffering. The following statement by the Buddha against giving consideration to certain philosophical questions posed by some of his followers, here taken from the *Cinta Sutta* in the *Papata Vagga* of the *Saṁyutta Nikāya*, is an often repeated formula found in several places in the *Suttapiṭaka*:

> You should not think of matters such as whether the world is eternal or not eternal, whether the world has an end or does not have an end . . . whether beings after having died yet live again or do not live again . . . Why should consideration not be given to such matters? Because such thinking is not beneficial. It is not the beginning [of the practice] of *brahmacariya*[8] which is undertaken for the sake of attaining tiredness [of worldly involvement], for the easing of lust, for extinction, peace, wisdom, enlightenment, for *nibbāna*.(T)[9]

Buddhism's emphasis on practice over doctrine and its ranking of reason below transcendent forms of wisdom does not mean, however, that the religion is inherently anti-speculative or incapable of producing an ongoing tradition of intellectual enquiry and debate. The early centuries of Buddhism saw multiple schisms over doctrinal issues and the production of a large body of interpretative literature which often included novel views and presentations of the original teachings and scriptures. It also does not mean that Buddhist doctrine is devoid of philosophical interest or of issues about which there is genuine theoretical debate. Indeed, the major part of this study is taken up with a philosophical consideration of the issues raised by Buddhadāsa's reinterpretations. Rather, Buddhism is based on a quite different understanding of the place of reason and of doctrinal debate from that which has characterized Western scholarship. And in turn, this different appreciation of the place of reason and reasoning in human knowledge has to an extent limited the development of an intellectual environment in which rational enquiry is not subject to extra-rational constraints.

Nevertheless, the general internal constraints on reason and doctrinal debate outlined above have been present in Buddhism since its inception and yet there have still been periods of significant intellectual activity and theoretical innovation in the history of the religion. The high degree of intellectual stagnation of traditional Thai Buddhism cannot therefore be attributed solely to any inherent anti-intellectual tendency of religion, although the above constraints have undoubtedly been important in discouraging the development of critical approaches to doctrine in all Theravada countries. Rather, it is necessary to turn to a more concrete consideration of the place of Buddhism in Thai society to understand the long uninnovative centuries of religious and doctrinal conservatism in Thailand. For, as an integral part of the Thai social order, Buddhism has also been subject to extra-religious influences which have historically restricted intellectual speculation on matters of doctrine.

## BUDDHISM AS STATE IDEOLOGY IN THAILAND

In addition to its message of salvation, Theravada Buddhism in Thailand has also had a distinctly this-worldly significance. Buddhist principles and ideas inform Thai notions of government, politics, and social interaction, and the religion's ostensibly spiritual teachings have long been used as justifications for political actions. The social and political implementation of Buddhist teachings and the governance of society by a Buddhist monarch are positively sanctioned by the canonical literature. The *Agañña Sutta*[10] recounts that because of greed and confusion amongst themselves, the first humans gathered together and argued for the need to select the best among them to "be wrathful when indignation is right . . . censure that which should be censured and banish him who deserves to be banished."[11] S. Tambiah describes this *sutta* as presenting an elective and contractual theory of kingship whereby a king is elected by a people and remunerated by the payment of a rice tax.[12]

The concept of a Buddhist monarch is further developed and reinforced by the notion of the *cakkavattin*, a morally inspired monarch who, in the *Mahāparinibbāna Sutta*,[13] is included in a list of four types of people described as *thūparāha*, those worthy of having a pilgrimage monument or stupa erected over their ashes. The other three types of *thūparāha* or "stupa-deserving" individuals all have a spiritual rather than a worldly character, that is, (1) a *tathāgata*, (2) a follower of a *tathāgata*, and (3) a *paccekabuddha*.[14] Further, in the *Cakkavatti Sutta*[15] the Buddha instructs the Emperor Dalhanemi in the *cakkavattivatta*, the vow of the universal monarch or *cakkavattin*, to depend on and honour the Dhamma, to protect the Dhamma in himself and his people, to provide property and subsistence to those in need, and to follow the counsel of those knowledgeable in the Dhamma.

But while sections of the canonical Theravada scriptures explicitly detail principles of moral governance, it was not until almost two hundred years after the Buddha's death that the Buddhist Sangha first became formally associated with a temporal regime. Under Asoka, ruler of an extensive North Indian empire from 272 to 232 B.C., Buddhism first acquired the role of a state religion, gaining the protection and support of a temporal monarch and also becoming dependent upon and subordinate to that monarch.

Asoka established the precedent whereby a Buddhist monarch was also charged with the authority to ensure that monks obeyed the *vinaya* or clerical code of conduct. The Buddhist king had no authority regarding doctrine or Dhamma, only over the Sangha's "purity," a term which traditionally connotes strict abidance by the *vinaya*. This definition of the monarch's religious authority as concerning matters of clerical practice, but not of doctrine, again reveals the strongly orthopractic character of Theravada Buddhism. The purity or strictness of practice maintained by members of the Sangha is the most common measure of the overall "health" or status of the *sāsanā* or religion. After Asoka the monarch's control over clerical practice came to be considered crucial to the maintenance of the Dhamma as a doctrine of liberation founded on the living practice of righteousness among the monks.

Following Asoka later Buddhist monarchs also acquired an institutionally sanctioned religious authority over the purity of the Sangha. Strong temporal power centralized in a monarch has traditionally been regarded as essential to the well-being of the *sāsanā*. This Asokan model provided the pattern for church-state relations in the early Thai kingdom of Sukhothai, and the association of the Buddhist Sangha with the Thai state has been significant since that time. As Niels Mulder notes:

> Throughout history Thai governments have been aware of the important integrative function of institutionalized Buddhism and repeated efforts have been made to control the monks and their practices, and to bring their organization under the supervision of the state.[16]

Somboon Suksamran concurs, stating that Buddhism

> has long served as one of the most important sources of political legitimation for the political rulers; one of the main socialising, acculturating and unifying forces in Thai society.[17]

At the same time, the order of monks has been rendered politically impotent because its integration into the political structure was effected in such a way that it had no means to exercise political influence. The drawing of a sharply defined distinction between a mundane religious path for the world-involved laity, *lokiyadhamma*, and a supramundane path for renunciates, *lokuttara-dhamma*, and the consequent radical separation of the role of the layperson from that of the monk, have provided a religious justification for proscribing clerical involvement in politics. For when world-involvement is equated with spiritual pollution, no monk can become directly involved in politics without irreparably damaging his clerical authority. In contrast to this traditional segregation of the lay or mundane from the clerical or supramundane, Buddhadāsa was concerned to abolish the distinction between the *lokiya* and *lokuttara* realms. This doctrinal stance amounts to a denial of the traditionally accepted apolitical character of the role of the Buddhist clergy and has drawn severe criticism from religious and political conservatives in Thailand.

However, Thai Buddhism's institutional isolation from explicit political involvement has not only resulted from the theoretical influence of the above doctrine but has also been enforced by direct control and supervision of clerical affairs by the Thai state. The history of church-state relations in Thailand amounts to a series of actions by the state—whether monarchy, military dictatorship, or civilian governments—to use the Sangha's authority to promote the policies and security of the government of the day, while at the same time depriving the monkhood of the capacity to interfere in the running of the state. One of the first acts of King Rama I (r. 1782–1801), founder of the present Chakri dynasty of Bangkok, was to reorganize and revivify Buddhism after the devastation of the earlier Thai kingdom of Ayutthaya by the Burmese. Political acumen as well as Buddhist piety can be read into the following account by a Thai prince of the activities of Rama I in rebuilding social order after the strife and chaos following the downfall of Ayutthaya in 1767:

> It is natural that the king's systematic mind would have promoted first a code of morality by which a standardisation of the conduct of the clergy could be established. He then set out with energy to see that his lay subjects as well as members of monastic orders behaved as good Buddhists. His effort in this direction is evidenced by the innumerable decrees governing the conduct of monks and laity.[18]

The twentieth century has seen two major shifts in the character of the use of Buddhism to legitimate the activities of the Thai state. The first shift was effected in the early decades of this century by King Vajiravudh or Rama VI (1910–1921), who emphasized that Buddhism not only underpinned the monarchy but also the entire nation. By stressing Thai nationalism and the importance of Buddhism to the security and welfare of the nation, Rama VI also laid the groundwork for the religion to become the ideological foundation of the civilian government which came to power in 1932. That is, when political power shifted from the monarch to politicians, and subsequently to the military, the legitimatory role of Buddhism also shifted and expanded. Since 1932, institutional Buddhism has become the ideological bulwark of the modern Thai state, just as it had previously been, and continues to be, the bulwark of the institution of monarchy. Thai political leaders since 1932 have placed just as much importance on maintaining and controlling the Buddhist Sangha as did earlier absolute monarchs. There is therefore a significant degree of continuity between the traditional Thai monarchy and the modern Thai state in terms of the use of Buddhist symbolism in the public legitimation of power. Rama VI's royalist-*cum*-nationalist slogan of *chat-satsana-phra mahakasat* (ชาติ-ศาสนา-พระมหากษัตริย์—Nation-Religion-Monarch), derived from the jingoistic British maxim of "God, King, and Country," has been touted as much by military rulers as it was by former absolute monarchs in their efforts to promote national unity and shore up their regimes.

A second shift in Sangha-state relations occurred after World War II, beginning with the regime of Field Marshal Sarit Thanarat (1957–1963), when the predominating concern of government became the promotion of national development. In political terms, Sarit's concern with development firstly translated into an emphasis on national unity and the integration of peripheral or marginal groups (for example, hill tribes) into the main body of Thai society. The second related emphasis of Sarit's development program was a concerted campaign to counter communism, which was interpreted as causing social divisions and so obstructing the goal of national development.

In 1962, Sarit passed a new Sangha act which effectively centralized power in the hands of those monks associated with or supported by his regime. Somboon Suksamran catches the political tenor of the changes introduced by the new act when he notes the major directives to the restructured Sangha administration were

> First, to follow the policies of the government; second to oversee and prevent the communist infiltration of the Sangha and monasteries;

> third, to prevent any attempt to use the monasteries for the propagation of communism.[19]

In the context of the Cold War and the civil wars in neighbouring Vietnam, Laos, and Cambodia, and in order to mobilize popular sentiment, successive Thai military regimes and military leaders have maintained that communism seeks the destruction of all religions, including Buddhism. And because Buddhism is regarded as the foundation of both the nation and the monarchy, communism has consequently been attacked as a threat to the foundations of Thailand's national integrity and to its most hallowed institutions. In Thailand, Buddhism has been officially defined as anticommunist and communism as anti-Buddhist. As the economist Puey Ungphakorn observed in 1969,

> According to a government slogan, broadcast on the radio, a person without religion must be a communist or a terrorist. Some school teachers also repeat this theory to their pupils.[20]

The continuing ideological significance of institutional Buddhism to Thailand's political and military leaders is shown by the fact that each major change in government policy this century has been accompanied by efforts to reform and reorganize the monkhood and to redefine its function in Thai society.

In this context, where Buddhism fulfils an important politico-ideological role, the Thai state exerts considerable control over both the organization and education of Sangha members. The maintenance of traditional interpretations of doctrine is seen by most of those in positions of influence and political authority in Thailand as part and parcel of preserving Buddhism as the ideological foundation of the nation. Consequently, the intellectual atmosphere within the Sangha, especially at the senior levels, is highly restrictive and not conducive to free intellectual enquiry or debate. While the emphasis on practice rather than doctrine and the relative devaluation of free intellectual enquiry in the Buddhist tradition have historically contributed to the intellectual conservatism of Thai Buddhism, the most concrete determinant of this conservatism has undoubtedly been the power and control of the Thai state over Sangha affairs. In recent centuries, and especially in the twentieth century, institutional Buddhism in Thailand has had no independent existence apart from the Thai state, which both supports and controls it. Maintenance of the traditional religious symbols and legitimation of the existing temporal order rather than doctrinal innovation or investigative scholarship have as a result been the predominating concerns of most monks.

State control over the Sangha, together with the community of interests between senior Sangha officials and the Thai monarchy and political elite, lead to strong pressures to maintain conservative views of the religion and of the social role of the Sangha. This is because the traditional character of Buddhist teaching, especially on social matters, provides justifications for the existing social order in which the senior clergy and political leaders symbiotically share in power.

Thai Buddhism has not been completely resistant to change in recent times. However, the innovations instituted have paralleled the changing political requirements and character of the state, and change has been restricted within fixed limits defined by the government of the day and overseen by the Department of Religious Affairs. King Mongkut's reforms not only aligned Buddhism more closely with Western ideas, but his reform order also provided the basis for much greater centralized control over the Sangha in succeeding decades. In recent years, conservative military governments have encouraged the use of Buddhism as a catalyst for the socioeconomic development of the countryside. However, the form of Buddhism propagated in this political and economic activity has been strictly controlled by ensuring that the monks involved undertake government-developed training programs. Buddhadāsa's unconventionality lay in the fact that he was prepared to innovate and reinterpret Buddhist teachings outside the limits implicitly and explicitly laid down by the government.

But despite the politically controlled atmosphere within the Sangha, which is resistant to reform in most aspects of the religion, it is nevertheless the case that the overriding orthopractic concern of the Sangha hierarchy to maintain strict, centralized control over correct clerical practice means that there is in fact no centrally enforced control on interpretations of doctrine. There is, for example, no central body in the Sangha which vets Buddhist publications in Thailand. Any monk or layperson is free to publish whatever interpretation of the scriptures and doctrines he or she wishes without first needing to obtain any ecclesiastical imprimatur. Because faithfulness to Buddhist tradition is in the main defined in terms of strict abidance by traditional practices, rather than in terms of adherence to a given orthodoxy, no specific institutional constraints exist on Buddhist writings or discussion. The only directly enforced intellectual control in Thailand is the general censorship of what the political authorities regard as politically inflammatory, communist, libellous, or immoral literature. While Buddhadāsa's reinterpretations of doctrine have been severely criticized by many religiously and politically conservative individuals, both monks and laypeople, he has never been criticized by the Sangha hierarchy. This is because, given that his work is neither illegal nor subject to secular censorship or restrictions, and that he strictly abides by clerical practices, there are no institutional means that can be used to criticize Buddhadāsa.

There are no formal or institutional barriers to doctrinal reform or theoretical innovation in Thai Buddhism. However, the combined power of the Thai state and senior Sangha hierarchy, whose interests coincide in seeking to maintain the dominance of doctrinally conservative views, and who together control both clerical education and lay religious education in Thailand, has resulted in the actual historical conservatism of Thai Buddhism.

Buddhadāsa's work is not only important because of his emphasis on the rational analysis of Buddhist doctrine. His views also conflict with the form of Buddhism used to legitimate the present social order in Thailand. This gives his work, even the seemingly abstract and theoretical sections, a direct political and social relevance in modern Thailand.

Buddhadāsa's doctrinal innovativeness thus broke with the long conservative tradition in Thai Buddhism which even today remains the dominating influence on the contemporary practice and understanding of the religion. In seeking to appreciate the significance of Buddhadāsa's reinterpretations in the context of contemporary Thai Buddhism, it is therefore necessary to consider how and why he made this theoretical break. When by far the majority of monks in Thailand continue either to support or to acquiesce in the conservative religious and political status quo, what motivated Buddhadāsa to set himself at odds with the generally accepted order of things? This issue is the focus of the discussion and analysis in the next chapter, in which some important theoretical and social aspects of Buddhadāsa's work are also outlined.

# 2 THE SOURCES OF BUDDHADĀSA'S INNOVATIVE VIEWS

IN CONTRAST to the historical conservatism of Thai Buddhism, Buddhadāsa's work represents a distinctly analytical and philosophical development. For example, Buddhadāsa took the all but unprecedented step of criticizing the traditional interpretation of the Buddhist theory of causation or *paṭiccasamuppāda*, and he questioned the reality of such generally assumed facts as rebirth. Underpinning these reinterpretations is a novel method of approaching the Theravada scriptures, a method whose objective is the demythologization of Buddhist doctrine. Buddhadāsa's work is characterized by the systematic reduction of metaphysical aspects of Buddhist teaching, such as notions of rebirth in heaven or hell, to psychological conditions.

The systematic demythologization of Buddhist doctrine is paralleled by Buddhadāsa's pervasive concern to give religious value to action in the material world. His reinterpretations of the religion's teachings are characterized by a shift of the theoretical focus of Buddhist doctrine from the transcendent to this world here and now. Buddhadāsa effects this shift by redefining the notion of Buddhist salvation as being a condition of life in this world, and then using this new definition to develop a more explicitly social thrust to Buddhist doctrine.

Traditionally Buddhism has taught that in the face of the transience of the things of the world, *anicca*, human beings should cultivate detachment and strive for the transcendent salvation of *nibbāna*. However, Buddhadāsa proposes that suffering is not always solely attributable to an individual's kammic inheritance but, on the contrary, is often caused by factors in the external world. Whereas Buddhism has traditionally taught that an individual's *dukkha* or suffering is a self-caused condition which is relieved through individual spiritual practice, Buddhadāsa maintains that the suffering caused by socioeconomic exploitation and political oppression has an external source and can be ended only by spiritually guided action in the social world. That is, for Buddhadāsa, liberation from suffering involves not only overcoming one's own ignorance and craving through spiritual insight, but also overcoming oppressive or *dukkha*-causing conditions in the external world. The focus of action to attain the religious goal of ending suffering is therefore expanded to include not only the self-directed moral and meditative practices of the individual who suffers, but also welfare-directed activity in the social context in which he or she suffers. In brief, for Buddhadāsa, activity in the material world has become an integral component of the religious goal of Buddhism.

The inclusion of the social world and social action within Buddhadāsa's interpretation of *nibbāna* can be interpreted as his recognition of the potential benefits afforded humanity by modern technology and scientific knowledge. Buddhadāsa accepts the results of science and tries to bring scientific knowledge within the scope of his reinterpreted version of Buddhism. He does this firstly by claiming that his view of Buddhism is in accord with the findings of science, and secondly by criticizing the animist and Brahmanical aspects of Thai Buddhism as being inconsistent with his scientific and rationalist interpretation of the scriptures.

In traditional Buddhist teaching and practice, in which there is a sharp distinction between the mundane and supramundane realms, world-involvement has been associated with the lay form of the religion. However, Buddhadāsa wishes to integrate a positive valuation of action in the material world with strict doctrinal Buddhism, that is, with what has traditionally been regarded as the *lokuttara* or world-renouncing form of the religion appropriate only for monks. He rejects the traditional lay or *lokiya* form of Buddhism not only because of the inconsistencies of its animist and Brahmanical features with his rationalist outlook, but also because he transfers the traditional world-involved or *lokiya* role to the doctrinal or *lokuttara* level. That is, Buddhadāsa seeks to integrate the *lokuttara* concern with salvation with the *lokiya* emphasis on world-involvement.

Buddhadāsa was a strong supporter of the modernist intellectual environment in Thailand and he found his most receptive audience among the Western-educated Thai intellectual elite. Buddhadāsa's intellectual modernism, a result of the influence of scientific and rationalist forms of knowledge on his thought, is further demonstrated by his emphasis on the authority of reason in interpreting the Buddhist scriptures over the authority of specific texts and revered commentators. Buddhadāsa's rationalism takes the form of a systematic doctrinalism, which involves reinterpreting doctrines by developing the logical relations between fundamental concepts such as *anattā* and *nibbāna*. This contrasts with the traditional slavish mouthing of the conclusions of commentaries or historically accepted authorities.

Because of the importance of the social world to his interpretation of Buddhism, Buddhadāsa also broke the traditional silence of Thai monks on political matters to express opinions on politics and social change in his country. But while his work has political significance, Buddhadāsa cannot be categorized as being aligned with any existing political group or faction, whether of the "right" or the "left." While offering Buddhist-based arguments providing qualified support for socioeconomic development and criticizing capitalist exploitation and oppression of the poor, he was at the same time critical of Marxism and all materialist philosophies, including what he regards as the sensualism of unfettered consumerism. He was thus critical of both the political East and West.

However, Buddhadāsa's radical reinterpretative efforts are not without their difficulties. His arguments are often vague and the sources of his views are rarely acknowledged and at times appear to be deliberately hidden. But over and above these academic details, important aspects of his thought, including his social philosophy, are flawed by fundamental contradictions. These contradictions are in fact forced on Buddhadāsa because of the practical conflicts arising from his decision to radically reform Buddhist teaching and practice while remaining within the conservative Thai Sangha. But even given these difficulties, Buddhadāsa's work remains important as the starting point and catalyst of a growing critical and modernist movement within Thai Buddhism which marks a real efflorescence of Buddhist intellectual activity.

But given the unquestioning acceptance of doctrine which has historically characterized Thai Buddhism, it is necessary to understand the sources of Buddhadāsa's innovativeness when analyzing the total phenomenon of his work. In this chapter I investigate what has altered in the traditional mix of Buddhism's internal theoretical constraints and external political limitations which permitted Buddhadāsa to develop his radical views. In particular, I analyze the cultural, social, and political changes which have impinged on the religion in the past century. Buddhadāsa's work is far from being a random irruption of reason and critical analysis in an otherwise stagnant tradition. His work was influenced by significant changes in Thai society and in Thai Buddhists' perceptions of themselves and their place in the world.

## PRECEDENTS FOR BUDDHADĀSA'S DOCTRINAL REINTERPRETATION

Buddhadāsa did not regard his reinterpretations of Theravada doctrine as innovations but rather as reforms based on the fundamental principles of the religion. He stated that his goal was to "revive the practice of Dhamma so that it is correct, as at the beginning [of Buddhism] or directly according to what is true."(T)[1] Religious reform is often characterized by innovation and change founded upon continuity with the past. Such a pattern of innovation based upon declared faithfulness to the past is necessary for any reformer working within a religion in which authority is traditionally invested in certain teachings, scriptures, or recorded insights. Reform is then expressed in terms of a return to the purity of the tradition's original sources, which Buddhadāsa took to be the teaching of salvation as passed down in the recorded words of the Buddha in the Theravada canon. In Buddhadāsa's work both the moments of conservatism and continuity and of innovation and change are equally important, and for each innovation he makes in reinterpreting Buddhism he takes an equally pronounced step back to refer to what he regards as the pure, original, and authoritative form of the religion.

Buddhadāsa based his effort to recover and re-express the fundamental truths of the religion on a return to the Buddha's original teachings in the *Suttapiṭaka* and to the ascetic practices of the Buddha. On this latter point Buddhadāsa remarked that

> The Lord Buddha himself did not have an umbrella, shoes, mosquito nets and lots of additional kinds of things . . . We call this [ascetic practice] the system of reviving or promoting the practice of the Dhamma. (T)[2]

However, Buddhadāsa's innovative work also has a number of historical precedents in the Buddhist reforms instituted in the nineteenth century by King Mongkut of Thailand and by the Anagarika Dhammapala in Ceylon. Mongkut sought to remove inconsistencies between monastic practices and the clerical code of conduct or *vinaya*, and between a doctrinal interpretation of Buddhism and popular views. When King Rama I restructured the Thai Sangha in the first years of the Chakri dynasty he referred to the established traditions of the earlier Thai kingdom of Ayutthaya as his model. Mongkut, however, went back even further into history to find a pristine source for his reforms in the Pali scriptures, and as John Butt notes

> Because the ideas he derived from these sources sometimes clashed with practices and beliefs which over the years had come to be accepted as orthodox by most Thai, Mongkut was frequently accused of supporting radically innovative changes in Buddhist faith and life.[3]

Popular Thai religion is a combination of many influences, with animistic and Brahmanical beliefs blending with Buddhist doctrines. However, the existence of non-Buddhist spirit worship, magical rites, and the honouring of Hindu deities has not traditionally been seen as conflicting with the canonical message of the religion. Rather, such features have been regarded as part of the overall heritage of Thai Buddhism. But Mongkut rejected many of the animist "accretions" to the canonical message of Buddhism, arguing that animism is inconsistent with the doctrines expressed in the Buddhist scriptures. Mongkut's studies of the Pali canon during the twenty-seven years he spent as a monk before disrobing and ascending the Thai throne led him to see discrepancies between the scriptures and the actual practices of Thai monks. As Thomas Kirsch notes,

> He [Mongkut] was so anguished about this discrepancy he vowed that he would disrobe if he did not receive some sign that the monastic line of succession back to the Buddha had not been broken in Thailand.[4]

Mongkut subsequently met a Mon monk whom he came to regard as upholding a tradition which continued the original Theravada practices. Mongkut then established a new, stricter order of monks, the Thammayut, "Those adhering to the doctrine or Dhamma," in accord with the Mon tradition. The Thammayut Order remains today as the second officially recognized sect of the Thai Sangha. The other sect is the Mahanikai Order (literally, "the great order"), which Mongkut characterized as "those adhering to long-standing habit" and with which the overwhelming majority of Thai monks, including Buddhadāsa, still remain associated.

Buddhadāsa's reinterpretations closely parallel aspects of King Mongkut's reforms. Mongkut had an intimate knowledge of Western ideas and the scientific views of his day, obtained from discussions with Christian missionaries dating from his early days as a monk in the 1830s. Kirsch comments that Mongkut's emphasis on reinstituting monkly conduct in strict accordance with the *vinaya* went hand in hand with certain ideological commitments:

For one thing, Mongkut rejected a great many traditional beliefs and practices as superstitious interpolations into Buddhism. He rejected the cosmogony and cosmology represented in the *Trai-phum*,[5] arguing that cosmology had to accord with the scientific views that he had learned in his contact with Westerners . . . Mongkut's monastic reform involved then, not only an effort to upgrade monastic practice and to make it more orthodox, but also included an attempt, in Western terms, to demythologize the world.[6]

Buddhadāsa also followed the principle instituted by Mongkut of following the Pali scriptures as closely as possible while avoiding interpretations of doctrine that contradict scientific knowledge or rationalist views.

For many Thais, including Buddhadāsa, nationalism has become an integral component of the reclamation and review of Buddhism, and in this context he appears to have been influenced by the reformist work of the Anagarika Dhammapala. Born Donald David Hevavitarana, this Ceylonese Buddhist later assumed the title of *anagārika*, denoting a wandering ascetic, and took the Pali name of Dhammapala ("protector of the Dhamma"). With the assistance of the Theosophical Movement, the Anagarika established the Mahabodhi Society in Colombo in the final decades of the nineteenth century with the goal of propagating Buddhism. However, his emphasis was as much social as religious and he became a symbol of a resurgent Sinhalese Buddhist nationalism and of a way to reclaim traditional cultural values which had been oppressed by colonialism while yet supporting socioeconomic modernization.

Balkrishna Gokhale describes Dhammapala as combating

> . . . the notion that Buddhism was a mere other-worldly philosophy calling upon man to turn his back on the world and all its affairs. He maintained that Buddhism was meant as much for the layman [*upāsaka*] as the monk and in the context of the modern age the *dharma* of the *upāsaka* needs reassertion and reinterpretation as much as the revival of monastic learning. Buddhism of the layman addresses itself to both material prosperity and spiritual growth.[7]

The Anagarika aimed for the fusion of modern technology and commercial enterprise with Buddhist values and cited with considerable admiration the achievements of Japan, which he saw as exemplifying the beneficial results of such a fusion. The similarities between the Anagarika's and Buddhadāsa's views are striking. Each of the above points—interest in a this-worldly religion, concern for laypeople, a desire for the integration of scientific and religious approaches, and admiration of Japan—are paralleled in Buddhadāsa's work. The commonality of the social contexts in which Buddhadāsa and the Anagarika worked provides a partial explanation of the closeness of their views. However, the fact that Buddhadāsa was in contact with the Mahabodhi Society and its publications in the 1930s through his brother Dhammadāsa also suggests that his views received some direct influence from the early Buddhist reform and nationalist movements in Ceylon.

There are precedents for aspects of Buddhadāsa's work in the recent history of Buddhism. However, while he was in part influenced by King Mongkut's reforms, and the Anagarika's Buddhist nationalism, Buddhadāsa's reinterpretations go far beyond those of Mongkut and the Anagarika. Indeed, the stark contrast between the novelty of Buddhadāsa's views and the long history of institutionalized conservatism of the tradition within which he worked suggests that the sources of his innovativeness are more likely to be found outside of Buddhism than within it. In particular, I suggest that the most important sources of Buddhadāsa's reappraisal of Buddhism can be traced to Western cultural, economic, and political influences in Thailand.

## WESTERN INFLUENCES ON THE STUDY OF BUDDHISM

The earliest Western intellectual engagements with Buddhism were the critical denunciations of the "pagan" beliefs and practices of the Buddhists by the early Christian missionaries. However, the European denigration of Buddhism and of Asian civilizations in the colonial period was much more than simply a religious phenomenon. In the face of the political, economic, and assumed cultural superiority of European civilization, all cultural and intellectual achievements were judged against the norm of Europe, in comparison with which Asian cultures were found to be severely lacking. This imputed backwardness of Asia was not only the view of Europeans but was also implicitly accepted by many of the Asians educated under colonial European education systems. However, this acceptance of Asia's intellectual and cultural inferiority was questioned by the nationalist and anticolonial movements established in the first decades of the twentieth century. For the members of the Asian nationalist movements, a renewed appreciation of indigenous language, religion, and culture went hand in hand with political attacks on the colonial powers. The twentieth century has consequently seen a resurgent interest among Asian Buddhists in the teaching and practice of Buddhism.

Even though Thailand was never colonized, Thai culture, education, and economic development have nevertheless been heavily influenced by Europe, and more recently by America. As a result, there are many parallels between the situation in Thailand and the colonized countries of Southeast Asia. As was the case among Buddhists in Ceylon and Burma, there has been a resurgent interest in Buddhism among those Thai Buddhists who are concerned to promote the value and significance of Buddhist thought and culture as symbols of Thai national identity and integrity.

Ironically, however, the resurgent interest in Buddhism has in many ways been spurred by the scholarly activities of the colonizing Europeans, from whom Thai, Burmese, and Ceylonese Buddhists have otherwise wished to distance themselves. Until Europeans began studying Buddhist thought systematically in the nineteenth century, doctrinal Buddhism—that is, the critical study of the scriptures of the Buddhist canon—had fallen into decline. Because of the long-established British domination of Ceylon, that country provided the most accessible source of the canonical scriptures, and it was the Ceylonese monks who first offered important source information on the Pali *Tipiṭaka* to Europeans. Indeed, with the Pali researches undertaken by scholars such as Thomas Williams Rhys Davids and Herman Oldenburg, and with the establishment of the Pali Text Society in the late nineteenth century, Ceylon became the focus for a revivified scholarly study of Theravada Buddhist doctrine. The pattern and character of those European studies have subsequently had a profound influence on Pali studies in all the Theravada countries, including Thailand.

The early European study of Theravada Buddhism had a pronounced doctrinal emphasis on the theoretical principles of the religion. This in turn led to a rejection of popular folk Buddhism in Ceylon as an irrational, demonological accretion. As Heinz Bechert notes,

> To be sure, the Indologists could not overlook the fact that monastic practice did not correspond to the precepts of the *vinaya*, that is, of canon law, and that the cult of the gods and the exorcism of demons had an important place in the religion of the Sinhalese . . . And yet representatives of this approach tried rather precipitously to explain away such observations or simply ignored them. Whatever could not be derived from Buddhist tradition was an "adulteration" of the religion, a Hindu influence or simply popular superstition.[8]

It was this sanitized doctrinal interpretation of Buddhism which was then taken up by the English-educated Sinhalese nationalists as a symbol of their cultural and national independence from Europe. This is because the educated Sinhalese elites rejected the popular form of their own religion as inconsistent with canonical principles, precisely the same reason given by the colonial scholars. And when Thai Buddhists subsequently looked to the example of Sinhalese Buddhist nationalism as a model for a modernist Buddhist movement in their own country, it was this same essentially European constructed, or deconstructed, form of Buddhism which was ironically held up as symbolizing "Thai-ness" and Thai independence from the West. Contemporary doctrinal Buddhism in Thailand, best exemplified by the work of Buddhadāsa, has thus been reconstructed and reinterpreted around the rationalist assumptions of the first European Indologists and Buddhologists, and strictly speaking is more a symbol of cultural fusion between East and West than of any inherent "Asianness."

In reasserting Buddhism's intellectual significance, some modernist and nationalist interpreters of Buddhism in Thailand, such as Buddhadāsa, have assumed the very principles of rationality, logical consistency, and scientific methodology which were previously used to denigrate Buddhism. There has been a tremendous intellectual effort by Buddhists to disprove the earlier criticisms of Western scholars that Buddhism is a superstitious and inconsistent religion by attempting to demonstrate that their religion is in fact rational, logical, and scientific.

The desire to demonstrate the intellectual significance of Buddhism by comparing it with Western ideas is most clearly shown in the attempts to prove the scientific character of the religion. As previously noted, science also had importance for Buddhadāsa in providing a means of alleviating or ending suffering, the Buddhist religious goal, at the material level. Demonstrating a harmony between Buddhism and science therefore is not only significant for Buddhadāsa in terms of imputing intellectual stature to Buddhism, but is also important in ensuring that there are no contradictions or barriers to integrating the material benefits of modern science and technology into a revised interpretation of Buddhist salvation. Buddhadāsa has said that Buddhism and science

> are alike in that scientific principles can stand proof—one may provide the proof himself for others to see, or be willing to let anyone scrutinise, test, or cross-question as he wishes, and it bears up until no further testing can be done and he must believe.[9]

The argument that the spiritual truths of Buddhism are open to experiential verification in a way that is assumed to be similar to the method of validating scientific results is a claim commonly made by Buddhists. For example, the Sri Lankan Buddhist thinker K. N. Jayatilleke says:

> I find that early Buddhism [i.e. Theravada] emphasises the importance of the scientific outlook in dealing with the problems of morality and religion. Its specific "dogmas" are said to be capable of

verification and its general account of the nature of man and the universe is one that accords with the findings of science rather than being at variance with them.[10]

And Robert Spencer, an English convert to Buddhism, adds:

> There can be no question that Buddhism is the one system, excepting perhaps science itself, which achieves an objective and detached view towards the nature and destiny of man.[11]

Nevertheless, while there is an enthusiasm for science and the scientific method among some contemporary Buddhist thinkers, this does not mean that there is a clear appreciation of the epistemological issues and debates about the scientific method. For example, while Buddhadāsa claimed that there is a congruence between the Buddhist approach to gaining spiritual insight and the verificationist methodology of science, he did not appear to be aware of the competing falsificationist view on the workings of science, for he did not attempt to demonstrate a relationship between Buddhist thought and falsificationism. In Buddhadāsa's works, science is presented as a static, abstract ideal rather than as the fuzzy-edged activity recent studies have shown it to be. The idealized view of science found in many recent Buddhist works suggests that the actual relation between science and Buddhism is not the real issue. Rather, modernist Buddhist scholars appear to be attempting to construct a justification or apologetic for Buddhist teachings which appeals to science because of its assumed authority.

That Buddhists are not prepared to accept fully scientific rationalism is shown by a careful reading of the *Kālāma Sutta*, the part of the canon most often referred to as providing a scientific basis for Buddhism. Many Buddhists, like Bhikkhu Ananda quoted below, regard the *Kālāma Sutta*[12] as a Buddhist charter for free scientific enquiry:

> In the *Kālāma Sutta* we are asked not to believe in anything merely because the Buddha happened to preach it . . . The true Buddhist is a free thinker, a seeker of the truth, who seeks to disarm the one enemy—Ignorance. He is self-dependent. . . In his quest for supreme

wisdom, the Buddhist will be guided by reason and knowledge rather than sentiment and emotion.[13]

In the *Kālāma Sutta* the Buddha advises the Kālāma people that the assumed authority of report, tradition, hearsay, or of a renowned teacher or text should not be accepted uncritically when considering the claims of competing or dubious doctrines. But while criticizing unthinking faith in traditional views and authorities, the Buddha is also critical of unrestrained rational investigations of different religious doctrines. He criticizes rational activity which does not arrive at the most beneficial or the most ethical result but instead accepts conclusions arrived at by purely logical analysis. In the *Kālāma Sutta* the Buddha also admonishes the Kālāma people to

> not be led by mere logic . . . by inference . . . by considering appearances . . . by agreement with a considered approved theory . . . by seeming possibilities.(T)[14]

The Buddha says that the deciding criterion when judging competing views should be whether a doctrine is *dosa* (morally corrupt) or *adosa* (free of moral corruption). That is, far from being what some Buddhists, selectively reading the *Kālāma Sutta*, have said is a Buddhist scriptural license for free intellectual enquiry, this *sutta* in fact presents a highly pragmatic approach to rational activity which gives ethical considerations primacy over logical or rational debate. According to the principle presented in the *sutta*, a logically "valid" theory would have to be rejected as "unprofitable" if it is not *adosa* or does not promote virtue and moral attainment, and thereby the attainment of *nibbāna*.

Buddhadāsa reads the *Kālāma Sutta* as warning not to believe blindly in either the *Tipiṭaka*, a teacher, what is reported or rumoured, what has been reasoned out, or what has been arrived at by logic. He says

> Although we may have read, listened and heard, we should not simply accept what is offered in these ways unless we have first

> thought it over, considered it carefully, fathomed it out, examined it, and seen clearly that it really is so.[15]

What distinguishes any scientific method from the Buddha's pronouncements in the *Kālāma Sutta* is that, according to the latter, one is to be as wary of the results of reason and logic as of rumour and report. Buddhadāsa acknowledged this when he said that "seeing clearly" means to apprehend truth or reality "without needing to use reason, without needing to speculate, without needing to make assumptions."[16] That is, despite claims for the scientific character of Buddhism, the *Kālāma Sutta* in fact calls for the development of direct spiritual insight into reality, not for a scientific or empirical method of enquiry. Nevertheless, while the *Kālāma Sutta* does not in fact contain a call for the implementation of the scientific method in Buddhism, Buddhadāsa and other Buddhist thinkers still consider the authority accorded science as rubbing off onto a Buddhism which has been shown to be "scientific." Buddhadāsa claimed:

> Thus is there not a clear indication of how Buddhism goes by nature with science, which the modern world everywhere honours? And the most important point is: When Buddhism alone is one with the world's science, then which religion is fit to be the religion of the world besides Buddhism?[17]

But while claims of the "scientific" character of Buddhism are strictly speaking invalid, it is nevertheless the case that there is a fundamental congruence between Buddhadāsa's doctrinal Buddhism and Western rationalism. As already noted, Buddhadāsa emphasized the doctrinal aspect of Buddhism and rejected the traditional popular or lay aspects of the religion in an attempt to integrate a positive valuation of action in the social world with core Buddhist doctrines. Popular Buddhism in Thailand is associated with beliefs in the power of supernatural beings which can intervene in human life, whether for good or for bad. In contrast, doctrinal Buddhism has always been dominated by notions of immutable impersonal law, the law of *kamma,* and the overarching cosmic-moral order of righteousness or Dhamma. In Buddhism the cosmos is a consistently and thoroughly ordered system in which both suffering and salvation result from the systematic operation of such principles as *kamma* and Dhamma. In Theravada Buddhism *nibbāna* results from systematically applying these universal principles in spiritual practice. In positing the existence of immutable universal laws, the doctrinal Buddhism which Buddhadāsa teaches, like Western rationalism, also emphasizes the consistent application of general principles.

As already noted, popular Buddhist beliefs are often in contradiction with doctrine. For example, belief in the transferability of religious merit or good *kamma* between individuals, that there is personal continuity after death, and that *nibbāna* can be attained as a result of an enormous accumulation of merit rather than through liberative insight, cannot be justified by Buddhist doctrine but are nonetheless widely adhered to. The contradictions of popular beliefs with doctrine have long been recognized and have been accepted as the unavoidable corruption of the Buddha's teachings by world-involved laypeople who are unable to grasp the subtleties of the transcendent doctrine. It is generally held that it is better that laypeople grasp things in their own inadequate way, and so act morally, than that they be left out of Buddhism entirely because of their spiritual turpitude.

Because knowledge has traditionally been judged in relation to its spiritual "benefit," rather than against any strict notion of rationality or logical consistency, such inconsistent views have been accepted where they are regarded as morally beneficial for those who hold them. However, Buddhadāsa rejected this epistemological duality and maintained that Buddhism should be doctrinally consistent throughout. This doctrinalism, which seeks to consistently apply the universal principles of Buddhist teaching throughout all aspects of the religion, is a rational potential which has been latent in Buddhism since its inception. However, this rational potential has not been fully developed because of the mitigating influence of the two-tiered mundane-supramundane structure of Buddhist practice and teaching, and because strict logical consistency has traditionally been regarded as having only secondary importance behind the moral benefit of beliefs held.

While European-derived rationalism has had a significant influence on contemporary Buddhist thought, the rejection of logically contradictory popular beliefs has in fact revealed and brought to the fore in Buddhadāsa's work a latent rationalism which has lain in the core of Buddhism. The rationalist implications of doctrinal Buddhism are only now being fully realized because, like the early European Buddhist scholars, Buddhadāsa rejects the distinction between an imperfect lay and a doctrinal clerical form of Buddhism because of his implicit acceptance of Western notions of rationalism and scientific reasoning. Buddhadāsa's rationalism is therefore a compound phenomenon, combining elements of both borrowed European and indigenous Buddhist rationalist methodologies.

It must be noted that there is a further source of Buddhadāsa's strict doctrinalist approach to Buddhism. Because his interpretations of Buddhism are so innovative and because some of his specific views are without direct precedents in either the canonical scriptures or in commentaries, Buddhadāsa must argue for his views and provide justifications for his interpretations. Because his reinterpretations therefore depend upon logical argumentation and demonstration, Buddhadāsa places much more emphasis upon reason than more traditional interpreters of Buddhist doctrine who can rely upon given and accepted sources.

## THE INFLUENCE OF SOCIOECONOMIC CHANGE IN THAILAND ON BUDDHADĀSA'S THOUGHT

In addition to the intellectual impact of the West, social changes specific to Thailand also had a significant impact on Buddhadāsa's thought. The relations between social and economic change and Buddhadāsa's reinterpretations of Buddhist doctrine are complex. But in general Buddhadāsa's views can be seen as responses to the religious and moral dilemmas facing the modernist, educated sections of the Thai elite, who make up Buddhadāsa's main audience in Thailand and of which Buddhadāsa was himself by birth a member. However, to detail these social and intellectual relations it is first necessary to describe the dynamic socioeconomic situation in modern Thailand.

While modernization is affecting the lives of all Thais, it is nevertheless only a relatively small urban elite of military and government bureaucrats, influential businessmen, teachers, students, writers, and artists who have any significant decision-making power in the process of modernization. Buddhadāsa's main audience and supporters are found amongst Buddhists who are directly concerned with the issues of Thailand's modernization and of the country's socioeconomic development. Nearly all Buddhadāsa's supporters are members of the numerically small, urban-based Thai elite who dominate the country politically, economically, and culturally. Furthermore, Buddhadāsa's supporters are drawn from only certain sections of the elite, and it is important to note that, while small in absolute terms, the groups controlling Thailand's political, economic, educational and cultural life are still highly heterogeneous. The Thai elite is split vertically into a hierarchy based on relative power and is also split laterally at each level of that hierarchy by conflicting ideological allegiances and political perceptions.

Writing in 1962, David Wilson divided the Thai elite into three hierarchical tiers[18] which make up a pyramid of power and influence. He locates a small group of ten to fifteen people—military commanders, civilian political leaders, and some aristocratic figures—at the top of this pyramid. These are the people who are potentially capable of dominating the elite and thereby the rest of the country because of their ability to manipulate key political forces. The second tier of the Thai elite isolated by Wilson is made up of about one thousand senior figures—high-ranking armed forces officers, special grade civil servants, some parliamentary leaders, and a few powerful businessmen. The third level, at the base of the pyramid, are, in the words of Daniel Wit, writing in 1968,

> The educated, interested and reasonably articulate thousands of persons resident in Bangkok and a few provincial towns who, whether within or without the public bureaucracy, are the Thai

equivalent of the middle classes . . . composed of high school and university graduates and their equivalent, most are middle-level bureaucrats with lesser numbers of professional and white collar personnel, writers and journalists and businessmen. They are attuned to the political currents and are even willing to be critical, but few are anxious for revolutionary changes.[19]

In addition to divisions arising from personal allegiances to one or other powerful military, bureaucratic, or political patron, there are ideological and political divisions within the elite between traditionalist and progressive groups. The same complex of issues focusing on national development, nationalism, Buddhism, and appropriate national political forms dominates the intellectual debate of both the traditionalist and progressive sections of the elite, but both sections systematically disagree on the best approach to deal with each issue. In brief, the traditionalist sections of the Thai elite support strong links with Western countries and reliance upon Western models of development based upon significant foreign investment together with an opening of the economy to high levels of foreign business penetration. The progressives, while not disagreeing with the capitalist model of socioeconomic development, are more critical of the deleterious cultural and economic effects of unrestricted reliance upon the West. In contrast, they tend to support the idea of a Thai-based model of development which refers to Buddhist rather than to capitalist paradigms. This emphasis on a Buddhist-based economic framework for development is reflected in such books as *Setthasat Choeng Phut* (Buddhist economics)(T),[20] a translation of and commentary upon E. F. Schumacher's *Small is Beautiful*, and in articles such as Wisit Wangwinyu's "Than Phutthathat kap setthasat chao phut" (Buddhadāsa and Buddhist economics)(T).[21]

The traditionalists' economic and technological reliance upon the West is associated with a vehement opposition to communism; the firing of a strong Thai nationalism among the populace to resist communist ideological infiltration; maintaining political and military links with the West, particularly the U.S.A.; and a preference for a strong, military-backed if not military-led government in

Bangkok. The progressives, on the other hand, seek to develop and strengthen Thai national identity as a cultural barrier to Western and Japanese as well as communist incursions into Thai sociocultural traditions. The progressives seek an independent rather than a derivative Thai cultural identity and support democratic political institutions as a vehicle for social justice within the country.

The progressives among the Thai elite are by and large liberals and democrats who have a strong commitment to establishing Thailand's political, economic, and cultural independence within the modern global order. A significant proportion of these progressives can be identified as the Thai intelligentsia, consisting of university and college teachers, students, writers, artists, some labour leaders, some outspoken monks such as Buddhadāsa, and lower-ranking but educated government officials committed to national development. Another large group of the progressive section of the Thai elite are members of what Ben Anderson calls the "new bourgeois strata," which have grown rapidly as a result of substantial post-World War II American and Japanese investment in Thailand. Anderson says that this "new bourgeoisie" is "rather small and frail to be sure, but in significant respects it is outside of and partially antagonistic to the old feudal-bureaucratic class."[22]

The new bourgeoisie consists of administrative, executive, and managerial workers, professionals and technicians, and service and recreation workers, most of whom have received some level of tertiary education. While strictly speaking neither radical nor leftist, this new bourgeoisie stands in some degree of opposition to the traditional military, bureaucratic, and aristocratic Thai elite whose established interests are often seen as hindering their social mobility and advancement.

Apart from a couple of brief interludes, such as the 1973–1976 period of civilian government, the traditionalists have dominated Thai politics since the 1932 revolution. More often than not the progressive members of the Thai elite have been in a defensive rather than offensive position. In terms of Wilson's conception of the Thai elite as a three-tiered pyramidal structure, the top rung and most of the positions of the middle rung are dominated by traditionalists and their supporters. Most progressives are isolated from any real exercise of power, being in the third and lowest rung of the elite hierarchy, with only a very few managing to establish themselves in influential middle-level management or decision-making positions.

The Buddhist Sangha has inevitably become involved in the conflicts between the traditionalist and progressive sections of the Thai elite. As already outlined, institutional Buddhism has been moulded by successive governments in order to provide a religious legitimation of their policies. The progressive elements of the Thai elite are consequently as dissatisfied with the conservative Sangha hierarchy as they are with the various regimes which have manipulated the official representatives of Buddhism. Because of the association of the Sangha with the dominant conservative, militarist, and monarchist sections of the elite, any significant reinterpretation or reform of Buddhism which broke or weakened the traditional politico-religious relations could not but have political implications. And indeed, the various criticisms of Buddhadāsa's reinterpretations of doctrine discussed in the following chapters have as much basis in political disputes between the traditionalist and progressive sections of the Thai elite as in disputes over strictly doctrinal matters.

Furthermore, a significant determinant of the high degree of support for Buddhadāsa's reinterpretative work from progressive sections of the elite derives from his dissociation from the conservative Sangha hierarchy. Progressive Thai Buddhists also support Buddhadāsa because of his commitment to a Buddhist-based notion of development which is founded upon a critique of the traditional interpretations of religion sponsored by both the official Sangha hierarchy and the majority of the traditionalist sections of the elite. Seri Phongphit, an academic philosopher, chacterized Buddhadāsa's popularity among progressive intellectuals as follows:

> His [Buddhadāsa's] line of thought has an influence on a large number of Thai intellectuals, thinkers and writers and he seems to be accepted and admired by intellectuals more than by other groups, especially since 14 October 1973[23] when his thought—as presented by himself and by others—has become increasingly clearly concerned with social and political affairs.(T)[24]

For progressive Thais, Buddhadāsa's reforms also had great sociocultural significance, for he was regarded as aiding efforts to define Thai national identity in terms other than the jingoistic ideal propounded by the Thai military and monarchy. The progressives seek a new Thai Buddhist identity which both defines their cultural uniqueness and their place in the world. This desire was expressed by Phra Pracha Pasannathammo, a follower of Buddhadāsa, who in a paper entitled "Than Phutthathat Kap Patiwat Watthanatham" or "Buddhadāsa and the cultural revolution,"(T)[25] gives one chapter section the heading, *Ekkalak khong Thai lae sakonniyom baep phut* or "Thai Identity and Buddhist Internationalism."(T)[26] Phra Pracha explains the cultural importance attached to Buddhadāsa's work when he says

> He [Buddhadāsa] enjoins us to see the value of a "Thai-ness" which is not simply a return to the former nationalism of self-infatuation that we are, or are of, a nation which is better than and superior to other nations. And it is different from the superficial nationalism of Rama VI [King Vajiravudh] and the mad nationalism current in the time of Field Marshal Phibunsongkhram.[27] And it is also different from the contemporary official propaganda [about Thai national identity] which is only the dregs of "Thai-ness" and which does not lead to an understanding of the core [of being Thai] itself.
>
> The fact that contemporary Thais have been separated from their "Thainess," that they feel alienated and have lost a sense of pride in their own country, is because the social leaders of the past one hundred years have not used their intellect to seriously question the true character of our identity. Because they have been blindly following the tails of the *farang* [Westerners] Indian-file . . . Buddhadāsa is an important person who points out the true core of being Thai that we should protect, that we should be proud of and should support and nurture. At the same time, he does not refrain from criticizing our weak points . . . But what is even more important is that he is a person who can progress from "Thai-ness" through Buddhism to also be a universalist. I regard this as finding the most appropriate type of identity.(T)[28]

Thai Buddhism's institutional role in legitimating the traditionalist military-monarchist elite has created disenchantment with official Buddhism among the rising middle and intellectual classes, who are outside of the system of Sangha-monarchy-military-bureaucracy alliances. The rising classes are seeking an alternative definition and approach to Buddhism which can be used both to oppose the traditional religio-social order which limits their chances for advancement and simultaneously to promote their own interests and view of the world. In this situation of conflict Buddhadāsa's modernist critical reforms have been taken up as an important component of the alternative Buddhist ideology sought by the Thai middle classes or new bourgeoisie.

In this context, it is significant that Buddhadāsa's family background and educational experience reveal him to be a member of the section of Thai society which constitutes his largest audience, the lower rung of the educated elite. Buddhadāsa was born in 1906 into a commercial family whose members valued education and social advancement through the traditionally recognized channels of the monkhood and the government service. For example, Buddhadāsa's younger brother, Dhammadāsa, was educated at Chulalongkorn University in Bangkok. Chulalongkorn University is the most prestigious tertiary institution in the country and was established in the first decades of the twentieth century to provide Thais with the training necessary to occupy posts in the expanding government bureaucracy of the newly modernizing country.

Dhammadāsa appears to have had a major influence on Buddhadāsa and to have taken as keen an interest in Buddhism as his older brother. Dhammadāsa was particularly impressed by the propagation of Buddhism in the West by Japanese and Ceylonese Buddhists. In letters written to Buddhadāsa while he was a student at Chulalongkorn University Dhammadāsa appears somewhat amazed by these Buddhist missionary efforts:

> Our Buddhism must certainly have something good, enough to be able to boast to the *farangs* about it.(T)[29]
>
> Foreigners who used to hold to other religions have become interested in Buddhism, and devote their time and energy to

propagating it and making it widespread. Why then don't we Thai, who are true Buddhists, think to do as the foreigners?(T)[30]

When he returned to manage the family business in Phumriang near Chaiya in 1929, Dhammadāsa continued his interest in Buddhism by setting up a small lending library on Buddhism at the family store. He also started a Buddhist discussion group called the Khana Sonthanatham (คณะสนทนาธรรม), The Dhamma Discussion Group, which in later years developed into the Thammathan Munnithi (ธรรมทานมูลนิธิ), the Dhammadāna Foundation.

Buddhadāsa's intellectual direction was also influenced by political and religious events during his stay in Bangkok at the beginning of the 1930s, when he attempted to obtain an ecclesiastical degree. At the time Buddhadāsa was in Bangkok one Narin Phasit arranged for his daughters to become *samaṇerī* or novice nuns. Narin wished to promote the Dhamma, which he regarded as having decayed because the Sangha no longer had the full complement of both monks and nuns as in the Buddha's time, the official order of Theravada nuns having fallen into decay before the Thais adopted Buddhism. Narin also established a monastery called Wat Nariwong for nuns in his attempt to revive the tradition of female ordination. Narin contacted the Khana Sonthanatham seeking support for his initiatives, because under Dhammadāsa's leadership and frequent letter writing to newspapers and journals his discussion group had become widely known as being interested in reforming Buddhism. Dhammadāsa at first supported Narin and informed him of Buddhadāsa's own reformist interests. However, Buddhadāsa disagreed with Narin, apparently not because of doctrinal differences but because he felt the way Narin had gone about his project of reestablishing the Theravada order of nuns amounted to an attack on the sanctity of the Sangha.

Narin and his ideas were generally criticized and his project was finally abandoned because of the vehemence of opposition both from within and outside the Sangha. Yet despite his opposition to the project, Buddhadāsa appears to have been deeply affected by the Narin episode. He became concerned that people like Narin could so easily criticize the Sangha and was led to consider what deficiencies there were in the Thai monkhood that left it open to attack. The problem of the degeneration of the Sangha occupied Buddhadāsa more and more and he began a deeper personal study of the scriptures in an attempt to glean the Buddha's actual intentions and teachings, and to judge the modern Sangha against them.

While issues such as modernization no doubt occupied Buddhadasa's mind at this time, and became more pronounced in his writings with the passage of the years, in and of themselves these were not the original motivating forces behind his reformist efforts. Rather, from his position inside the Sangha, he appears to have been more concerned with preventing the attacks of such modernist, educated laypersons as Narin. In coming to regard Narin's and other's criticisms of the Thai Sangha as valid and as flowing from a degeneration of the monkhood, Buddhadāsa also accepted the modernist intellectual values and rationalism which underlay those criticisms. However, like any true conservative, he did not see the solution to the degeneration of Thai Buddhism as lying in a one-sided accommodation of the Sangha to modernist views. Instead Buddhadāsa sought to purify Buddhism by returning to the original teachings and instructions of the Buddha. He thought that because the Sangha had so degenerated as to become the object of attacks from the lay populace, the original teachings must have been lost or at least suffered misinterpretation. In Buddhadāsa's view, criticisms that the Sangha was out of line with contemporary society, and even a retarding and negative social influence, were not to be met by simply modernizing the monkhood. With faith in the universality of the Buddha's message of salvation, Buddhadāsa thought that once the original form of Buddhism was refound and expressed anew the religion's universal and thus current relevance would once again become transparently clear.

Over and above these formative intellectual influences, it is also important to note that Buddhadāsa received encouragement from his family when it became clear that he wished to use his obvious intellectual talents in the religious domain. Because of his family background Buddhadāsa would have had a keen personal awareness of the aspirations of the upwardly mobile but non-aristocratic educated

Thais of his generation. This is shown by his strong identification with the bureaucrats and junior army officers who overthrew the Thai absolute monarchy in 1932 in order to establish a popular government under a reconstituted constitutional monarchy. Buddhadāsa saw a close relationship between the political revolution of 1932 and his own mission to reform Buddhist teachings and practice, which began in the same year:

> In the country there was a revolution, a reform concerning the governance of the land. For we temple-dwellers, we religious, there was the intention to revolutionize or reform activities relating to religion. We wanted the revival, promotion, study and practice of religion, to improve it to the extent that it could be called a reform.(T)[31]

The strong support for Buddhadāsa's views from members of the new Thai bourgeoisie was due to the reflection in his work of the social, political, and religious issues which preoccupy the educated Thai middle class. In his various reforms of doctrine and teaching Buddhadāsa not only addressed what he saw as the need to change Thai Buddhism but also at the same time the new bourgeoisie's perceived need for religious reform. In particular, Buddhadāsa's work directly addresses some difficult religious and ideological dilemmas facing the lay Thai Buddhist intelligentsia.

The life of the modern Thai urban dweller, pervasively influenced by the "revolution of rising expectations," the ethic of progress, and the spoils of modernity, is radically different from the traditional ways of living for which Buddhism has historically provided the integrative value system. As a consequence there is a growing questioning of the relevance of Buddhism to the new Thai society now in the process of developing. More and more Thais, especially educated urban dwellers, are questioning the appropriateness of Buddhist practices and doctrines which developed from and were directed towards an altogether different social order. Siddhi Butr-Indr echoes the feelings of many educated Thai Buddhists when he says:

> Unless the spiritual principles of religion can be translated in terms of social ideals, values and interests or can influence worldly affairs, they will not survive as far as society as a whole is concerned.[32]

Social modernization has raised two broad sets of issues for traditional Buddhism. At the social or institutional level the question is whether a religion which has historically legitimized the socioeconomic and political structures of traditional Thai society can be reinterpreted and used to provide ideological support for and legitimation of fundamental social change. And secondly, at the level of personal ethics, Buddhists supportive of modernization must deal with the fact that Buddhist teachings have traditionally defined material values as being in opposition to the religious ideal of transcendent enlightenment or *nibbāna.* As George Rupp observes, for a religious system to remain viable in a modernizing twentieth-century society it cannot avoid the issue of the religious significance of "man's increasing capacity to shape his personal and corporate life within the sphere of phenomenal existence."[33] This ethical problem can be summarized as whether, in attaining salvation from suffering, the emphasis of religion should be on adjusting one's desires to the reality of a hostile world or whether it should be on changing the world to fit in with one's desires. Underlying the doctrinal reforms of Buddhadāsa can be seen a desire to establish the pursuit of material well-being as a religious value in its own right while yet not denying or devaluing the traditional spiritual verities. Buddhadāsa thus tackled the contemporary religious dilemma of the need to resolve the conflict between upholding traditional Buddhist teachings and practices and risk seeing Buddhism become increasingly socially irrelevant, and accepting the benefits of modernization and risking the materialization of the religion and the loss of its spiritual values.

Many intellectual Buddhists wish Buddhism to act as the ideological foundation of a religious and moral approach to socioeconomic development, as a unique Thai alternative to both capitalism and communism. As a key focus of Thai national and cultural identity, Buddhism is regarded as having the potential of providing a cultural and institutional link between Thailand's rich cultural past and the hope for a more prosperous and independent future. In this context the twin demands being placed upon Buddhism by progressive intellectuals are, firstly, that it support economic development and modernization and, secondly, that it direct a primary emphasis to the concerns of this world, here and now.

But while these broad issues of the relevance and place of Buddhism in modern Thailand underlie the concerns of educated Buddhists for the future of their religion, most contemporary religious analyses and debates are couched in much more specific terms, in terms of the perceived failure of institutional Buddhism or the Thai Sangha to meet the needs of Thai men and women in the twentieth century. It is the Sangha, the traditional monastic organiszation of Buddhism in Thailand, which is the focus of criticisms which arise from the disillusionment of the progressive sections of the Thai educated elite with the intellectual, political, and ritualistic conservatism of officially sponsored institutional Buddhism. As Donald Swearer notes,

> The generally low educational level of the average monk and monastic preoccupation with ritual and ceremony led to widespread alienation of the intelligentsia from institutional Buddhism.[34]

Pun Chongprasoet, the late founder of a lay Buddhist revivalist movement, The Sublime Life Mission[35] and long-time supporter of Buddhadāsa, concurs with Swearer's view:

> These days the majority of those who have been ordained are devoid of knowledge about either the world or Dhamma. This is because they are too lazy to study and seek out knowledge, and because their only aim is looking for money. Consequently they are incapable of correctly answering questions about the Dhamma. What those who have been ordained propagate has in the main become mere ignorant nonsense.(T)[36]

The Sangha is the focus of criticism because in Theravada Buddhism religious authority in matters of doctrinal interpretation has traditionally been centralized in the hierarchy of monks.

Historically the Buddhist layperson has not been regarded as having significant religious standing, and as a result lay frustrations deriving from the perceived irrelevance of the religion in the face of modern expectations tend to be directed towards the traditional holders of spiritual authority, the monks.

However, there is a countervailing factor in Thai Buddhism which might be considered to provide a way to resolve these lay frustrations. This is the fact that Buddhism has traditionally had two distinct levels of ethics and religious expectations—one for the world-involved layperson and one for the renunciate aspiring to spiritual perfection. Buddhist lay ethics and practices, *lokiya-dhamma*, have always been more worldly, encompassing economic, political and social concerns which in general are well suited, perhaps with some minor adjustments, for guiding activities related to modernization and socioeconomic development. Siddhi Butr-Indr summarizes the attributes of the ideal Buddhist layperson, which are presented in the *suttas,* as being one who

> seeks wealth by lawful and non-violent means, in so doing gets ease and enjoyment for himself, shares it with others and does meritorious deeds, utilises it without greed and craving, and is guiltless of offence, heedful of danger and alive to his highest value.[37]

Given that the roles of monk and layperson are institutionally compartmentalized and the *lokiyadhamma* has traditionally sanctioned active world-involvement, the reasons for lay Thai intellectuals' disenchantment with Buddhism and their criticisms of the Sangha are not immediately apparent. The source of the dissatisfaction in fact lies in the changes which have occurred in their view of the world and in their religious aspirations, changes which have been taking place apace with modernization. The relatively small stratum of educated Thais is the social group whose values and outlook have come to differ most radically from the traditional Thai conceptions of life and religion. Contemporary tertiary educated Thais consider themselves part of the international intellectual community and, as has already been noted, accept the Western-derived criteria of theoretical criticism and argumentation and the methodological principles of science which underpin the technology being used for modernization. And more importantly, like the British-educated Sinhalese elite in Ceylon, they also judge traditional and popular lay Buddhism by these same Western-derived rationalist and scientific standards, often rejecting or criticizing it as being superstitious and unsubstantiated by the scriptures. For example, Pun Chongprasoet often spoke of modernist religious reforms as being like "operating to remove the cancer of superstition from Buddhism,"(T)[38] a cancer he defined as including, among other things, belief in magic, spirit houses, magic bracelets and amulets, trances and spirit possession and conversing with celestial beings.

The divergence between popular Buddhism and the doctrinal religion ascribed to by many educated Thai Buddhists has been apparent for some time. In 1947 one Araya Nikonthai[39] made the following observations in a newspaper article entitled *Phutthasatsana champen samrap khon thai rue* (Is Buddhism necessary for Thais?"), a plea for modernization in Thai Buddhism:

> If we had persisted in following the ways of our ancestors how could we have got the constitution?[40] The differences between the religious beliefs of our ancestors and of people today are thus so great that we can say there is a Buddhism for the people of the past and a Buddhism for contemporary people.(T)[41]

John Van Esterik notes that in desiring to reform Buddhism in accordance with their modernist views, progressive Thai intellectuals cut across the traditional institutional divisions of Thai Buddhism, appropriating to themselves not only such formerly clerical aspects as meditation but even the monarch's traditional role as upholder of the religion:

> The reformation of Buddhism by laity is a modern movement. Educated and elite laity have taken up the role normally bestowed upon the king, to purify the religion and, at the same time to make it relevant to present day society, as they perceive it. Instead of restoring the monkhood, which many of them denigrate, they seek

"salvation" in a religious involvement that will purify each and every individual in the state.[42]

Being lay yet adhering to a traditionally clerical, monastic form of Buddhism means that progressive Thai intellectuals face more moral and ideological tensions than do the monks, the general populace or the power elite of the aristocracy, military, and large business interests. These tensions are manifested in their disenchantment with the traditional religion. In contrast to the religious conservatism of most other sections of Thai society, those Thais who bring the critical insights of their Western-styled education to bear on the problems of contemporary Thai society and religion must deal with the full force of the ideological conflict generated by placing modernist material demands and expectations for social development on a system of religious doctrine which grew from a pre-modern social order and which sought an altogether other-worldly goal. For example, there is a pronounced tension between the ultimate religious goal of *nibbāna,* now appropriated by many lay Buddhist intellectuals as their private religious ideal, and the traditional Theravada interpretation of *nibbāna* as a purified mental state attainable only by years if not lifetimes of intense moral and meditative effort undertaken in seclusion away from everyday social interaction. This is only one of a number of fundamental tensions which result from educated laymen's and laywomen's rejection of the traditionally defined lay system of Buddhist belief and practice and their consequent attempts to hold to the clerical system of religious practice and doctrine, which has been exclusively monastic for over two millennia.

However, the traditional separation of lay Buddhism from the clerical form of the religion means that educated lay Buddhists face a practical dilemma in addition to the theoretical problem of developing a doctrinally pure religion by removing what are seen as non-Buddhist accretions. Underlying this practical dilemma is the historical restriction of Dhamma or religious studies to the leisured scholar monks. But more fundamental is the problem that, according to the clerical tradition now inclined towards by the educated laity, a world-involved layperson is regarded as lacking the religious authority necessary to develop acceptable reinterpretations of Buddhism. While desiring to reform or purify Buddhism, the critical lay Buddhist lacks the religious status needed to authorize any significant reinterpretations. Only the clergy possess such authority but, as already noted, the Sangha is by and large conservative, with few monks feeling any responsibility to adjust either the interpretation of the Dhamma or their own practice of the *vinaya* to suit the modernist predilections of a critical intellectual minority .

The continuing acceptance of this traditional centralization of religious authority in the hands of members of the Sangha is reflected in the fact that not even the most radical lay Thai Buddhists have suggested that they appropriate full religious authority to themselves. Among all the calls for doctrinal purification and reforms of the Sangha there are no calls for a Protestant-like reformation of Thai Buddhism. This reticence of the laity to seek to obtain complete religious authority for themselves is a consequence of the long-standing political support for the orthopractic character of Buddhism, where the greatest religious status is ascribed to those who most strictly follow the ascetic codes of the *vinaya*, i.e. the renunciate monks. This officially recognized and sanctioned tradition of orthopraxy, which denies full religious authority to the laity, is not challenged by even the most radical of Buddhists. This is because the appropriation of the full religious authority of the clergy by the laity would undermine the traditional role of the monk and thus the institution of the Sangha. And such action is seen, even by the most critical layperson, as a threat to Thai Buddhism itself. This reluctance to do anything which might be seen as undermining the Sangha, such as an explicit lay assumption of religious authority, follows from the Sangha being included as an inalienable part of one of the most central of all Buddhist articles of belief. This is the Buddha's pronouncement that all those who seek salvation from suffering should maintain faith, *saddhā,* in the three unimpeachable jewels, *tiratana*, of the Buddha, the Dhamma, and the Sangha.[43] It is out of the question for a doctrinally strict lay Buddhist to breach such a central canonically recorded doctrine by arrogating to him- or herself the spiritual authority invested in the Sangha and vouchsafed by the Buddha's own recorded words.

What the critical Buddhist layperson, caught at the crossroads of a clerical ideology and worldly involvement, would therefore seem to require is a monk, preferably with a reputation for both scholarship and practical insight, to develop a new outlook upon Buddhism on their behalf. For, as outlined above, educated lay Buddhists face doctrinal and practical dilemmas which they as laypersons cannot resolve. I suggest that a key to understanding the significance of many of Buddhadāsa's doctrinal reinterpretations lies in realizing that both his teachings and his personal history, as a renunciate monk, meet the pressing social and religious needs of that group of educated Thai Buddhists who desire a religion which is consistent with their modernist view of the world and with their roles as agents of their country's socioeconomic development. In interpreting Buddhadāsa's work I will often return to this argument, that the central aspects of his reinterpretations of Buddhism, whatever their doctrinal authority or spiritual validity, can also be seen as fulfilling the needs of modernist Thais looking for a Buddhism consonant with their social aspirations for a modernized, developed Thailand.

As already noted, Buddhadāsa is by birth and rearing a member of the social group which now constitutes his largest audience. While sections of Buddhadāsa's work can be seen as straightforward attempts to demythologize or rationalize Buddhist teachings, other sections of his work are explicitly concerned with the social and political role of Buddhism in modern Thailand. This social aspect of Buddhadāsa's work clearly shows that he shares the concerns of his lay audience and that he does feel responsible to develop a modernist interpretation of the religion which is relevant and directed to resolving the dilemmas faced by lay Buddhists. Buddhadāsa thus sympathizes with his lay supporters and is explicitly concerned to deal with their difficulties in his work. Consequently, it must be acknowledged that Buddhadāsa's work is not only a response to modernist and rationalist intellectual trends but also to the religious dilemmas faced by the rising new bourgeois stratum of Thai society, of which Buddhadāsa himself can be regarded as a member.

It is not only Buddhadāsa's ideas which are important to his lay audience. Buddhadāsa's way of life is also important in authorizing and giving legitimacy to his radical views in the face of a generally antagonistic and conservative religious establishment. Buddhadāsa's strict ascetic life gives authority to his views, something of vital importance to the insecure new bourgeoisie which is seeking to find a recognized place for itself and its views in modern Thailand.

Religious authority in Theravada Buddhism is more than an institutionally recognized right to speak on and interpret matters of doctrine. Because of the orthopractic character of the religion and the absence of centralized censorial controls on interpretations of the Buddha's teachings, whether by laypeople or by monks, there is in effect a universal right to speak on matters of doctrine within certain legally and traditionally defined bounds. Religious authority within Thai Buddhism denotes the right to be listened to and to be regarded as a person whose views should be treated with due gravity and respect. Essentially, religious authority in Thailand is equivalent to the institutionally recognized standing of a person within the official hierarchy of the Buddhist Sangha rather than the standing of his analyses or arguments. The religious authority of monks is defined by two factors, strict adherence to the ascetic code of conduct and intellectual acumen or knowledge of the scriptures.

Unlike most monks, Buddhadāsa fulfilled both of the traditional authority-conferring criteria. Buddhadāsa's double-sourced religious authority lies, firstly, in his being a renowned and capable scholar who is well-versed in the Buddhist scriptures and, secondly, in his conservative ascetic approach to Buddhist practice. In 1932, at the age of twenty-six, he proclaimed that the only way to reach the truth of Buddhism was to literally follow the Buddha's path of renouncing the world for the forest. Buddhadāsa decided to repenetrate to the heart of the Buddha's realization by discarding the diversions of the Sangha hierarchy and its associated ritualism and returning to the ascetic roots of the religion. For several years he lived as a solitary recluse in an abandoned monastery in the jungle of Southern

Thailand, a fact that for many Thai Buddhists endows him with a greater religious authority than that of purely scholarly monks, who are not regarded as having so strong a practical insight into the truths of Buddhism. After this solitary phase during which Buddhadāsa began to formulate his reinterpretations of doctrine, he also began to promote and publish his views and today is recognized as a learned teacher of Buddhist doctrine. As a monk, Buddhadāsa is therefore in a strongly authoritative position and he has used this to develop a wide-ranging reinterpretation of Buddhist doctrine which parallels the ideological concerns of the progressive lay Buddhists.

Buddhadāsa's popularity amongst modernist lay Thai Buddhists can be regarded as resulting from his resolution of certain intellectual and practical religious problems facing that group, both in the authority of his person, which is founded upon both practice and scholarship, and in the innovative character of his teachings. However, it is his reformist views rather than the precise details of his ascetic practice that draw the most praise and which are the object of this study. In the words of one lay supporter,

> Buddhadāsa has been called a reformer . . . a reformer is someone astute in returning to the ancient teachers and in returning to the original teachings. Such a person is an opponent of teachings which have been so embellished as to lose the way, interpreting the original teachings so that they are in line with the changing society and with the new generation. A reformer communicates the culture and basic institutions of old by steadfastly keeping to their core and to *saccadhamma*,[44] interpreting appropriately for the situations which actually arise in the new society. (T)[45]

## SUMMARY

The sources of Buddhadāsa's reformist work and of his break with the doctrinal conservatism which has historically characterized Thai Buddhism are complex. External political, economic, and cultural influences from the West have triggered the development of Buddhist reform movements. These reform movements have acted as bases for reinterpreting doctrines and views, an activity which Buddhadāsa has justified and authorized by a declared return to the original wisdom and insight of the Buddha. Western-derived criticisms of popular animist beliefs have also freed a latent rationalism lying within doctrinal Buddhism itself, whose development and application has provided an indigenous source of innovation and reform. Furthermore, social conflicts and changes in the structure of Thai society resulting from modernization have given immediate sociological and political relevance to what otherwise may simply be taken as abstract theoretical issues of religious doctrine. The nascent Thai middle classes, like the entrenched conservative establishment, regard Buddhism as a vital institutional source of social and religious legitimacy. However, given that the social advancement of the new bourgeoisie is dependent upon socioeconomic development and change, rather than upon maintenance of the status quo, they wish to see a new interpretation of Buddhist doctrine and practice which supports their interests. The "new Buddhism" they desire is precisely the rationalist, doctrinal, and world-involved doctrine of Buddhadāsa.

Buddhadāsa's work thus exists at a juncture of trends: of Buddhist reform movements, of the rationalization of the religion due to the impact of Western notions, and of the need of Buddhadāsa's own social stratum of the educated Buddhist elite for an alternative Buddhist ideology to promote their interests within the Thai social order. All three forces are manifest in and overdetermine Buddhadāsa's work, the details of his reinterpretations having sources in both theoretical and social influences. In developing a complete understanding of Buddhadāsa's work it is consequently necessary to consider all of these factors.

# 3

# *PHASA KHON–PHASA THAM*: BUDDHADĀSA'S METHOD OF SCRIPTURAL INTERPRETATION

THE THEORETICAL pivot of Buddhadāsa's reinterpretation of Theravada doctrine is the notion of *chit wang*, "voided-mind" or "freed-mind", which is analyzed in detail in chapters 5 and 6. *Chit wang* denotes a mind which is free from moral impurities and is in a state of peace and equanimity, the foundation of *nibbāna*. For Buddhadāsa, *chit wang* is the key to understanding the religious goal of Buddhism and is the basis of the practice to attain that goal both in individual life and in social life. But while Buddhadāsa's interpretation of *chit wang* is based upon notions found in the canonical literature, in particular the notion of *suññatā* or "voidness," it has not historically received much attention in Theravada Buddhism. *Suññatā* or *chit wang* has in general been a secondary concept used to explain more central notions such as *anattā*, non-self, and *anicca*, impermanence. Because of the peripheral character of the notions of *suññatā* and *chit wang* in the traditional readings of the *Tipiṭaka* in Thailand, Buddhadāsa cannot justify his emphasis on them by referring to either the Thai tradition of scriptural interpretation or to the later commentary literature used to support that tradition. In placing *chit wang* at the centre of his presentation of Theravada doctrine, Buddhadāsa has in fact drawn heavily on Mahayana and Zen Buddhist teachings. Indeed, in order to support his interpretation of Theravada Buddhist doctrine, Buddhadāsa has had to break radically with the doctrinal analyses and readings of the scriptures historically taught by the Thai

Sangha. This break with the Thai interpretative tradition has three main components.

Firstly, Buddhadāsa developed an alternative hermeneutic or interpretative approach to the canonical scriptures which allowed him to argue that significantly more sections of the *Tipiṭaka* provide support for his views than superficial readings appear to provide. He calls this interpretative theory *phasa khon–phasa tham*, "everyday language–Dhamma language," and the theory of *phasa khon–phasa tham* is the focus of this chapter. Secondly, Buddhadāsa reads the Theravada scriptures selectively, rejecting as irrelevant to his reinterpretative enterprise the entire final section of the *Tipiṭaka*, the *Abhidhammapiṭaka*. In brief, he rejects the *Abhidhammapiṭaka* because it is not written in the Buddha's words. Buddhadāsa accords the greatest authority to the Buddha's recorded discourses in the *Suttapiṭaka* because he regards those sermons and conversations as embodying the Buddha's original insights. Buddhadāsa's rejection of the *Abhidhammapiṭaka* is detailed in chapter 4 below. Buddhadāsa also rejects the exegesis of the scriptures contained in Buddhaghosa's *Visuddhimagga*, which has been the most important commentary on the Pali canon since the fifth century of the Christian era. In criticizing Buddhaghosa's system of exegesis, Buddhadāsa opens the way for his altogether different interpretation of the scriptures based on the hermeneutic theory of *phasa khon–phasa tham*. In addition Buddhadāsa reads selectively those sections of the canonical literature that he does retain. For example, in reading the *Suttapiṭaka* he concentrates on the *Dīgha*, *Majjhima*, *Aṅguttara*, and *Saṁyutta Nikāyas*, which contain the greatest number of direct quotes from the Buddha. On the other hand, he all but ignores the *Khuddaka Nikāya* of the *Suttapiṭaka*, a section of the scriptures which contains a larger proportion of the popular, "superstitious" Buddhist teachings that he rejects.

But in addition to his theory of scriptural interpretation and his critique of the canonical scriptures and commentaries, there is a third important component to Buddhadāsa's reinterpretative enterprise, namely, his reliance upon rational argumentation. That is, instead of seeking to justify his views solely in terms of scriptural precedents, a methodological approach he nevertheless follows in places, Buddhadāsa also argues for his central theory of *chit wang* from first principles. Buddhadāsa's views must stand on the strength of arguments presented to support them because he is unable to rely on traditional sources of authority such as the commentaries, which present an interpretation of Buddhism that he rejects.

But even though the radical nature of his views forces Buddhadāsa to rely more heavily upon rational analysis in presenting his views, he is still severely constrained by institutional factors. He must at all times be seen to be maintaining religious tradition and must avoid being regarded as harming the social or official role of Buddhism in Thailand. Buddhadāsa thus cannot afford to be seen as radical or innovative but must present his views as being founded upon genuine Buddhist principles. But this very need to demonstrate his faithfulness to Buddhist principles, as opposed to conforming to established interpretations of the doctrine, introduces a far greater emphasis on rational argument into Buddhadāsa's work than has traditionally characterized doctrinal studies of Buddhism in Thailand.

The fact that Buddhadāsa ultimately does break from traditional notions and interpretations of doctrine is shown by his preparedness to accept into Theravada Buddhism non-Theravada notions that he regards as having religious value. Because he argues for his views in terms of what he sees as the principles of Buddhism and because he places his primary allegiance in those principles rather than in any specific text, commentary, or traditionally accepted view, Buddhadāsa is free to draw on ideas which he regards as being theoretically compatible with his interpretation of Buddhist doctrine.

## THE THEORY OF *PHASA KHON–PHASA THAM*

Buddhadāsa distinguishes two hermeneutic levels of the Buddha's words in the *Suttapiṭaka*, calling these two levels *phasa khon* (ภาษาคน) or everyday language and *phasa tham* (ภาษาธรรม) or Dhamma language.[1] He gives the following definitions:

> Everyday language is worldly language, the language of people who do not know Dhamma. Dhamma language is the language spoken by people who have gained a deep insight into the truth, Dhamma.[2]

Buddhadāsa says *phasa khon*, or everyday language, "has as its foundation a meaning dependent upon matter (it does not fundamentally rest upon Dhamma) and consequently speaks only about material things."(T)[3] On the other hand, *phasa tham*, or Dhamma language, "has to do with the mental world, with the intangible nonphysical world."[4]

While Buddhadāsa speaks of two kinds of language, in fact the distinguishing point between *phasa khon* and *phasa tham* is that they represent two different types of knowledge which underlay the original composition of the scriptures and which inform the reading of those scriptures today. According to Buddhadāsa, the Buddha's recorded statements in the scriptures fall into two general categories, depending upon whether the Buddha himself was speaking in a mundane or literal way about everyday things, that is, *phasa khon*, or whether his words were in fact expressing transcendent insights and so were founded on supramundane or spiritual knowledge, in which case they are *phasa tham* or Dhamma language. The *phasa khon–phasa tham* theory is then concerned with the recognition of which sections of the scriptures are expressions of everyday language and which express spiritual insights in Dhamma language. To be able to recognize this distinction, Buddhadāsa maintains, requires a degree of spiritual insight on the part of the reader, lacking which all the Buddha's statements will mistakenly be read with a mundane awareness simply as *phasa khon*. This is because language itself, being a feature of the rational or discursive functioning of the mind, is incapable of adequately expressing transcendent knowledge. Such knowledge is only symbolically or metaphorically alluded to in language and is incapable of being explicated within the rational domain. But if the reader does not recognize when language is being used to allude to that which cannot in fact be linguistically expressed, he or she will mistakenly concentrate on the literal or *phasa khon* sense of the terms, and will misread the author's original intent.

Buddhadāsa claims that it is possible to read some *suttas* or sections of the scriptures in two ways with two different meanings, depending on the mode of knowing which informs the reader's act of interpreting. Should the reader's awareness be based solely on sense-based experience of tangible things, then the *sutta* will be read as expressing the meanings of *phasa khon* or everyday language. But if the reader is spiritually aware and knowledgeable of the intangible realm then the same *sutta*, if it was in fact composed as an expression of transcendent knowledge, may be read as expressing the meaning of *phasa tham*, Dhamma language. The same linguistic expression may thus be taken as referring to the abstract and supramundane. Thus the two types of language in Buddhadāsa's theory do not refer to any objectively discernible quality of the grammar, syntax, or vocabulary of the scriptures. Rather, the theory is concerned with detailing the types of interpretative frameworks a reader may apply to religious texts, with the intention of permitting the original spiritual or mundane character of *suttas* to be recognized.

A *phasa khon* interpretation of a term is then simply its conventional or literal meaning while the same term's *phasa tham* rendering is its spiritual or symbolic sense. Buddhadāsa uses this distinction to argue that many of the traditional readings and interpretations of the Buddhist scriptures in Thailand remain at the literal or *phasa khon* level. He also argues that these traditional interpretations are wrong, or at least inaccurate, insofar as they do not take into account the transcendent *phasa tham* sense of terms or passages. In general, Buddhadāsa is opposed to literal or *phasa khon* interpretations of the scriptures, arguing that the true import of the Buddha's words is only found when their metaphorical or *phasa tham* significance is appreciated. He does not claim that every expression in the scriptures has both a *phasa khon* and a *phasa tham* reading. It is not the case that the entire body of the recorded words of the Buddha can be read as a consistent system solely at the literal level of *phasa khon* or at the metaphorical level of *phasa tham*. There is only an overlap, and thus possible confusion over interpretation, at certain points. He maintains that both hermeneutic levels need to be considered in order to accurately understand the Buddha's teachings, "not just either one of them alone."[5]

In his work Buddhadāsa places more emphasis on the notion of *phasa tham*, and those sections of the *Suttapiṭaka* that he regards as being expressed in Dhamma language, than on *phasa khon* and those sections of the scriptures which can be read literally. This is because it is his reinterpretations of doctrine in terms of *phasa tham* which differ from the traditional views of Buddhist teachings and which therefore need to be discussed and justified. The parts of the scriptures which he regards as being written in *phasa khon* are not of great interest to Buddhadāsa because they are the sections where, by and large, he agrees with the traditional literal reading of the texts.

## THE NOTIONS OF SPIRITUAL DEPTH AND CONTEMPORARY RELEVANCE IN BUDDHADĀSA'S WORK

Buddhadāsa's notion of Dhamma language as an appreciation of the underlying spiritual sense of a term or statement, is closely related to his concern to inject new relevance into Buddhism. He has said that he hopes his reinterpretations will enable Thai Buddhism to "effect results that will satisfy today's students."(T)[6] By "student" Buddhadāsa here means educated Thais with a modernist and progressive outlook. Buddhadāsa regards his *phasa tham* interpretations as not only revealing the hidden truth of Buddhist teachings but also as simultaneously demonstrating the contemporary relevance of those teachings to "today's students." That is, he regards returning to the original truth of the religion as equivalent to establishing the importance of the saving message of Buddhism in the modern world. This equation of truth or spiritual depth with contemporary relevance is seen by some of Buddhadāsa's critics as opportunistic, as seeking to justify a modernist Buddhist social ideology by what is presented as a return to the original truth of the religion. Such claims are not without some substance given the apparent preparedness of some of Buddhadāsa's lay followers to support his modernist interpretations for pragmatic reasons rather than because his views are perceived as necessarily manifesting spiritual truth. For example, a biographer of Buddhadāsa gives the following quote as indicative of the views of those who support Buddhadāsa's work:

> If the religious officialdom does not effect a revolutionary renewal in Buddhism so that it becomes appropriate and relevant to the expectations of Thais of today's civilization then the disintegration of Buddhism will become more clearly manifest every day . . . As for the state of mind of Thais with strong nationalist feelings, at this time they have already begun to be widely alert in religious matters. That is, they would be glad to accept every kind of religion or ideology so long as that religion or ideology helps promote the development of cooperation . . . for suppressing the power of other lands in our economic and political affairs.(T)[7]

But whether Buddhadāsa's views are regarded as representing the original teachings of the Buddha, or as simply being a conveniently adjusted interpretation presented under the guise of conforming to Buddhism's original insights, depends on what is regarded as the true core of the religion. Buddhadāsa's conservative critics take the historically and institutionally sanctioned interpretations of doctrine as the most reliable guidelines to the Buddha's message. As a consequence, the fact that Buddhadāsa's views are in general at odds with the traditional presentations of the doctrine is regarded by these authors as discrediting his work.

However, Buddhadāsa believes that religious truth lies in faithfulness to doctrinal principles rather than to historical tradition as embodied in the institution of the Sangha, which he regards as often maintaining erroneous and inconsistent interpretations of Buddhist teachings. Buddhadāsa assumes Buddhism to be a universal religion, in the sense that its message of salvation from suffering is universally true and relevant to all people in all times and in all places. He then regards the criticisms of modernist Thais that Buddhism in Thailand is no longer relevant to contemporary life as indicating that the true meaning of the Buddha's message has been obscured. Buddhadāsa claims that the source of the obfuscation of the Buddha's universally relevant message of salvation lies in the influence of Brahmanical and animist beliefs, which have become associated with institutional Buddhism and which have distorted the original pristine character of the religion. Buddhadāsa believes that when these accretions are removed and the doctrine is once again revealed in its original purity the contemporary relevance of Buddhism's universal message will become clear and the problem identified by intellectual critics will be resolved. At the same time, Buddhism will have been cleansed of the irrational and supernatural elements which many educated Thais find unacceptable. Buddhadāsa's rationalist approach to interpreting Buddhist doctrine, justified by his interpretative theory of *phasa tham*, simultaneously brings Buddhism into conformity with a particular view of modern scientific rationality and with a doctrinal view of the religion that seeks to make the teachings of Buddhism wholly consistent with its basic theoretical principles.

Buddhadāsa's return to religious principles can be seen as a genuinely motivated attempt to "purify" Buddhism and to reveal its universal message of salvation. But at the same time, his related interest in establishing Buddhism as a scientific and rational religion, if considered in isolation, can also be regarded as a pragmatic attempt to instil relevance into the religion by responding to changing public opinions and social trends. However, Buddhadāsa's work is not a "pure" phenomenon, whether purely a response to Buddhist principles or purely a pragmatic or political development. His work is a compound phenomenon which can only be expected to manifest its diverse sources. Consequently, neither Buddhadāsa's claims that he is returning to the truth of Buddhism, nor the counterclaims of his critics that his theory of *phasa tham* is merely a cover for pragmatic adjustments of doctrine to meet contemporary expectations, can be ignored.

## DOCTRINAL REINTERPRETATIONS BASED ON *PHASA THAM* READINGS OF THE BUDDHIST SCRIPTURES

In the Pali scriptures the Buddha and his disciples often refer to celestial beings and to demons and the various levels of heavens and hells inhabited by these beings. Traditionally other worlds and superhuman and subhuman beings have been regarded as real in Buddhism, respectively representing the heights and depths a human may either rise or sink to in subsequent lives as a result of the consequences of their good or bad deeds. Celestial beings or *devatā*, heavens and hells, are all taken as real by Buddhaghosa in his interpretative text, the *Visuddhimagga*. Speaking of the supernatural powers attained by concentration meditation and the attainment of *jhānas* or trance states, Buddhaghosa says that with the super-normal power of clairaudience one may hear "right up to the Brahma world,"[8] that is, the heavenly domain inhabited by the god Brahma and his retinue. Elsewhere he says that because of a strong desire for heavenly bliss one may, by the effect of the *kamma* created by such a desire, be reborn in the Brahma world.[9] Buddhaghosa supports his interpretation with quotes from the Buddha's scriptural pronouncements on the benefits of attaining *jhānas*:

> Where do they [meditators] reappear after developing the first *jhāna* limitedly? They reappear in the company of the deities of Brahma's retinue.[10]

However, Buddhadāsa does not interpret such references to the "deities of Brahma's retinue" as being actual celestial beings. He says such a view is a limited *phasa khon* reading and instead defines *devatā* (Thai: *thewada*) in *phasa tham* as, "A person free of suffering, who is beautiful, lives in ease and is glorious."(T)[11] He adds:

> If in this human world there are some people who need not work, be anxious, or bear heavy burdens but who can continually relax, play, and be at ease, then, according to the above definition, they can be called *thewada*. Moreover, if they do not obtain this status of ease for a few hours they may burn with worries and unease like beings in hell. When they work at tiring duties they are human. But in the hours they are sensually satisfied they are *thewada*.(T)[12]

As for the nature of the abodes of these *thewada* and hellish beings, Buddhadāsa says that

> Heaven is in one's breast, hell is in one's mind, *nibbāna* exists in the human mind. Hence what is meant by the term "world" exists in the human mind.(T)[13]

Talking specifically of the various grades of hell described in the Pali canon, Buddhadāsa maintains that their interpretation as "woeful states" of mind, *apāya*, "coincides in meaning and purpose with what the Buddha taught,"[14] while the belief that they represent actual realms of being "should be recognised as superstition."[15]

There is a common pattern across all Buddhadāsa's *phasa tham* reinterpretations which reveals an implicit criterion underlying the use of the theory. Notions which in the *Visuddhimagga* and popular interpretations of the scriptures refer to actual supramundane or submundane realms and beings are reduced to psychological states or conditions. That is, in Buddhadāsa's *phasa tham* readings the traditional Buddhist cosmology is collapsed and brought within the range of the life and mind of the individual. Heaven or *sugati* in *phasa tham* is not a realm of happy rebirth but the state of mind of a happy person. Similarly, a *thewada* is anyone who is "in heaven," in the popular sense of someone alive here on earth who is overjoyed or pleasantly satisfied.

Taken as a whole Buddhadāsa's *phasa tham* reinterpretations represent a systematic demythologization of the Buddhist scriptures whereby cosmological realms become psychological states and deities and demons are interpreted as individuals experiencing those states. Whenever a concept or term is traditionally interpreted in a way which is at odds with a modernist or scientific world view then that term or concept is demythologized and subjected to a *phasa tham* reinterpretation. Buddhadāsa eschews metaphysical interpretations of the doctrine and attempts to bring all the significant notions of Buddhist thought within the experiential ambit of the human mind.

However, this demythologization appears to be at odds with sections of the scriptures which unequivocally refer to supernatural states and beings. The commonness of the Buddha's unqualified scriptural references to heavens, hells, deities, and demons gives the strong impression that he himself believed in the metaphysical rather than simply psychological reality of such realms and beings. For example, it is difficult to interpret the following passages from the *Puggala* and *Cittanayi Suttas* as referring to anything other than an actual hell and an actual heaven:

> If at this time the person [who has a mind turbid with *kilesa*] should die they would go to *naraka* [hell] because of their turbid mind . . . All beings inevitably go to *dugati* [hell] because of that mental turbidity.(T)[16]
>
> If at this time this person [who has a mind bright and clear of *kilesa*] should die they would go to *sugati* [heaven] because of their clear mind . . . All beings inevitably go to *sugati* because of that mental clarity.(T)[17]

However, Buddhadāsa's demythologization of the Theravada scriptures does obtain some support from the fact that the authority of the traditional system of scriptural exegesis taken from the *Visuddhimagga*, in which heaven and hell are regarded as real, is based solely on tradition. There is no literature supporting the interpretative position taken in the *Visuddhimagga* because historically it has never been questioned in Thailand. Because heaven and hell have been generally accepted as referring to actual supernatural conditions there has been no need to justify the literal reading of these and similar terms in the scriptures. This means that the interpretative system presented by the *Visuddhimagga* and related commentaries is only as strong as the regard and reverence in which that text and its interpretative tradition has customarily been held. Should the regard for the traditional interpretative tradition falter, then, in the absence of any canonical justification for reading the scriptures literally, the interpretations hallowed by that tradition would be substantially weakened. Buddhadāsa is therefore able to argue that his radical reinterpretations are consistent with the Buddha's teachings.

The superficiality of the criticisms of the *phasa tham* theory made by Buddhadāsa's opponents demonstrates the lack of a theoretical basis for the traditionally accepted exegetical system. Those criticisms which are not directed at the political implications of Buddhadāsa's theory amount to statements of faith and *ad hominems*. In countering Buddhadāsa, Anan Senakhan says,

> There really is a hell. It denotes every kind of being which must be

> born in the realm of suffering called hell... beings having wholesome *kamma* are born in heaven.(T)[18]

He accuses Buddhadāsa of, "explaining [the doctrine] like a mentally backward person."(T)[19]

In the absence of reasoned arguments for accepting the traditional Theravada exegetical system, any competing system of interpretation need not have so strong a theoretical foundation as might be expected. This point is brought out clearly by a follower of Buddhadāsa in a book on interpreting religious symbolism, that is, *phasa tham*:

> Since there exists no simple set of rules for the deciphering of religious allegories, each individual is more or less at liberty to propose whichever interpretation strikes him as the most reasonable. Whether he then manages to convince others that his view is correct depends on how well he can put his case and defend it against the attacks of critics.[20]

Yet it must be noted that Buddhadāsa does not in fact completely deny the cosmological reality of heaven and hell:

> True enough, the heaven and hell of everyday language are realms outside—though don't ask me where—and they are attained after death. But the heaven and hell of Dhamma language are to be found in the mind and may be attained anytime depending on one's mental makeup.(T)[21]

To be precise, Buddhadāsa does not deny the traditional supernatural interpretations of doctrine but rather renders them irrelevant for the purpose which he takes to be the goal of Buddhism. That is, they are irrelevant to the attainment of *nibbāna* in this life. For, as Buddhadāsa so often insists, "*nibbāna* must be something we can have in this life."(T)[22] He maintains that

> Buddhism exists in order to allow everyone to live in the world victoriously; we needn't flee the world.(T)[23]

As for that which is called Dhamma or *satsana* (religion), it exists in order to be the refuge of the people of the world. I don't want good people to abandon the world but I want people to live in the world beneficially and without suffering.(T)[24]

Buddhadāsa defines Buddhism as a religious system which is concerned only with this life and, while not denying the existence of an afterlife in heaven or hell, he places them outside the focus of concern of the religion. This means that from a *phasa tham* standpoint all the references to an afterlife in the Buddhist scriptures must be interpreted as symbols of some condition or process in this life. Buddhadāsa maintains, "The Dhamma of the Lord Buddha does not talk about the period after death in the coffin as something important."(T)[25] He justifies his disinterest in the afterlife by saying that, "If we rectify and correct this life then without doubt the next life will be rectified accordingly."(T)[26]

From a purely theoretical perspective the denial of the significance yet non-denial of the reality of supernatural phenomena might seem an unnecessary complication. However, we should look to the ideological significance of *phasa tham* when seeking to understand the emphasis Buddhadāsa places on it. One of the functions of Buddhadāsa's reinterpreted system of Buddhism is to endow the material world and human activities in this world with religiously sanctioned value. This sanctification of the mundane is achieved by integrating mundane activities and aspirations into the effort to attain spiritual salvation. This shift, to view the material world as a positive domain of human activity and aspirations, is radically opposed to the traditional clerical view of the world as a retarding and almost inherently evil influence. The traditional scriptural view of life in the world, as a householder, is made clear in the following quote from the *Dīgha Nikāya*:

Full of hindrances is the household life, a path for the dust of passion. Free as the air is the life of him who has renounced all worldly things. How difficult it is for the man who lives at home to live the holy life (*brahmacariya*) in all its fullness, in all its purity, in all its bright perfection.[27]

The attitude among many monks in Thailand today is little different. The biographer of the famous ascetic monk Achan Man (died 1947) recounts that at an early point in his life the sage

> came to realise that the life of the householder is the conglomeration of all kinds of suffering, being like an immense thicketed forest where lurk all kinds of dangers, whereas the chaste life (*brahmacariya*), supported by the efforts of renunciation, would serve to carry him through that dangerous land.[28]

The denial and opposition implicit in the theory of *phasa tham* is not directed solely at supernatural and other "unscientific" views, but also against the world-negating outlook inherent in the traditional *lokuttara* standpoint. This indicates that the deeper function of Buddhadāsa's theory, over and above the demythologization of the Buddhist scriptures, is the establishment of the social world as a domain with religious importance. It is because science values the material world, as the source and object of human knowledge and as the domain for the finding of human well-being, that Buddhadāsa so values it and uses *phasa tham* as a method to effect a rationalist demythologization of Buddhism. The proposition that there are two levels at which the Buddhist scriptures can be understood is thus fundamental to Buddhadāsa's attempt to make activity in the material world a positive part of the religious effort to end suffering, and this contributes to the significance of Buddhadāsa's thought and to his popularity among progressive Buddhists.

## SOURCES OF THE THEORY OF *PHASA KHON–PHASA THAM*

Given the importance of the *phasa khon–phasa tham* theory to Buddhadāsa's work, it is important to know what standing or validity the theory has in the Theravada tradition which he seeks to reform. In fact, the theory of *phasa khon–phasa tham* has a precedent in well-established principles laid down for interpreting the Theravada scriptures. Buddhadāsa observes that "The Buddha laid down a principle for testing: examine and measure against the *suttas* and compare with the *vinaya*."[29] This interpretative principle is based on advice given by the Buddha on his deathbed on how to deal with statements on the doctrine which are dubious or disputed. In the *Mahāparinibbāna Sutta* the Buddha says

> Then you should study well those [disputed] paragraphs and words, and investigate whether they occur in the *sutta*, and compare them with the *vinaya*. If having investigated the *sutta* and compared with the *vinaya* they can neither [be found] in the *sutta* nor [be found to be] comparable with the [teachings in the] *vinaya*, then you should reach agreement on these points that they are certainly not the words of the Bhagava [the Buddha], and that the *bhikkhu* in question [who made the disputed statement] has incorrectly remembered [the Buddha's teaching]. You should discard those statements completely.(T)[30]

The principle of interpretation laid down here is that disputed or dubious statements on the doctrine should be compared with the recorded words of the Buddha, the *sutta*, and with the ethical principles recorded in the *vinaya*, to gauge whether they are accurate and in accord with Buddhist ethical principles.

The Buddha gave this strict and literalist interpretative method at a time when Buddhism was an oral tradition. Before the Buddhist canon was written down several centuries after the Buddha's death, monks were primarily concerned to remember faithfully the Tathāgata's precise words. The Buddha's statement in the *Mahāparinibbāna Sutta* is thus meant as an injunction to monks to adhere closely to the actual teachings of the Buddha which they had committed to memory.

However, once the Buddhist scriptures were written down the interpretative principle laid down in the *Mahāparinibbāna Sutta* was considerably revised. One of the most important methodological texts of the literary period of traditional Theravada Buddhism is the *Netti-Pakaraṇa*. George Bond maintains that the following method is presented in the *Netti-Pakaraṇa*[31] as leading to the "right construing" of the Buddha's words: "These terms and phrasing [in question] must be placed beside the *sutta*, compared with the *vinaya* and patterned after the essential nature of Dhamma."[32] The principle that interpretations of the doctrine should "be patterned after the essential nature of the Dhamma" is more general than that put forward by the Buddha, proposing that a view or opinion should be theoretically consistent with the doctrinal basics of the religion, rather than being a literal restatement of the Buddha's words, as required by the *Mahāparinibbāna Sutta*.

The *Netti-Pakaraṇa* develops the canonical interpretative principle into a form more appropriate to a literary tradition in which the demands of simple memorization have been lifted and detailed textual analysis can be undertaken. The principle that scriptural interpretations should be patterned after the Dhamma amounts to a recognition that in a literary tradition faithfulness to the Buddha's teaching no longer necessitates a strictly literal adherence to his actual words but may also be based upon views which follow the spirit of the Buddha's teachings. This more liberal principle of interpretation is then very close to Buddhadāsa's method of interpreting the scriptures.

Bond proposes that the interpretative method put forward in the *Netti-Pakaraṇa*

> not only requires the interpreter to elicit from a text the semantic essence of the Dhamma [phrasing], but also to indicate how a text points to the goal of the Dhamma [i.e. *nibbāna*].[33]

That is, the *Netti-Pakaraṇa* teaches that the scriptures can be interpreted at two levels: at the level of understanding the literal meaning of statements and terms, and at the level of understanding how those terms and statements point towards or are suggestive of *nibbāna*. These two levels closely parallel Buddhadāsa's distinction between *phasa khon*, as the literal sense of a term, and *phasa tham*, as the transcendent insight alluded to by what otherwise can be read as a quite ordinary expression. And just as Buddhadāsa proposes that those lacking spiritual insight may read the scriptures in terms of *phasa khon* while missing their higher or *phasa tham* import, so too Bond says that the *Netti* implies that every authentic text implicitly points to the *attha* [sense or meaning] of the Buddha's teachings, but unless an interpreter is aware of the guidelines this indication of the goal could be overlooked or misunderstood.[34]

Thus, the basic similarity between the method of the *Netti-Pakaraṇa* and Buddhadāsa's interpretative theory is, as Bond puts it, the proposition that "the interpreter must not only understand the words of the Buddha's teaching but must also grasp how they point to the aim of the Dhamma."[35]

Buddhadāsa aims to present the doctrines of Buddhism in a way that clearly reveals their relevance to contemporary life. In attempting to fulfil this aim by using the interpretative licence conferred by his notion of *phasa tham* or Dhamma language, Buddhadāsa is in fact re-expressing the interpretative principle which the author of the *Netti-Pakaraṇa* implored all interpreters of the Buddha's words to adhere to: namely, to go beyond the immediate sense or presentation of a term to appreciate its underlying spiritual import.

In addition to the methodology of the *Netti-Pakaraṇa*, there is an even older precedent for the *phasa khon–phasa tham* distinction in the tradition that the Buddha varied the level of his instruction according to the ability of his audience to understand the spiritual truths revealed. This tradition supports Buddhadāsa's claim that different sections of the *suttas* were given by the Buddha in different ways, whether as *phasa khon* or as *phasa tham*. The view that there are two levels to the Buddha's discourses is related to the traditional division between the two paths to salvation taught by the Buddha; that is, the division between the *lokiya* path for the layperson, which promotes well-being but does not end the process of rebirth, and the *lokuttara* path for the renunciate, which leads directly to the cessation of rebirth and to liberation from suffering. The view that the Buddha spoke in different ways depending on the level of spiritual development of his audience is also related to the Buddha's pragmatic approach to knowledge, where that which is beneficial is given priority over that which is strictly true.

Using this theory some passages in the scriptures have been interpreted as referring to the *lokiya* path where, say, "right view" or *sammādiṭṭhi* does not mean direct insight into religious truth but rather an outlook with spiritually or morally beneficial results. On the other hand, other passages in the scriptures have been taken as referring more directly to the *lokuttara* path and *sammādiṭṭhi* has then been interpreted as meaning spiritual insight or wisdom.

Buddhadāsa expresses a similar view in the following passage:

> At the basic level, right view *(sammādiṭṭhi)* is understanding which is correct in the respect that it effects beneficial development of this world in every way the worldlings want.[36] Right view of the middle level is understanding which is correct insofar as it effects beneficial development in worlds higher than those that worldlings wish for, and which are called the "other world;" the world beyond or the next world[37] and which are better than or different from this world. As for the high level of right view, that denotes understanding which is correct in the respect that it effects crossing over or transcendence of each and every world in all ways, which is called the attainment of *nibbāna* or *lokuttara* and which is interpreted as being beyond the world.(T)[38]

The tradition that there are two levels of the Buddha's discourses has been systematically expressed in the *Abhidhammapiṭaka* as the Buddhist theory of two truths, *sammatisacca* and *paramatthasacca*. *Sammatisacca* or conventional truth denotes the everyday level of knowledge, while *paramatthasacca* denotes a form of knowledge based directly on underlying truth or reality. In the *Abhidhamma-piṭaka* these two modes of knowing are also related to two modes of expounding the Dhamma. *Sammatisacca* or conventional truth is related to *puggalādhiṭṭhāna*, exposition of the doctrine in terms of persons or by personification, and *paramatthasacca* or absolute truth is related to *dhammādhiṭṭhāna*, exposition in terms of elements or concepts. Exposition of Buddhist doctrine in terms of elements, *dhammādhiṭṭhāna*, denotes the consistent presentation of the teachings in terms of the doctrine of *anattā* or non-self, interpreting everything as being composed of naturally occurring elements or aggregates, *khandhas*, combining and functioning in accord with natural laws or Dhamma. To be wholly consistent with the doctrine of *anattā* one must completely eschew speaking of individuals (Pali: *puggala*) or persons. Instead, one must speak only of *khandhas* acting in accord with natural laws.

A consistent account of Buddhist teaching which eschews reference to people who suffer or attain liberation, talking only of aggregates of form, consciousness, volition, etc., is called *dhammādhiṭṭhāna*, where Dhamma has the special sense of an element or constitutive aggregate, *khandha*. *Dhammādhiṭṭhāna* thus denotes a true or faithful exposition of the doctrine based upon spiritual insight into Dhamma. Like Buddhadāsa's notion of *phasa tham*, *dhammādhiṭṭhāna* denotes a spiritually informed exposition of Buddhist doctrine which is based upon insight into the truth of *anattā* and is in accord with absolute truth, *paramatthasacca*.

On the other hand, *puggalādhiṭṭhāna* is regarded as an inferior and inadequate exposition of the doctrine because it continues to refer to people and individuals as if they in fact have an essential self. *Puggalādhiṭṭhāna* accounts of Buddhist teaching are, like *phasa khon*, based on everyday awareness or conventional knowledge, *sammatisacca*, which is devoid of spiritual insight. While expositions of the doctrine in terms of *puggalādhiṭṭhāna* may have value in encouraging moral practice among those who lack the spiritual insight to appreciate the core doctrines, such expositions in terms of conventional concepts and terms are, strictly speaking, false. And while such false but morally and spiritually beneficial accounts of the doctrine are sanctioned in the instructional texts of the *Suttapiṭaka*, the authors of the *Abhidhammapiṭaka* presented the doctrine in a way wholly consistent with the principle of *anattā*. That is, the *Abhidhammapiṭaka* represents an attempt to present Buddhist teachings solely in terms of *dhammādhiṭṭhāna*.

Buddhadāsa has related his notions of *phasa khon* and *phasa tham* to *puggalādhiṭṭhāna* and *dhammādhiṭṭhāna,* respectively. He equates the Thai word for person, *khon* (found in the term *phasa khon*, "everyday language"), with the Pali loan word *bukkhon* or *puggala* denoting "individual", which is found in the term *puggalādhiṭṭhāna*. That is, Buddhadāsa regards his neologism, *phasa khon*, as a Thai version of the Pali term *puggalādhiṭṭhāna*. Buddhadāsa says that *phasa khon* "is called speaking in the way of *puggalādhiṭṭhāna*, for those who cannot work out deep things."(T)[39] Buddhadāsa also equates *dhammādhiṭṭhāna* with the absolute truth or *paramattha-sacca* which underpins his *phasa tham* interpretations of the scriptures:

> This [*paramatthasacca*] is held to be truly speaking in the way of *dhammādhiṭṭhāna*, and to reach to the end point of those matters [of doctrine] which ordinary people still cannot see.(T)[40]

The word *tham* (found in *phasa tham*) is the Thai equivalent of the Pali term Dhamma, and Buddhadāsa appears to regard his term *phasa tham* as a contemporary Thai rendering of the Pali term *dhammādhiṭṭhāna*.

While Buddhadāsa presents *phasa khon* and *phasa tham* as being related to the notions of *puggalādhiṭṭhāna* and *dhammādhiṭṭhāna*, respectively, there is, however, an important difference between the two sets of terms. Traditionally the *Suttapiṭaka* as a whole has been called *vohāradesanā*, "the teaching [presented in terms] of conventional speech," because it is composed predominantly of conversations or *vohāra* expressed in conventional speech. That is, the entire *Suttapiṭaka* has traditionally been categorized as *puggalādhiṭṭhāna*. On the other hand, the *Abhidhammapiṭaka* has been called *paramatthadesanā*, "the teaching (presented in terms) of ultimate truth," because its doctrinal tracts are in the main expressed in terms of the constitutive elements of existence. That is, the *Abhidhammapiṭaka* is traditionally regarded as an exposition in terms of *dhammādhiṭṭhāna*. The theory of *phasa khon–phasa tham*, however, breaks with this convention. Buddhadāsa maintains that many of the Buddha's statements in the *Suttapiṭaka* should be read as *paramatthadesanā*, i.e., as *phasa tham*. He says that to regard all the discourses recorded in the *Suttapiṭaka* simply as conventional speech or *vohāradesanā* and to interpret them as *puggalādhiṭṭhāna* or *phasa khon* is to miss their real spiritual significance. That is, Buddhadāsa transfers the notion of *dhammādhiṭṭhāna* from its traditional referent of the *Abhidhammapiṭaka* to the discourses and discussions of the *Suttapiṭaka*, which have historically been regarded as being presented solely in terms of *puggalādhiṭṭhāna*. Thus, while being derived from the notion of *dhammādhiṭṭhāna*, Buddhadāsa's notion of *phasa tham* has a different referent from its parent notion. Similarly, while the notion of *phasa khon* is derived from that of *puggalādhiṭṭhāna*, Buddhadāsa's term also has a different referent. Instead of being a generic term for the direct speech recorded in the *Suttapiṭaka*, *phasa khon* denotes an inadequate and uninformed reading of the Buddha's words.

## DIFFICULTIES WITH THE THEORY OF *PHASA KHON–PHASA THAM*

There is a difficulty, however, in the derivation of the notions of *phasa khon* and *phasa tham*. For while Buddhadāsa wishes to use these notions to develop his reinterpretation of the doctrine contained in the *Suttapiṭaka*, the two terms' respective parental notions of *sammatisacca* and *paramatthasacca* and of *puggalādhiṭṭhāna* and *dhammādhiṭṭhāna* are not found in the *Suttapiṭaka* but first appear in the later *Abhidhammapiṭaka*,[41] whose authority Buddhadāsa by and large rejects. In fact, the distinction between absolute and relative truth defined above is only explicitly developed in the later commentaries, which Buddhadāsa considers even less authoritative than the *Abhidhammapiṭaka*. Buddhadāsa's views on the canonicity and authority of the Theravada scriptures and commentaries are discussed in detail in chapter 4. However, it is important to note here that Buddhadāsa rejects the authority of the literature which he himself has stated is the source of the crucial hermeneutic theory of *phasa khon–phasa tham*. He rejects the *Abhidhamma* literature in order to cleanse Buddhism of the superstitious, cosmological views commonly associated with it in Thailand and in order to avoid what he regards as the *Abhidhammapiṭaka's* excessive analytical detail. The motivation behind setting up the *phasa khon–phasa tham* theory is similarly to develop a method of interpreting the key scriptures of the *Suttapiṭaka* in a way that is scientific and non-superstitious. However, these two prongs of Buddhadāsa's reinterpretation of Theravada doctrine—the rejection of the *Abhidhamma* and the positing of the theory of *phasa tham*—are in fact in conflict, with the rejection of the *Abhidhamma* undermining the scriptural basis of his hermeneutic theory.

Nevertheless, as discussed above, the notions of *puggalādhiṭṭhāna* and *dhammādhiṭṭhāāna* found in the *Abhidhamma* literature are not the only sources of the theory of *phasa khon–phasa tham*. Both the interpretative method put forward in the *Netti-Pakaraṇa* and the generally recognized tradition that the Buddha varied his discourses to suit the level of understanding of his audience also provide a firm basis for Buddhadāsa's theory within the Theravada tradition. Nevertheless, it is still the case that Buddhadāsa explicitly cites *puggalādhiṭṭhāna* and *dhammādhiṭṭhāna* as the respective sources of his notions of *phasa khon* and *phasa tham*, and it is also the case that he rejects the authority of the *Abhidhamma*, which is the canonical source of those notions. While Buddhadāsa does not discuss his justifications of the *phasa khon–phasa tham* theory and his rejection of the *Abhidhamma* in the same texts, this does not lessen the logical contradiction, a contradiction which he neither acknowledges nor deals with.

However, another Thai scholar monk also interested in developing modernist and relevant interpretations of Buddhist theory, *Phra* Rajavaramuni, has provided a possible resolution of the above contradiction in his reference work on Theravada doctrine, *Phutthatham* (พุทธธรรม)(T).[42] While Rajavaramuni is not explicitly concerned with Buddhadāsa's work or with the theory of *phasa khon–phasa tham*,[43] large sections of his book *Phutthatham* are directed to an analysis and justification of interpretations of the scriptures which correspond closely to Buddhadāsa's own views. Even though Buddhadāsa and Rajavaramuni have worked independently, they share common views about the need to reinterpret and represent Theravada teachings in a way that demonstrates their relevance to modern life. These common views have in several places independently led the two scholar monks to similar interpretative positions. Like Buddhadāsa, Rajavaramuni places the greatest emphasis on the Buddha's own recorded words in the *Suttapiṭaka* as the source of doctrinal authority. Wherever possible he attempts to trace the origins of his interpretations of doctrine back to statements in the

*Suttapiṭaka* rather than justifying his views by referring to later commentaries on the scriptures.

In *Phutthatham* Rajavaramuni provides a detailed discussion of the origins of the *sammatisacca-paramatthasacca*(T) distinction,[44] which is one precedent of the *phasa khon–phasa tham* theory. Rajavaramuni observes that the immediate source of this distinction is a comment made by a nun or *bhikkhunī* named Vajira[45] in the *Vajira Sutta*, who is quoted as condemning the conventional approach to understanding reality which is ignorant of the truth of *anattā* or non-self:

> This is Mara [delusion]! How can you have this clinging-informed thought that it [a human being] is an entity? Inasmuch as it is only a pile of *saṅkhāra* [compounded things] no entity at all can be found. Just as when the necessary components are assembled together it is said that there is a "cart," so when all the *khandha* are present it is [conventionally] assumed that there is an entity.(T)[46]

Rajavaramuni adds that the *sammati-paramattha* distinction developed in the *Abhidhammapiṭaka* is in fact founded on the Buddha's advice to "recognize the use of language as a medium of meaning without being attached to the [conventional] assumptions as a slave of language."(T)[47] He supports this view by citing passages such as the following from the *Poṭṭhapāda Sutta*, where the Buddha says, "these are worldly appellations, worldly expressions, worldly usages and worldly designations that the Tathagata uses in speaking but is not attached to."(T)[48] Here Rajavaramuni is saying that the conceptual distinction of *sammatisacca* and *paramatthasacca*, which underpins both Buddhadāsa's *phasa khon–phasa tham* theory and the interpretative distinction of *puggalādhiṭṭhāna* and *dhammādhiṭṭhāna*, has its actual source in the Buddha's own recorded words found in the *Suttapiṭaka*. That is, Rajavaramuni's account circumvents the difficulty caused by Buddhadāsa's denial of the *Abhidhammapiṭaka* and related commentaries by tracing the sources of the distinction back to the *Suttapiṭaka*, whose authority Buddhadasa does recognize. However, Buddhadāsa himself does not detail this source of his notions in the *Suttapiṭaka* and so it still remains the case that within the body of his own writings there remains a contradiction between his assertion of the theory of *phasa khon–phasa tham* and his denial of the authority of that theory's immediate scriptural source in the *Abhidhammapiṭaka*.

In addition to the theoretical difficulties associated with the scriptural sources of the *phasa tham* theory, there are also practical difficulties in applying Buddhadāsa's theory of scriptural interpretation. Firstly, Buddhadāsa provides no explicit principle to indicate which parts of the *Suttapiṭaka* should be read in terms of either *phasa khon* or *phasa tham*. His theory is consequently particularly susceptible to attack, for without a clearly expressed criterion of how the two types of interpretation should be applied, disputes over the respective *phasa khon* or *phasa tham* character of particular *suttas* cannot easily be resolved. And secondly, Buddhadāsa does not provide a theoretical criterion for judging the accuracy of any particular interpretation of a *sutta* which he claims is the true *phasa tham* rendering of that *sutta*. This means that it is difficult for Buddhadāsa to prove that in reinterpreting the Pali scriptures he is not simply following his own whim or twisting the original text to suit his own purposes, as has been claimed by some of his critics. This is not to say that Buddhadāsa's interpretations are in fact wrong or twisted, but that he provides no criterion which might allow others to decide independently the accuracy of his renderings of the scriptures. That is, he does not provide a theoretical criterion which would allow an independent observer to determine from an analysis of the text or scriptures in question whether that text should be read as *phasa tham* and, if it is to be read as *phasa tham*, whether the Dhamma language interpretation Buddhadāsa gives to that text is in fact correct.

But while Buddhadāsa does not present any explicit criteria for applying his interpretative theory, a close reading of his works does reveal the operation of some implicit criteria. One of these criteria is sociological, in that Buddhadāsa bases judgements of the inaccuracy of traditional readings of the scriptures and of the accuracy of his *phasa tham* readings on the social and religious consequences of those respective interpretations. This criterion is related to Buddhadāsa's ecumenical interests for, as discussed in chapter 9, harmony between religions is a major plank of

Buddhadāsa's proposal for a better world, seeing as he traces social problems to weaknesses in or conflicts between religions. He thereby regards ending social problems which hinder improvements in human well-being as fundamentally a religious matter, saying that

> The true objective of the founders of all religions with regard to the completion or perfection of what is most useful and needful for humanity is not being achieved, because the followers of the respective religions interpret the language of Dhamma wrongly, having preserved wrong interpretations and preached wrongly to such an extent that the world has been facing turmoil and problems created by the conflicts among religions.[49]

Thus for Buddhadāsa the key to religious harmony is that each religion's doctrines should be interpreted correctly according to *phasa tham*, and because of what he sees as historical accretions to and misinterpretations of original religious teachings he warns that "We should be extremely careful with [religious] interpretations of a rigidly traditional nature."[50] To promote mutual understanding and agreement about the correct rendering of each religion's doctrines Buddhadāsa calls for "enlightened flexibility as regarding interpreting."[51] Concretely this "enlightened flexibility" means that

> We should maintain that if an interpretation of any word in any religion leads to disharmony and does not positively further the welfare of the many, then such an interpretation is to be regarded as wrong; that is, against the will of God, or as the working of Satan or Mara.[52]

Here Buddhadāsa is restating the Buddha's epistemological criterion of "moral benefit" discussed in chapter 1. That is, he proposes that the criterion for judging the accuracy of a *phasa tham* interpretation is ethical. A term or *sutta* should be subjected to a *phasa tham* reinterpretation if its traditional interpretation does not produce social and religious harmony. And a *phasa tham* rendering is correct if it then permits or promotes universal welfare and interreligious harmony.

This sociological criterion for the application of *phasa tham* interpretations demonstrates that Buddhadāsa's theory is not based solely in Theravada doctrine although, as has already been discussed, it is closely related to the tradition of Theravada thought. Rather, Buddhadāsa's hermeneutic theory incorporates his perception of the social role and importance of Buddhism in Thailand, for the sociological criterion for applying *phasa tham* interpretations of the scriptures is based upon his judgements about the social impact of particular interpretations of religious texts and doctrines. The sociological criterion for the application of *phasa tham* interpretations does not deal with the character of the texts in dispute, but is based on extra-textual judgements of the beneficial or deleterious impact of scriptural interpretations. For Buddhadāsa *phasa tham* interpretations are valid and true if and because they promote moral and religious well-being and ultimately assist in the attainment of *nibbāna* or salvation from suffering. As already noted, this criterion is in accord with the practical or ethical epistemological emphasis of Theravada Buddhism, where a theory is judged as "true" if it has practical benefit in assisting the attainment of salvation, not because that point or theory is true per se.

This practical and ethical epistemological criterion is, however, founded upon implicit theoretical principles. It is based firstly on the assumption that *nibbāna* is an actual and true condition. Furthermore, the ethical criterion of truth assumes that any activity which promotes the attainment of *nibbāna* must of necessity be guided by knowledge which either reflects that ultimate truth or participates in it to such an extent that it is capable of ultimately effecting its realization. That is, only action based upon principles which are in fact in accord with the ultimate truth of *nibbāna* are in practice capable of leading to the understanding of that truth. Because the ethical goal of Buddhist spiritual practice is a state of wisdom or absolute knowledge, epistemology and practice are thereby interrelated. For this reason Buddhadāsa's practical or sociological criterion for applying his *phasa tham* theory must be regarded as in fact being based upon sound Buddhist epistemological criteria. However, he himself has not explicitly detailed these matters and has, as a consequence, left his interpretative theory somewhat in a state of theoretical confusion.

## CRITICISMS OF THE *PHASA THAM* THEORY

The confusions associated with Buddhadāsa's presentation of the theory of *phasa khon–phasa tham* make it particularly susceptible to attack, and indeed there are vehement critics of Buddhadāsa's two-language theory. However, the attacks of these critics in general reveal either a misunderstanding of what the theory actually proposes or the criticism is more political than theoretical, which perhaps is to be expected given the practical and social emphasis of the *phasa tham* theory. In general it is the political and social implications of Buddhadāsa's views on the language of the Buddhist scriptures which are criticized, not the views themselves nor the means by which he arrives at them. The polemical character of many of the criticisms raised against the *phasa khon–phasa tham* distinction in fact demonstrates that in fundamentally reforming Buddhist teachings in Thailand, Buddhadāsa provides not just an intellectual but an ideological challenge to traditional and conservative Thai Buddhists, who respond with political and ideological rather than strictly theoretical attacks on his work.

For example, the late Thai prime minister Kukrit Pramoj criticized not only the *phasa khon–phasa tham* distinction but also said that the overall style of Buddhadāsa's language in his works and sermons is confusing for the average Thai. In one public debate with Kukrit, Buddhadāsa remarked that "The more one studies Buddhism the less one understands it."(T)[53] Buddhadāsa had a fondness for paradox and irony, being much influenced by the Zen school of Buddhism. And, as in Zen, Buddhadāsa often liked using language provocatively with the object of stimulating his audience to reconsider their customary views. In the above quote Buddhadāsa is emphasizing that purely theoretical studies of Buddhism not only do not lead to correct spiritual understanding, but the convolutions of an intellect caught at the level of *phasa khon* may also actually prevent insight into Buddhist truths. However, in reply to Buddhadāsa's above statement Kukrit quipped, "You should go and teach the Japanese, you speak like a Zen Buddhist."(T)[54] As a politician Kukrit has the accessibility of Buddhism to the Thai masses in mind when he criticizes the purported difficulty of Buddhadāsa's style.

There have also been specific theoretical criticisms of Buddhadasa's interpretative theory, such as the following by Winai Siwakun, an economist and political scientist working in the Department of the Budget.[55] Winai argues that

> In regard to explaining the Dhamma understandably, how will we speak unless we use *phasa khon* for talking and explaining so as to obtain knowledge and understanding of Dhamma?(T)[56]

Here Winai has in mind the traditional notion of religious language in Thailand, which he mistakenly thinks is what Buddhadasa means by *phasa tham*. Historically the language of Buddhism in Thailand has not been the vernacular but the ancient language of Pali, which is unintelligible to the uneducated. Winai asks how Buddhism can be understood if Buddhadāsa intends using such a remote and unintelligible language. But Winai has not only misunderstood what Buddhadāsa means by *phasa tham*, namely, a spiritually insightful reading of the scriptures and not a special scholarly religious language; he also fails to understand what is meant by *phasa khon*. He takes *phasa khon* as meaning literally "human speech," with the implication of speaking in an understandable and reasonable way. While in common usage in Thailand *phasa khon* has the positive import of being clear, down to earth and sensible, for Buddhadāsa it has the negative import of denoting an inadequate and limited appreciation of the Buddha's teaching. This inversion of the term's usual import in Thai is a deliberate linguistic ploy by Buddhadāsa to emphasize that what most people take to be a sound and reasonable interpretation of the scriptures is, from a spiritual perspective, quite unsound. Winai asks how deep things can be understood without using the clear language of *phasa khon*.

It is Buddhadāsa's point, however, that what Winai purports to be clear and reasonable language is based upon a material rather than a spiritual mode of knowing. Consequently, a *phasa khon* analysis is incapable of appreciating the actual import of the Dhamma simply because it has not penetrated to the epistemological realm of Dhamma, remaining in the "sensibleness" of mundane awareness.

Buddhadāsa's point is that without spiritual insight into Dhamma, no amount of explaining, no matter how clear and reasonable, will ever succeed in instilling in the listener an actual appreciation of the Buddha's teaching. In Buddhadāsa's view *phasa khon*, or language taken literally as expressing the conventionally accepted wisdom of the average person, no matter how perspicuous, forever fails to grasp the truths of the Dhamma.

Nevertheless, in his criticism of Buddhadāsa's theory Winai invokes a powerful ally in his emphasis on ease of understanding in accounts of Buddhism, namely the present Thai king, Bhumiphol Adulyadej or Rama IX. In a 1965 address to the Khana Kammakan Sun Khonkhwa Thang Phutthasatsana (คณะกรรมการศูนย์ค้นคว้าทางพุทธศาสนา), or the Committee of the Centre for Buddhist Research, at Wat Saket, Bangkok, King Bhumiphol Adulyadej emphasized that despite the progress of science, Buddhism retained its traditional importance, as indicated by the number of Europeans and Americans interested in it. The king then suggested that foreigners' interest in Buddhism should be facilitated and that

> Buddhism should be taught so that it can be easily understood, by means of language everyone can listen to without having to spend a long time.(T)[57]

This speech is referred to by another critic of Buddhadāsa's, the former monk, Phra Chayanantho Bhikkhu, or Anan Senakhan,[58] in a book called *Khamson Diarathi* (Heretical teachings), a text which is directed solely at condemning Buddhadāsa and his ideas. The clear implication of this book is that Buddhadāsa's teachings, by not fitting with the king's expressed wish for Buddhism to be expounded simply and straightforwardly, not only show disobedience to the monarch but also subvert the propagation of Buddhism to foreigners, which the king and many other Thai Buddhists regard as an important cultural activity.

However, these criticisms by Winai and Anan are not directed at the actual theory of *phasa tham*, but rather criticize the political implications of Buddhadāsa's work. This failure to deal with theoretical issues and the corresponding concentration on politics is a systematic characteristic of many of the criticisms directed against Buddhadāsa's interpretations. This indicates that the crucial point of disagreement between Buddhadāsa and his critics is not in fact strictly doctrinal but rather is a question of fundamentally differing appreciations of the nature of Buddhism in modern Thailand. The response of Anan Senakhan, Winai Siwakun, and similar conservative critics of Buddhadāsa to socioeconomic modernization and development has been to resist change in what they perceive as key elements of Thai culture and identity, symbolized in the traditional teaching and practice of Buddhism. For the conservatives change is regarded negatively as a threat, but for liberal Buddhists like Buddhadāsa the changes brought about by modernization are seen as challenges, to be met by judicious adjustment of existing ideas and outlooks to the new circumstances. As discussed in later chapters, these two polarized responses to change are also associated with polarized political stances in contemporary Thai secular life.

## SUMMARY

The *phasa khon–phasa tham* theory of interpreting the Buddhist scriptures is not without theoretical difficulties, most notably caused by Buddhadāsa's denial of the validity of the very scriptures which provide some of the theoretical foundations for his interpretations and by his failure to provide an explicit criterion for applying the theory. However, the theory of *phasa tham* does follow the spirit of Theravada Buddhist teachings and does have significant precedents both in the canonical scriptures and in the commentary literature. Leaving aside the question of the precise historical and scriptural precedents for Buddhadāsa's theory of *phasa tham*, it is also the case that his interpretative theory is a consistent development of basic doctrinal principles. That is, given the assumption that Buddhism contains a universally true and relevant message and the recognition that the religion is no longer seen as relevant by many Thais, an interpretative effort which demonstrates the vitality of the original message of salvation must have in fact penetrated to and incorporated that message.

But in judging Buddhadāsa's work it is also important to note that, independent of the theoretical status of the theory, *phasa tham* has a broader social and ideological significance in Thailand. This is because of its use in the demythologization of Buddhist doctrine and the related conferring of religious value on activity in the social world. Despite its limitations and failings, the theory of *phasa tham–phasa khon* must be recognized as a positive attempt to develop a new system of interpreting the *Tipiṭaka*. However, Buddhadāsa not only champions his new hermeneutic by buttressing it with supporting arguments, he also undermines the doctrinal credibility of his critics, which does not amount to a specific defence of the *phasa tham* theory but is rather an attempt to discredit those who attack it. This subversive approach is manifested in Buddhadāsa's denial that the scriptures emphasized by his major opponents, the *Abhidhammapiṭaka* and its commentaries, are authoritative sources of Buddhist doctrine. These critical claims are considered in the next chapter.

# 4 BUDDHADĀSA ON REBIRTH AND *PAṬICCASAMUPPĀDA*

## CRITICISMS OF THE *ABHIDHAMMAPIṬAKA*

BUDDHADĀSA'S REINTERPRETATIONS of Buddhist doctrine are not only based on his hermeneutic theory of *phasa khon–phasa tham* but also on a selective and critical reading of the Buddhist canon, the *Tipiṭaka*, and of the commentary literature. He rejects large sections of both the *Abhidhammapiṭaka* and Buddhaghosa's *Visuddhimagga* as either unnecessary or inaccurate. Buddhadāsa undertakes this radical critique of the Theravada scriptures and commentary literature as part of his effort to eradicate supernatural beliefs from Thai Buddhism and to refocus the religion on the immediacy of human life here and now. Buddhadāsa is particularly critical of the traditional Buddhist concern with *kamma* and rebirth, which he regards as being most strongly supported by the *Visuddhimagga* and traditional interpretations of the *Abhidhammapiṭaka*.

The *Abhidhammapiṭaka*, the third major division of the Theravada canon after the *Vinayapiṭaka* and the *Suttapiṭaka*, is a set of seven complex texts. The intention of the authors of the *Abhidhammapiṭaka* was to re-present Buddhist teachings as detailed in the recorded words of the Buddha in the *Suttapiṭaka*, as a consistent theoretical development of the doctrines of *anicca* and *anattā*. The *Abhidhamma* literature eschews describing objects as entities or *attā*, that is, as individuals. Instead, in accord with the *anattā* doctrine, the *Abhidhammapiṭaka* refers to the objects of experience only in terms of elements and shifting relations of compounding between those elements. The analyses of the *Abhidhamma* were developed as spiritual aids for overcoming delusion and for developing insight into reality. By analyzing the minutiae of experience in terms of the transitory relations of elements, the authors of the *Abhidhamma-piṭaka* aimed to assist the aspirant to give up his or her delusory belief in the substantial nature of the objects of experience.

Despite the canonicity of the *Abhidhammapiṭaka*, Buddhadāsa is highly critical of the emphasis placed on this section of the Buddhist canon in Thailand, and he claims that Thai Buddhism would in fact be better off without its complex theoretical details. Buddhadāsa regards the complexity of the *Abhidhammapiṭaka* as being unnecessary and even potentially misleading. He translates the Pali prefix *abhi* as meaning "extreme" (*ying* – ยิ่ง) or "excessive" (*koen* – เกิน), calling the *Abhidhammapiṭaka* an "excessive part" or "superfluous part" (*suan koen* – ส่วนเกิน)(T)[1] of the scriptures, and he argues that "It is part of the *Dhamma* which is not directly or immediately related to the extinction of suffering."(T)[2] By this Buddhadāsa means that the *Abhidhammapiṭaka* is an intellectual system that is only an adjunct to the meditative practice which is the sole source of spiritual insight. He regards the *Abhidhammapiṭaka* as unnecessary for the purpose of attaining *nibbāna*:

> On some occasions the Lord Buddha mentioned [in the *Suttapiṭaka*] the words *abhidhamma* and *abhivinaya*. These denote the parts of the Dhamma which are excessive or the parts which provide too deep an explanation, beyond what is necessary for a person to know or to have in order to attain *nibbāna*.(T)[3]

However, Buddhadāsa's interpretation of the term *abhidhamma* is problematic. The term *abhidhamma* is rare in the *Suttapiṭaka*, the section of the scriptures which Buddhadāsa accepts as the authoritative source of Buddhist doctrine. Where the term does occur in the *Suttapiṭaka* it has a special sense, and does not specifically denote the *Abhidhammapiṭaka*. This is because the final section of the Theravada canon postdated the compilation of the *Suttapiṭaka* by at least a couple of centuries. Suchip Punyanuphap, complier of *Phra Traipidok Samrap Prachachon* (The *Tipiṭaka* for the common man),[4] observes that in the *Kinti Sutta*[5] of the *Suttapiṭaka* the term *abhidhamma* denotes "the highly distinguished Dhamma."(T)[6] In particular, it denotes the *bodhipakkhiyadhamma* or the thirty-seven qualities regarded as contributing to enlightenment.[7] In the *Mahāparinibbāna Sutta* these thirty-seven qualities are also described as the practice of Dhamma beyond the basics of Buddhist ethics. The difficulty in interpreting the two terms *abhidhamma* and *abhiññāvisesitahamma*, which both denote a "higher" or "distinguished" Dhamma, is that the notion "distinguished," *visesita*, can denote both "excellent" or "superior" as well as simply the notion of "having many distinctions" or "having many parts." Noting this ambiguity, Buddhadāsa maintains that the prefix *abhi* in *abhidhamma* may mean either "great" or "excessive," depending on the context. He also acknowledges that, depending on who uses it and how it is approached, the *Abhidhammapiṭaka* may either be of "great" use or it may be "excessive" and a hindrance to spiritual practice. Buddhadāsa says that the *Abhidhammapiṭaka* may

> be either beneficial or non-beneficial, it can cause confusion or not cause confusion because it contains both that which is real or true and that which is excessive and unnecessary.(T)[9]

He concedes that the study of the *Abhidhammapiṭaka* is appropriate for those with penetrating understanding who wish to undertake an intellectual study of Buddhist principles. But he also claims that the *Abhidhammapiṭaka* is both excessive and a spiritual hindrance to the ordinary person. Buddhadāsa defines the true *abhidhamma* or "great Dhamma" as *suññatā* or voidness, which he calls "the *abhidhamma* which does not go by the name of *abhidhamma*."(T)[10] The notion of *suññatā*, in particular as interpreted in the notion of *chit wang*, is central to Buddhadāsa's interpretation of Buddhist practice and is discussed in detail in subsequent chapters.

Buddhadāsa further defines the term *abhidhamma* by first drawing a distinction between philosophy and science:

> Buddhism as such is not a philosophy, it is a science. It is of a kind with material science but it is a mental science or a science of *nāmadhamma* (mentality).(T)[11]

Here Buddhadāsa takes "philosophy" to denote intellectual speculation while he describes "science" as knowledge which is both definite and immediate. Using his theory of *phasa khon–phasa tham,* Buddhadāsa says that for those who do not know spiritual truth, that is, those who interpret the scriptures at the level of everyday language, the term *abhidhamma* simply denotes a speculative system of thought such as is found in the *Abhidhammapiṭaka.* But for those who "know" and who read the canon at the level of *phasa tham, abhidhamma* denotes "scientific knowledge" of absolute truth or *paramasacca*, which he defines as *anattā* or *suññatā*, or in Thai *khwam wang* (ความว่าง)—"voidness." That is, for Buddhadāsa *abhidhamma* does not denote a certain text or theoretical doctrine but rather the existential condition of knowledge of *anattā* or the "voidness of self" attained through meditative insight.

However, in the final analysis Buddhadāsa concludes that the *Abhidhammapiṭaka* is superfluous or excessive. This is because, in his opinion, it is not necessary to know the *Abhidhammapiṭaka* in order to become an *ariyapuggala,* an enlightened or liberated personality,[12] and he cites the *Yodhājīva Vagga* in the *Tikanipāta* of the *Aṅguttara Nikāya*[13] as supporting his claim. Buddhadāsa in fact proposes that Theravada Buddhism would be better off without the *Abhidhammapiṭaka* altogether:

> Should we toss the *Abhidhammapiṭaka* away completely . . . nothing would be lost because we would still retain the *Suttanta [Suttapiṭaka],* which is the practical aspect of the scriptures for attaining *nibbāna* quickly . . . But what! Now we have just the opposite [in Thailand]: attempts to throw out the *Suttantapiṭaka* completely and leave only the *Abhidhammapiṭaka.* Buddhism is going to the dogs!

> . . . If all the *Suttantapiṭaka* is thrown out leaving only the *Abhidhammapiṭaka* humanity will go to the dogs! We could not correctly follow the Noble Eightfold Path (*ariyamagga*) that leads to *nibbāna.* But if we were to get rid of every last bit of the *Abhidhammapiṭaka* . . . we could still follow the path to *nibbāna,* and easily at that, because we would not have the path obscured or our minds confused by that *Abhidhammapiṭaka.* (T)[14]

These criticisms of the *Abhidhammapiṭaka's* "excessiveness" are not purely theoretical but are related to Buddhadāsa's concern to make Buddhist practices accessible to the layperson. Mastery of the complex analyses of the *Abhidhammapiṭaka* has historically been associated with one type of clerical meditative practice. However, the use of the *Abhidhammapiṭaka* as a guide to meditation is not the only Buddhist meditative system and Buddhadāsa's criticisms can be read as indicating that laypeople do not need to devote years to an academic study of the *Abhidhammapiṭaka* before they can practice meditation.

Buddhadāsa's criticisms are also related to the fundamentalist character of his reinterpretative enterprise. Despite the novelty of some of his views, Buddhadāsa authorizes his reinterpretations by claiming that they are consistent with the original teaching of the Buddha as recorded in the *Suttapiṭaka.* The *Suttapiṭaka* is consequently the most important section of the Buddhist canon for him, especially those sections containing the reputed words of the Buddha. Buddhadāsa follows this fundamentalist course in order to cut through what he regards as the misinterpretations of later commentaries and so penetrate to the original, pure core of Buddhism. Thus when Buddhadāsa states that "the *Abhidhammapiṭaka* does not exist in the form of the Buddha's words," (T)[15] he is also saying that, in his opinion, the *Abhidhammapiṭaka* lacks the religious authority of the *Suttapiṭaka* and so should not be given equal standing with the authentic discourses recorded in the *Suttapiṭaka.*

Buddhadāsa also criticizes the way the *Abhidhammapiṭaka* has historically been studied in Thailand and the purpose for which it has been used. He claims that the monks who study *Abhidhamma* teachings in Thailand in fact content themselves with the even less authoritative commentaries on the *Abhidhammapiṭaka*, avoiding study of the more difficult original text. Buddhadāsa notes that around the twelfth Buddhist century (sixth to seventh centuries of the Christian era), Ceylonese commentators summarized the *Abhidhammapiṭaka* into a more compact text called the *Abhidhammatthasaṅgaha*.[16] Over the centuries many further commentaries were based on this radically abridged version of the original canon. Mrs. Rhys Davids observes that

> *The Abhidhammatthasaṅgaha*, whether on account of its completer survey of what is known as *Abhidhamma*, or because of its excessively condensed treatment, or because of its excellence as a handbook, stimulated a larger growth of ancillary works than any of the foregoing [list of Pali commentaries.][17]

Buddhadāsa asserts that the commentaries based on the *Abhidhammatthasaṅgha* came to emphasize the supernatural and the miraculous instead of the original analytical emphasis of the *Abhidhammatthasaṅgha* itself. He claims that this trend towards supernaturalist readings of the *Abhidhamma* has developed so far in Thailand that the *Abhidhamma* studied and taught there today should be called "rat's nest *Abhidhamma*" (อภิธรรมรังหนู),[18] because it is full of odds and ends. That is, he claims that the *Abhidhammapiṭaka* has become associated with the popular supernatural religion, in contradistinction to the original intentions of its authors. One of the most common supernatural associations of the *Abhidhammapiṭaka* is in Thai funeral practices, sections of the *Abhidhammapiṭaka* traditionally being chanted at funeral services because of a mythical association with communicating with the dead. Kenneth Wells comments,

> The *Abhidhamma* is used at funerals both because it is considered to contain the essence of the teaching of the Buddha and because it was used by the Buddha when he preached to his mother after her death and ascension to the *tavatiṁsa* heaven.[19]

It is not because of the specific relevance of its teachings that sections of the *Abhidhammapiṭaka* are recited at Thai funerals. In fact the content of the *Abhidhammapiṭaka* is largely irrelevant in this context, the mere recitation being more important because of the belief that the spirit of the deceased may benefit from the teachings. In this context Buddhadāsa is not critical of the *Abhidhammapiṭaka* per se. Rather, he is critical of the supernatural interpretation of Buddhism which is often justified by the *Abhidhamma* or by specific supernatural interpretations of the *Abhidhammapiṭaka* itself.

Those Thai Buddhists who base their interpretation and practice of the religion upon the *Abhidhammapiṭaka* are some of Buddhadāsa's most vocal critics, for he attacks the foundation of the form of Buddhism they follow. For example, in opposition to Buddhadāsa's claim that the *Abhidhammapiṭaka* is "not in the form of the Buddha's words," Winai Siwakun retorts that "the science for the transcendence of the suffering of life which is found in the *Abhidhammapiṭaka* is a result of the realization of the Lord Buddha."(T)[20] That is, Winai claims that although the *Abhidhammapiṭaka* is not composed from the Buddha's actual discourses, it is nevertheless consistent with the spiritual insights revealed in the *Suttapiṭaka*.

Buddhadāsa vehemently criticizes the association of spirit cults with Buddhism, saying that "We should not let our most perfect Buddhism become an animistic faith like that of the uncivilized."(T)[21] He presents rationalist interpretations of supernatural phenomena and describes belief in ghosts and spirits as possibly resulting from a collective psychological or hypnotic effect:

> The influence of the collective mental flow of many ignorant people can have enough power to possess the minds of foolish individuals . . . and accordingly develop in them the feeling that such things are true and so cause them to believe in ghostly and magical things . . . the thing called *avijjā* (ignorance) builds up such erroneous beliefs.(T)[22]

That the primary focus of Buddhadāsa's criticisms of the *Abhi-*

*dhammapiṭaka* is on attacking supernatural beliefs is indicated by the fact that, in defending their views against Buddhadāsa's attacks, the proponents of the *Abhidhamma* in Thailand are most concerned to assert the reality of the supernatural beings that Buddhadāsa denies. For example, in defending the *Abhidhammapiṭaka* in the face of Buddhadāsa's criticisms, Anan Senakhan notes the four *yoni* or modes of generation mentioned in the *Suttapiṭaka*, where all beings are classed as either womb-born, egg-born, moisture-born or *opapā tika*. This last category denotes creatures having "spontaneous" births, that is, without the instrumentality of parents. Anan regards this mode of generation as referring to the process by which superhuman and subhuman beings are "born" or come into existence in heaven and hell. In contrast, Buddhadāsa interprets the notion of "birth" (Pali: *jāti*, Thai: *chat*) in *phasa tham* as referring to the deluded idea of individuality—that there is an essential self or *attā:*

> The word "birth" refers to the arising of the mistaken idea of "I", "myself." It does not refer to physical birth, as generally supposed. The mistaken assumption that this word "birth" refers to physical birth is a major obstacle to comprehending the Buddha's teaching.[23]

Buddhadāsa interprets *opapātika* in *phasa tham* as metaphorically referring to the processes by which the notions of "I am a suffering individual" and "I am a happy individual" come into being. Anan rejects this reduction of the supernatural to psychological states, saying,

> *Opapātika* are beings which have both concrete (*rūpa*) and abstract (*nāma*) existence. They have both bodies and minds but their bodies are composed of translucent atomic particles.[24] One could say they have divine bodies but the truth is that they have fine material bodies. *Opapātika* are people we cannot see with our unaided eyes.(T)[25]

In his *phasa tham* interpretations Buddhadāsa gives supernatural beings such as *thewada* and demons only an abstract existence. For him demons and *thewada* are no more than mental states and have no concrete or material existence. By emphasizing the material or fine atomic nature of *thewada* and spirits, Anan attempts to counter their reduction to purely abstract psychological states.

Buddhadāsa has not remained completely silent in the face of Anan's criticisms. However, his response is indirect and is presented in the context of a discussion of the doctrine of *paṭiccasamuppāda* or dependent origination. Buddhadāsa considers Buddhist teachings about *paṭiccasamuppāda,* specifically about death and rebirth, to have long been misinterpreted because of an implicit acceptance of the notion of *attā*, that there is an individual self or soul. He maintains that the mistaken views that there is a self and that there is entitative continuity between one life and the next have been implicitly accepted within Theravada Buddhism since the Third Buddhist Council, which was held only three hundred years after the Buddha's death. He acknowledges that this scriptural misinterpretation may have arisen unintentionally and because of ignorance and intellectual slackness in interpreting the subtleties of Buddhist doctrine. However, he also suggests that its acceptance may have been the result of a conspiracy to destroy Buddhism:

> There may have been rebellious traitors acting as destructive agents inside Buddhism who [deliberately and] maliciously explained *paṭiccasamuppāda*, the foundation of Buddhism, incorrectly. That is, so that it would become the eternalist doctrine (*sassatadiṭṭhi*) found in Hinduism, or [in other words] change into Brahmanism ... If there were such harmful intentions it would mean that someone must have made up an explanation [of *paṭiccasamuppāda*] in order to create a channel for the *attā* doctrine to come into Buddhism. And then Brahmanism would swallow Buddhism ... This is a supposition from the standpoint that there could have been harmful [influences within Buddhism].(T)[26]

With uncharacteristic sectarianism Buddhadāsa adds that the motivation behind such a treacherous plot is that "Brahmanism is an enemy of Buddhism; it wants to swallow Buddhism."(T)[27] These criticisms do not have a merely historical import. The implication of Buddhadāsa's statements is that if Brahmanical ideas of an eternal self or soul were dangerous over two thousand years ago then they, and those purported Buddhists who teach that human beings are reborn as spirits and demons, are equally harmful today. Buddhadāsa thus accuses those who claim that he is destroying Buddhism of precisely the same crime.

## CRITICISMS OF THE *VISUDDHIMAGGA* AND TRADITIONAL INTERPRETATIONS OF THE *PAṬICCASAMUPPĀDA*

The *Abhidhammapiṭaka* is not the only Buddhist text whose authority Buddhadāsa questions in order to establish his *phasa tham* or demythologized interpretation of Buddhist doctrine. He also criticizes the *Visuddhimagga* of Buddhaghosa. Written in the fifth century as a summary of Buddhist teachings, the *Visuddhimagga* has become the most revered of all Theravada commentaries. Sunthorn Na Rangsi says of the *Visuddhimagga* that it is "regarded by the Theravadins as an authentic source of Buddhist teachings second only to the Pali *Tipiṭaka* itself."[28] Perhaps because of the respect traditionally accorded the *Visuddhimagga*, Buddhadāsa's criticisms of Buddhaghosa's views are somewhat guarded:

> I don't respect or believe in Buddhaghosacariya one hundred percent, because there are parts [of the *Visuddhimagga*] I have quite some disagreement with. I can respect up to ninety or ninety-five percent of Buddhaghosa's teachings.(T)[29]

Buddhadāsa's main point of disagreement with Buddhaghosa concerns the interpretation of *paṭiccasamuppāda*, the doctrine of dependent origination. Through a series of causally linked stages the *paṭiccasamuppāda* demonstrates how ignorance, *avijjā*, leads to attachment, *upādāna*, and how attachment in turn leads to suffering. The *paṭiccasamuppāda* is a systematic explanation of the Buddhist doctrine that ignorance of reality is the root cause of human suffering. Conversely, the *paṭiccasamuppāda* is also taken as detailing how attaining wisdom and overcoming ignorance lead to the cessation of suffering and so to *nibbāna*. The twelve causally linked stages of the *paṭiccasamuppāda,* also called *bhavacakka* or the cycle of becoming, are in order as follows:

| | | |
|---|---|---|
| 1. | *avijjā* | ignorance |
| 2. | *saṅkhāra* | mental "formations" associated with volitional or *kamma*-creating actions |
| 3. | *viññāṇa* | consciousness |
| 4. | *nāmarūpa* | the five aggregates or *khandhas* constituting individual existence |
| 5. | *saḷāyatana* | the six bases of sense impressions[30] |
| 6. | *phassa* | sense contact, the six types of sense impressions |
| 7. | *vedanā* | feelings resulting from sense impressions |
| 8. | *taṇhā* | craving for the six types of sensorily cognizable objects |
| 9. | *upādāna* | attachment or clinging to sensed objects |
| 10. | *bhava* | coming into being, becoming |
| 11. | *jāti* | birth conditioned by *bhava* |
| 12. | *jarāmaraṇa* | old age and death |

*Jarāmaraṇa* denotes suffering which results from birth, *jāti*,[31] which has itself been conditioned by all the preceding ten factors beginning with ignorance. The suffering of *jarāmaraṇa* is in turn regarded as a condition for the arising of ignorance, and is consequently the starting point for another cycle of the *paṭiccasamuppāda*. The *paṭiccasamuppāda* is in every sense a vicious cycle, with each stage feeding on the former and contributing to the next.

The *paṭiccasamuppāda* has also traditionally been regarded as providing the theoretical basis for an explanation of the process of rebirth. Buddhaghosa interpreted the twelve spokes of the *bhavacakka* as spanning three separate lifetimes and in the *Visuddhimagga* he wrote

> The past, the present and the future are its [i.e., the *paṭiccasamuppāda's*] three times. Of these it should be understood that, according to what is given in the texts, the two factors ignorance and formations

(*saṅkhāra*) belong to the past time, the eight beginning with consciousness belong to the present time, and the two birth and ageing-and-death, belong to the future time.[32]

In Buddhaghosa's interpretation rebirth is explained by the postulation of a special relation between consciousness, *viññāṇa*, and formations, *saṅkhāra*. As Sunthorn Na Rangsi comments, in the *paṭiccasamuppāda*,

> the function of consciousness is twofold: to cognise the object presented and to constitute the subterranean stream of consciousness (*bhavaṅga*) which is the basis of individuality.[33]

Traditionally, consciousness in a "subterranean" or *bhavaṅga* mode is regarded as forming the basis of individual identity. In order to remain consistent with the doctrine of *anattā* and avoid the implication that the rebirth doctrine denotes that there is an entity which reincarnates in successive lives, this subterranean mode of consciousness is described as not being a self-existing entity or self. Rather, it is described as being a process with a definite origination and end. It is maintained that the *bhavaṅga* consciousness underlying each successive life is distinct and discrete, beginning at conception and ending at death. The actual link between successive births (i.e., between the cessation of one *bhavaṅga* condition at death and the origination of the next *bhavaṅga* at conception) is called the *paṭ isandhiviññāṇa*. It is this *paṭisandhi* consciousness which transfers the *kammic* impressions or *saṅkhāra* which determine an individual's character or fate from one existence to the next. That is, traditional Theravada teachings propose that *kammic* residues are transferred from one life condition to another (via the discrete transferal process called *paṭisandhiviññaṇa*), but that successive existences are in fact distinct and discrete. This is because the identity-giving *bhavaṅga* consciousness underlying each existence is posited as being a finite phenomenon specific to each individual existence.

However, Buddhadāsa denies that the causal linkages of *paṭiccasamuppāda* provide an account of literal rebirth. Instead he maintains that the cycle of dependent origination should be taken as explaining the arising of suffering at any given moment. Buddhadāsa denies that rebirth is central to Buddhist doctrine. As noted above, he says that "birth" should be interpreted in *phasa tham* as the psychological arising of the deluded sense of selfhood, not as denoting literal birth or rebirth.

Buddhadāsa's denial of the importance of the notion of "rebirth" to Buddhist teachings is one of his most radical claims, which not only stands in opposition to the Theravada interpretative tradition as represented by the *Visuddhimagga* but also counters the explicit references to rebirth in the canonical scriptures of the *Suttapiṭaka*. Sunthorn Na Rangsi says,

> In the Pali scriptures there are many stories telling about some of the Buddha's disciples who passed away and assumed new births in some realm of existence or other. All such stories stand as scriptural proofs of rebirth.[34]

The recollection of past lives, such as indicated in the following passage from the *Potaliya Sutta*, is commonly reported in the *Suttapiṭaka*:

> Behold householder, this *ariyasāvaka* (follower of the Buddha) abiding in *upekkhā* (equanimity) as the cause of a pure mind without any greater Dhamma, can recall many past lives, can recall one life, two lives . . . ten lives . . . a hundred lives, a thousand lives, a hundred thousand lives through many eons of world development and many eons of world dissolution.(T)[35]

While it is possible to interpret the term "life" or "birth" (*jāti*) in the above passage in *phasa tham* as the arising of the sense of self, and the term "world" as denoting a psychological condition, there are other passages in the *suttas* where the reference to literal rebirth is less easily interpreted metaphorically. For example, in the *Siṅgālaka Sutta* the Buddha admonishes the layman *Siṅgālaka*, saying that one who follows the *vinaya* or discipline of the Buddha

> naturally practices for victory over both worlds . . . both this world

> and the next. In the future after having died because of the body's breakdown that *ariyasāvaka* will naturally attain to the *sugati* heavenly world.(T)[36]

Buddhaghosa clearly indicates in the *Visuddhimagga* that he does not intend *jāti* or birth, the eleventh spoke of the *paṭiccasamuppāda*, to be interpreted metaphorically when he says that birth

> should be regarded as the aggregates (*khandhas*) that occur from the time of rebirth-linking (*paṭisandhiviññāṇa*) up to the exit from the mother's womb.[37]

Buddhadāsa's opposition to this long-established teaching is consequently no light matter. However, it should also be noted that in the *Suttapiṭaka* belief in rebirth is not included among the central articles of belief or among the key doctrines of Buddhism. In denying rebirth, Buddhadāsa thus flounts both tradition and sections of the scriptures but he does not contradict any fundamental doctrine such as *anattā, anicca, dukkha,* or *nibbāna*. Buddhadāsa's preparedness to contradict even sections of the *Suttapiṭaka*, in addition to denying the authority of the *Abhidhammapiṭaka* and its commentaries, reveals that his approach to reinterpreting Buddhism is doctrinal rather than scriptural. That is, Buddhadāsa is concerned to present an interpretation of Theravada teachings which is consistent with doctrinal principles. For Buddhadāsa, logical consistency with the doctrinal fundamentals of Buddhism is the most important determinant of authoritative interpretations of the teachings. While providing guidelines and insights, the Buddhist scriptures are not taken as the ultimate source of religious authority and are discarded by Buddhadāsa wherever they contradict his strictly doctrinal and modernist views.

Buddhadāsa argues for his metaphorical interpretation of the notion of "birth" by claiming that the belief in rebirth, as presented in the *Visuddhimagga* and as generally understood in Thailand, contradicts the doctrine of *anattā*. He claims that belief in rebirth may easily become the false doctrine of *sassatadiṭṭhi*, that there is an eternal self. Buddhadāsa warns,

> Be careful in this matter of the "next life." One small error will make it the *sassatadiṭṭhi* (eternalist doctrine) of the Brahmins. That is, believing that when some person has died that he himself will be reborn again.(T)[38]

He contends that according to the traditional interpretation of "birth" in Buddhism,

> A person's *kilesa* in a previous life effect *kammic* results in this life . . . those *kammic* results in this life then cause *kilesa* to arise anew in this life, which then effects *kammic* results in a subsequent life. When *paṭiccasamuppāda* is taught like this it becomes a teaching about *attā*. It becomes a teaching that there are *attā*, selves, beings and individuals.(T)[39]

In contradistinction to the interpretation presented in the *Visuddhimagga*, Buddhadāsa denies that *viññāṇa*, the third element in the *paṭiccasamuppāda* series, means "rebirth-linking consciousness" or *paṭisandhiviññāṇa*.[40] Instead he maintains that *viññaṇa* straightforwardly refers to the six modes of sensory consciousness recognized in Buddhist teachings. Buddhadāsa makes this claim despite the clear association of the notion of *paṭisandhi* with rebirth in the *suttas*, as in the following passage from the *Ñaṇakathā* in the *Khuddaka Nikāya*:

> In a previous *kammicly*-determined existence delusion was *avijjā*, the aggregate of *kamma* was *saṅkhāra*, satisfaction [in sensuality] was *taṇhā*, immersion [in sensuality] was *upādāna*, and consideration [of being] was *bhava*. These five Dhammas in the previous *kamma*-existence were the determining factors of *paṭisandhi* in this life. *Paṭisandhi* was consciousness and it developed into *nāmarūpa* and nerves, which became the twelve sense spheres (*āyatana*).(T)[41]

Buddhadāsa does not acknowledge that his denial of rebirth contradicts such explicit references in the canonical scriptures, and this further indicates that the guiding principle of his reinterpretations is consistency with what he regards as the basic doctrines of Buddhism, not faithful abidance by any specific text.

Buddhadāsa's critique of the notion of literal rebirth raises anew an ancient difficulty of Buddhist doctrine, namely, how to reconcile the doctrine of *anattā* with belief in rebirth. If there is rebirth what is it that is reborn if, as the Buddha taught, there is no self or soul which reincarnates? The interpretation that consciousness has subliminal (*bhavaṅga*) and rebirth-linking (*paṭisandhi*) aspects, as described above, has traditionally been regarded as resolving this problem. In this interpretation, consciousness or *viññāṇa* is defined as a dependent characteristic of each individual existence, having no independent existence and not continuing beyond death. However, in its subliminal or *bhavaṅga* mode consciousness is regarded as having the capacity to transfer *kammic* momenta to another, subsequent existence, passing some of its own characteristics on to the *bhavanga* consciousness associated with that subsequent existence.

However, Buddhadāsa resolves the conflict between the doctrines of *anattā* and rebirth by an altogether different approach, by redefining what is meant by "birth." Buddhadāsa develops his interpretation of "birth" by focusing on the teaching that "True happiness consists in eliminating the false idea of 'I' (*asminanassa vinaya etam ve paramam sukham*)."[42] He defines "the false idea of 'I' or *attā*" as denoting the subjective sense of self together with the self-centred attitudes associated with it. According to this definition, *anattā* not only denotes the ontological doctrine of "non-self" or "non-essentiality" but also the ethical notion of "non-self-centredness" or "unselfishness." Buddhadāsa interprets the teaching that true happiness results from eliminating the false idea of "I" as meaning that suffering is ended by ending self-centredness. In this context he also cites the Buddhist maxim, "Birth is perpetual suffering (*dukkha jāti punapuññam*)."[43] Here, Buddhadāsa maintains that the "birth" which engenders suffering is not physical birth but rather the arising of the false idea of "I" and of self-centredness. He asks,

> Just what is this rebirth? What is it that is reborn? The birth referred

> to is a mental event, something taking place in the mind, the non-physical side of our make-up. This is birth in *Dhamma* language.[44]

In Buddhadāsa's system one is "reborn" when one's notion of selfhood or self-identity shifts:

> The word "birth" merely means a single change of thought about "I" and "mine." It is one birth if we think like a thief and are born a thief and it is another birth the moment we have returned to thinking like a normal person and so have been born as a person.(T)[45]

That is, in *phasa tham* to be "born" a thief is to psychologically identify with being a thief, and to be born a "person" is to regard oneself as a "person." Buddhadāsa interprets the notion of "death" in a similar way, saying that "To die means that 'I' and 'mine' die completely."(T)[46] That is, in *phasa tham* death is not the physical end of life but the ending of the deluded notion of individuality. Furthermore, since ending the delusion of selfhood is to be free of the "rebirth" which causes suffering, it is also to be freed of suffering, which is the definition of *nibbāna*. As Buddhadāsa notes,

> In the words of an old saying, "*nibbāna* is to die before dying . . ." That is, the *kilesa*—the causes of the feeling that there is an "I" or a "mine"—it is they that die.(T)[47]

Buddhadāsa systematically reinterprets all notions associated with rebirth, such as *saṁsāra* or the cycle of rebirth and suffering, in terms of *phasa tham*. For example, he says that if

> at any time there exists the idea "I"–"mine," at that time there exists birth, suffering, and the cycle of *saṁsāra*. The "I" is born, endures for a moment, then ceases; is born again, endures for a moment and then again ceases—which is why the process is referred to as the cycle of *saṁsāra*.(T)[48]

Because the notion of "birth" in the *paṭiccasamuppāda* series has traditionally been interpreted as meaning physical birth, and because it is a causal precursor to suffering or *dukkha* in the *paṭicca-samuppāda*, in traditional Theravada thought physical existence has been regarded as being inherently associated with suffering. This is made clear from the inclusion of the physical processes of aging and death and of pain in the traditional explanation of *dukkha* or suffering in the *Visuddhimagga*: "With birth as condition there is aging and death, and sorrow, lamentation, pain, grief and despair; thus there is the arising of this whole mass of suffering."[49]

However, for Buddhadāsa, *dukkha*, the condition from which Buddhism seeks release, only follows from the birth of self-centredness, not from physical birth. He consequently defines *dukkha* solely as mental suffering:

> A person has a physical birth only once, and finally dies just once, but they can have mental birth and extinction many times. Even in a single day there can be many cycles of birth and extinction . . . and each time it [that mental birth] is suffering. For this reason, the *dhammic* doctrines which mention suffering denote mental suffering.(T)[50]

That is, for Buddhadāsa the only religiously significant suffering is mental pain or mental disease. Physical suffering is not denied by Buddhadāsa, but he does not regard it as religiously significant. That is, because the cause of physical suffering lies in the material world he regards its alleviation as being a matter of applying material rather than religious or spiritual remedies. Thus in Buddhadāsa's system, suffering, in the religious sense of ignorance-caused *dukkha*, is not regarded as being inescapably inherent in physical birth. For Buddhadāsa existence in the material world is not necessarily a state of imperfection. This elimination of the negative connotations associated with existence in the material world is one of the most important aspects of Buddhadāsa's reinterpretative system. For, as discussed in later chapters, he wishes to abolish the traditional role division between the world-involved layperson and the renunciate monk, by giving the layperson access to traditionally clerical practices and by according spiritual value to the layperson's activities in the social world.

Buddhadāsa interprets this world and this life as the domain of Buddhism's concern and as the locale of salvation. Traditionally the notion of "world," *loka*, in Buddhist doctrine, as in English, connotes materiality—the earth and all that constitutes and populates it. The term "world" is also used in the sense of supernatural heavenly and hellish "worlds." However, in Buddhist thought the term *loka* has an additional, negative association with impermanence, *anicca*, and with suffering. However, Buddhadāsa's *phasa tham* interpretation of the term "world" should be noted here:

> In Dhamma language (*phasa tham*) the word "world" refers to the worldly (*lokiya*) mental state, the worldly stage in the scale of mental development . . . the condition which is impermanent, changing, unsatisfactory (i.e., *dukkha*) . . . Hence it is said that "world" is the unsatisfactory condition (*dukkha*); the unsatisfactory condition is the world.[51]

The traditional negative valuation of existence and activity in the material world is completely absent from Buddhadāsa's work. He systematically reduces the field of Buddhist spiritual action from a cosmic to a psychological level, which implies that not only may this material life be freed of *dukkha* (i.e. mental sufferings) but also that it is only within the psychological dimension of this material life that liberation can be sought. In other words, Buddhadāsa's reinterpretation of Theravada Buddhism implies that the material world, here and now, is the only field of Buddhist spiritual activity and the only domain in which its benefits, i.e., enlightenment and *nibbāna*, are enjoyed. In his reformulation of the doctrine of *paṭiccasamuppāda*, his denial of rebirth and in his emphasis on the here and now, Buddhadāsa thus lays the groundwork for a more "worldly" or socially involved interpretation of Buddhism. There is in fact a fundamental continuity between Buddhadāsa's theoretical reinterpretations of spiritual theory and his social theory which is analyzed in later chapters.

## CRITICISMS OF BUDDHADĀSA'S REINTERPRETATIONS OF "BIRTH"

The supporters of the *Abhidhamma* in Thailand vehemently disagree with Buddhadāsa's *phasa tham* interpretation of birth and rebirth. Anan Senakhan affirms that "'Birth' denotes the birth of all sentient beings, according to their respective categories in the thirty-one realms of existence."(T)[52] That is, he affirms the traditional Buddhist cosmology of rebirth in various heavens or hells according to one's merit or demerit. An associate of Anan's and a senior member of the Abhidhamma Foundation, Bunmi Methangkun, maintains that "If the cycle of birth and death [i.e., *saṁsāra*] as a being in various worlds should not be, Buddhism will fall into decay."(T)[53] By this Bunmi means two things. Firstly, he means that if the cycle of *saṁsāra* does not in fact exist and "If we are only born for a single life and there is no rebirth, then there is no need to have the Buddha, and his teachings are meaningless."(T)[54] And secondly, Bunmi implies that if the metaphysical phenomenon of *saṁsāra* does exist but people like Buddhadāsa deny its reality, then that misguided view can only mean that liberation from the cycle of rebirth will not even be sought for, let alone be attained. Buddhism would consequently utterly fail to provide salvation and would amount to a meaningless religion.

However, there is a sense in which Anan's and Bunmi's criticisms of Buddhadāsa are misdirected. Buddhadāsa does not in fact completely deny the actuality of rebirth. What he does deny is the relevance of literal rebirth to the spiritual enterprise of Buddhism. Buddhadāsa says,

> If we can master this kind of birth [of "I"] here and now we will also be able to master the birth that comes after physical death. So let's not concern ourselves with the birth that follows physical death. Instead let us concern ourselves seriously with the birth that happens before physical death.[55]

Buddhadāsa thus does not deny that *kamma* accumulated from actions performed now can influence the quality of existence in some future incarnation. However, he refocuses Buddhism, defining Buddhist doctrines as referring solely to this life. By saying that a life led well now will augur well for any future birth Buddhadāsa implicitly retains the traditional belief in literal rebirth. The contradiction between Buddhadāsa's above statement on the reality of rebirth and a previously quoted passage where he says "A person has a physical birth only once" is only apparent. If, as proposed by the *anattā* doctrine, there is no soul then even if actions in this life do lead to rebirth, it is not the same person who is reborn. Strictly speaking, each person as a unique individual is born only once. As a conditional phenomenon, *attā* or individuality does not transcend any specific concrete existence.

Nevertheless, it must be acknowledged that Buddhadāsa walks a theoretical tightrope between denying and accepting literal rebirth. He criticizes Buddhaghosa's use of the *paṭiccasamuppāda* to account for rebirth and he also says that reference to "birth," "death," and to the "cycle of birth and death" in the Buddhist scriptures should be interpreted metaphorically. However, he does not explicitly deny the reality of rebirth. In denying Buddhaghosa's interpretation of the *paṭiccasamuppāda*, Buddhadāsa is consequently left without any theoretical explanation of the mechanism of rebirth and without any resolution of the contradiction between simultaneously maintaining the doctrine of non-self and the reality of rebirth. However, Buddhadāsa is not concerned with this theoretical contradiction because he maintains that Buddhism is solely concerned with life here and now. He is consequently under no obligation to resolve theoretical difficulties that he has defined as being outside his field of concern.

Despite his explicit concern to define Buddhism as a teaching of salvation relative to life here and now, Buddhadāsa is unable to completely deny the reality of rebirth because of the large numbers of scriptural references to rebirth and also because rebirth is in fact a theoretically essential notion in the structure of Buddhist thought.

Some passages in the *Suttapiṭaka*, when taken in isolation, suggest that the Buddha did not sanction belief in rebirth or an emphasis on the afterlife. For example, in the *Poṭṭhapāda Sutta* the Buddha says, "Behold, Poṭṭhapāda, these points we cannot determine, whether beings after death either continue to exist or do not continue to exist."(T)[56] When pushed on why this could not be determined the Buddha replied,

> Behold, Poṭṭhapāda, because that is not meaningful, is unrelated to the Dhamma, is not the start of *brahmacariya*, does not proceed for the sake of tiredness [of worldliness], for extinction, for peace, for higher knowledge, for realization, for *nibbāna*. Thus for these reasons we cannot determine [this matter].(T)[57]

This *sutta* provides scriptural support for Buddhadāsa's this-worldly emphasis on that which is of immediate practical benefit to the ending of suffering. This *sutta* also provides support for Buddhadāsa's disinterest in providing an alternative to Buddhaghosa's account of the rebirth process. Like the Buddha, Buddhadāsa regards such an intellectual exercise as having no direct relevance to the practical goal of ending suffering and consequently as being outside the purview of Buddhist concern. However, the above excerpts must be balanced against the many references to literal rebirth and to the next world in the main body of the *Suttapiṭaka*. For example, in *suttas* such as the *Pāyāsirājañña Sutta,*[58] disbelief in the unreality of *kamma*, rebirth, and the next world are respectively presented as false views which hinder acceptance of Buddha's teaching of salvation.

However, there is also a theoretical necessity in Buddhist thought to maintain the reality of rebirth. If the accumulations of *kamma* and *saṅkhāra* are acknowledged as real, and if not all *kammic* reactions or *vipāka* are experienced in this life, then rebirth is essential for the future exhaustion or outworking of *kamma* acquired in this life plus that remaining from previous lives. Without rebirth Buddhism is left without an account of moral justice. Without rebirth Buddhism cannot explain why the good sometimes suffer or why the evil sometimes prosper, for by the law of *kamma* good actions reap good results and evil actions result in evil consequences. Because there is no immediately apparent relation between the moral quality of a person's actions and the actual quality of their life here on earth, Buddhism must postulate the existence of a future life in which the good, bad, or neutral consequences of present intentional actions are experienced. Rebirth is necessary in order to make sense of the entire Buddhist moral and spiritual enterprise. Because of the close relation between the notions of *kamma* and of rebirth it is then no accident that, given his emphasis on this life, the notion of *kamma* and of suffering originating from past *kamma* is significantly downplayed in Buddhadāsa's system. Buddhadāsa's views on *kamma* are discussed in detail in chapter 8.

Because of the conceptual structure of Buddhist teachings, and because of the prevalence of references to actual rebirth in the scriptures, Buddhadāsa cannot completely deny either rebirth, *kamma,* or the reality of future existences. In attempting to make Theravada Buddhism a religion of the here and now, the most he can do is de-emphasize these aspects of the Buddha's teaching and correspondingly emphasize the more immediate, this-worldly aspects.

## POLITICAL OPPOSITION TO BUDDHADĀSA'S VIEWS

Buddhadāsa's selective emphasis on certain aspects of the Theravada scriptures and the vehemence with which he attacks long-held views and beliefs is an important source of the criticisms which have been directed against him. As Niels Mulder notes, for most Thais Buddhadāsa's criticism of the traditional view of Buddhism is "shocking:" "all these people have always thought themselves to be good Buddhists, and now they have to hear they are not. Necessarily they feel threatened."[59]

This sense of threat goes some way to explaining the opposition to Buddhadāsa, but it should be emphasized that the threat he poses is not purely intellectual or religious. Buddhadāsa's views challenge the traditional institutional character of Thai Buddhism and its ideological role in the structure of politics and culture in contemporary Thailand. Because the religious heritage he and other reformers seek to reinterpret is an essential factor in the traditional structure of Thai society, even apparently theoretical debates on Buddhist doctrine may have political implications. This explains why, in Mulder's words, religious reformers in Thailand are so "easily branded as heretics, a danger to the stability of society, and thus are often called 'communists.'"[60]

Bunmi Methangkun, head of the Abhidhamma Foundation (Wat Phra Chetuphon), criticizes Buddhadāsa's demythologizing of Buddhist doctrine and his emphasis on the religion as a this-worldly doctrine in the following way: "He is one who has opened the door wide to accept those who like politics and do not hold to our religion . . . in order to destroy Buddhism."(T)[61]

That is, Bunmi regards Buddhadāsa as accommodating Buddhism to non-Buddhists (read communists), whom he and the members of organizations such as the Abhidhamma Foundation seek to nullify by propagating their own traditional form of Buddhism. The above criticism that Buddhadāsa is destroying Buddhism, both doctrinally and by allowing non-Buddhists to infiltrate and subvert the religion, is not purely religious, for in their ideological campaign against communism conservatives promote the notion that traditional Buddhism is the foundation of the monarchy and of national security. Bunmi notes,

> Buddhism is still the collective nucleus of the sympathies of the Thai people; in this they are solidly united. When Buddhism gradually degenerates what will happen? How could the nation and king continue?(T)[62]

Opposing communism, maintaining traditions, and supporting the monarchy, which is viewed as a symbol of Thai tradition and independence, are three recurring themes in the writings of Buddhist conservatives.

However, the criticisms of reformist monks such as Buddhadāsa, who are regarded as "Abandoning traditions which are good and which have existed from ancient times,"(T)[63] also transcend politics per se. The conflict is also over the character of Buddhism. For Buddhist conservatives, Buddhism is the key social institution of Thailand, the basis of Thai society and social order. For Buddhadāsa, on the other hand, Buddhism is first and foremost a doctrine of individual salvation. That is, the conflict between traditionalist and reformist Buddhists is at one level a conflict between competing individualistic and a institutional views of the religion. If, as Anan proposes, the institutional character of Buddhism is most important, then it follows that all the things that maintain the solidarity of that social institution are also of paramount importance. Conformity to defined goals and traditional sources of unity, such as the power of the state and the symbol of the monarchy, will rank above innovation and reform, which may well threaten solidarity and unity. But if Buddhism is, as Buddhadāsa views it, a doctrine of personal salvation, then the pressure to conform to traditional beliefs and practices may well be in contradiction with the individual's spiritual quest for enlightenment.

This debate is outside of religion because it is unable to be resolved by a purely doctrinal discussion or by reference to the Buddhist scriptures. The Theravada scriptures are ambiguous and contain conflicting tendencies which, when taken alone, can be used to justify either Buddhadāsa's individualistic doctrinal interpretation or the institutional perspective of Anan and other conservatives. Sections of the Buddhist scriptures appear to unequivocally treat heaven, hell, spirits, and other supernatural phenomena as real states and real beings, while other sections appear to reject such supernatural belief. Trevor Ling observes that Buddhism has historically exhibited a spirit of tolerance towards belief "in the many supernatural beings who are respected, venerated, propitiated or worshipped by the mass of the common people."[64] Nevertheless, in contrast to this general tolerance towards lay beliefs, Ling also notes that the Buddha specifically forbade monks to be involved in supernatural activities. Citing a *Vinaya* text, Ling notes the following injunction of the Buddha:

> You are not, O *Bhikkhus*, to learn or teach the low arts (lit. "brutish wisdom") of divination, spells, omens, astrology, sacrifices to gods, witchcraft and quackery.[65]

Theravada Buddhist doctrine is open to widely varying readings and can be used to support divergent spiritual and social positions. For this reason it is difficult to evaluate Buddhadāsa's reformist interpretation of Theravada doctrine simply in terms of his faithfulness to Buddhist teachings or to the canonical texts. Viewed theoretically or doctrinally, one can conclude that, despite numerous inconsistencies of detail, Buddhadāsa has by and large succeeded in creating an important and innovative reading of the Pali canon which is broadly consistent both with the texts he accepts as authoritative and with modernist intellectual expectations. But when viewed politically or sociologically, one can just as easily conclude that Buddhadāsa is an idealist who, in rejecting popular beliefs, fails to appreciate the importance of institutional Buddhism to the Thai populace, whether farmers, labourers, civilian bureaucrats, or soldiers. The criticisms of conservative Buddhists like Anan Senakhan and Bunmi Methangkun can be taken as an indicator of Buddhadāsa's failure to develop a popularly acceptable reform of Theravada Buddhism.

At the same time, however, Buddhadāsa's work is regarded as having great social and religious significance by the small section of modernist Thai Buddhists in the new bourgeoisie. For example, in a survey of the religious beliefs of 284 Thai academics at five state universities, David Gosling found that only 25 percent believed in the reality of rebirth and most expressed no opinion on the reality or unreality of other Buddhist doctrines such as *nibbāna* and *kamma*. However, the majority regarded the principle of impermanence, *anicca*, to be in substantial agreement with science and regarded it as being compatible with a doctrinalist interpretation of Buddhism. Significantly, Gosling reports that

> between 30% and 70% of the questionnaire respondents at Chulalongkorn, Mahidol and Chiengmai Universities and Payap College (respectively) mentioned Putatat [i.e. Buddhadāsa] on the questionnaire.[66]

Gosling notes that his correspondents usually mentioned Buddhadāsa approvingly, especially in the context of supporting his interpretation of rebirth as a psychological phenomenon occurring in this life. Gosling's conclusions show that the Thai scientists he interviewed do indeed hold very similar views on Buddhism and Buddhist doctrine to Buddhadāsa:

> Very few respondents had any desire to reject Buddhism, and as has already been pointed out, the rejection of rebirth as a literal statement of what happens at and beyond death often went hand in hand with a dynamic this-worldly interpretation of the cardinal Buddhist doctrines.[67]

There are therefore multiple levels at which Buddhadāsa's reinterpretations of Theravada doctrine can be criticized. Firstly, his denial of the authority of the *Abhidhammapiṭaka* and of the reality of spirits and rebirth is a direct threat to those whose interpretation of Buddhism is founded on those scriptures and teachings. Secondly, the contradiction between Buddhadāsa's desire to interpret Buddhism as a religion of the here and now and the scriptural emphasis on the reality and importance of rebirth creates theoretical tensions in his work. Buddhadāsa's doctrinalism and his emphasis on individual salvation as opposed to the traditional institutional role of Buddhism in Thai society also cuts across and opposes what most Thais regard their religion to be. But despite these theoretical and sociopolitical difficulties, it is nevertheless still the case that among progressive Thai Buddhists he is one of the most popular and respected academic monks in modern Thailand. This is not simply because of his demythologization of Buddhism. Buddhadāsa also commands the respect of intellectual Buddhists because the view of Buddhist practice that he develops upon the base of his *phasa tham* interpretations provides access for laypeople to the spiritual core of the religion, from which they have historically been isolated. Buddhadāsa's incorporation of the laity into the spiritual heart of Buddhism—the quest of *nibbāna*—is considered in the following chapter.

# 5 *CHIT WANG* AND THE ABOLITION OF THE MONK-LAY DISTINCTION

BUDDHADĀSA IS highly critical of the supernatural elements of popular Thai Buddhism and he argues for a return to doctrinal basics interpreted in terms of their relevance to the experience of life on earth here and now. However, those features of Buddhism which Buddhadāsa rejects as superstitious have traditionally been the dominant and most important aspects of the religion for the Buddhist layperson. Concern with Buddhist doctrine has in general characterized only the clerical religion of the monks. Therefore, if the Buddhist laity are not to be excluded from Buddhadāsa's system he must incorporate them within his doctrinal view of Buddhism. But given that laypeople cannot relinquish their involvement in social affairs and, furthermore, that Buddhadāsa rejects the traditional world-oriented lay or *lokiya* path, the only way he can incorporate the layperson within his doctrinally purified system is by making the traditional clerical and doctrinal view of salvation compatible with the mundane life and commitments of the laity. Indeed, the integration of the socially involved role of the layperson with a rationalist and doctrinal interpretation of Buddhist teachings is a major focus of Buddhadāsa's work. The theory of *phasa tham* and the rejection of the supernaturalism and otherworldliness of traditional interpretations of the *Abhidhammapiṭaka* and the *Visuddhimagga* are the methodological levers he uses to effect a fundamental restructuring of the entire edifice of Theravada Buddhist thought and practice.

Buddhadāsa's theoretical reconstruction of Theravada Buddhism can be divided into two aspects. Firstly, by integrating the world-involved lay role with doctrinal Buddhism, Buddhadāsa undermines the validity of popular, supernatural Buddhism. Secondly, he is concerned to give authentic religious value to the lay role, to world involvement, and to the social and material world itself. Buddhadāsa aims to sanctify the social and material world, *loka*, which has traditionally been regarded as the antithesis of spirituality. The theoretical pivot upon which Buddhadāsa attempts his reconstructive effort of integrating world involvement with spiritual practices is a special interpretation of the notion of *anattā* or "non-self," which Buddhadāsa calls in Thai *chit wang* ("voided-mind" or "freed-mind"). Buddhadāsa defines "freed-mind" as being the base or foundation of *nibbāna*. However, unlike traditional interpretations of *nibbāna*, which define salvation as a transcendent condition attained by breaking the snares of world involvement, Buddhadāsa maintains that *chit wang* is based in the everyday experience of mental calm and peace available to all, whether monk or layperson. He maintains that there is a fundamental continuity between ordinary mental peace or *chit wang* and the absolute imperturbable peace of *nibbāna*. The notion of *chit wang* is the most important positive concept in Buddhadāsa's system.

## *CHIT WANG* AND *SUÑÑATĀ*—BUDDHADĀSA'S INTERPRETATION OF *ANATTĀ*

The term *chit wang* is Buddhadāsa's rendering into Thai of the Pali term *suññatā* (Sanskrit: *śunyatā*),[1] literally "voidness" or "emptiness," and the Thai term can be literally translated as "void-mind." However, caution needs to be exercised in interpreting the expression *chit wang* because there are two quite different but related aspects to the notion of "void" or *suñña*[2] in Theravada thought. Firstly, *suññatā* is used in reference to the doctrine of *anattā* to denote the non-substantial, phenomenal character of reality—the fundamental void underlying being. *Suññatā* also has a second, ethical import of being "devoid of lusts, evil dispositions and *karma*."[3]

In the Theravada tradition the term *suññatā* has most commonly been used to denote the notion of *anattā* as applied to the external world, that is, to denote the notion of the non-substantiality of the objects in the external world. This sense of *suññatā* is commonly called the voidness or emptiness of the world, as in the following passage from the *Khuddaka Nikāya*: "Because of being void of self or of things due to a self it is consequently said that the world is void."(T)[4]

The second sense of *suññatā* denotes being devoid of moral impurities, which in Buddhist thought is regarded as being in a state of mental equilibrium, *upekkhā*, wherein one is neither attracted to nor repelled by anyone or anything. While the traditional emphasis in Theravada Buddhism has been on the first sense of *suññatā* described above, i.e. denoting *anattā* or the "voidness" of the objects of the world, it is the second sense, i.e. to be devoid of "lusts," which is most emphasized by Buddhadāsa in his notion of *chit wang*. Buddhadāsa's primary emphasis in his interpretation of *anattā* is upon the mental attitude of non-self-centredness or selflessness. The former interpretation of *anattā* is not absent from Buddhadāsa's writings but it is significantly downplayed. His justification for this ethical emphasis in the interpretation of *anattā* and *chit wang* is pragmatic:

> The interpretations of *anattā* and *attā* have never been fully beneficial. They must be reinterpreted to be fully beneficial and useful for everyone in restraining suffering.(T)[5]

That is, Buddhadāsa maintains that the traditional interpretation of *anattā* as denoting the absence of an essence or self has not realized the full benefits of the notion in practical efforts to attain the goal of ending suffering. Buddhadāsa regards his interpretation of *attā* as denoting "self-centredness" and *anattā* as denoting "non-self-centredness" as being more beneficial to the goal of ending human suffering.

Buddhadāsa renders the term *attā*, "self" or "selfhood," into Thai by the compound term *tua ku–khong ku* (ตัวกู-ของกู), "I"–"mine,"[6] and says that realizing the truth of *anattā* is equivalent to ending the self-centred view that there is an "I" and that there are things which are "mine:" "Don't identify as 'I' or 'mine'; act with clear awareness and there will be no suffering."[7] For Buddhadāsa, it is the false view that there is an "I" which is able to possess objects of desire as being "mine" which is at the root of emotional attachment. According to the doctrine of *anicca*, the desiring of impermanent things in the long run can only lead to the "I" or desirer suffering the loss of those things. Thus, in accord with Buddhist teaching, ending identification as an "I" or self is essential for liberation from suffering. When there is no longer any sense of "I", there is correspondingly no possessive sense of "mine," and so both clinging and its concomitant suffering are ended.

For Buddhadāsa, *chit wang* denotes having a mind, *chit* (จิต), which is free, *wang* (ว่าง), from the possessive and deluded attitude of "I"–"mine." That is, *chit wang* denotes a mind in ethical equilibrium which is free from disturbing moral stains or hindrances to salvation. *Chit wang*, "freed-mind," is therefore as much an ethical as a psychological notion, denoting the state of mind which should be established if one is to attain *nibbāna*. The following passage, called "Eating the Food of 'Freedness'," is a description of living in the condition of *chit wang*, devoid of "I" and "mine:"

> Both the thing that eats and thing that is eaten are "*freedness*" (*khwam wang* ความว่าง), are "freed-things" (*khong wang* ของว่าง). He who eats thus is "freed" (*wang*) because he is neither a being nor an individual. The thing which is eaten is a "freed-thing," or simply the natural elements.(T)[8]

This "freed-ness" or *suññatā*, i.e. the state of being *wang* or "voided" of moral impurities and delusions of selfhood, is in no sense an ontological void. What is "voided" is simply the self-centred attitude of "I"–"mine." In the above passage Buddhadāsa indicates that the *chit wang* attitude to eating should not be that "'I' am eating this food," but rather that "the elements which are this individual are eating the elements which are this food."(T)[9] He makes the psychological and ethical character of *chit wang* clear in the following statement:

> Mental emptiness [sic][10] is the state in which all the objects of the physical world are present (and being perceived) as usual but none of them is being grasped or clung to as "mine."[11]

> Thus *chit wang* is not a vacuous mental state. It is not "void" of content. All objects are there as usual and the thinking processes are going on as usual, but they are not going the way of grasping and clinging with the idea of "I" and "mine."[12]

Buddhadāsa defines *chit wang* as a condition in which "one does not cling to anything, is not anything, does not feel that one gets anything or that one gets to be anything."(T)[13] When the mind is freed it is "free from suffering, free from dogmatic clinging and attachment."(T)[14]

Because the Buddhist notion of "world," *loka*, is often described in the scriptures as being "voidness" or *suññatā*, the notion of *suññatā* (Thai: *wang* ) has often been misinterpreted as denoting a literal void or vacuum. Buddhadāsa continues the tradition of describing the world as being *wang*, but it should be kept in mind that by this he means that the world is "freed" or "voided" of moral defilements, not that it is a literal "emptiness:"

> The Lord Buddha said, "*suññato evekhassu mogharāja sada sato*— One should be a person with mindfulness, always seeing the world in the condition of being a freed-thing (*khwam-wang*)." ... Whoever sees the world in the condition of being a freed thing will not have suffering because they will see it [the world] as something completely without birth and extinction, and so there cannot be suffering.(T)[15]

In interpreting the expression "the world is *suññatā*," one must remember that in Buddhist thought the notion of "world" does not denote an objective thing totally independent of consciousness, although Buddhism does not deny that there is an external world. Rather, in Buddhism the "world" is always conceived in terms of its relation to human experience and desires. There may well be an external world independent of human experience but insofar as it is external to human experience such a world is, according to Buddhist teachings, irrelevant to any human concerns. The Buddhist "world," *loka*, is that part of the external cosmos which can be perceived and which can therefore become an object of human sense-based desire. Sunthorn Na Rangsi says,

> The existence of the world according to Buddhism is nothing apart from the existence of sentient beings and vice versa . . . When a man is no more in the world the world is no more for him.[16]

Therefore, when Buddhadāsa calls the world a "freed-thing" he does not mean that it is a literal void but that it is a realm of experience freed of clinging and so of suffering. A "freed-world" is one no longer clung to or craved for. Buddhadāsa makes this clear when he says,

> The *suññatā* of the Buddha means the absence of anything that we might have a right to grasp at and cling to as an abiding entity or self . . . . The world is described as empty because there is nothing whatever that we might have a right to grasp at. We must cope with an empty world, with a mind that does not cling.[17]

Thus Buddhadāsa's description of the world as a "freed-thing" is not a comment on the character of the external world but is an injunction about the non-attached state of mind which should be brought to bear in all relations with the world in order to attain salvation from suffering.

## *CHIT WANG* AS THE FUNDAMENTAL CONDITION OF MIND

Following on from his wish to interpret *anattā* "beneficially," that is, to make doctrinal Buddhism accessible to and of benefit to the layperson, Buddhadāsa defines *chit wang* as the fundamental condition of the mind:

> I consider a mind freed from *kilesa* to be fundamental . . . . Normally the mind is fundamentally free from *kilesa*; hence our only [spiritual]

> duty is to wait and block their way with mindful wisdom. Don't give them [*kilesa*] the chance to arise. Let there continually be the freedness of the fundamental, original freed-mind.(T)[18]

Here Buddhadāsa states that the mental impurities or *kilesa*[19] which bar the way to salvation have no essential existence but, like all other things, exist dependently. The condition which permits *kilesa* to arise and pollute the mind is the absence of mindfulness or *sati*. *Sati* denotes self-watchfulness, which is to distance or detach oneself from one's thoughts and actions and so attain mental and moral equilibrium. *Sati* or mindfulness is the basic Theravada meditative practice, usually developed by the practice of observing the inward and outward breath. On this Buddhadāsa advises, "Having mindfulness is to wait and be cautious with every inward and outward breath. Don't get lost in attached clinging, to having, taking, and being."(T)[20]

When one lacks mindfulness one ignorantly identifies with one's thoughts and actions, which in turn is regarded as giving rise to mentally disturbing *kilesa*. But *kilesa* do not have to be dug out or extricated from the mind because, according to Buddhadāsa, they have no essential character. Thus to try to get rid of *kilesa* by actively suppressing them is to mistakenly regard them as having a positive nature. In Buddhadāsa's system *kilesa* are not to be removed, but rather prevented from developing by remaining mindful and so not allowing their necessary preconditions to arise. This interpretation of *chit wang* is important to Buddhadāsa's reinterpretative effort because it implies that the human mind is fundamentally pure and undefiled. Given that Buddhadāsa defines *chit wang* as the basis of attaining *nibbāna*, in his view all that is required to begin working for *nibbāna* is to remain "mindful" in order to prevent the mind's original purity from being defiled. This is a much more accessible spiritual practice for attaining *nibbāna* than the traditional complex system of Buddhist meditation. That is, Buddhadāsa's interpretation of *chit wang*, as denoting both the fundamental condition of mind and the foundation of *nibbāna*, radically simplifies traditional Buddhist spiritual practices, making them much more accessible to the layperson.

However, this interpretation of *chit wang* has attracted considerable criticism. Bunmi Methangkun, for example, has theoretical objections to Buddhadāsa's claim that *chit wang*, a pure mind completely free of any moral impurities, is the fundamental condition of mind. Bunmi observes that "There are *anusayakilesa*, that is, a fine kind of *kilesa* which hide, completely obscured inside the mind, and which no one anywhere can comprehend."(T)[21]

In Buddhist doctrine *anusaya* are regarded as latent or subconscious morally unwholesome (*akusala*) proclivities which underlie the observable expressions of *kilesa*.[22] The following passages from the *Visuddhimagga* reveal the non-conscious nature of *anusaya* and their fundamental role in perpetuating the clinging which creates *kamma* and which leads to rebirth:

> The defilements (*anusayakilesa*) that are the roots of the round (of rebirth) are inherent in one's own aggregates (*khandhas*) not fully understood by insight from the instant those aggregates arise.[23]

Elsewhere in the *Visuddhimagga* it is said

> These things are called proclivities (*anusaya*) since, in consequence of their pertinacity, they ever and again tend to become the conditions for the arising of ever new sensuous greed (*kāmarāga*), etc.[24]

These passages suggest, in contradistinction to Buddhadāsa's contention that the mind is fundamentally pure, that moral impurities are inherent in the factors or *khandhas* from which mind is constituted. Bunmi claims that *chit wang* cannot be the basis of *nibbāna* because even when the mind is free from explicit *kilesa* (i.e. Buddhadāsa's definition of *chit wang*) the implicit or unexpressed *anusayakilesa* still remain, potentially capable of becoming manifest and of destroying the mental peace of *chit wang*. Buddhadāsa does not deny that *anusaya* exist, for he claims that *chit wang* is the fundamental condition of the conscious mind. He does not deny that morally unwholesome *kammic* residues may remain subconscious or latent. Indeed, he invokes the notion of latent *anusaya* when explaining why the *sakadagāmī*, the enlightened Buddhist saint who is "reborn" only once more before attaining salvation, must yet still take one more "birth:"

> *Sakadāgāmī* translates as "a person who will return once more," meaning that the *sakadagāmī* already traverses the correct path [towards *nibbāna*] but because of the germs of some kinds of original *kilesa* [i.e. *anusaya*] which remain, he still reverts once more to recollecting and missing the condition of living like an average person.(T)[25]

The debate over whether the mind is fundamentally pure or defiled, and over whether *chit wang* should, as Buddhadāsa maintains, denote only the conscious mind or, as Bunmi holds, should also include the non-conscious mind, is at root a disagreement over the definition of *nibbāna*. It is a debate over the degree of mental purity which must be developed before it can be said *nibbāna* has in fact been attained. If, as Bunmi maintains, *nibbāna* is defined as the absence of all disturbances or *kilesa*, even including potential *anusaya*, then such a state of mental purity could only be attained after considerable spiritual effort. However, if, as Buddhadāsa holds, *nibbāna* is simply the absence of impurities from the conscious mind, i.e. *chit wang*, then Buddhist salvation is not only readily accessible to both the layperson and the monk but is also a mental state that each person experiences whenever they are not particularly angry, hateful, or desirous.

## *NIBBĀNA* AS A UNIVERSALLY ACCESSIBLE SPIRITUAL GOAL

The most important result of Buddhadāsa's equation of *chit wang* with the basis of Buddhist salvation is that *nibbāna* is not a transcendent condition attainable only after years or perhaps lives spent purging the mind of impurities, but, like *chit wang*, is the original condition of the mind. In other words, in Buddhadāsa's system *nibbāna* is the mind's characteristic state. *Nibbāna* is the mind's basic condition, an original state of mental equilibrium to be retained or reattained by remaining mindful and by not allowing the delusions and ignorance of "I"–"mine" to arise.

Buddhadāsa recognizes three levels of *nibbāna*. The first level of *nibbāna* is called *tadaṅganibbāna* and is defined as "a state that comes about momentarily when external conditions happen, fortuitously, to be such that no idea of 'I' or 'mine' arises."[26] That is, *tadaṅganibbāna* denotes the attainment of mental calm because of the influence of a peaceful environment. The second level of *nibbāna* recognized by Buddhadāsa is called *vikkhambhananibbāna*, which denotes mental calm attained because of the mental control exercised in *samādhi* meditation, in which intense concentration arrests or paralyzes the arising of *kilesa*. But neither of these two forms of *nibbāna* are regarded as permanent. In the case of *tadaṅga-nibbāna*, any disturbance in the external environment would in turn re-effect the disturbing influence of *kilesa* upon the mind. And in the case of *vikkhambhananibbāna*, *kilesa* are not in fact abolished but only paralyzed from acting by the force of meditative concentration. In contrast to these preliminary forms of *nibbāna*, Buddhadāsa calls the highest form of *nibbāna samucchedanibbāna* or *parinibbāna*, which is when mental peace results from the actual ending rather than the simple repression of mind-disturbing *kilesa*. However, Buddhadāsa nevertheless regards *tadaṅganibbāna* and *vikkhambhananibbāna* as actual modes of *nibbāna*, while his traditionalist opponents regard only *parinibbāna* as true *nibbāna*. That is, Buddhadāsa accepts conscious states of mental peace which may still be underlain by *anusaya* as actual but basic forms of *nibbāna*. For Buddhadāsa, the supreme *parinibbāna* is foreshadowed by the less profound and impermanent but, for him, nevertheless actual *nibbānic* states of *tadaṅganibbāna* and *vikkhambhana-nibbāna*. However, Anan Senakhan recognizes only a mind totally freed of *anusaya* as having access to *nibbāna* and he is highly critical of Buddhadāsa's broader interpretation:

> Buddhadāsa tries to twist the explanation that the term *nibbāna*, which is the extremely difficult and profound Dhamma, denotes

> something that is easy [to attain]. It is as if he holds in contempt the realization of the Lord Buddha.(T)[27]

In fact, however, Buddhadāsa does not present *nibbāna* as something easily attained. He acknowledges that *nibbāna* is an ineffable condition not able to be adequately described in words or rational concepts:

> This is the difficulty or depth of its [*nibbāna*'s] meaning, for the world [of human learning] still lacks any linguistic term to denote a condition which is far, far beyond the world—a condition that is attained by following neither goodness nor evil, neither happiness nor suffering—but which we must yet request to call, in the manner of a supposition, the blessed *nibbāna*.(T)[28]

But, for Buddhadāsa, *nibbāna* is not beyond description because it is beyond the material world, but rather because while being based in everyday experience it still transcends the usual mental world of human beings which is disturbed and clouded by ignorance.

This debate over the definition of *nibbāna* reflects Anan's and Buddhadāsa's differing views on the nature of Buddhism as a religion. Anan Senakhan supports the preservation of the traditional distinction between the lay and clerical forms of Buddhism and denounces Buddhadāsa's populist interpretation of salvation as shallow. Buddhadāsa, however, wishes to make the core spiritual aspects of Buddhism relevant and accessible to all Buddhists, whether world-involved laity or renunciate monks. His definition of the lower forms of *nibbāna* as actual conditions of salvation, while to some extent a matter of semantics, reflects his concern to emphasize the accessibility of Buddhist practice and salvation to all. He maintains that the layperson who experiences the occasional peaceful bliss of *tadaṅganibbāna* has tasted true salvation, even if only momentarily.

Buddhadāsa also acknowledges two other traditionally recognized types of *parinibbāna*, *sa-upādisesanibbāna* and *anupādisesanibbāna*, defining the former as follows:

> When the five *khandhas* which have been freed of *avijjā* (ignorance) have yet to disperse, and there is still the enjoyment of the taste of *nibbāna*, such a state is called *sa-upādisesanibbāna.*(T)[29]

*Sa-upādisesnibbāna*, also called *kilesaparinibbāna* or the full extinction of defilements, denotes "*nibbāna* with the groups of existence (*khandhas*) still remaining."[30] That is, *sa-upādisesanibbāna* is a condition of salvation traditionally regarded as being attained while alive, when the *khandhas* or constitutive factors of human existence remain to sustain life. *Anupādisesanibbāna*, on the other hand, denotes "*nibbāna* without the groups (*khandhas*) remaining."[31] *Anupadisesanibbāna* is also called *khandhaparinibbāna* or the full extinction of the *khandhas* which sustain life, and is traditionally regarded as a post-death condition of salvation. Chinda Chandrkaew expresses the traditional Theravada view of salvation when he says of *sa-upādisesanibbāna* and *anupādisesanibbāna*

> These are not two different kinds of *nibbāna*; they, in fact, refer to the one and the same *nibbāna* which is given as two according as it is experienced before or after death.[32]

However, Buddhadāsa denies that supreme or *parinibbāna* is only attained upon death, citing the fact of the Buddha's life mission which was undertaken after his enlightenment:

> The Buddha and all the other *arahants* were completely free of desires, yet succeeded in doing many things far more useful than any of us are capable of . . . . If the defilements responsible for the desire to be and get things had been completely eliminated, what was the force that motivated the Buddha and all the *arahants* to do all this? They were motivated by discrimination coupled with goodwill (*metta*).[33]

In Buddhadāsa's interpretation there is no relation between *parinibbāna* as a mental state and death. On the contrary, for Buddhadāsa an *arahant* who is *anupādisesa* is not dead but in a state of unperturbable balance beyond the influence of any mentally or morally disturbing factors. This interpretation is supported by the following passage from the *Dhātu Sutta*. In this *sutta* the two types of *nibbāna* are not distinguished in terms of respectively denoting pre-death and post-death conditions of salvation. Rather, *sa-upādisesanibbāna* is described as a condition in which remaining mental impurities, i.e. *anusayakilesa*, may yet cause mental confusion and so attachment and suffering, while *anupādisesanibbāna* is described as a completely unperturbable condition:

> When a *bhikkhu* partakes of mental objects that are both liked and disliked, when he yet partakes of pleasure and pain because the five naturally arising sense organs have not yet decayed and the five senses still remain, behold, O *bhikkhus*, the ending of *rāga* (passion), the ending of *dosa* (anger), the ending of *moha* (delusion) of such a *bhikkhu* is what is called the *sa-upādisesanibbāna* factor . . . . When all feelings in the selfhood of a *bhikkhu*, that is, factors born of *kilesa*, or *taṇhā* and so on, cannot cause him to be engrossed [in sense objects] and are extinguished and cooled, behold, O *bhikkhus*, this we call the *anupādisesanibbāna* factor.(T)[34]

Two issues are at stake in Buddhadāsa's disagreement with the traditional view that *anupādisesanibbāna* is a post-death condition. The first issue has already been raised above and is a matter of definition related to the question of the accessibility of *nibbāna* to the layperson. Anan Senakhan and other traditionalists define true *nibbāna* as the supreme condition of salvation or *parinibbāna*, whether *sa-upādisesanibbāna* or *anupādisesanibbāna*. Buddhadāsa, on the other hand, takes a broader view, including the *tadaṅga* and *vikhambhana* states of *nibbāna* as conditions of true salvation. However, there is also a second theoretical issue involved in this disagreement. Buddhadāsa's and Anan's conflicting interpretations of *nibbāna* represent alternative views of the actual character of *nibbāna*. In Buddhadāsa's interpretation, *nibbāna* is founded upon the everyday experience of mental calm, and rather than being qualitatively distinct, the higher state of *parinibbāna* is described as being the acme of a single continuum of ever more exalted states of salvation which progressively approach the final condition of unperturbable mental equipoise. For Anan, on the other hand, *nibbāna* is intrinsically transcendent and outside of everyday life, being qualitatively distinct from everyday experience.

In Buddhadāsa's system, *chit wang* is defined as the immediate precursor of *nibbāna* and he defines both conditions in the same terms, as the absence of "I"–"mine" or self-centredness:

> *Nibbāna* translates as "extinction without remainder" but, one may well ask, extinction without remainder of what? It is simply the extinction without remainder of "I"–"mine," which is simply the feeling of attached clinging . . . . That is, the state in which there is nothing to be taken or to be.(T)[35]

That is, Buddhadāsa regards *nibbāna,* like *chit wang*, as being a condition in which there is neither identification, or "being someone," nor possessive attachment, or "taking something." And, like *chit wang*, Buddhadāsa defines *nibbāna* as the fundamental or natural condition of the mind:

> The blessed *nibbāna* is the destination point of every person. There is an attraction towards the condition of *nibbāna,* or to put it another way, the inherent tendency of desire is always towards a naturally existing freedness (*khwam wang*). But this tendency suffers some kinds of interfering influences, such as the fruits of *kamma,* which retard it and pull it off its natural course.(T)[36]

Buddhadāsa's interpretation of *nibbāna* as being a "natural" goal of every person, which is founded upon the everyday state of mental equilibrium that he calls *chit wang*, is fundamental to his attempt to make Buddhist salvation a universal goal accessible to all, whatever their life circumstances:

> This is a *nibbāna* in which everyone should be interested. It is a natural matter, something that everyone can understand and do. It is of many kinds and levels of calm and we can attain it according to our own ability.(T)[37]

## BUDDHADĀSA'S THEORETICAL ABOLITION OF THE MONK-LAY DISTINCTION

Buddhadāsa's view of the universal relevance of *nibbāna* contrasts sharply with the traditional Thai view that striving for ultimate salvation is an activity appropriate only for spiritually advanced monks. Slater summarizes the traditional view of the assumed inaccessibility of *nibbāna* to the ordinary person when he notes, "only the saint can experience *nibbāna,* only the saint can know."[38] Jane Bunnag concurs, saying,

> According to orthodox Theravada doctrine only a monk . . . can have any hope of achieving *nirvāṇa;* the layman, or householder who remains firmly rooted in the material world, can entertain no such aspirations.[39]

In the context of criticizing Buddhadāsa's view of the universal relevance of *nibbāna,* Kukrit Pramoj has supported the traditional Thai distinction between the lay and monastic Buddhist roles:

> Buddhism has two grades of Dhamma which are established on different kinds of truth or *sacca,* and which proceed towards different kinds of goals. They are not the same at all. These two grades of Dhamma are *lokiyadhamma* (worldly Dhamma) and *lokuttara-dhamma* (supramundane Dhamma), which are different varieties of Dhamma that could be called different levels or different compartments. But they are in the same religion and both are the instructions of the Lord Buddha.(T)[40]

Buddhadāsa does not deny that one must become a saint or an *arahant* in order to attain *nibbāna,* but he does deny that it is first necessary to be a monk in order to become a saint. Buddhadāsa believes that it is more difficult for the layperson to attain *nibbāna* but he is nevertheless concerned to break down the traditional monk-lay distinction, ascribing the same religious aspirations and hopes to all. He says that "an *arahant* has transcended monkhood and laity alike."[41] That is, he denies that an enlightened person must be a monk, saying that an *arahant* is in a condition which is beyond such social distinctions. Buddhadāsa claims that because the life of a layperson has more disturbing problems than the monk's sheltered monastic existence, the laity are in greater need of *nibbāna*'s quenching of the fires of suffering than are monks.(T)[42] Regarding the practice of *sati* or mindfulness, the basis of *chit wang* or the "freed-mind" state necessary to attain *nibbāna*, he says that the term "practitioner" (*khon patibat tham*) does not refer to

> those who practise alone in the forest. The people who live at home, who act and work with duties and the burden of whatever responsibilities are all called "practitioners." That is, they practise Dhamma.(T)[43]

However, Buddhadāsa does not seek to abolish the actual roles of monk and layperson but only to place both on an equal spiritual footing, with equal access to the fruits of the path. For example, he proposes that Thais should uphold the tradition of laymen seeking ordination for at least one three-month *phansa* or rainy season retreat during their life: "Ordaining for three months, which even today many arrange to do, is something which should be done and which should be encouraged."(T)[44]

Buddhadāsa says that this practice should be retained to ensure that the religion does not decline, and in order to allow laymen to obtain a better understanding of the principles of Buddhism. While he criticizes many other non-canonical practices and beliefs, Buddhadāsa says that the particular non-canonical custom of short-term ordination should be retained because of its benefits:

> Even though being ordained for three months is not something that existed in the time of the Buddha, if it is done with pure and good intentions it is still something reasonable for collectively holding to and performing the practice [of Dhamma] into the future.(T)[45]

While opening up access to ultimate salvation from suffering to the layperson, Buddhadāsa does not equate the layperson with the monk on all counts. He still maintains that:

> It occurs in the Pali scriptures themselves that the holy life, *brahmacariya,* is not something that the layperson can practise flawlessly well . . . because the state of being a layperson has many [worldly] concerns and obstacles.(T)[46]

Because of the limitations of being a layperson Buddhadāsa says "We still cannot enter into [the meaning of] the religion itself until we have truly led the life of monk."(T)[47] He therefore does not abolish the institution or role of the renunciate. What he abolishes is the traditional barrier to lay practice of meditation and related salvation-oriented activities. Buddhadāsa shifts the focus of his critique away from the question of social roles by defining the terms "lay" and "monk" in *phasa tham* as mental states rather than as religious roles:

> Don't take living in a house or a temple as the criterion of being a layperson or a monk. You must consider what is the person's state of mind. . . . These days those living in a monastery may have a mind like one living at home . . . . a householder may well have a mind like a monk or even an ascetic.(T)[48]

By this definition both a monk and a layperson may have the practical experience of living the Dhamma in the world, which Buddhadāsa says is vital to true religious attainment. However, Buddhadāsa takes this argument one step further when he says, "The layperson's Dhamma is necessary for the person who would attain *nibbāna* . . . . If one cannot be a layperson well then one cannot attain *nibbāna.*"(T)[49]

In other words, Buddhadāsa claims that the fruits of the supramundane *lokuttara* path are unrealizable without being founded on the mundane level of activity. This unconventional claim, the converse of the traditional view that *nibbāna* is only attainable by maintaining a radical separation between the *lokiya* and *lokuttara* domains, follows from Buddhadāsa's opinion that "being a layperson has the meaning of studying the Dhamma itself,"(T)[50] that is, in one's actual life. Buddhadāsa regards following the Dhamma in lay life as giving one a practical understanding of Buddhism as opposed to the often theoretical understanding of the monks. Furthermore, this practical understanding, born of adhering to the Dhamma throughout all life's vicissitudes, is regarded as breeding a more effective approach to attaining salvation. In Buddhadāsa's *phasa tham* interpretations the terms *lokiya* and *lokuttara* are stripped of their traditional associations with being a layperson and a monk, respectively. Instead they refer to states of mind which are independent of one's lifestyle or social role: "The *lokuttara* domain denotes a mind which is without 'self,' that has neither 'I' nor 'mine'."(T)[51]

The traditional justification for lay sponsorship and material support of the Sangha has been the belief that giving alms to monks and donations to monasteries are meritorious acts which lead to the accumulation of good *kamma* and so to a felicitous rebirth. But if, according to Buddhadāsa, such supernaturalist views of *kamma* and rebirth are to be rejected, and if laypeople themselves possess all the spiritual authority and ability required for their own salvation, then the traditional bases of the Sangha's support would appear to be threatened. This need not mean the collapse of the Thai Sangha, but if Buddhadāsa's reformist ideas were widely accepted it would mean that the Sangha which did continue would have to have its socioreligious role radically redefined.

A radical restructuring of institutional Buddhism would seem to be a practical consequence of Buddhadāsa's abolition of the spiritual distinctions between laity and monks. However, Buddhadāsa is concerned to uphold the traditional practice of Buddhism which confers religious authority upon his reinterpretative work and he does not mention this logical consequence in his writings. Instead, and in contradiction to the thrust of his theoretical abolition of the monk-lay distinction, he reaffirms the practical retention of these two traditional roles on pragmatic grounds. As noted above, Buddhadāsa says that ordaining as a monk ensures the continuation of the religion by giving laymen a first-hand knowledge of renunciate practices. But while he does not recognize the potentially disruptive consequences of his ideas for the institution of Buddhism in Thailand, Buddhadāsa's conservative critics have focused their attacks on precisely this point. Bunmi Methangkun and Anan Senakhan accuse Buddhadāsa of seeking to destroy Buddhism and the Sangha. Bunmi criticizes the abolition of the traditional monk-lay distinction when he says Buddhadāsa has put forward his teachings in order to "destroy Buddhism and to have the monks go out to till the fields."(T)[52] However, because his ideas have not yet led to any action which has concretely affected the status or role of the Sangha, Buddhadāsa's doctrinal declericalization of *nibbāna* has not yet met any practical opposition from within the Sangha hierarchy, although individuals have attacked his views.

## DEBATE ON THE *LOKIYADHAMMA-LOKUTTARADHAMMA* DISTINCTION

In a handbill attacking Buddhadāsa's notion of *chit wang*, Phra Kittiwuttho[53] cites the traditional canonical basis for the distinction between the worldly and the supramundane paths in the *Dhammadinna Sutta.*[54] Kittiwuttho claims that Buddhadāsa's rejection of the traditional *lokiya-lokuttara* distinction contradicts the teachings of the Buddha in the *Suttapiṭaka*. In the *Dhammadinna Sutta* a layman, Dhammadinna, asks the Buddha to describe the path to happiness and well-being. The Buddha replies that the best and most expeditious path to well-being or *nibbāna* is to study and put into practice the "profound teaching of the Tathagata on the voidness (*suññatā*) of *lokuttara*," an injunction which Buddhadāsa equates with abiding by *chit wang*. However, Dhammadinna replies that it is too difficult for a layperson to appreciate the profundity of the Buddha's teaching of *suññatā* and instead asks to be instructed in the Dhamma in a way appropriate for a layperson like himself who is already established in Buddhist moral practice. The Buddha then provides an alternative instruction, the *sotāpattiyaṅga* or four "limbs" of spiritual practice which lead one into the stream, *sotāpatti*, which flows towards *nibbāna.* These four limbs are defined as: (1) faith in the Buddha, (2) the Dhamma and (3) the Sangha, as well as (4) abiding by the *sīlas* or moral practices for the purpose of developing *samādhi*. When Dhammadinna says that he and his retinue are already established in these four *sotāpattiyaṅga* the Buddha replies that they have then attained the fruit of *sotāpatti*, i.e., they have entered the stream that flows towards *nibbāna*.

The four *sotāpattiyaṅga* have traditionally been regarded as the bases of *lokiyadhamma* or the layperson's practice, whose goal is not *nibbānic* salvation but a felicitous rebirth. The above *sutta* has also traditionally been interpreted as meaning that the practice of *suññatā* is too difficult for the layperson and that the higher or more expeditious path to salvation is open only to the monk. It is also taken to mean that following the most expeditious path to salvation requires complete renunciation of *lokiya* concerns in the socio-cultural world, whose influences are regarded as retarding or obstructing the attainment of *nibbāna*.

However, in talking of the same *sutta*, Buddhadāsa claims that in providing a practically more accessible path for the layperson the Buddha has not thereby given up the goal of *nibbāna* as being appropriate for the laity. Rather, he claims that the four *sotāpattiyaṅga* given by the Buddha to Dhammadinna are not *lokiyadhamma* in the traditional sense but are fully fledged aspects of the path that leads to *nibbāna*. This is because he maintains that the term *sotāpatti* or "entering the stream" implies the beginning of the practice of the Noble Eightfold Path, *ariyamagga*, whose culmination is not worldly success but *nibbāna*. Indeed, the Buddha says nothing in the *Dhammadinna Sutta* about the *sotāpattiyaṅga* constituting a distinct *lokiya* path and the term *lokiya* is not mentioned in this context. Consequently, it would appear that the popular interpretation of this *sutta* referred to by Kittiwuttho in criticizing Buddhadāsa has no immediate scriptural basis.

Buddhadāsa maintains that not only is the traditional interpretation of the *Dhammadinna Sutta* wrong but that "the misunderstandings of some people who try to separate *lokiya* and *lokuttara* concerns will destroy the very truth of Buddhism."(T)[55] While acknowledging the different social roles of the monk and the layperson, Buddhadāsa says that the Buddha never spoke of *lokiyadhamma* as something different from and opposed to *lokuttaradhamma*. Instead he says that the Buddha taught:

> *Lokiyadhamma* is the duty or business of the layperson who has to practise Dhamma in accordance with their common character. But, at the same time, the Buddha also gave knowledge of *lokuttara-dhamma* for the purpose of governing those *lokiya* duties so they would be performed without suffering.(T)[56]

The debate over what practices the Buddha actually prescribed for the layperson is complicated both by some basic confusions and by conflicting views presented in different parts of the scriptures. Firstly, there appears to be a common confusion on the part of Buddhadāsa's critics between the terms *lokadhamma* and *lokiyadhamma*. In the *Catukka Nipāta* of the *Aṅguttara Nikāya*,[57] *lokadhamma* is defined as the eight "worldly factors" or "worldly conditions" of: (1) *lābha*–acquisition, (2) *alābha*–loss, (3) *yaso*–renown, (4) *ayaso*–ignominy, (5) *ninda*–blame, (6) *pasaṁsa*–praise, (7) *sukham*–well-being, and (8) *dukkham*–suffering. These conditions characterize someone who is still attached to the objects of the world. *Lokiyadhamma*, on the other hand, refers to the notion of a separate path for the layperson which has a different goal from the *lokuttaradhamma* of the *bhikkhu*. It is true that in places in the scriptures, such as in the *Lokavipatti Sutta*,[58] the Buddha says that the *puthujjana* or "worldling" is caught in *lokadhamma* while the *ariyasāvaka* or "noble follower" of the Buddha is not. However, it is not the case that the Buddha associates *lokiyadhamma* with *puthujana*, and it appears that the two terms *lokiyadhamma* and *lokadhamma* are often wrongly equated. In fact, the Buddha himself does not use either of the terms *lokiyadhamma* or *lokuttaradhamma* anywhere in the *Suttapiṭaka*, their first canonical occurrence being in the *Dhammasaṅgani* of the *Abhidhammapiṭaka*.[59]

Another commonly confused point is that the terms *puthujjana* and *ariyasāvaka* are often mistakenly read as denoting "layperson" and "monk," respectively. But in the canon it is not specified whether either an *ariyasāvaka* ("noble follower") or a *puthujjana* ("worldling") is either a layperson or a monk. Buddhadāsa's position that the Buddha did not specify a lay path distinct from the path of the monk is therefore vindicated by a strictly literal reading of the *Suttapiṭaka*.

However, it is nevertheless understandable how the popular views and confusions arose. Firstly, scattered throughout the *suttas* are numerous statements denigrating the status of the layperson and extolling the renunciate role: "[To be] a restricted layperson is the way of dust, [to enter] the monkhood is the way free and clear."(T)[60] As Siddhi Butr-Indr notes, the path to *nibbāna*

> is open to monk and lay adherent alike, yet due to the lesser opportunities a lay adherent has for a spiritual life, he is mostly considered to be second to the monk, whose monastic life offers greater possibilities of spiritual advancement.[61]

And the traditional identifications of the term *puthujjana* with layperson, and the term *ariyasāvaka* with monk, do appear to have the implicit support of the Buddha. This is because when he comments that *puthujjana* or "worldlings" are caught in *loka-dhamma*, the Buddha is almost invariably addressing an audience of *bhikkhus* and encouraging them in their vocation by showing the benefits of their life of renunciation when compared with the troubled life of the householder. There is, therefore, a tension between Buddhadāsa's strictly literal reading of the scriptures on this issue and the more contextual reading favoured by Buddhist traditionalists.

Indeed, Buddhadāsa's own writings exhibit an unresolved tension resulting from his taking a literal interpretation of the scriptures in some places but using a more contextual or metaphorical reading in others. As mentioned in chapter 3, a major difficulty with the *phasa khon–phasa tham* theory is Buddhadāsa's failure to provide a clear criterion for determining whether a specific section of the scriptures should be read literally, as *phasa khon*, or metaphorically, as *phasa tham*. Without such a criterion Buddhadāsa's alternation between literalist *phasa khon* readings and metaphorical *phasa tham* interpretations of different parts of the scriptures cannot completely avoid the charge of being cloaks for his own bias.

## SUMMARY

A major determinant of Buddhadāsa's denial of the traditional monk-lay distinction is the fact that the popular lay religion contains the Brahmanical and animist features which conflict with his rationalist and modernist outlook. In seeking to make Buddhism consistent with both a modernist world view and with the fundamental principles of the religion, Buddhadāsa must reject the customary beliefs and practices of the lay populace which conflict with his doctrinal interpretation of the religion. The lay Buddhist populace can then only be given a significant religious place in Buddhadāsa's system by including them within the ambit of his reformed doctrinal Buddhism, an aspect of the religion which was previously open only to monks.

However, Buddhadāsa also often writes with his modernist lay Buddhist audience in mind and he is concerned to respond to the expectations of that audience. That Buddhadāsa has this audience in mind when he redefines *nibbāna* is made clear in the following statement:

> What benefit is there in the teaching that we will get *nibbāna* after we have died? It is as a result of this that modern people are not interested in *nibbāna*. And furthermore, Buddhism is made barren by such teachings.(T)[62]

Buddhadāsa's use of the notion of "benefit" as a criterion for gauging the correctness of doctrinal interpretations provides a channel for the introduction of the contemporary social expectations of Buddhadāsa's lay audience into his system. For, as is clear from the above quote, Buddhadāsa regards a "beneficial" interpretation of doctrine to be one which is sufficiently in tune with people's attitudes to make them "interested" in the doctrine. His systematic reforms are thus not exclusively motivated by his personal scholarly desire for a rationalist and doctrinally consistent Buddhism. His reforms have also been motivated by a desire to mould Buddhist teachings in response to the expectations of his lay audience, in an attempt to re-establish the relevance of Buddhism to the lives and aspiration of that lay audience.

As discussed in chapter 2, modernist Thai Buddhists, like Buddhadāsa, also reject the popular animist and supernatural forms of Buddhism as irrational and unscientific. They have consequently turned their interest to the traditionally clerical, doctrinal level of Theravada Buddhism. While Buddhadāsa's concern to abolish the theoretical distinctions between monks and laypeople can be regarded as flowing from his wish to make Buddhist doctrine consistent with modernist and rationalist principles, the dominance of this concern in his work can also be interpreted as a response to the demands of his lay audience, to his attempt to make Buddhism socially relevant. Buddhadāsa's work should be read as a confluence of these two influences.

But because of his emphasis on ending the monk-lay distinction, Buddhadāsa must also resolve tensions which arise from making the formerly clerical ideal of *nibbāna* both theoretically and practically consistent with the life of the layperson in contemporary Thailand. For example, it is no longer acceptable that *nibbāna* be defined as a condition attainable only by years of intense meditative practice undertaken in monastic isolation. It is precisely this traditional view of the Buddhist goal which has both in theory and in practice barred the layperson from sharing in the fruits of *nibbāna* and which has contributed to what Buddhadāsa recognizes as the growing irrelevance of Buddhism in Thailand. Defining *chit wang* both as the naturally existing unperturbed state of mind and as the basis of *nibbāna* provides a much more lay accessible view of the religion's goal. Nevertheless, it is a measure of the unconventional nature of this interpretation that Buddhadāsa has first had to develop a new hermeneutic approach to the scriptures and also criticize the authority of almost a third of the Theravada canon plus the historically accepted system of scriptural exegesis in order to present his views. Without the *phasa tham* theory and without rejecting the *Abhidhammapiṭaka* and parts of the *Visuddhimagga* Buddhadāsa would have found it much more difficult to deny the traditional supernatural interpretations which he regards as being inconsistent with the doctrines of Buddhism and with modern scientific knowledge.

Buddhadāsa's notion of *chit wang* and his interpretation of *nibbāna* provide a religious goal which has its basis in everyday life—the higher spiritual states require only the development and deepening of the naturally existing condition of "freed-mind." By this theoretical development Buddhadāsa brings the Buddhist spiritual goal out of the monastery and into the stream of everyday life. However, *chit wang* is far from being just a theoretical notion. It is also the basis of Buddhadāsa's interpretation of Buddhist spiritual practice, and just as in his doctrinal interpretations he defines the state of *chit wang* as being integrally related to everyday experience, so too the practices Buddhadāsa describes as developing this condition are also related to the domain of everyday life. As detailed in the next chapter, *chit wang* is the basis of Buddhadāsa's Buddhist philosophy of action in the social world.

# 6 THE PRACTICE OF *CHIT WANG*

*CHIT WANG*, defined as the base of Buddhist spiritual attainment founded in everyday life, is the central plank of Buddhadāsa's attempt to resolve the difficulties created by his advocacy of a modernist, scientific interpretation of Theravada Buddhism and his rejection of the traditional lay religion. Buddhadāsa has met these problems by developing an interpretation of doctrinal Buddhism which, he maintains, is as accessible and relevant to the world-involved layperson as it is to renunciates. However, in order to fully resolve the difficulties created by his rejection of the traditional lay religion, Buddhadāsa must provide more than simply a theoretical explanation of the relevance of doctrinal Buddhism to the layperson. In addition to arguing for lay access to the *nibbānic* form of Buddhism, Buddhadāsa must also demonstrate that a layperson's adherence to the teachings and practices of the traditionally clerical aspect of Buddhism is compatible with activity in the social world. He must demonstrate the compatibility of simultaneously working for both material well-being and striving for *nibbāna* if he is to provide full and unqualified lay access to doctrinal Buddhism.

Because of the high level of social awareness and concern for social development among Buddhadāsa's lay audience, any interpretation of Buddhism which perpetuated the traditional devaluation of social activity relative to spiritual practice would fail to produce what he has stated is the goal of his work, namely, the development of an interpretation of Buddhism which educated Thais can regard as relevant to their lives and to their work. For Buddhadāsa to achieve this goal he must demonstrate, firstly, that the practice, as well as the theory, of salvation in his interpretation of Buddhism is accessible to the layperson. Secondly, he must show that this practice is compatible with and supportive of progressive social activity. In this chapter these two requirements are discussed in the context of an analysis of Buddhadāsa's teachings on the practice of *chit wang*, firstly, in terms of the relationship between *chit wang* and Buddhist meditation, and secondly, in terms of the relationship between meditation and "work" in the social world.

## TRADITIONAL BUDDHIST MORAL AND MEDITATIVE PRACTICE

Traditionally Buddhist spiritual practice has had a three-tiered structure, the base of which is *sīla* or virtuous conduct. *Sīla* or moral practice, combined with an understanding of Buddhist teachings on the causes and methods of ending human suffering, is regarded as the foundation of *samādhi* meditation, the second stage of spiritual practice. The purpose of *samādhi* or concentration meditation is to calm the mind and develop one-pointedness or undivided mental attentiveness. In the third stage of Buddhist practice, *vipassanā* or insight meditation, the concentrated power of consciousness is focused on a quest for insight into the truths of existence—*anicca, dukkha,* and *anattā*. With the attainment of such insight, ignorance is dispelled and the root cause of suffering is eradicated. The ultimate fruit of insight meditation is salvation or *nibbāna*.

However, while this graded series of practices is generally accepted as the structure of Buddhist religious practice, historically varying degrees of emphasis have been placed on the different stages. In particular, there has been an historical emphasis in Thailand on *samādhi* or concentration meditation, often to the exclusion of insight meditation or *vipassanā*. The emphasis on *samādhi* meditation in Thailand may be related to its traditional association with supernormal powers and supernatural experiences. *Samādhi* meditation induces trances or states of introspective absorption called *jhānas*. There are many levels of increasingly deep "absorptions" or *jhānas* which, Spiro observes, produce "a certain type of concentration, which (it is believed) determines which of the Buddhist heavens one will eventually enter."[1] It is also believed that the *samādhi* practitioner, through the attainment of certain trance states, may also develop supernormal powers such as clairvoyance and clairaudience. Supernatural powers or *iddhis* are associated with the second level of *samādhi* concentration, called *upacāra* or access concentration. *Phra Maha* Boowa Nyanasampanno, author of a biography of *Achan* Man, a monk famed for his psychic achievements, describes the *upacāra* level of *samādhi* concentration as allowing telepathic communication with invisible spiritual beings. *Phra Maha* Boowa observes that the first or *khaṇika* level of *samādhi*

> is not enough to pick up messages from outside or to communicate with these kinds of invisible beings. The third level of concentration is called *appanā* or full (absorption) concentration and is too profound for the picking up of messages and communicating with invisible beings.[2]

Buddhadāsa is critical of this traditional emphasis on the development of psychic powers or *iddhis* through *samādhi* meditation, and he is opposed to practising Buddhist meditation with the specific intention of developing *iddhis*:

> The Buddha did not deny mental *iddhis*, but he strongly disapproved of demonstrating them because they are mere illusions .... We don't come across it in the *Tipiṭaka* that the Buddha demonstrated *iddhis*. There do exist accounts of the Buddha demonstrating *iddhis*, but they occur only in commentaries and other works. Consequently the truth of these accounts is dubious; and there really is no need for us to judge them true or false.[3]

Despite the emphasis on *samādhi* meditation and supernaturalism in Thailand, many doctrinally strict Buddhist teachers have nevertheless regarded the *jhānas*, or *samādhi*—induced trance states—as in fact being spiritual hindrances to the attainment of liberative insight into reality. This is because, in Spiro's words, "The meditator prefers to perpetuate his *jhānic* pleasures rather than proceed to *nibbāna*."[4] Buddhadāsa agrees with this view, saying that

> While the mind is concentrated [in *samādhi*] it is likely to be experiencing such a satisfying kind of bliss and well-being that the meditator may become attached to it or imagine it to be the fruit of the path [i.e. *nibbāna*].[5]

Nevertheless, as Spiro comments, for many monks and for the majority of Buddhist laypeople,

> It is the supernatural products of meditation which they view as holy and for which they venerate monastic meditators who, allegedly, have achieved these supernormal states.[6]

## BUDDHADĀSA'S EMPHASIS ON *VIPASSANĀ* MEDITATION

In addition to its value as the base for insight meditation or *vipassanā*, *samādhi* is also important to traditional Thai Buddhists because of its association with supernatural powers and psychic communication with celestial beings. It is for this same reason that Buddhadāsa de-emphasizes *samādhi* and is critical of the traditional emphasis on concentration meditation in Thailand. In contrast, he maintains that it is *vipassanā* or insight meditation which is the most important aspect of Buddhist spiritual practice. He says of *samādhi* that it

> may come about naturally, on the one hand, and as a result of organised practice on the other. The end result is identical in both cases; the mind is concentrated and fit to be used for carrying out close introspection. One thing must be noticed, however, the intensity of concentration [i.e., *samādhi*] that comes about naturally is usually sufficient and appropriate for introspection and insight, whereas the concentration resulting from organised training is usually excessive, more than can be made use of.[7]

Buddhadāsa goes on to denounce the organized practice of *samādhi* which is central to the supernaturalist view of Buddhism:

> A deeply concentrated mind cannot practice introspection at all. It is in a state of unawareness and is of no use for insight (*vipassanā*). Deep concentration is a major obstacle to insight practice.[8]

In the above quote Buddhadāsa is in fact championing one of the canonically recognized meditative paths to *nibbāna*, the *vipassanā*-based *sukkhavipassaka* or "dry-visioned" attainment of *nibbāna*, so-called because its practice does not result in the meditator experiencing the supernatural delights attained through *jhāna* or *samādhi* meditation. The "dry-visioned" attainment of *nibbāna* results from a direct, unelaborated insight into liberative truth. *Sukkhavipassaka* is to attain *nibbāna* after a penetrating insight into reality based upon the foundation of the basic concentration level called *upacāra samādhi* or "access concentration." Buddhadāsa is in accord with canonical teachings when he says that a mind in any *samādhi* state higher than *upacāra* cannot practise *vipassanā* meditation and that to develop liberative insight via *vipassanā* the mind must first come out of the higher trance states.

However, the Buddhist scriptures also describe another much more elaborate meditative path to *nibbāna* than the *sukkhavipassaka* or *vipassanā* method supported by Buddhadāsa. This alternative meditative path in fact uses the very *jhānic* trances or *samādhi* concentrations which inhibit the development of the liberative insight into reality obtained from *vipassanā* meditation. This path to *nibbāna* via *samādhi* concentrations has nine stages. The first eight stages constitute the four *rūpajjhānas* or meditative absorptions of the fine material sphere and the four higher absorptions of the immaterial spheres, which are called the four *arūpajjhānas* or *arūpāyatana*. These *jhānic* trances all involve intense concentration,

> during which there is a complete, though temporary, suspension of the fivefold sense activity . . . The state of consciousness, however, is one of full alertness and lucidity.[9]

The four higher *jhānas* are based on a process of "voiding" or "emptying" consciousness of the sense of entitative existence or *attā*. Objects of consciousness are systematically broken down into their components in order to develop insight into the truth of the nonessential character of phenomenal existence. The culmination of this process is meditative concentration on pure voidness or *suññatā* itself. In the *Cūḷasuññatā Sutta* the Buddha describes the practice of "voiding" the mind of entitative awareness by subtracting, one after another, the perceived entitative or *attā* qualities of various objects, in this case a house:

> He [the meditating monk] knows clearly that this ideation is emptied of the awareness that it is a house, that it is something human, and he has clear awareness only of that single thing which it is not emptied of . . . . Thus he considers the voidness (*suññatā*) of those things which do not [in fact] exist in that ideation [of a house] and he knows clearly that which does continue to exist and which still is. *Ānanda*, such as this is the *bhikkhu's* progress towards voidness according to truth which is pure and not in error.(T)[10]

After having subtracted all the material qualities and attributes of the object of meditation the mediator proceeds to concentrate, in succession, on the increasingly abstract and "voided" states of (i) the realm of the infinity of space, *ākāsānañcāyatana*; (ii) the realm of the infinity of consciousness, *viññāṇañcāyatana*; (iii) consciousness of the realm of nothingness, *ākīñcaññāyatana*; and finally (iv) consciousness of the realm of neither perception nor non-perception, *nevasaññānāsaññāyatana*. These four higher meditations or *arūpajjhānas* involve a process of gradually extricating the meditator from his or her sense of selfhood as well as of the entitative character of the objects of consciousness.

A state beyond all these stages of *samādhi* is identified in the *Pañcala Sutta* where it is called *saññāvedāyitanirodha*.[11] This ninth stage is described as the cessation of consciousness and sensation in which all *āsava* or latent mental impurities disappear because of the attainment of penetrating wisdom, *paññā*. After this mental purification through intense concentration *nibbāna* can then be attained.

The *Cūḷasuññatā Sutta* also provides a detailed account of *saññavedāyitanirodha*. In this *sutta* the ninth stage of *samādhi* is described as a concentration devoid of any signs or distinguishing features where *suññatā* or absolute void is the object of consciousness. But this meditative state nevertheless still has "combining factors" or *saṅkhāra*, that is, *kammic* residues, capable of arising and destroying the concentration-induced condition of mental calm. For this reason, the ninth *samādhi* stage is still an impermanent condition, because it may still be subject to disturbances or disruptions. But when the meditator attains the realization that even this exalted state is subject to cessation and can pass away, then he or she is released from the *āsavas* of lust, desire for being, and ignorance (i.e., *kamāsava, bhavāsava,* and *avijjāsava*), and the mind then attains *ñāṇa* or liberating wisdom. At this point,

> It is the end of birth. The practice of the moral life has reached its end. The work that should be done is finished and no other work for existing in this [liberated] way need be performed.(T)[12]

In other words *nibbāna* can be attained by a transcendence of even the highest *samādhi* meditation on voidness, *saññāvedāyitanirodha*.

However, Buddhadāsa rejects this elaborate and difficult meditative system for attaining *nibbāna* via *samādhi*, which requires a life devoted solely to meditative practice. Instead, he maintains that the most appropriate spiritual practice is the practice of *chit wang* or *sati*, mindfulness of breathing. Buddhadāsa proposes that in practising the most basic form of Buddhist meditation, mindfulness of breathing or *ānāpānasati*, sufficient concentration or *samādhi* is developed to permit liberative insight into reality. Spiro describes the general practice of mindfulness as "where one attends to, and is self-consciously aware—in the minutest detail—of one's every act, thought, sensation and emotion."[13] In the specific practice of the mindfulness of breathing, "one not only attains total concentration, but also becomes aware in one's own body of one of the characteristics of existence, that is, impermanence."[14]

Buddhadāsa rejects the intricacies of the *samādhi* system of meditation because he says the Buddha has provided a shortcut system to enlightenment. He maintains that the practices detailed in the Noble Eightfold Path or *ariyamagga*, whose acme is *sammā-samādhi* or "right *samādhi*," is for "people who will not take shortcuts. It is not the wrong path; it is the right path. But it is on the ordinary level, and takes a long time."[15]

He says that the shortcut or *sukkhavipassaka* method involves not clinging to sensed objects or to the notion of self. That is, he proposes that the development of *chit wang* is the key to Buddhist spiritual practice and he says that once *chit wang* or the attitude of non-self-centredness is developed the rest of Buddhism's spiritual practices are developed automatically:

> Not to hold that there is selfhood (*attā*) in eye, ear, nose, tongue, body or mind, causes the arising of the entire Noble Eightfold Path (and thus of *samādhi*) in a single moment.[16]

Buddhadāsa does not dispute the traditional gradation of Buddhist practices into *sīla-samādhi-vipassanā*, but he proposes that the mindfulness attained through the practice of *chit wang* provides sufficient concentration to operate as a basis for insight practice, thus rendering the elaborate *jhānic* concentrations and their supernatural products irrelevant:

> If we set the mind right or prevent it from craving and clinging then that is *samādhi*, it is the very thing of *samādhi* itself. Then whether we are acting, speaking, walking, eating, or whatever, we will remain in that *samādhi*. That is, the mind is free from "I" and "mine." We will have both the well-being and the penetrating keenness to think, consider, and work with our heart and mind in everything. Hence I say that to have *samādhi* is easy, as easy as rolling a stone down a hill.(T)[17]

## *CHIT WANG*—A LAY-ACCESSIBLE PATH TO *NIBBĀNA*

Spiritual practice based on *chit wang* is of central importance to Buddhadāsa's system of doctrinal reinterpretation and reform. *Chit wang* is the basis of Buddhist spiritual practice aiming at the attainment of *nibbāna* which, while preserving the traditional graduated *sīla-samādhi-vipassanā* schema of Buddhist practice, also purges Buddhist meditation of the supernatural emphasis on *samādhi* meditation supported by religious traditionalists. Mindfulness or *sati* based on *chit wang* also provides a meditative system which bypasses the complexities of the monastically oriented *samādhi* system and which is not accessible to the layperson who has little free time available for meditative practice. Buddhadāsa emphasizes the general accessibility of the practice of *chit wang* or non-self-centred mindfulness, and thus the accessibility of salvation, by maintaining that if it is practised correctly the mindfulness of *chit wang* can itself lead to *nibbāna*. Buddhist doctrine details a series of stages on the path to ending suffering and Buddhadāsa claims that each of these stages follows on from one another in a natural succession, starting from the fundamental mindful practice of *chit wang* or non-self-centredness. He claims that it is

> just by making our own daily living so pure and honest that there develop in succession spiritual joy (*pīti, pamoda*), calm (*passadhi*), insight into the true nature of things (*yathābhūtañāṇadassana*), disenchantment (*nibbidā*), withdrawal (*virāga*), escape (*vimutti*), purification from defilements (*visuddhi*), and then peace or *nibbāna*.[18]

Buddhadāsa says that once the basic practice of *chit wang* is established, the entire process of liberation culminating in *nibbāna* is set in motion: "Because the fruit of the path arises automatically once the path is established, the attainment of the path is regarded as the culmination of the practice."[19] Thus, just as there is no need for special concentration or *samādhi* practices, according to Buddhadāsa spiritual insight and salvation also develop as natural consequences of being established in the mindfulness of *chit wang*. He supports his case by citing scriptural instances of people who are described as having attained *nibbāna* naturally, without following any specific system such as *jhānic* or *samādhi* concentrations: "These people did not go into the forest and sit, assiduously practising concentration on certain objects, in the way described in the later manuals."[20] For Buddhadāsa, *nibbāna* requires neither the special learning of the scholastically trained monk nor the retreatist monastic life-style:

> Through the power of just this naturally occurring concentration, most of us could actually attain liberation. We could attain the fruit of the path, *nibbāna, arahantship,* just by means of natural concentration.[21]

Buddhadāsa does not deny the value of the systematic *samādhi* approach to meditation, saying that it may be of use to those who are still at a relatively undeveloped spiritual stage and "who still cannot perceive the unsatisfactoriness of worldly existence with their own eyes, naturally."[22] But the general import of his system of practice, like his interpretation of the doctrine, is to declericalize salvation and to provide a path to *nibbāna* for the layperson, negating the spiritual distinction between layperson and monk. Buddhadāsa is not concerned with the doctrinal details of enlightenment or salvation, with the different types of saving wisdom or *paññā,* or with the various meditative states listed as producing that wisdom in the *Abhidhamma* and commentary literature. Rather, in accord with his rationalist emphasis, Buddhadāsa, believes that the attainment of *nibbāna* is guaranteed once the proper moral and meditative basis is established. For Buddhadāsa, *nibbāna* is not a miraculous or supernatural condition but rather it is the culmination of systematic spiritual practices which operate in full accord with the general laws of existence realized by the Buddha.

For Buddhadāsa, the foundation of correct spiritual practice is the most important thing in attaining salvation. For when the foundation, that is, *chit wang*, is laid correctly, he maintains that the structure arises automatically through the operation of the natural laws which the Buddha utilized and systematically followed. Buddhadāsa consequently sees his duty as a monk and spiritual instructor as being to demonstrate and detail how the path to salvation may be begun, or how the stream to *nibbāna* may be entered, from the position of being an individual living in contemporary Thailand. There is no need for elaborate descriptions of supernatural mental states or for detailed descriptions of different conditions of wisdom or insight in Buddhadāsa's system. For once the path is correctly followed, all the rest, right up to salvation, follows as an inevitable and natural consequence.

## DEBATE ON THE COMPATIBILITY OF *CHIT WANG* WITH SOCIAL ACTION

Buddhadāsa's opening up of Buddhism's spiritual practices to the laity has not been universally welcomed. Former Thai prime minister Kukrit Pramoj voices the following objection:

> In olden times when a child asked its elders about *vipassanā* [insight meditation] . . . no one spoke. They said it was a secret. The instructors ordered not to let just anyone be taught, the student had to be chosen. It was not a widespread teaching. Hence, up until now Buddhism has not gone against national development or the foundation of government.(T)[23]

Kukrit believes that the attainment of higher spiritual states is incompatible with worldly involvement and so he lauds the traditional practice of restricting access to the soteriological aspects of Buddhism to the few, that is, to monks. Kukrit is consequently concerned by the popularization of Buddhist meditation techniques among the lay populace, maintaining that if people attain *chit wang* through meditation they will be in no position to aid the development of the country:

> Because the person who has no cravings or attainments, the person whose mind is freed [that is, *chit wang*], holds to nothing as himself or as his own, he is in no condition to be able to develop the country, develop the land, or even to develop himself.(T)[24]

Kukrit is here expressing the widely held view that the spiritual path to *nibbāna* and the path of worldly involvement cannot both be traversed at the same time. A Sri Lankan monk, Somathera, makes a similar comment:

> In those who seek immortality (*nibbāna*), all kinds of endeavour and exertion to acquire worldly power and possessions become slack through the perception of death (*anicca*) but they do all that has to be done for attaining the deathless state.[25]

In this context, Buddhadāsa observes that his notion of *chit wang* has been criticized as a threat to Thailand's national security: "[It has been accused that] if the Thai people have *chit wang* completely they will not love their country and they will not protect their country."(T)[26] But Buddhadāsa claims that the emotional detachment and calm of *chit wang* is not the same as the social disinterestedness which Kukrit and others maintain follows from the cultivation of "freed-mind." Rather than hindering the attainment of social or material goals, Buddhadāsa says that by removing the confusions caused by self-centredness such goals will in fact be attained more efficiently and with less suffering:

> I want the layperson to be able to work with less suffering and to have completely successful results. By what means will we attain this? Will it not be done with *chit wang*, or would a confused mind be better?(T)[27]

Buddhadāsa appears to take his lead on this point from the *Subha Sutta*,[28] where the Buddha is asked about the relative statuses of the work of a layperson who has many concerns and of a monk who has few distractions, regarding their relative abilities to follow the path to *nibbāna*. The Buddha replied that work undertaken with great desire and great effort, if struck by disaster, will come to naught while a work undertaken with little desire and little confusion, if fortuitous, can produce grand results. In other words, working in an unattached way, as in working with *chit wang*, does not of itself prevent "great results," of whatever kind, from being produced.

But Kukrit remains skeptical of the possibility of work or worldly activity for social development being "pleasurable":

> I think that if one wants to obtain successful results in the world those results must be bought with suffering . . . [If one wants] true *wang* without suffering, one must completely sacrifice worldly success . . . . When one is a layperson there must be some happiness and some suffering, it is not *wang*.(T)[29]

Buddhadāsa retorts that the example of the Buddha's strenuous propagatory and teaching activities carried out after his enlightenment shows that having the mental peace of *chit wang*, and of *nibbāna*, in no way hinders the fulfillment of demanding worldly tasks:

> There has never been any evidence anywhere [for the supposition that] those who are free of *kilesa* will not work. The Lord Buddha and the *arahants* worked more than us, sacrificed more than us and became more tired than us, and all their work was for helping others.(T)[30]

But Kukrit holds fast to his traditionalist views for, unlike Buddhadāsa, he does not regard the Buddha's life as a realistic model for the average person. Talking of *nibbāna* he says,

> The person who reaches a state such as this naturally cannot live in the world like an ordinary person. They cannot live as a householder in the society of householders . . . They must try to get away from society. This is the usual thing upon attaining the fruits of the path.(T)[31]

Kukrit's criticisms of Buddhadāsa's abolition of the *lokiya-lokuttara* distinction and of the propagation of the notion of *chit wang* may, however, be motivated by political considerations as much as by religious conservatism. Kukrit maintains that monks should have no mundane associations or direct social involvement whatever:

> It is a sin for a saint to establish a foundation,[32] even if that foundation has the object of helping our fellow man. Because, if established, a foundation will cause attachment and craving to arise. When there is not enough money there is suffering, doing anything will lead to suffering.(T)[33]

Here Kukrit is assuming that involvement in the world is intrinsically linked with suffering, and the moment a saint (i.e., one who is free from suffering) enters the mundane domain, even to help another, that worldly involvement must have the unwholesome or *akusala* effect of causing the saint to suffer or fall from his state of spiritual attainment. Buddhadāsa, however, maintains that it is not worldly involvement per se but the attitude of attachment when acting in the material world which leads to suffering. However, Kukrit's assertion that a saint cannot enter the world without soiling his saintly status—coming from a seasoned politician and former prime minister—may be as much a call for the complete separation of church and state as an expression of religious belief. There are several reasons why a politician might seek to keep the Sangha out of politics, not the least of which is to ward off the development of a potential alternative source of power in the country. As a strongly organized body, the Sangha would be a potent political force if its energies were directed into the mundane realm. As noted in chapter 1, successive Thai governments have maintained tight control over the Sangha to strip it of effective power and to prevent the order of monks from using its strong organization and prestige in Thai society against those governments. In addition to the explicit legal and political controls on the Sangha's activities, the doctrines that the worldly domain is the sinful antithesis of the spiritual realm and that a monk's entering the social world entails a spiritual pollution which destroys his spiritual authority also function as ideological barriers to the expansion of the Sangha's activities into the sociopolitical realm. Buddhadāsa's views threaten this traditional isolation of the Sangha from politics and Kukrit's criticisms can be read as an attempt to maintain the ideological status quo. But despite the criticisms of traditionalists, Buddhadāsa insists that his interpretations are in strict accordance with the Buddha's teachings.

In replying to criticisms that the doctrinal teachings of *anattā* or *chit wang* are too abstract or remote for the average person, he retorts,

> But I have tried to do what is best, to follow just what the Lord Buddha suggested, that the lay people should know about *suññatā* or *chit wang* as is appropriate for them.(T)[34]

The average person should know about the central doctrines of Buddhism because "It is clearly written in Pali, in the blessed scriptures, the Lord Buddha said *suññatā* is a matter having eternal benefit in helping the laity."(T)[35]

## BUDDHADĀSA ON *KAMMA* AND SUFFERING

In contrast to Kukrit's views, Buddhadāsa denies that lay people are fated to suffer: "If one acts well and correctly as a lay person one may be able to avoid suffering."(T)[36] Buddhadāsa denies that suffering is something intrinsic to lay life and says that it need not be accepted passively as the unavoidable result of past fate or *kamma*. Commenting on the distractions and confusions of the householder's life he says:

> Those things do not exist for the sake of giving suffering or for either directly or specifically being suffering. They may have come into being as lessons or as tests to advance the [spiritual] level of human beings.(T)[37]

Buddhadāsa does not deny the traditional view that the sufferings of a layperson are fated because of their *kamma*, but he does oppose the interpretation that suffering is a spiritual impediment:

> If we look at it from the point of view of suffering then it is suffering, but if we look at it from a better perspective then it is just. That is, it is something that teaches and drives us forward quickly . . . . obstacles or suffering are tools to help us subsequently become spiritually intelligent.(T)[38]

For Buddhadāsa suffering is just, not simply because it is retribution for misdeeds, but more importantly because it leads to the future benefits of learning how to avoid suffering and how to progress quickly on the spiritual path. Buddhadāsa inverts the traditional notion that *kamma* is a spiritual block or hindrance. He regards the suffering that human beings are fated to as a positive tool which, rather than holding one back or barring one from salvation, is in fact capable of accelerating one's attainment of *nibbāna* if correctly appreciated and acted upon. He advises that if suffering arises because of the concerns of being a layperson, "Don't accept it as suffering and torture, take it as a problem which must be solved."(T)[39] Buddhadāsa maintains that suffering is not something humans should passively endure as their fated moral due but is a tool which should be used as a spur to the attainment of greater things.

The implications of this reinterpretation of *kamma* and suffering are profound, because it represents a fundamental shift in the Buddhist view of human existence and activity in the world. Buddhadāsa does not regard mundane existence as a punishment for past sins but as the domain in which human beings actively control and improve their lives in the quest to end the problems and sufferings of everyday life. Suffering is no longer ended only in a transcendent realm. For Buddhadāsa, suffering is both created and destroyed at the mundane level and it cannot only be ended mentally through spiritual practice but also physically through material activity to better the social and material world. In other words, in Buddhadāsa's interpretation the Buddhist goal of the cessation of suffering is placed within the very social world or mundane realm, *lokiya*, which in traditional Buddhism is the complete opposite of salvation. On this point Tambiah has commented that

> What Buddhadāsa's ideas forcefully refute and deny is the fatalism, the postponement of action, the unreality of this world and therefore apathy towards it attributed to Buddhism by certain stereotype commentaries. He is in fact saying that the world here and now . . . comprise[s] the stage for urgent and immediate action in the form of

Buddhist practice. Perhaps an even more important ideological assertion on his part is that the quest for *nirvāṇa* does not mean a negation and renunciation of action in the world.[40]

## *CHIT WANG* AND WORK

Buddhadāsa's conception of human beings as active controllers of their own material and spiritual progress is most clearly presented in his view of work as integrating both social and spiritual activity. While fundamentally derived from the notion of *kamma* or action, Buddhadāsa's interpretation of work has a much more this-worldly import than the traditional Buddhist notion of *kamma*. Whereas *kamma*—that is, world-involved activity inherently infected with craving and clinging—is traditionally regarded as something to be avoided because it leads to further entanglement in the cyclical net of suffering, Buddhadāsa defines work as an inherently liberative activity because it is related to the practice of Dhamma, and, he maintains, "the actual practice of Dhamma is the work."[41] The basis of Buddhadāsa's notion of work is *chit wang* or, more precisely, the non-self-centred activity which he interprets as meaning to work for the sake of Dhamma rather than for any self-interested motivation. His ideal is to be able to "work for the work, to work for the sake of Dhamma."(T)[42] Buddhadāsa instructs that

> we should do every kind of work with a "freed-mind." All the results of work should be given up to "freed-ness." We should eat the food of "freed-ness" the way a monk eats. We should die to ourselves completely from the beginning.(T)[43]

To give up the results of working to "freed-ness" means not craving or clinging to those results but, like an ideal monk, to eat or act with the awareness that it is merely a congeries of essenceless (*anattā*) elements which are being eaten or acted upon. The result of such working with "freed-ness" is to eat without "tasting" the food, or to act without "tasting" the fruits or results of the action. That is, to act with *chit wang* is to maintain equanimity and not to be perturbed by either the good or bad results of acting, and so not to suffer from the vagaries of impermanent existence. It is Buddhadasa's intention to render all human activity, including mundane material work, suffering-free: "If we have Dhamma it will make working or development free of suffering."(T) [44]

Yet Buddhadāsa promises more than a simple absence of suffering as the result of working with *chit wang*. He maintains that work carried out with *chit wang* will be successful—because activity is no longer confused by "I"–"mine"—and that working will be a pleasurable rather than just a neutral or suffering-free experience:

> We will consequently feel successful in our work. That is, the work will go well and the person who does it will be happy and want to work because he or she enjoys working. If we act in this way, it is Buddhism or going to the heart of Buddhism.(T)[45]

He maintains that spiritual practices and principles should guide and be integrated with worldly activities, including activity associated with socioeconomic development:

> Development which gets results must have the *lokuttara* type of Dhamma integrally governing it. That development will as a consequence be correct and will not proceed to create ongoing crises or to cause corruption.(T)[46]

Buddhadāsa makes no distinction between work defined as a spiritual activity to establish oneself in *chit wang* or as the mundane activities of everyday life and making a living. For him the two amount to the same thing: "Working is the same thing as practising Dhamma—there are no ways of the world [distinct from] the ways of Dhamma."(T)[47] This is very much a philosophy of action in the world which brings salvation into the world of everyday life while also imbuing mundane work and activities with a religious or sanctified quality. Buddhadāsa does not distinguish between mundane and spiritual activity but only between correct and incorrect activity, a distinction based not on the objective character of an action, such as its location either within or outside the monastery precincts, but rather on the psychological attitude which is brought to bear on an action. All actions performed with *chit wang* are regarded as having the same spiritual status on the path to *nibbāna*. Thus, in Buddhadāsa's system the "monastery" or the site of spiritual practice is no longer a geographical location but a state of mind. This integration of work with spiritual activity is made manifest in the following definition:

> The word "working" [*kan tham ngan*] is Thai. If it were rendered into Pali it would be the word *sammākammanto*, which translates as "having right work." When there is right work then it is one component of the Noble Path's [*ariyamagga*] set of practices for advancing towards the blessed *nibbāna*.(T)[48]

By defining work in terms of whether it is carried out with the non-self-centred attitude of *chit wang* or with the self-centred attitude of "I"–"mine," rather than in terms of either its mundane or supramundane character, Buddhadāsa removes Buddhism's negative sanctions against what has historically been seen as the non-spiritual and even anti-spiritual character of mundane activity. The above identification of work with the spiritual practice of "right action" or *sammākammanto*, the fourth of the eight injunctions of the Noble Eightfold Path, means that in Buddhadāsa's system mundane work has the status of a moral injunction. For Buddhadāsa, worldly activity is an integral and necessary part of the path to *nibbāna*. In other words, instead of being the antithesis of the state of salvation, the sociocultural world is essential to what Buddhadāsa means by the attainment of salvation. Working, the fundamental activity underlying the industrial mode of production, is, according to Buddhadāsa, not simply necessary for socioeconomic development but also for spiritual salvation.

The Marxist notion that man realizes himself through productive labour appears to underlie the following proclamation by Buddhadāsa:

> Humans must act in order to be human . . . Working is something sublime, holy, exalted. As for being human, if that which is called work is abandoned we will inevitably lose our correct humanity.(T)[49]

Here "humanity" denotes a state achieved through the spiritual effort of practising *chit wang*. Being "human" or a "man" is not, according to Buddhadāsa, something one is born with but rather is a state which is attained: "'man' . . . refers to the higher qualities implied in the word 'human'."[50] Buddhadāsa implies that we are made human through our work in the world, as practised with *chit wang*. Man as a spiritual being is thus equated with man as an economic being, because for Buddhadāsa economic activity and spiritual activity cannot be separated without making life pointless and meaningless:

> The world is working and working is the world, life is working and working is life—they are one and the same thing. If we were to live in the world or have a life devoid of working then such a life would be without meaning; it would, moreover, already to be dead.(T)[51]

*Chit wang*, when interpreted as being the basis of Buddhist practice, provides the link between Buddhadāsa's spiritual philosophy and his treatment of social and political issues. *Chit wang* incorporates all the diverse concerns of Buddhadāsa's reinterpretative program. That is, it is a focus of his criticisms of supernatural readings of Buddhism and of the separation of lay and clerical forms of the religion. It is also a focus of his concern to give social activity spiritual standing and to grant the Buddhist laity direct access to salvation. Buddhadāsa describes *chit wang* as being both a development of the everyday experience of mental calm and the direct precursor of *nibbāna*. That is, *chit wang* is the link between the world of the everyday mundane awareness of the layperson and the supramundane condition of spiritual salvation. According to Buddhadāsa, *chit wang* provides the layperson with direct access to *nibbāna*. Similarly, the practice of *chit wang*, or the conscious development of mindfulness or *sati*, is interpreted as being integral to activity and work in the social world. Indeed, Buddhadāsa regards working and *chit wang* as integrally related. Consequently, for Buddhadāsa *chit wang* is the key to the resolution of the theoretical problem of developing a lay-accessible interpretation of both the theory and the practice of doctrinal Buddhism. Just as the theory of *phasa tham* is the basis of Buddhadāsa's methodological approach to the task of reinterpreting Theravada Buddhism, so is the notion of *chit wang* the conceptual hub of that reinterpreted system.

# 7

# *CHIT WANG* AND ZEN

BUDDHADĀSA'S INTERPRETATION of Theravada Buddhist doctrine, in particular his emphasis on *chit wang* or "freed-mind," has been significantly influenced by the teachings of Zen Buddhism, a sect of Mahayana Buddhism traditionally found in China, Japan, and Vietnam. The Mahayana tradition of Buddhism, however, is founded on notions which differ fundamentally from those which underpin Theravada Buddhism. In terms of metaphysics, the most important difference between the two traditions is the Mahayana claim that voidness or *śunyatā* (Pali: *suññatā*), as the fundamental nature of reality, has a positive character and is not the ontological void or emptiness denoted by the Theravada notion of *anattā* (Sanskrit: *anatman*). The Mahayana proposition that the "void" is not empty but an originating "fullness" which forms the undifferentiated substratum of all existence is presented in Zen teachings as an intellectual paradox whose truth can only be realized by a transcendence of mundane rationality. Zen masters have historically emphasized the penetration of paradoxical statements, called *koan*, as an important meditative tool in striving to attain transcendent spiritual awareness. In contrast, the Theravada tradition contains no explicit doctrines of the paradoxical nature of reality, instead presenting the basic teachings of Buddhism, including that of *anattā* or non-self, as unambiguous descriptions of the actual character of existence. Soteriologically, Mahayana Buddhism differs from

Theravada in its acceptance of the ability of spiritually advanced personalities to directly assist the spiritual enlightenment of others by acts of grace. In contrast, salvation in Theravada Buddhism is a wholly individually attained condition.

In using Zen and Mahayana notions in his reform of Theravada doctrine Buddhadāsa must come to terms with the important doctrinal differences mentioned above in order to justify his borrowing of non-Theravada ideas. He does this in several ways, such as by claiming that Zen is not in fact part of the Mahayana tradition but rather represents a return to the fundamental core of Buddhism which has relevance for all Buddhists of all traditions and backgrounds. However, Buddhadāsa's main justification for employing Zen-derived ideas is contained in his attempt to demonstrate the existence of similarities and even identities between the Zen ideas that he borrows and the undeniably Theravada character of his teachings. However, these arguments are often weak and in places rely upon misinterpretations of Zen notions and somewhat managed readings of Zen texts which avoid detailing points that show up the actual differences between Theravada and Mahayana doctrine. The failings of Buddhadāsa's justifications of his use of Zen ideas do not, however, ultimately detract from the significance of his Zen-influenced reinterpretations of Theravada doctrine. Whether or not his ideas strictly follow Theravada notions, Buddhadāsa still remains faithful to what he interprets as the spirit of Buddhist doctrines. And it is this emphasis on the broader principles of Buddhist teachings rather than on scriptural details which has allowed him to reinvigorate the theoretically stagnant Theravada tradition by introducing views and concepts from other Buddhist traditions.

## THE TEACHINGS OF ZEN BUDDHISM

John Blofeld describes the central tenets of Zen Buddhism as follows:

> Zen submits that, while all Buddhist sects present the truth in varying degrees, Zen alone preserves the very highest teaching of all—a teaching based on a mysterious transmission of Mind which took place between Gautama Buddha and Mahakas'yapa, the only one of his disciples capable of receiving this transmission.[1]

Zen emphasizes that the central teaching of Buddhism cannot be caught within an intellectual web of words but is a mystical, wordless doctrine whose truth is realized directly and immediately rather than being approached gradually through a systematic gradation of practices as in Theravada Buddhism. This truth beyond words, in which the intellectual polarities of everyday consciousness and rationality dissolve, is variously called the "void," *śunyatā,* "Mind" or "One Mind."[2] To the intellect this truth is impenetrable, and so a conceptual void, but Zen teachers maintain that it is nevertheless the source of all being, a substratum of Mind upon which all phenomenal existence is grounded. The Zen scholar Suzuki describes Mind as that "from which this universe with all its multiplicities issues, but which is itself simple, undefiled and illuminating as the sun behind the clouds."[3]

In Zen, enlightenment, *satori* in Japanese, is an all or nothing experience: one either intuits Mind or One Mind in toto in a sudden inspiration or not at all. Nevertheless, Zen still teaches that one can only prepare the mind for its sudden realization of truth through meditation and it is from the practice of *dhyāna* meditation (Chinese: *chan*, Japanese: Zen) that the sect in Japan takes its name.

According to tradition, the wordless doctrine or direct spiritual insight of the Buddha first passed to Mahākaśyapa (Pali: Mahākassapa) and from him to Ānanda, who became the second of twenty-eight patriarchs who received the wordless doctrine in an unbroken line of succession. The last Indian patriarch, Bodhidharma, is regarded as having gone to China in the sixth century of the Christian era, becoming the first of six Chinese patriarchs, the last of whom was Hui Neng (also called Wei Lang). Subsequent divisions in the sect broke the direct line of spiritual succession.

## BUDDHADĀSA'S JUSTIFICATION FOR BORROWING ZEN NOTIONS

Buddhadāsa in no way hides his indebtedness to Zen and by explicitly supporting Zen teachings opens himself to the criticism of being an apostate to his Theravada roots. The Theravada Sangha has historically regarded itself as the bearer of the true Buddhist doctrine and practice, on the argument that its traditions and scriptures can be traced back further into history than those of any other existing Buddhist school. The Theravadins have been highly protective of their "purer" tradition and extremely wary of its pollution with Mahayana doctrines. Buddhadāsa's critics correctly regard the pivotal notion of *chit wang* as a Thai equivalent of *śunyatā* or void, but mistakenly claim that this is solely a Mahayana and not a Theravada concept. *Phra* Kittiwuttho says:

> This Theravada section of Buddhism does not talk about *chit wang*. In the *Tipiṭaka* . . . nothing at all is indicated about the matter of *chit wang*. The Buddha's words in Pali show nothing like it . . . *chit wang* is a matter outside of the blessed *Tipiṭaka*. It is not a principle of this pure Theravada section of Buddhism, but is an opinion of the Mahayanists.(T)[4]

Buddhadāsa defends himself against such criticisms by claiming that *chit wang* "is the heart of all Buddhism, [having existed] since before the separation into Theravada or Mahayana."(T)[5] In opposition to critics like Kittiwuttho, Buddhadāsa claims that *suññatā* is not only a term used by the Buddha but that in the *Dhammadinna Sutta* the Buddha calls it the basis or heart of Buddhist practice. Buddhadāsa also cites other *suttas* as providing support for his emphasis on *suññatā* and on *chit wang*. He maintains that in the *Mahāvara Vagga* of the *Saṁyutta Nikāya* the Buddha says:

> Emptiness (*suññatā*) is what I teach. A teaching that does not treat of emptiness is someone else's teaching, an unorthodox teaching composed by some later disciple.[6]

And he quotes the Buddha as saying in the *Pañcaka Nipata* of the *Aṅguttara Nikāya* that:

> A discourse of any kind, though produced by a poet or a learned man, versified, poetical, splendid, melodious in sound and syllable, is not in keeping with the teaching [of the Buddha] if not connected with *suññatā*.[7]

After claiming that *chit wang* is at the heart of Buddhism, Buddhadāsa attempts to further weaken Kittiwuttho's attack by saying, "True Buddhism is neither Theravada nor Mahayana,"(T)[8] and he opens the way for the further incorporation of Mahayana ideas into Theravada by saying that "We should not regard Zen as being Mahayana."(T)[9] This last claim is based on a rather narrow and chauvinistic definition of Mahayana Buddhism as being concerned more with the worship of Mahayana saints or *bodhisattvas* than with following the practical teachings of the Buddha. Buddhadāsa attempts to show that Zen does not fit this narrow definition and so should not be called a part of Mahayana Buddhism. Despite the narrow character of the definition of Mahayana Buddhism used by Buddhadāsa in supporting his case for borrowing Zen notions, it must nevertheless be acknowledged that this is the same definition used by his critics when they raise the spectre of the purported purity of Theravada being subverted by the introduction of Mahayana teachings. And so, inasmuch as Buddhadāsa is here conducting a polemical rather than a scholarly debate, his demonstration of the supposedly non-Mahayana character of Zen can be regarded as politically expeditious even if it is theoretically superficial. In trying to dissociate his borrowing of Zen notions from what most Thai Buddhists regard as being Mahayana, Buddhadāsa claims that:

> The Zen sect arose in order to ridicule those Mahayanists who worship only [the *bodhisattvas*] Amitabha and Avalokiteśvara with pleadings and implorings.(T)[10]

Here Buddhadāsa is saying that Zen criticizes the same ritualistic faith which Theravadins fault in popular Mahayana practice. However, he does not acclaim Zen as being any better or as having any more insights than Theravada:

> Zen is not any better than the type of Buddhism we already have . . . . Zen is interesting. Whoever studies it well must become more intelligent than before.(T)[11]

It has been Buddhadāsa's own translations into Thai of various Zen works[12] which have led to the popularization of that sect's ideas among a formerly uninterested Thai readership. And in the introduction to one of those translations, *The Teachings of Huang Po*, he appeals to his audience's modernist aspirations by saying that while the work is the acme of Zen Buddhist thought it is still largely unknown in Thailand, and if they do not acquaint themselves with it, "Thai Buddhists will be said to be behind the times."(T)[13]

## ZEN INFLUENCES ON THE NOTION OF *CHIT WANG*

It is not the specific term *suññatā* which Buddhadāsa has borrowed from Zen, for this term does occur in the Pali canon. Rather, it is the view that *chit wang* is the fundamental state of mind which has been taken from the Zen school. Suzuki quotes the Zen master Hui Neng as making the following statement on this point: "Mind as it is in itself is free from ills . . . . The Mind as it is in itself is free from disturbances. . . . The Mind as it is in itself is free from follies."[14]

Blofeld, whose English translation of Huang Po's teachings was in turn translated into Thai by Buddhadāsa, says that Zen refutes the view

> that the mind is a mirror to be cleansed of the defiling dust of phenomena, passion and other illusions, for this view leads to dualism . . . the dust and the mirror are one intangible unity.[15]

The Zen master Hui Neng taught the paradoxical doctrine that *nirvāṇa* is the same as *saṁsāra* or the cycle of suffering and rebirth from which liberation is sought. Hui Neng taught that defilements are the same as pure Mind, and that to distinguish between these polarities is to be caught in the delusory net of dichotomous thinking. Hui Neng then did not seek to end defilements or the cycle of *saṁsāra* but rather the polarized way of thinking in which *nirvāṇa* is distinguished from *saṁsāra*, and in which *kleśa* (Pali: *kilesa*) or mental defilements are considered distinct from pure Mind. According to Hui Neng, mental defilements and the suffering of rebirth are all essentially the same as Mind or One Mind.

Buddhadāsa adopts a view similar to Hui Neng's on the fundamental purity of the mind when he criticizes some *Abhidhamma* scholars as holding that "people fundamentally have *kilesa*. That is, that the mind is fundamentally disturbed. They then try to extract *kilesa* in order to abolish them."(T)[16] It follows from the doctrine of *anattā* that even *kilesa* such as ignorance (*avijjā*) and craving (*taṇhā*), despite their great power to obstruct the attainment of *nibbāna*, are non-essential and dependent phenomena. The dependent nature of *avijjā* is detailed in the *Avijjā Sutta*[17] where it is stated that *avijjā* has the *pañcanīvaraṇa* or five hindrances of lust, ill will, sloth, restlessness and anxiety as its "food" or dependent sources of origination. These five hindrances are further described as having three kinds of *duccarita* or bad conduct as their "food," while lacking control of the senses is in turn given as the "food" of *duccarita*. The list of dependent causes then proceeds through many successive stages.[18] This means, as Chinda Chandrkaew states, that:

> In spite of the fact that in the causal formula of Dependent Origination (*paṭiccasamuppāda*) *avijjā* is first mentioned . . . the attempt to interpret *avijjā* as the first principle or cause, out of which everything comes, cannot be sustained.[19]

But despite the above scriptural description of *avijjā* as being a compounded or dependent phenomenon, ignorance is nevertheless still popularly hypostatized as a self-existing evil, personified by the demonic figure of Mara. Venerable Boowa Nyanasampanno reflects this popular view of *avijjā* when he says:

> Ignorance is clever, not only in its defensive manoeuvres whereby it is adroitly evasive, but also in aggressive strategy, whereby it can launch a surprise attack on its opponent with devastating results.[20]

Like Hui Neng, Buddhadāsa opposes this hypostatization of ignorance and mental defilements, saying that the attitude of attacking *avijjā* and other *kilesa* is to deludedly confer on them a substantial character which, as impermanent dependent phenomena, they do not possess. He instead proposes using mindfulness or *sati* to prevent the necessary conditions for *kilesa*, such as *avijjā*, from arising. That is, he teaches that one should remain in the original state of *chit wang*.

## DIFFICULTIES IN BUDDHADĀSA'S USE OF ZEN NOTIONS

But while agreeing with the Zen doctrine that the mind is fundamentally pure and that attacking defilements is the wrong way to attain enlightenment, Buddhadāsa's reasons for holding these views differ from the Zen injunctions to avoid thinking in terms of rational polarities. And despite the superficial similarities between Zen teachings and his own views, Buddhadāsa creates some confusions in his work by not clearly acknowledging the differences between his outlook and that of Zen.

A fundamental confusion arises from Buddhadāsa's identification of his notion of *chit wan*g with the Zen idea of One Mind or Original Mind. For while Buddhadāsa's interpretation of Theravada doctrine in large part rests upon a reduction of supernatural phenomena to psychological states, the Zen teaching of One Mind, unlike the notion of *chit wang*, has an explicitly ontological component. This contrasts sharply with both Buddhadāsa's view and the traditional Theravada view of *anattā*. Blofeld notes a Zen criticism of the Theravada view of *anattā*, a view which Buddhadāsa strongly supports:

> If the Theravadins are right with their "no ego and no Self," what is it that reincarnates and finally enters *nirvāṇa?* . . . . For if the

> temporarily adhering aggregates of personality are not held together by an ego-soul or by a Universal Self or the One Mind, whatever enters *nirvāṇa* when those aggregates have finally dispersed can be of no interest to the man who devotes successive lives to attaining that goal.[21]

Buddhadāsa avoids the ontological problem posed by Blofeld (i.e., what is it that reincarnates and ultimately attains *nibbāna*?) by defining the scope of Buddhism as covering only the psychological domain of this life on earth. As already described, Buddhadāsa reinterprets rebirth as denoting the continual re-arising of ego-centredness or "I"–"mine." In contrast, Mahayanists maintain that there is a transcendent "Self," the One Mind, pre-existing all things and which is the pure ontological foundation of being. This Mahayana notion differs fundamentally from the deontologized idea of *chit wang*, which Buddhadāsa maintains is the same as the Zen notion of One Mind. *Chit wang* is a basic, undefiled mental condition while the Zen One Mind is not only a fundamental mental state but is also regarded as being the basic mental substratum. Buddhadāsa, on the other hand, eschews all discussion of substrata and of fundamental substances as soteriologically irrelevant.

In a previous chapter it was noted that Buddhadāsa does not deny that non-conscious mental impurities, *anusayakilesa*, continue to exist even in saintly personalities who are established in *chit wang*. From this it was concluded that *chit wang*, which Buddhadāsa defines as the fundamental mental condition, denotes the basic state of the conscious mind. For if *chit wang* is not restricted to being a condition of the conscious mind, Buddhadāsa's notion of "freed-mind" would contradict the proposition that there are *anusaya* or latent, non-conscious *kilesa* or mental defilements. In contrast, however, the Zen One Mind, as the source of all being, is much more than a state of the conscious mind. That is, *chit wang*, as a condition of the conscious mind, is markedly different from the all-encompassing character of the Zen One Mind, and Buddhadāsa's attempt to identify the two only creates confusion as to the actual character of *chit wang*, and of One Mind.

Some confusion also enters Buddhadāsa's work because of his

equation of the Zen notion of *śunyatā* with the concept of *wang* or *chit wang*. As noted above, *chit wang* denotes a mental state which is freed or emptied of defilements. In contrast, however, the Zen and the Mahayana notion of *śunyatā* denotes an all-pervasive, underlying principle of reality which, while being an absolute void in which all dualities are abolished, paradoxically also has the positive quality of being the "essence" of being. Neither *chit wang* nor the Theravada notion of *suññatā* can be described as paradoxical. Both denote the absence of psychological and moral defilements, not the absence of conceptual dualities. The Theravada concept of *suññatā* underpinning Buddhadāsa's notion of *chit wang* straightforwardly describes phenomena as being characterized by *anattā* or non-essentiality. The Zen *śunyatā*, on the other hand, is a much more absolute philosophical notion than either the Theravada *suññatā* or the psychological condition of *chit wang*.

In attempting to identify *chit wang* with what Blofeld translates as One Mind, Buddhadāsa maintains that the original Chinese expression for the term Mind is in fact ambiguous in that it could be rendered as either "original mind" or "true mind." He decides to translate it as "true original mind," *chit doem thae* (จิตเดิมแท้) and admits that "These words, 'original mind' or 'pure original mind,' are found in the Dhyāna Sect [i.e. Zen]. They don't occur in our Theravada Sect."(T)[22] However, Buddhadāsa goes on to equate this Zen notion of "pure original mind" with the Theravada Pali term *pabhassara* (Sanskrit: *prabhaśvara*, Thai: *praphatson* ประภัสสร), literally "to shine very brightly," saying that like "true original mind" this denotes the original mental state which is free from unwholesome defilements:

> The mind is naturally *pabhassara*. That is, it is without *kilesa* and is not saddened or clouded because of *kilesa*. That original mind shines as *pabhassara* but when *kilesa* enter it changes into a [morally] clouded mind.(T)[23]

In an article comparing Zen and Theravada, Walpola Rahula refers to the term *pabhassara* as demonstrating the existence of a link between the two schools. Rahula offers the following explanation of the Zen symbolism of a black ox which through taming and training gradually becomes white:

> The underlying idea is that the mind, which is naturally pure, is polluted by extraneous impurities and that it could and should be cleansed through discipline and meditation.
>
> There are in the *Aṅguttara-nikāya* (Ang. I (PTS), p. 10) two very important and essential *suttas* which serve as an index to the concept of the black ox gradually becoming white. One *sutta* says: *Pabhassaram idam bhikkhave attam, tañ ca kho agantukehi upakkilesehi upakkilittham.* ("Bhikkhus, this mind is luminous and it is defiled by adventitious defilements.") The other one says: *Pabhassaram idam bhikkhave attam, tañ ca kho agantukehi upakkilesehi vippamuttam.* ("Bhikkhus, this mind is luminous and it is freed from adventitious defilements.")[24]

That is, there is a Theravada scriptural basis for Buddhadāsa's view that the mind is originally pure and only "adventitiously" or incidentally clouded and so not fundamentally defiled. Rahula Walpola also notes that the Pali term *pabhassara* is found in its Sanskrit form, *prabhaśvara*, in the important Zen text, the *Laṅkavatara Sutra*, where mind is described as *prakṛti-prabhaśvara*, "luminous by nature," a description which is paired with *prakṛti-pariśuddhi*, "pure by nature." Thus, in addition to having a basis in the Theravada canon, Buddhadāsa's view that mind is originally pure also bears some relation to the Zen view. But despite these scriptural precedents for Buddhadāsa's interpretation of *chit wang* as denoting *pabhassara* or the Zen "true original mind," it is nevertheless still the case that *chit wang* is an incomplete rendering of the Zen notion of Mind. As Blofeld notes:

> Zen adepts, like their fellow Mahayanists, take *anatman* to imply, "no entity to be termed an ego," nought but the One Mind, which comprises all things and gives them their reality.[25]

Buddhadāsa's interpretation of *anattā* as *chit wang*, or the absence of the self-centredness of "I"–"mine," catches the Zen emphasis on the absence of ego as a psychological function but not the Zen view of one mind as ultimate reality. Buddhadāsa nowhere talks in terms of entities or of the mind or "Mind" as a basis of reality.

The spiritual goal of Zen is identification with the "void" or the One Mind, as expressed in the following excerpt from a Vietnamese Zen manual for which Buddhadāsa has significant regard:

> People normally cut reality into sections and divide it into compartments, and so are unable to see the interdependence of all phenomena. To see one in all and all in one is to break through the great barrier which Buddhism calls the attachment to the false view of self. . . . We are life and life without limits. . . . If our lives have no limits, the assembly of the five aggregates (*khandhas*) which makes up ourselves also has no limits. The impermanent character of the universe, the success and failures of life can no longer manipulate us. Having seen the reality of interdependence and penetrated deeply into its reality, nothing can oppress you any longer.[26]

This emphasis on loss of self through identification with One Mind is absent from Theravada, and from Buddhadāsa's writings. Buddhadāsa defines *anattā* as the absence of the defiling or immoral quality of self-centredness, and he mistakenly represents this as being the central teaching of Zen:

> The Chinese Buddhist Sect of Zen teaches us to live without needing to have a self . . . to eat without there needing to be an eater, to work without there needing to be a doer. That is, to have a mind suffused with wisdom.(T)[27]

In the introduction to his Thai translation of the work of the Zen master Huang Po, Buddhadāsa uncritically mentions the ontological Zen view of One Mind: "All beings are the same thing as that which is One Mind, or is the Buddha."(T)[28] But he does not present this interpretation in any other of his writings, and even in the same passage from which the above statement is taken he shifts from Zen's ontological view to his own Theravada-based, psychological and moral interpretation of One Mind as being equivalent to *suññatā*, and thus to *chit wang*: "One Mind has a meaning equivalent to being freed from all distracting things."(T)[29]

When further explaining Huang Po's ideas Buddhadāsa says that before birth, "One Mind already exists: no-one knows how long it has been in existence."(T)[30] Huang Po means by this that One Mind is the pre-existing ground of all being, while it must be recalled that for Buddhadāsa "birth" means the arising of the self-centred sense of "I"–"mine" or of ego-centredness, a psychological rather than a metaphysical phenomenon. Thus in terms of *phasa tham* to say that One Mind exists before "birth" is, in contradistinction with the Zen view, simply to say that *chit wang* is the mental state which pre-exists the arising of self-centred defilements.

There is a further significant difference between Theravada and Zen in their respective accounts of enlightenment, *nibbāna* and *satori*. Buddhadāsa implies that both Theravada and Zen aim for the same goal. However, not all Theravada scholars agree that the spiritual goals of the two traditions are in fact identical. After a study of the respective scriptural descriptions of *satori* and *nibbāna*, a Sri Lankan scholar monk, Bhikkhu Ananda, concludes that

> though the description of one who has attained *satori* and *nirvāṇa* may seem similar, yet, however, the attributes belonging to one who has attained *nirvāṇa* are never heard of nor mentioned of the person who has attained *satori* in Zen.[31]

Differences arise from the ways in which Zen and Theravada adepts, respectively, attain their ideal states. *Nibbana* is something attained through individual moral and meditative practice while, ideally, the Zen enlightenment or *satori* is regarded as a special transmission from the mind of the teacher to the mind of the aspirant. Unlike in Theravada, a teacher is therefore essential in Zen not only for instruction in meditation practices but also for the actual attainment of enlightenment. The Zen teaching that this mind-to-mind enlightenment is sudden also differs from the Theravada emphasis on meditation as leading one gradually closer and closer to *nibbāna*. Suzuki says of Zen: "That the process of enlightenment is abrupt means that there is a leap, logical and psychological, in the Buddhist experience."[32] This is completely at odds with Buddhadāsa's interpretation of *chit wang*, and *nibbāna*, as being continuous with and developing out of everyday experiences of mental calm.

Thus while Buddhadāsa often refers to Zen teachings, claiming them to be compatible with if not identical to Theravada doctrine, the view of Zen he presents is heavily coloured by Theravada notions. In fact, Buddhadāsa's misinterpretation of the Zen notion of One Mind shows that, contrary to Kittiwuttho's claim, he is not an apostate to Theravada Buddhism. Buddhadāsa misinterprets Zen notions precisely because he keeps to Theravada's non-ontological principles. Kittiwuttho's criticism is misplaced, for while Buddhadāsa's emphasis on *chit wang* and *suññatā* has its source in Zen, his actual interpretation of *chit wang* in fact remains strictly within the bounds of Theravada orthodoxy. Buddhadāsa nowhere introduces the ontological import of the Zen notions of *śunyatā* and One Mind.

Rather than actually introducing Zen ideas into Theravada Buddhism, Buddhadāsa has instead used Zen terms and Zen-like arguments to justify a shift of emphasis within Theravada doctrine. While he tends to use language which has a strong Zen flavour, he does not reject or replace any Theravada position with its opposed Zen view. Instead of introducing actual Mahayana or Zen notions into Theravada Buddhism, Buddhadāsa draws on Zen to create a new terminology to differentiate his particular interpretative emphasis from the traditionally accepted versions of Theravada teaching in Thailand. This borrowing of Zen terms and idioms gives Buddhadāsa's work a Zen-like appearance while also obscuring the fact that his interpretations of *chit wang*, *suññatā*, and *nibbāna* are in fact continuous with Theravada tradition rather than being a "heretical" acceptance of Mahayana teachings as claimed by his critics.

## BUDDHADĀSA'S MANAGEMENT OF ZEN SCRIPTURES

Buddhadāsa's "sanitization" of Zen in order to make it fit better with his version of Theravada extends beyond subtly eliding the ontological implications of terms such as One Mind and *śunyatā*, and avoiding discussing the differences between *satori* and *nibbāna*. In translating Blofeld's book on Hui Neng into Thai, Buddhadāsa also omits some sections which show Zen criticisms of Theravada doctrines. For example, while including most of Blofeld's footnotes in his own translation, Buddhadāsa leaves out the following note on the term *srāvaka*, found on page 39 of the English translation:

> Huang Po sometimes stretches this term to imply Hinayanists [i.e., Theravadins] in general . . . . Huang Po implies that Hinayanists pay too much attention to the literal meaning of the scriptures, instead of seeking intuitive knowledge through eliminating conceptual thought.[33]

Buddhadāsa also omits large sections of the second part of Blofeld's translation called "The Wan Ling Record of the Zen Master Huang Po (Tuan Chi)." Section 37 of the Wan Ling Record in Blofeld's English version contains the warning: "If you accept the doctrine of *anatman* [Pali: *anattā*] the concept '*anatman*' may land you among the Theravadins."[34] This is a Zen criticism of the Theravadins' purported attachment to intellectualisms and to the precise linguistic meaning of the term "non-self," rather than attempting to go beyond the intellectual polarities of whether there is or is not a self in order to penetrate to transcendent truth itself.

It is not immediately clear why Buddhadāsa should manage his sources in order to artificially create an appearance of compatibility between Zen and Theravada doctrine. It is also unclear why he overlooks the ontological assumptions underpinning the Zen and Mahayana teachings on One Mind when he is in contrast so critical of the ontological beliefs in spirits, demons, and heavens of his fellow Thai Buddhists. These inaccuracies, confusions, and the straightforward avoidance of troublesome aspects of the Zen scriptures may, however, result from religio-political constraints. It is clear that Buddhadāsa sees much in Zen that he feels is both of value to Thai Buddhism and compatible with Theravada principles. However, in the purist and intellectually xenophobic atmosphere of the Thai Sangha he perhaps feels it necessary to justify his enthusiasm for Zen by maintaining that there is an absolute identity between Theravada and the Japanese school. Because his view of Buddhism is clearly unconventional within the conservative Theravada tradition in Thailand, Buddhadāsa seeks to avoid portraying himself as an innovator and as a doctrinal renegade by constantly putting forward precedents for his ideas. Nevertheless, that the precedents Buddhadāåsa draws on must in several cases be taken from outside Theravada (in the Zen and Mahayana traditions) indicates the actual innovativeness and unconventionality of his ideas. In the face of the novelty of his views on Theravada doctrine and the often intransigent conservatism of his critics, and of the Thai Sangha hierarchy, Buddhadāsa takes the extreme position of identifying his central notion of *chit wang* with Zen ideas of One Mind and *śunyatā*, even though this requires a stretching and management of the Zen sources. Any admission of inconsistencies or incompatibilities between Zen and Theravada might be seen by Buddhadāsa as providing his conservative critics a theoretical stick with which to beat him. Buddhadāsa may fear that any self-admitted chink in the armour of his arguments might be used to pull down the entire edifice of his reformist enterprise.

However, the sources of the inconsistencies in Buddhadāsa's use and treatment of Zen materials and notions remain speculative. But given the intellectual ardour and capability systematically expressed in Buddhadāsa's work, I am reluctant to attribute the various inconsistencies noted above to either a simple intellectual slip or to deliberate duplicity. I am more inclined to the view that the inadequacies in his treatment of Zen result from religio-political pressures to maintain an appearance of absolute conformity to Theravada principles and traditions.

## SALVATION HERE AND NOW— THE ZEN INFLUENCE ON BUDDHADĀSA

While the version of Zen described by Buddhadāsa as important for modernist Thais to know and appreciate is a particularly Theravada interpretation, there is no denying the significant influence of various aspects of Zen doctrine on his work. It is not only terminology and literary styles that Buddhadāsa has borrowed but also aspects of the ethic or approach of Zen to the quest for enlightenment. Buddhadāsa finds a soulmate in such Zen authors as Suzuki, who writes: "Zen disregards conventionalism, ritualism, institutionalism, in fact anything that is binding and restricting."[35] He finds in Zen a kind of Buddhism with the common goal of cutting through the encumbrances of past interpretations of the scriptures by returning to the practical core of the religion.

There are also specific emphases of interpretation borrowed from Zen without which Buddhadāsa would not have been able to develop his radical, modernist interpretation of Theravada. For example, the doctrine that *chit wang* is the fundamental mental state (as already seen, an idea borrowed, with variations, from the Zen teaching of One Mind) has important implications regarding whether human existence on earth is seen as essentially involving suffering or as only conditionally inadequate, and so potentially subject to amelioration and betterment. Traditional Theravada teachings equate material existence with being caught in *saṁsāra*, the cycle of rebirth and suffering, and maintain that the mere association of mind or *nāma* with the physical or bodily factors of existence, *rūpa*, is the compounded state of existence of *saṅkhāra*, which the Buddha taught underlay all suffering. It is a necessary conclusion of this interpretation that the mind can never be totally free of defilements or the causes of suffering so long as it is associated with the material factors of the body. Mere association with the material world is regarded as a defiling experience. In criticizing Buddhadāsa, Anan Senakhan summarizes this traditional interpretation as follows:

> Insofar as *nāmarūpa* [the compound of mind and body factors] yet remain, there must be compounding (*saṅkhāra*) and when there is compounding it is *vaṭṭasaṁsāra* . . . When there is *nāmarūpa* there must be arising and passing away. When there is arising and passing away that itself means there is *vaṭṭasaṁsāra*. Where there is *vaṭṭasaṁsāra* there cannot be *nibbāna* because *nibbāna* is devoid of *nāmarūpa*, devoid of compounding, it is *asaṅkhatadhamma* [unconditioned]. (T)[36]

The compounding of *nāma* and *rūpa* (that is, of mental factors and materiality) is traditionally regarded as leading to the cycle of birth and death, becoming and unbecoming, which in turn is regarded as leading to suffering. And so according to this traditional view, any compounded state (that is, any embodied state) cannot attain *nibbāna* because embodiment necessarily entails the suffering which is the antithesis of *nibbāna*. Buddhadāsa disagrees completely with this traditional view. For him, *saṅkhāra* or compounding is not essentially the relation of body to mind but rather is the purely psychological attachment of volition and consciousness to the objects of desire. Buddhadāsa conceives of compounding as the association of consciousness with cravings which grow from delusion and ignorance. In *phasa tham, vaṭṭasaṁsāra* is consequently interpreted as the psychological cycle of suffering resulting from the arising or "birth" of the deluded outlook of ego-centredness, "I"–"mine." Buddhadāsa maintains that "At whatever moment the mind is not compounded with 'I'–'mine' there is no *vaṭṭa-saṁsāra*."(T)[37] In *phasa tham*, *vaṭṭtasaṁsāra* is not an ontological condition, as it is for Anan, but a psychological state which is not fundamentally characteristic of human mental life but rather only arises periodically, when delusion and desire compound with consciousness:

> Whenever the mind has compounding [*saṅkhāra*] boiling and gushing up it is *vaṭṭasaṁsāra*. Whenever there is no compounding and the mind remains in original peace it is *nibbāna*.(T)[38]

Rajavaramuni also considers the problem of material existence and suffering, and offers an interpretation similar to Buddhadāsa's. He notes that if the mind is still pervaded by *kilesa* then the process of perception will be "tainted." Perceptual consciousness or *saññā* tainted with the defilements of attachment and ignorance is an obstacle to salvation from suffering because, being imbued with ignorance, it cannot attain the clear and objective perception of reality as transient and non-essential which is necessary for salvation. Rajavaramuni calls this defilement-tainted consciousness *papañcasaññā* or *kilesasaññā*, which is, "*saññā* (perception) that arises from *kilesa* or is combined with *kilesa*."(T)[39] Rajavaramuni also observes that it is this *kilesa*-infected knowledge or delusion, *moha*, which is the energy of *saṁsāravaṭṭa*, the cycle of suffering as detailed in the *paṭiccasamupāda*. But he maintains the process of perception does not intrinsically produce deluded awareness or necessarily lead to suffering, for: "*Arahants* yet have *saññā* but it is a *saññā* that is devoid of *āsava*. That is, it is free from *kilesa*."(T)[40] When *kilesa* are absent perception is called *kusalasaññā* or "wholesome perception," and this is said to lead to the process of *vivaṭṭa* or the opposite of *saṁsāravaṭṭa*, that is, the process of the ending of suffering. And Rajavaramuni describes *vivaṭṭa* as taking place within the scope of the liberated life here on earth, in opposition to the traditionalist claim that life is equivalent to *saṁsāra* or suffering.

Boyd also presents an interpretation similar to Buddhadāsa's, arguing against the traditional view as put forward by Anan Senakhan. Boyd notes that the Buddha explicitly denied the teaching that *nibbāna* was annihilation. Consequently, if *nibbāna* is the end of *saṁsāra*, and thus the end of suffering, but it is not physical annihilation, then the ending of *saṁsāra* cannot be equivalent to annihilation or death, which is implied in traditional Theravada views that define life as inextricably permeated by suffering and the web of *saṁsāra*. Using this argument Boyd then says, in terms very similar to Buddhadāsa, that notions such as rebirth, becoming, ageing and dying, as they occur in the *paṭiccasamupāda*, "can refer as much to the rise and fall of sensations-with-attachment (*saṁsāra*) as they do to physical failure or death."[41]

But while Buddhadāsa's view of the relations between *saṁsāra* and *nibbāna* can be argued to be strictly in accord with Theravada principles, he nevertheless supports it by referring to the Zen view on *saṁsāra*. Following the Zen idiom, Buddhadāsa claims that *nibbāna* or salvation exists in the condition of *saṁsāra*, or the cycle of rebirth and suffering.[42]

Blofeld notes that Zen scholars have criticized the traditionalist Theravadins as being "dualistic in that they seek to overcome their *saṁsāric* life in order to attain *nibbāna*; while Zen perceives that *saṁsāra* is none other than *nibbāna*."[43]

Rupp notes that this charge of dualism derives from the fact that

> Whereas for the Theravadins the fundamental motif in the interpretation of the relation between *nirvāṇa* and *saṁsāra* has been that of contrast, the Mahayanist has typically expressed the conviction that they are ultimately identical.[44]

But despite drawing on Zen notions of the identity of *saṁsāra* and *nibbāna* and using Zen-styled rhetoric, Buddhadāsa nevertheless still retains the traditional Theravada duality of *saṁsāra* and *nibbāna*. He emphasizes that both *vaṭṭtasaṁsāra* and *nibbāna* exist in this life here on earth but he does not claim, as does Zen, that both are paradoxically simultaneously present, that is, that *saṁsāra* is *nibbāna*. While both *saṁsāra* and *nibbāna* are psychological states for Buddhadāsa, they do not both paradoxically exist together. For Buddhadāsa, *saṁsāra* or the delusions of "I"–"mine" still exclude *nibbāna*. He does not borrow the Zen notion of the mystical union of opposites. When Buddhadāsa says that *nibbāna* exists in *saṁsāra* he in fact means that what he takes as *nibbāna* exists in what other Theravadins mistakenly believe to be characteristically *saṁsāra* or suffering, that is, human existence here on earth. This is a further instance of Buddhadāsa's use of Zen-like language to describe and justify Theravada or reinterpreted Theravada notions.

Yet while Buddhadāsa does not, like Zen teachers, paradoxically identify *saṁsāra* with *nibbāna*, he does maintain that even in *saṁsāra*, or the worldly state of compounding and suffering, the mind still remains fundamentally pure, or *chit wang*. In contradistinction to the traditional Theravada view, the notion of *chit wang* presents a picture of human beings as fundamentally good and as having in themselves all the qualities required for attaining their own liberation in this life. In the traditional view ordinary humans are fundamentally flawed by their *kilesa* and so are morally inferior to those greater spiritual beings, the Theravada saints, who are regarded as having purified their minds of the defilements which still compound the mental states of the average person. By his reforms Buddhadāsa has introduced into Theravada what Rupp has described as the strength of Mahayanist teachings:

> Its [Mahayana Buddhism's] insistence that *nirvāṇa* and *saṁsāra* are ultimately one constitutes an at least potentially positive valuation of the whole of being. Hence the concern of the Mahayana Buddhist is with all of reality. All beings participate in the Buddha-nature (One Mind); all are already ingredient in *nirvāṇa*.[45]

That is, Buddhadāsa has imbued Theravada Buddhism with something of the universal spirit of Mahayana while not actually introducing the notions of One Mind, Buddha-nature, and other ontological elements of Mahayana teaching. In endowing each person with spiritual perfection, *chit wang*, as their basic character, Buddhadāsa also endows each Buddhist individual with the potential authority to govern their own spiritual lives and to strive for the ultimate salvation of *nibbāna*. His effort to abolish the spiritual distinction between monks and laity by opening up *nibbāna* to all thus has a distinctly Mahayana character, paralleling the Mahayana emphasis on the universal potentiality of all human beings to attain salvation.

At the same time, Buddhadāsa retains what Rupp views as the strength of the Theravada view, which derives from the retention of the distinction between *nibbāna* and *saṁsāra*. Rupp says that in Theravada Buddhism

> the religious task entails a straightforward confrontation with moral limitations and a concerted effort to overcome them—an effort, that is, to change the existing state of affairs. The result is a conception of

*nirvāṇa* which emphasises differences and consequently the need for changes in the prevailing patterns of phenomenal existence or *saṁsāra*.[46]

In other words, at an ideological level Buddhadāsa's interpretation of Theravada provides a basis for action in the world, for change and development, and for notions of universal access to the benefits of such actions and changes. Buddhadāsa overcomes some basic ideological limitations of both traditional Mahayana and Theravada teachings, when viewed in the contemporary context. His views counter Mahayana Buddhism's undermining of the need for action or change which flows from the teaching that *nirvāṇa* is already present in every *saṁsāric* or worldly condition, no matter how much it is imbued with suffering. And he also opposes Theravada Buddhism's elitist view of who is capable and deserving of attaining *nibbāna*.

## ZEN AND SOCIAL ACTION— THE INFLUENCE ON BUDDHADĀSA

The ideas and emphases adopted from Zen are important to Buddhadāsa's system of thought because in the Theravada and Thai contexts they reinforce and support the ideological shift effected by the introduction of pivotal notions such as *chit wang* and the interpretative theory of *phasa khon–phasa tham*. It is significant that the interpretation of Zen which seems to have most influenced Buddhadāsa is contained in a Vietnamese book whose author's explicit intention was to develop a Zen Buddhist foundation for social activism in what was then South Vietnam. The book, *The Miracle of Being Awake—A Manual on Meditation for the Use of Young Activists* by Thich Nhat Hanh, was originally written in Vietnamese for the author's friends in the South Vietnamese Schools of Youth for Social Service. In a description of the time, it is said these schools were composed mostly of "young Buddhists who have left the more comfortable life in the cities to share the difficulties of the peasants and refugees in the countryside."[47]

The goal of these young Buddhists was to improve the life and situation of the South Vietnamese peasants by following an ideology which was neither communist nor capitalist but Buddhist. For political reasons Thich Nhat Hanh's book was not published in South Vietnam and in fact was first published in translation, both in Thai and English,[48] and subsequently became very popular in Thailand. The significance of the book for Buddhadāsa, and his association with its Thai publishers, can be gauged from the following quote from the preface to the 1976 English version, printed in Thailand:

> On the 27th May, Ven. Buddhadāsa *Bhikkhu*, the most learned monk in Siam, will complete his 70th birthday anniversary. On the same day Mrs. Nilchawee Sivaraksa[49] will observe her 40th birthday. As she has a great regard for the Mahathera, she has ordered a number of copies of "The Miracle of Being Awake," which has been very much admired by the venerable *bhikkhu,* to be especially presented to him.[50]

Buddhadāsa's emphasis on mindfulness as the practice of *chit wang* and on *chit wang* as underlying productive and fruitful work is closely paralleled in "The Miracle of Being Awake." After asking how a worker can practise mindfulness all day and yet do all "that needs to be done to change and to build an alternative society,"[51] the author answers himself by saying that

> There is no reason why mindfulness should be different from focusing all one's attention on one's work, to be alert and to be using one's best judgement.[52]

Buddhadāsa's integration of both *samādhi* and *vipassanā* techniques of meditation and his dual account of *chit wang* as both the original mental state and as the practice to reattain it can also be seen to be related to the following description of mindfulness as being

> at the same time a means and an end, at the same time the seed and

> the fruit. When we practise mindfulness in order to build up concentration, mindfulness is a seed. But mindfulness is the life of awareness . . . and therefore mindfulness is also the fruit.[53]

While it is clear that Zen teachings have significantly influenced Buddhadāsa's views, his whole system cannot be explained by referring only to this influence. The ideas Buddhadāsa has borrowed from Zen all fit into the pattern of his reformist ideology, and they all buttress his attempts to develop a modernist interpretation of Buddhism in line with the principles outlined in chapter 2. There is a convenient parallelism between Zen teachings and the modernist, socially relevant reading of Theravada that Buddhadāsa aims for. However, it is always Theravada rather than Zen that stands paramount in Buddhadāsa's mind and this is shown most clearly by the fact that when there are discrepancies between Zen and Theravada, as is inevitably the case, it is always Zen that gives way to Theravada teachings and not the converse.

# 8 BUDDHADĀSA ON MODERNIZATION AND DEVELOPMENT

BUDDHADĀSA'S IMPORTANCE in Thailand is not limited to his reinterpretation of Buddhist doctrines of salvation or to his having laid the theoretical groundwork for a world-involved and socially involved Buddhism. For his supporters among modernist Thai Buddhists, Buddhadāsa's statements on socioeconomic development and on politics, which are developed from the theoretical foundations of his doctrinal reinterpretations, are equally important. It is Buddhadāsa's explicit statements on contemporary social and political issues which have given his work sociological as well as doctrinal and religious significance in Thailand. But while his social philosophy is socially significant, it is nevertheless marked by certain theoretical tensions. These tensions do not result from simple theoretical slips or lapses but rather arise from the way in which Buddhadāsa has carried out his modernizing reform of Thai Buddhist doctrine. The contradictions arise from his championing of a world-involved and socially relevant interpretation of Buddhist teachings while still maintaining strict conservatism in the area of clerical practice. That is, there are inconsistencies between Buddhadāsa's strict orthopraxy, which gives religious authority to his reinterpretations, and his actual reinterpretations of doctrine.

## BUDDHADĀSA'S QUALIFIED SUPPORT FOR SOCIOECONOMIC DEVELOPMENT

Buddhadāsa has contributed to debate on the role of Buddhism in Thailand's socioeconomic development by presenting arguments supporting material development, provided such development remains tied to clearly specified religious goals. Buddhadāsa has based his suggestions for a Buddhist approach to national development on general arguments such as the following, where he links notions of evolution and progress with his interpretation of the Buddhist world view:

> According to the law of evolution as put forward by contemporary sciences like biology and, in particular, Darwinism; as expressed by Buddhism in the law of the twenty-four kinds of causal relations[1] and the *paṭiccasamuppāda*; and finally as can easily and generally be observed, this world gradually advances towards higher and higher levels—if not materially then of necessity mentally. Stagnation and decline are not found . . . . All this shows that the internal instincts [of living things] together with all the external, surrounding promoting factors only pull things towards increasing betterment, because such is the inherent desire of all living things.(T)[2]

However, when he turns to speak of progress in the social rather than the natural sphere, Buddhadāsa maintains that development is no longer inevitable but is dependent upon a conscious integration of both material and spiritual values in human work. Buddhadāsa acknowledges that single-minded material and spiritual activity are respectively capable of effecting progress in their own spheres:

> Whenever we are strongly inclined towards the material side of things we reach the end point of material development, an example being the rapid advances of contemporary science. And whenever the world is collectively inclined towards the mental side of things we will reach the end point of mental development just as in the ancient period of the *arahants*.(T)[3]

However, he maintains that whatever material developments modern science may produce, working on only the material or physical level of activity cannot of itself lead to mental or spiritual development. And Buddhadāsa regards the political conflicts and social tensions of the modern world, arising according to him from moral laxity, as showing that: "Solving problems materially is inadequate; problems must be solved mentally as well."(T)[4]

But Buddhadāsa also claims that a purely mental or spiritual approach to social problems and to the issue of development is equally inadequate, saying that: "In fact it is impossible for us to live by either mind or matter alone. Development has both."(T)[5] Nevertheless, he still regards spiritual factors as having the greatest importance and as being the main determinants of attaining successful or problem-free development: "It must be the correct and important things that lead. For example, the mental, the intellectual, the spiritual should lead the material."(T)[6]

By way of example of what he regards as a correct approach to development, Buddhadāsa offers Japan, home of Zen, as evidence for the productive power of social activity informed by the spiritual condition of "freed-mind" or *chit wang* to provide a basis for all-round welfare:

> Japan took the path of mental instead of material development and now Japan's material development has progressed to the point that the foreigners [i.e. Europeans and Americans] are afraid of the birthplace of that mental development. Japan has a high level of mental development . . . it is in everyday life, in the very culture, that is, the kind of Buddhism we call Zen.(T)[7]

Significantly, Buddhadāsa regards Zen-influenced mental development as promoting qualities such as resoluteness, industriousness, vigour in work and forbearance as well as politeness and gentleness —which together could be considered a manager's checklist of the attributes of an efficient worker. In other words, Buddhadāsa would like to see a Zen-styled mental culture promoted in Thailand in order to promote the kinds of qualities which would lead to Thai workers becoming more efficient agents of material development. This reveals another side to Buddhadāsa's interest in ending the distinction between the layperson's and the monk's religious paths. He regards the qualities acquired by laypersons through meditation and strict spiritual practice as not only permitting them to reach *nibbāna* but as also enabling them to work more efficiently at the material level. For Buddhadāsa, working with *chit wang* or a "freed-mind" not only frees one from suffering but also helps to achieve better material results. This allows him to say: "Developing the mind according to Dhamma or by following the correct worldly way amount to the same thing."(T)[8] That is, provided people act morally Buddhadāsa does not distinguish between either material or mental development, seeing both as necessarily following from abiding by Dhamma and developing *chit wang*.

Because of the importance placed on spiritual practice in his view of development, Buddhadāsa is a strong critic of the present approach to development in Thailand, which he regards as being too one-sidedly materialist:

> We have been born in a primitive, underdeveloped country, although that is in fact only true of the minority. But we follow the backsides of countries which are developed or run after materialism. We are people who are able to become *paccekabuddhas*, but we don't want to. We still run after the tail end of the progress of those who are materially developed. Why do we worship the material side of development? . . . . It is more, more, more, because we don't know . . . that it is dangerous to humanity.(T)[9]

By materialism Buddhadāsa means the psychological or spiritual domination of the mind by desires for material objects and physical pleasures. Buddhism teaches detachment from the objects of the material world and defines *nibbāna* as a condition which is unaffected by suffering because it is totally independent of the impermanent things of the world. Thus, when he criticizes development in Thailand as being overly materialist, Buddhadāsa means that it is being gone about with a mental attitude of attachment and in such a way that it promotes further attachment to material things, which in turn leads to suffering among those who participate in such development. According to Buddhadāsa, confusion and social disorder result from undertaking development with an immoral attitude of craving or attachment to material results:

> The world now aims only for material development because of cowardice and the fear of not keeping up with "Them," of not having the equipment to fight "Them" or to live well . . . . Consequently, the whole world is in a state of disorganization and confusion. There are complicated problems without end which have arisen from moral degeneration.(T)[10]

Moral degeneration here means attachment and the self-centeredness of "I"–"mine," which Buddhadāsa regards as the root causes of the confusion and lack of peace in the world.

The notion of peace or *santi* is central to Buddhist doctrine because the spiritual goal of *nibbāna* is conceived of as being the stilling and extinction of confused attachment and its concomitant suffering. As Chinda Chandrkaew observes,

> peace is the intrinsic value about which all others move. Hence it is stated that there is no bliss higher than peace (*Dhammapāda* verse 202), which itself here means the attainment of *nibbāna*.[11]

Buddhadāsa maintains that "Nature wants there to be peace. If there isn't peace there will be destruction and ruin."(T)[12] The nature spoken of here is the cosmic-moral order of Dhamma, and the destruction and ruin is consequent upon the factionalism and conflict which arise from self-centred attachment and greed. "Keeping the peace" is a strong value in Thai culture, where it is most commonly expressed as an aversion to *wun-wai* (วุ่นวาย), or confusion and disorder, which are believed to lead to instability and anarchy. Morell and Samudavanija comment that:

> The proper [Thai] behavioural mode is to be quiet, calm and submissive. In contrast, *wun-wai* and its confusion upset peace and order in society, the most un-Thai action of all.[13]

Buddhadāsa thus approves of the material benefits of socioeconomic development but not the cultural and social costs of the associated loss of spiritual values.

## BUDDHADĀSA'S INTEGRATED THEORY OF ACTION

It was noted in chapter 2 that many of Buddhadāsa's supporters among progressive, educated Thai Buddhists seek in Buddhism an independent and indigenous ideology of development—a set of intrinsically Thai guidelines for the overall progress of the country. Buddhadāsa and his lay audience desire Buddhist doctrine to be a theoretically consistent unity. Thus if Buddhism is to fulfil an ideological role supportive of socioeconomic development then the religion's teachings must be interpreted in such a way that material activity in the social world is integrated with and seen to develop from the fundamental principles of doctrine. Because progressive Buddhists repudiate the traditional lay forms of Buddhism as superstitiously concerned with merit and rebirth, it is not sufficient that notions of modernization or development be interpreted simply in terms of the historically given lay aspect of the religion. Rather, material social activity must be integrated with the doctrinal core of the religion, i.e. with the attainment of ultimate peace or *nibbāna*. While not posing this problem explicitly, Buddhadāsa nevertheless provides the foundation of an integrated Buddhist interpretation of action. For example, he implies that socioeconomic development and social justice are essential for spiritual attainment and thus for salvation. In the context of discussing the injustices of the contemporary capitalist approach to socioeconomic development in Thailand, Buddhadāsa says: "If the political system in the world is not good (in promoting justice and development) the people of this world will not have the hope of attaining *paramadhamma* [ultimate *nibbāna*]."(T)[14] He equates the social injustices of capitalism with immorality and materialism:

> If in any country there are still people . . . in need it must mean that there is not equality in that society. As a consequence, disorganiza-

> tion of many kinds and varieties will necessarily arise; as, for example, conflicts in the country, the breaking up of social harmony, insurrection, changes in the system of government, changes in the economic system to socialism or communism. Because when the poor can bear their situation no more they tend to look for a way to destroy the extremely selfish wealthy people with no regard for anything at all. And many other kinds of disruption then follow, such as making war and killing each other. (T)[15]

Thus Buddhadāsa thinks that in unjust societies where the rich selfishly hoard social wealth the poor have no opportunity for spiritual attainment because of the unbearable nature of their worldly existence. And the disorder and confusion which result from the poor rebelling against social injustice and inequality only make the spiritual peace of *nibbāna* an even more remote and unattainable goal. Morally guided social activity for overcoming what Buddhadāsa regards as the related problems of poverty and social injustice is consequently a prerequisite for making spiritual attainment or *nibbāna* a universally accessible goal.

Buddhadāsa's emphasis on work, which he takes as meaning "That which human beings must do, both physically and spiritually, for both physical and spiritual results,"(T)[16] provides a further basis in his doctrinal reinterpretations for an integrated theory of action. He implies that work is essential to spiritual attainment when he says that in regard to learning about the path to *nibbāna*, "work itself is the best teacher."(T)[17]

However, there are theoretical difficulties associated with integrating the doctrine of transcendent salvation with any notion of material activity and in making both spiritual and worldly activity part of the same fundamental effort for salvation. Wit summarizes the difficulty when he says that the core of Theravada doctrine has traditionally involved:

> a belief in the virtue of non-involvement in the struggles of society. Man's physical labour or the application of human intelligence to the solution of worldly problems is not eulogised or even considered [by the religious] to be the means to a better life . . . . Neither individual

nor collective economic, social or political action is suggested as the appropriate means of improving man's lot.[18]

Buddhadāsa deals with this difficulty by no longer conceiving of *nibbāna* solely as an individual spiritual goal but also as a social goal whose realization necessitates social action as well as personal spiritual practice. In contrast to the traditional Theravada view that *nibbāna* is only accessible to world-renouncing monks, Buddhadāsa regards Buddhist salvation to be open to all, lay and monk. At the level of individual salvation Buddhadāsa retains the traditional teaching that *nibbāna*, as a condition which is independent of all changing things, is attainable no matter what one's material circumstances. However, at the social level he maintains that a supportive social order is a necessary prerequisite for every person to in fact have the opportunity to work for and attain *nibbāna*.

Buddhadāsa denies the traditional view of spiritual practice in which aiming to attain *nibbāna* necessitates retreating from social involvement to the monastery or forest hermitage. When, as in the traditional Buddhist view of salvation, the quest for *nibbāna* is limited to a small elite, equating the attainment of salvation with detachment from social involvement does not pose any great difficulty. But when *nibbāna* is regarded as a universally accessible ideal it is clearly impossible to equate the quest for salvation with retreatism. It is impossible for every member of society to avoid or retreat from mundane distractions without social order collapsing, and so for Buddhadāsa *nibbāna* must be defined as a goal attainable within the social sphere. And given that the ability of a layperson to work for *nibbāna* is dependent upon a supportive social order, such as having sufficient wealth and free time to be able to practise meditation or study Buddhist teachings, salvation in Buddhadāsa's system consequently becomes conditional upon the state of the social world. For when retreating from social involvement is no longer an acceptable path to *nibbāna*, and when injustice and inequality inhibit some people's ability to work for that spiritual goal, then removing those inhibiting social factors is essential if *nibbāna* is in fact to be a universally relevant and accessible goal.

While the realization of *nibbāna* as a universally accessible social goal is dependent upon a relatively prosperous and just social order, Buddhadāsa does not repudiate the traditional teaching that any given individual can always strive for and attain *nibbāna* whatever his or her social circumstances. An individual whose circumstances inhibit his or her ability to undertake spiritual practices and strive for *nibbāna* always has the option of renouncing social involvement and becoming a monk or recluse. Buddhadāsa consequently does not contradict the teaching that *nibbāna*, as a condition of personal salvation, is independent of all changing phenomena. It is only as a social ideal that the attainment of *nibbāna* is dependent upon the realization of a supportive social order. Similarly, it is only as a social ideal that the attainment of *nibbāna* necessarily implies action in the world to better society; the personal attainment of *nibbāna*, as in traditional Buddhism, necessitates no social involvement whatsoever, and in Buddhadāsa's system remains a condition attainable totally outside of society. That is, the path to *nibbāna*, as an individual state of salvation, in theory remains independent of one's material circumstances. But *nibbāna*, as the universally relevant social goal Buddhadāsa defines it as, cannot be realized without a just and equitable social order.

Buddhadāsa's emphasis on the relation between social order and justice and the opportunity for spiritual attainment has a well-established precedent in the Theravada notion of the *cakkavattin* or righteous monarch. The traditional Thai view of the *cakkavattin* is presented in the *Traibhumikatha*, and Andaya notes that in this text:

> The legendary Buddhist king, Dharmaśokaraja, is cited as the ideal example of a *cakravartin* who practised meritorious works and eased the lot of his people so that they could devote more time to spiritual matters.[19]

That is, there is an explicit recognition in the Buddhist tradition of the importance of social order to the general populace's spiritual welfare, and on this point Tambiah makes the relevant observation that

> From early times Buddhism has been positively related to a conception of an ideal politico-social order, whose cornerstone was a righteous monarch who would promote a prosperous society and religion. This Buddhist conception of a moral polity readily fits with a formulation that only a materially prosperous society can be ready for the pursuit of spiritual concerns; it also fits equally with a political ideology of benevolent absolutism combined with welfare socialism.[20]

However, the welfare of the populace has traditionally been regarded in terms of their following the lay or *lokiya* path. In contrast, Buddhadāsa integrates the social welfare tradition of Buddhist political teachings with the formerly monastic ideal of attaining *nibbāna*. According to Buddhadāsa, a social order should not only promote the moral welfare of the populace, it should also meet the much more exacting criterion of contributing to the actual spiritual salvation of the populace.

## BUDDHADĀSA ON THAILAND'S SOCIAL ILLS AND THE FAILURE OF TRADITIONAL RELIGION

For Buddhadāsa the fundamental cause of social problems, and of the disorder and confusion which hinders the realization of *nibbāna* as a social goal, is inadequate or improper morality: "All disorganization (*wunwai*) is the result of a lack of morality."(T)[21] Moral failures, that is, not maintaining *chit wang* or detached mindfulness, lead to the self-centredness of "I"–"mine," which Buddhadāsa regards as the immediate cause of social problems: "Self-centredness is the basic cause of suffering, both individually and socially."(T)[22] Without the mindfulness and self-restraint involved in moral practice, the truths of *anattā* and *anicca* are lost sight of. Misguidedly thinking that there is a self which can possess and things that can be possessed, people selfishly crave material objects, and this selfish craving causes social suffering when some consequently hoard wealth while others go in need. When there is hoarding by the "haves" there are attempts by the "have nots" to take the stored wealth, and so social conflict and confusion arise. Thus for

Buddhadāsa the causes of turmoil or the lack of social peace are traced to the same moral lapses and self-centredness which produce personal suffering and lack of mental peace.

Buddhadāsa further traces the moral failings which cause social problems to the failure of religions to effectively communicate their spiritual message:

> Because of wrong interpretations people fail to apply themselves to religious practice so that their so-called "religion" ceases to be an effective device for solving the problems of everyday existence. Only when a religion has failed to do its duty does materialism come into existence in the world . . . . if religious institutions interpret the tenets held by them correctly, especially the tenets expressed in the language of *Dhamma* [i.e. *phasa tham*], then religious practice itself will prove to be the "decided opponent" of materialism in all its forms.[23]

Buddhadāsa regards his *phasa tham* interpretations of Buddhism as not only revealing the correct way to personal salvation but also as correcting doctrinal misinterpretations which have led to people becoming disenchanted with religion. He attempts to re-interest his Thai audience in what he sees as the universally relevant truths of Buddhism, and implores Thais to take a fresh look at their religion, as interpreted in *phasa tham*:

> Don't get the impression that morality is reactionary. Children, adults, and people with political and economic power tend to look on religions or morality as reactionary and as following the ways of our grandparents . . . . The truth is that it [religion] has reached the point of being reactionary because it has been going in the wrong direction for so long.(T)[24]

According to Buddhadāsa, not only has the history of doctrinal misinterpretation made world-involved people disenchanted with religion, it has also led to devout people abandoning important areas of social activity. The historical division between the mundane and the supramundane has led many to regard active world-involvement directed towards ameliorating social problems as antithetical to their religious life, and Buddhadāsa decries Buddhists' avoidance of political involvement and the abandonment of political activity to the self-centered and self-seeking:

> In society people who have sharp and pure spiritual intelligence usually prefer to avoid getting involved in politics, accordingly aiming only for the pure, in-depth study of the humanities, literature, ancient history or the natural sciences. In Thailand there are people who don't dare utter a word about politics, who don't dare speak about the problems of morality, who are afraid of being accused that they are involved in politics. Consequently they don't dare mention the word "peace" or consider the thing called peace. They detest and are afraid of the word "politics." They are afraid because they think that politics is something dirty and deceitful . . . . When it happens that intelligent people like this prefer not to get involved in politics, it consequently seems that it will be left only to the stupid or to people with worldly [materialist] mentality to get involved in political affairs. The people with true and pure intelligence have deserted it. This is called the degeneration of the world because of the failure to use intelligence for the purposes of peace.(T)[25]

In a similar vein Buddhadāsa has also said:

> Here even among us Buddhists some may doubt, "Why should we play a leading role in all the affairs of the people in the whole world? Let us only be interested in our own internal Buddhist affairs . . ." If there is anyone who thinks like this please let him recollect the words of the Buddha who says: "The Tathāgata is born in the world for the happiness of all beings." Moreover, when the Buddha first sent groups of monks out to spread the teaching, He emphasised this as well, saying, "Go you forth, Oh *bhikkhus* . . . to preach the divine life for the benefit and happiness of the world . . ." It is proper for us to sacrifice ourselves to play a leading role in the affairs of the whole world as the Buddha intended us to do.[26]

In response to the traditionalist claim that spirituality or

Dhamma is the antithesis of involvement in the social world, Buddhadāsa replies,

> In one sense Dhamma is indeed the opposite of the world, but it is opposite in that it helps get rid of problems. When the world is pointed towards evil, Dhamma will point it towards good . . . . Whenever there is peace and happiness it can be said that Dhamma and the world have been able to show their amicable relations.(T)[27]

For Buddhadāsa the association of Dhamma or morality with politics, that is, the participation of Buddhists in the political process, would prevent politics becoming corrupt and a source of conflict. This is his justification for saying: "I am of the opinion that Dhamma is a political ideology."(T)[28] Buddhadāsa thus views social problems as resulting from an inadequate level of moral understanding and moral practice in the lay society, a failing whose cause lies in the inadequacies of the Buddhist church. He regards Buddhism as having failed because of its promotion of erroneous interpretations of doctrine which fail to show the relevance of religion to modern life and so turn people away from the religion and render those who do stay with the official church socially and politically impotent.

Buddhadāsa's views on the need for moral people to become politically involved not only counter the traditional Buddhist view that spiritual attainment is opposed to worldly involvement but also go against the traditional Thai view of political activity. As Morell and Samudavanija note, "The image of politics in Thailand is of an activity that is dirty, immoral, manipulative, corrupt and chaotic."[29] A corollary of this traditional view is the belief that political involvement is spiritually corrupting, and Somboon Suksamran observes that, while there is in fact a fundamental structural relation between institutional Buddhism and the Thai political establishment, the view that only a "pure" or politically disinterested Sangha can ensure the moral welfare of the nation leads both the Thai rulers and the Sangha authorities to "maintain that the Sangha is divorced from mundane affairs."[30] Buddhadāsa thus goes against tradition by bringing the political import and significance of Buddhism into the open, and this is one of the main attractions of his system of thought to progressive Thai Buddhists. As one anonymous commentator and supporter states:

> He [Buddhadāsa] has done things differently from the customary activities of usual religionists and moralists, especially in Thailand. That is, he has criticized contemporary society and politics.(T)[31]

## EDUCATION AND THE SOLUTION OF SOCIAL PROBLEMS

Given that Buddhadāsa isolates the roots of social problems and conflicts as lying in inadequate and improper moral knowledge, education has a pivotal role in his blueprint for solving social ills: "Education . . . is the thing we take to be of the greatest importance. It is the foundation of everything."(T)[32]

Buddhadāsa's emphasis on the importance of education in his view of a better Thai society has strong historical precedents. Historically, it was Buddhist monks who were the educators in Thailand and the monasteries were the only schools, a situation which only changed significantly after World War II, when the state education system was able to take over the role of the old monastery schools. In the early years of Thailand's modernization, the state school system and the monastery schools were often one and the same. In 1898 when King Chulalongkorn (Rama V) sought to establish government-sponsored primary education in the Thai provinces, he did it through the monasteries, by using monks as teachers, because the then Siam lacked both the teachers and the finances to build an education system from scratch. Craig Reynolds observes that this decision

> took advantage of the traditional practice of schooling young boys in the monasteries, and it kept secular and religious learning bound together as they had always been. In Vajirañāṇa's words [the then Supreme Patriarch]: "Secular and religious learning flow in the same

channel. Each will sustain the burdens of the other so that both may move forward and progress."[33]

However, Buddhadāsa regards the increasing secularization of education in Thailand as a negative development and would like to return to the old historical norm where religious and worldly education were integrated. He criticizes the trend towards purely vocational education, calling it education for mere survival rather than for spiritual development. In particular, Buddhadāsa condemns Thai educators and educational administrators who base education in Thailand on what he considers to be the materialist, career-centred systems common in Western countries, instead of following spiritual principles:

> Because they [Thai educators] believe the foreigners more than the Lord Buddha, more than Jesus Christ, more than the Prophet Mohammed, they consequently arrange the educational system to follow the foreigners.(T)[34]

Buddhadāsa contends that concern for the details of material survival has become so great that it has been forgotten that without a religious code of ethics such things are devoid of meaning. To counter this trend he says that the central purpose of education should be to teach children spiritual fundamentals. And the result of the sort of education Buddhadāsa proposes would be people reaping the spiritual and material benefits of living according to *chit wang*.

## TENSIONS IN BUDDHADĀSA'S SOCIAL THOUGHT

While it is Buddhadāsa's social and political thought which has been a major determinant of his popularity among modernist Thai Buddhists, ironically it is this aspect of his work that exhibits the most tensions. For example, Buddhadāsa has not acknowledged or considered the serious implications that his doctrinal reinterpretations have for the Thai Sangha. If, as Buddhadāsa teaches, spiritual and social activity are integrated, and if the layperson thereby has access to the traditionally clerical aspects of Buddhism, it is not clear what role is left for the monks or the Sangha in his proposed system of Buddhist-based socioeconomic development. Furthermore, despite all his calls for the active involvement of Buddhists in socially oriented activities, the tension remains that Buddhadāsa himself is not concretely involved in social welfare activities, and in fact he explicitly denies that this is the proper role of the monk:

> Monks should not directly co-operate in social welfare activities or in any of the people's development works . . . They should be a group that provides the people with mental and spiritual development, progress and safety.(T)[35]

In the opening chapters it was noted that, in accord with the significance placed upon orthopraxy in Theravada Buddhism, Buddhadāsa's innovative doctrinal reforms were founded on and authorized by his strict adherence to traditional clerical practices. However, the doctrinal reforms Buddhadāsa authorizes by his practical conservatism imply a radical restructuring of the traditional roles of the Buddhist monk and layperson. That is, his reinterpretations of Buddhist teaching imply a radical change in the very practices whose traditional forms he clings to and continues to support. However, Buddhadāsa does not acknowledge that he himself undermines the traditional historically accepted bases for maintaining the strict monk-lay role division in Theravada Buddhism. Neither does he acknowledge that there is a fundamental tension between his conservative practice and his radical reinterpretations of doctrine, which imply an utter reformation of Buddhist practice.

This tension between, on the one hand, maintaining a traditional role division between monks and laity, and on the other hand, supporting modernist world-involved interpretations of doctrine in which that role division has no place, is an inconsistency that is not unique to Buddhadāsa's writings. It is a characteristic of the work of many other modernist Buddhists. For example, there is a growing trend in Thailand, with advocates across the political and social spectrum, to promote the training of monks as community development workers. *Phra* Rajavaramuni (Prayut Prayutto) has offered the following rationale for giving monks secular as well as religious training and for expanding their traditional role to include secular activities:

> It is not that we are trying to secularise the Buddhist monk. Rather, we are attempting to restore his traditional place as religious leader and guide of the people.... Besides their own peculiar duties towards the goal of self-enlightenment, monks are bound with many social obligations to serve their community and to render reasonable services for the benefit of the layman's society.[36]

However, such clerical involvement in society in fact jeopardizes the traditional symbolic value of the Sangha, eroding the religious and spiritual standing of the monk by his performance of acts perceived as essentially secular. When it is argued that the layperson should have complete access to the traditional *lokuttara* or clerical aspect of the religion, and conversely that the monk should become involved in secular development and welfare projects, then the monk can no longer claim any special religious status or respect. The monk's hands are tainted by worldly involvement just as the layperson's role is sacralized. Despite the groundswell of support for clerical involvement in society as a means of refinding and rejustifying the monkly role, the notion is nevertheless regarded with considerable ambivalence by many senior members of the Sangha. As Morgan opines,

> It is not the particular standard of living [of the Thai people] that is in question, but the style, rate and effects of continual changes in standards. The restless generation of wants and desires has such great affinities to the burning thirst or insatiable craving which lies at the very core of Buddhist concern, that the Sangha leadership could scarcely escape ambivalence about the whole process of economic development and growth, the process of modernisation.[37]

I agree with Morgan's contention that those who support the expansion of the activities of the monks and the enhancement of the aspirations of the laity do not seem to perceive these notions as blurring the distinction between monk and laity.[38]

Even though he supports socioeconomic development and an expansion of the layperson's role into the traditionally clerical domain, Buddhadāsa is not in practice prepared to correspondingly deconstruct the barriers that separate the monk from the social world. Despite the tension that it creates in his arguments for active Buddhist involvement in society, Buddhadāsa is perhaps unwilling to deal with the implications of being seen as explicitly blurring the traditional demarcation between lay and monkly roles, a development which Morgan argues is almost universally regarded as

> a threat to the internal stability of the Sangha, to the prestige of the Sangha in Thai society and to the health of Thai society so dependent upon the functioning of the Sangha.[39]

Given these difficulties it would appear that if Buddhadāsa's reinterpreted system of Buddhism is to be saved, his notion of Buddhist social action must be interpreted as a modernist, world-involved ideology which is applicable more to the layperson than to the monk. Buddhist teachings have never placed negative sanctions on lay involvement in the social world, and Buddhadāsa confers on the laity all the spiritual rights to salvation that were traditionally reserved for the clergy. However, he denies monks the right to participate in the worldly activities which he otherwise defines as central to his modernist notion of Buddhism. In insisting that monks refrain from becoming involved in secular or development activities, Buddhadāsa simultaneously denies the Sangha a place in his integrated view of Buddhist spiritual and social action. Indeed, Buddhadāsa's own role as a monk is somewhat undermined by this tension between his radical theory and conservative practice. But while the tension is glaring it is neither acknowledged by Buddhadāsa nor resolved.

In addition to the tension between Buddhadāsa's theories and his conservative practice there is, however, a further theoretical difficulty associated with his attempt to integrate the mundane and supramundane aspects of Buddhist teachings. This difficulty lies in the very character of Theravada ethical doctrines. As discussed above, for *nibbāna* to be a universally accessible social goal would require cooperative effort to create a just and prosperous society. That is, cooperating and working with other people are central to the attainment of the social goal of *nibbāna* and of the social conditions under which all can work for *nibbāna*. But such cooperative activity is not at all essential for individual effort aimed at attaining *nibbāna*, which on the contrary has traditionally been defined as the activity of the social recluse and renunciate. Theravada ethical teachings have likewise traditionally extolled the virtues of self-restraint and mental control that are essential for calming and focusing the mind and for facilitating the development of meditative insight. Theravada ethical writings on the *lokuttara* or supramundane path concentrate exclusively on the virtues of individual spiritual practice rather than on collective or cooperative activity. Traditional Theravada ethical notions are defined more in terms of attitudes than actions, emphasizing the individual's state of mind towards others more than any concrete expression of assistance to others. Consequently, it is not clear what scriptural sources Buddhadāsa can refer to in justifying his notion of Buddhist social involvement. For example, the important Buddhist ethical goals of *metta*, loving-kindness, and *karuṇā*, compassion, are defined in the *Visuddhimagga* as follows:

> Loving-kindness is characterised here as promoting the aspect of welfare. Its function is to prefer welfare. It is manifested as the removal of annoyance. Its proximate cause is seeing lovableness in beings. It succeeds when it makes ill-will subside, and fails when it produces [selfish] affection.[40]
>
> Compassion is characterised as promoting the aspect of allaying suffering. Its function resides in not bearing others' suffering. It is manifested as non-cruelty. Its proximate cause is to see helplessness in those overwhelmed by suffering. It succeeds when it makes cruelty subside and it fails when it produces sorrow.[41]

Compassion and loving-kindness are manifested by the removal of one's own cruelty and of one's annoyance of others, not necessarily by any positive contribution of assistance. And compassion is defined as not meaning to bear others' suffering. The individual rather than cooperative character of Theravada ethics is shown by the fact that even the above attitudinal virtues must be given up at certain stages of spiritual practice in order for the mind to be totally concentrated on attaining salvation. *Achan* Mun's biographer gives the following account:

> The mind that is still worrying about other things or other people is like a ship overloaded with cargo and soon doomed to a watery grave. For such a mind no hope for the cessation of suffering can be expected. Whatever loving-kindness there is towards others must cease for the time being. When the Final Goal is being attained, loving-kindness for others must die away, for it will interfere with the attainment of the goal itself.[42]

The Buddhist notion of welfare, from the spiritual perspective of the follower of the Dhamma, does not necessarily incorporate actually aiding other people in a material or concrete sense by changing the condition of the world. Rather, Buddhist ethics emphasize making people feel happy by helping them adjust their desires to the world. As Wit observes:

> Certain individual acts of charity and benevolence are suggested, but there is no philosophical or religious justification of human struggle to change the world.[43]

It is the above notion of spiritual welfare which underlies the following passage from the *Loka Sutta*, which describes three types of people who "help the world:" an enlightened *tathāgata*, an *arahant* follower of a *tathāgata*, and a *tathāgata's* follower who aspires for *arahant*ship:

> Behold, O *bhikkhus*, these three types of people who, when they are

born into the world, are necessarily born for helping many people, for the happiness of many people, for the welfare, for the benefit, for aiding, for the happiness of *devatā* and of human beings.(T)[44]

All of the terms, "helping," "welfare," "benefit," and "aiding" above denote spiritual and not material welfare. Rahula notes that in ancient Ceylon, source of many of the traditions of Theravada Buddhism, opinion was divided as to whether monks should engage themselves in humanitarian activities. He says,

There were two classes of monks. One class of monks devoted themselves only to meditation, with the sole purpose of saving themselves, without taking any interest in the welfare of the people. The other class of monks seems to have taken an interest in the welfare of the people—both spiritual and material—in addition to their own salvation.[45]

However, Rahula observes that the consensus which gradually arose among the monks, and which remains the general opinion in Thailand today, was that monks

could serve the people best by leading a holy life themselves. Their way of life was an inspiration and example for the people to follow a righteous life.[46]

Siddhi Butr-Indr agrees that this moral-exemplary role is the view of correct monkly practice current in Thailand, saying,

The fundamental duty of the monk towards the lay adherent is to conduct himself as the model, teacher, instructor, guide and promoter of morality and other spiritual values in society.[47]

As discussed above, Buddhadāsa concurs with this traditional isolation of the monk from active social involvement. But leaving aside the practical difficulties Buddhadāsa's position creates for the Sangha, it is still the case that if his system is to be saved, and to function as a lay rather than clerical Buddhist ideology of socio-economic development, it is necessary to provide for the layperson a clear link between the personal spiritual practice required for salvation and cooperative moral activity in the social world. But given that, on the one hand, Buddhadāsa rejects popular lay forms of Buddhism which have been the traditional source of cooperative ethical notions in Buddhism and, on the other hand, that *lokuttara* ethics provide no clear basis for cooperative social welfare activity, it is not clear how personal practice and social involvement can in fact be integrated in Buddhadāsa's system.

Because of the individualistic character of efforts at attaining salvation in traditional Theravada doctrine, social relations are not a necessary or integral part of the path to *nibbāna*, but like all interactions with the world are something to be treated warily if they cannot be avoided. But once Buddhadāsa universalizes the religious goal and makes it the acme of both the clerical and the lay paths, as well as the ideal and goal of social activity, then the precise relation between social interaction and involvement with others and the personal attainment of *nibbāna* must be made explicit. Buddhadasa himself emphasizes that

> As for the matter of *nibbāna*, which is the chief or head of peace, we should arrange for it to be something manifest in the pages of general publications as a matter of everyday study for each person. This is because the matter of *nibbāna* denotes salvation, which follows the wants and inclinations of the instincts of every sentient being. (T)[48]

In traditional Theravada Buddhist societies social relations were not viewed as crucial to personal salvation but as the obligation of laypeople to abide by the king's laws, to pay the king's taxes, and to serve in his army in exchange for the monarch's maintenance of both the social and spiritual orders. Being solely of the supramundane realm, *nibbāna* was totally outside the jurisdiction of the king and so the activities of those one-pointedly engaged in attaining salvation, i.e. the monks, also fell outside those social obligations. *Nibbāna* was regarded as the antithesis of the world of social relations. But having spiritualized the social domain, making it an integral part of the path to personal salvation, this concept of monarchical relations in traditional Buddhist societies is inadequate for Buddhadāsa's purposes. For he must show that social relations are not simply an obligation to an external temporal-spiritual authority but are integral to one's own spiritual practice and to the attainment of one's personal salvation. Buddhadāsa attempts to demonstrate the necessary relation between social and spiritual practice by proposing that not to help or assist others who are in need is to suffer from the same self-centredness which bars one from spiritual attainment:

> Religion doesn't only mean the actions of individuals to pass beyond suffering. We must still help others to pass beyond suffering also. That is, we must have loving-kindness (*karuṇā*) towards our fellow man and towards all sentient beings, because if we are completely without loving-kindness we will be a self-centred person . . . . As is said in the Pali words of the Lord Buddha in the *Nipāta Sutta* of the *Khuddaka Nikāya* . . . , "A person who only has wisdom in seeking out his own benefit is an impure human being . . ." Hence a religious person must assist others as one type of necessary human duty, or else it will be to have a religion in words only.(T)[49]

Unlike Buddhaghosa, Buddhadāsa regards loving-kindness as denoting explicitly assisting others, and not simply as the development of the intention of benevolence. Buddhadāsa also claims that every human being must be a member of the world society and that all have three unshirkable duties: to nature, such as nourishing the body and maintaining a healthy physical existence; to Dhamma, to be upright and moral and so maintain a healthy mental life; and thirdly, to relate together in a peaceful social life:

> Whoever evades these duties as a matter of course forfeits his humanity or his membership of the world society. Even though he is still alive it is as if he were already dead.(T)[50]

Buddhadāsa also says that serving others is a good opportunity to make merit. However, here he carefully distinguishes his *phasa tham* interpretation from the popular view of merit as a metaphysical quantity which can be accumulated through good deeds and whose amount determines the quality of one's rebirth, and ultimately one's salvation. In order to clearly dissociate himself from such popular interpretations of merit-making Buddhadāsa gives the warning that

> Of all tempting things there is nothing more tempting than merit. So he [the Buddha] said that merit is *upadhi* (that is, it is also a bait of *kilesa*) . . . . Because merit inevitably leads to birth in one realm or another, if not in the condition of a human then as a *devatā*. That is, it is an instrument that keeps us always swimming in the cycle of mental birth and death.(T)[51]

Buddhadāsa also dissociates himself from the popular view that merit is best acquired by giving alms to monks, citing the *Navaka Nipāta* of the *Aṅguttara Nikāya* and saying that the Buddha taught that

> Developing awareness of change (*aniccasaññā*) for just as long as it takes to click the fingers has more effect, or more merit value, than providing meals for the whole Sangha along with the Buddha as leader.[52]

For Buddhadāsa, merit is not something stored up for the sake of going to heaven. Rather, to perform merit (Thai: *tham bun)* is to act selflessly for the benefit of others in order to reduce the power of deluded self-centred thoughts in one's life and consequently to also reduce the suffering self-centredness produces.

## BUDDHADĀSA ON *KAMMA*

Buddhadāsa also indirectly shows the need for Buddhists to help others progress and to be involved in social welfare activities by avoiding talking of suffering and poverty in terms of *kammic* retribution:

> We should regard poverty and being in material need as a person's greatest bad luck or as the most pitiful kind of basic human bad luck. We must not be indifferent towards those who are still in need.(T)[53]

When, as in traditional Theravada Buddhism, physical or material suffering is seen as just, and moral retribution for past misdeeds is regarded as something inevitable and unavoidable, then the theoretical basis for helping others overcome material difficulties is very weak. And it is in order to promote his reinterpretation of Theravada doctrine as a Buddhist ideology of social welfare and socioeconomic development that Buddhadāsa instead speaks of poverty in a way that attempts to overcome the traditional acquiescence and moral indifference by arousing sympathy for others' suffering.

The notion of *kamma* and of fate is significantly underplayed in Buddhadāsa's system. In Buddhist teachings the suffering of *kamma* or fate is regarded as misfortune which cannot be avoided. But because Buddhadāsa regards some of the major sources of physical suffering, such as hunger, disease, and ignorance, to be amenable to eradication, or at least to amelioration, then such suffering is no longer included within the category of inevitable and unavoidable suffering due to *kammic* determinants. By contributing to the elimination of material suffering, modern technology and education in certain circumstances have the potential of relieving what has traditionally been regarded as fated and inevitable suffering. Thus it is to be expected that fate and the inevitability of material suffering will be de--emphasized by Buddhadāsa, who wants Buddhists to take advantage of the benefits of modern technological developments. When Buddhadāsa does mention suffering he talks more of mental unease and disease, aspects of human life which are as much a part of modern material culture as of any past society. Buddhadāsa regards Buddhism as a solution to mental ills and mental suffering, being happy to leave the improvement of material well-being and the ending of material suffering to scientists and technocrats.

As in other aspects of his reinterpretation of Theravada Buddhism, Buddhadāsa does not reinterpret the doctrine of *kamma* by denying traditional interpretations out of hand but by providing an alternative emphasis and a new focus on the notion. Buddhadāsa nowhere denies that personal suffering is in fact a result of *kammic* reactions, determined by previous actions performed with ignorant attachment. However, he chooses not to talk of suffering in a way that emphasizes its inevitability and human inability to change it. In line with the propagation of an ideology proclaiming that beings are responsible agents capable of actively changing their circumstances for the better, he chooses to focus on those aspects of human suffering which are open to amelioration and are able to be softened by the provision of one or other form of material assistance. The primary focus in Buddhadāsa's system is on suffering which can be ended by another's assistance.

However, by de-emphasizing *kamma* and the related notions of merit and demerit in an attempt to provide an ethical justification for involvement in the world, Buddhadāsa simultaneously undermines the traditional political legitimating role of Theravada Buddhism. Traditionally the Thai king has been regarded as the person with the greatest merit in the kingdom and to hold the highest secular rank by virtue of that merit. As Charles Keyes observes,

> Not only was the right of a man to occupy the throne legitimised in the popular mind by the idea that only a person with an exceptionally meritorious component to his *karmic* legacy could occupy the throne, but it was also believed that the welfare of the kingdom during a man's reign was dependent upon the degree to which he possessed a "merit" which could be shared with his subjects.[54]

Historically, the welfare of the kingdom has been regarded as being tied up with the individual merit possessed by the king. This ideology of kingly merit has changed somewhat since the abolition of the absolute monarchy in 1932, but despite transformation it does remain, as indicated in popular rituals where a holy merit-transferring thread or *sai sin* (สายสิญจน์) is connected to both a picture of the king and to a Buddha image. This ritual symbolizes the idea that the source of merit, in the sense of a "merit" whose benefits can be shared by all who participate in the ritual, lies at the top of a spiritual hierarchy where the Sangha and the monarchy link. Keyes continues:

> The King is conceived of today, as in the past, as being the one with by far the greatest legacy of merit of any within the realm. This conception of the King as "having merit" serves today, as in the past, to legitimise the contemporary sociopolitical order. The political leadership of the country are known to receive from the King their [symbolic] mandate to rule.[55]

Thus when Buddhadāsa in effect denies the notion of participatory merit[56] and even the spiritual significance of *kamma* per se he simultaneously undermines the basis of Buddhism's use of it as a means of popular political legitimation. However, it is not only Buddhadāsa's critical view of *kamma* which undermines Buddhism's traditional political legitimating role. His concern to demythologize Theravada Buddhism also leads him to discard what in Thai history has been the most important Buddhist text justifying the monarch-led social order, the *Traibhūmikathā*.

The elaborate cosmological descriptions of the *Traibhūmikatha* have traditionally been taken as describing the various levels of heavens and hells attained as a result of different qualitative and quantitative accumulations of merit and demerit. As a result of Buddhadāsa's denial of both participatory merit and the traditional Thai view of society and the cosmos, based on the notions which are contained in the *Traibhūmikathā*, Theravada Buddhism's social and political legitimatory role is seriously jeopardized. If Buddhism is to be the progressive social ideology which Buddhadāsa and his supporters desire it to be, there is therefore a need for a new Buddhist theory to provide legitimacy for Thai political forms.

While not defining the problem so clearly, it would seem that Buddhadāsa regards the following Buddhist principle as underpinning a contemporary social order which takes its legitimacy from Buddhism: namely, the promotion of welfare in such a way as to enable the populace to strive for *nibbāna*. Political legitimacy then would not flow from symbolic association with or participation in the king's merit but rather from the visible, individually practised morality of political and social leaders. That is, the new Buddhist legitimacy would lie in individual merit, in both the Western and Buddhist senses, not in mere association with the traditional symbols of authority. This notion of Buddhist "meritocracy" is dealt with further in the next chapter when discussing Buddhadāsa's idea of *dhammocracy*.

However, Buddhadāsa himself presents no explicit resolution of the difficulties of needing to provide, firstly, a doctrinal justification for social action and, secondly, a new interpretation of the ideological relation between Buddhism and the Thai state. And these omissions, both manifested at points of juncture between his reinterpreted theory and actual social practice, are further indications of the tensions within Buddhadāsa's social thought. This does not mean that the issues dealt with in his social thought are any less important than his work on spiritual philosophy. On the contrary, the future of Theravada Buddhism in Thailand will be determined by how the Sangha administration and lay Thai Buddhists resolve the questions raised by social, economic, and political change. What the limitations in Buddhadāsa's social thought do reveal, however, are the tensions created in Theravada Buddhism between the relative freedom in the domain of doctrinal interpretation and the enforced conservatism of practice within the Sangha.

## MAHAYANA INFLUENCES ON BUDDHADĀSA'S SOCIAL THEORY

In the process of developing a Theravada social doctrine Buddhadāsa maintains that aspects of suffering may be softened if not ended through another's benevolent assistance rather than through one's own moral effort and spiritual insight. This seems to imply that at least part of the way to salvation, i.e. the ending of suffering, can be attained through no effort of one's own but rather through a gracious external intervention. Such a view has similarities with the doctrines of some schools of Mahayana Buddhism, which teach that salvation can be attained through faith in the liberative grace of either the Buddha or a Mahayana saint, a *bodhisattva*. This tendency of Buddhadāsa's Theravada social doctrine to incorporate aspects of Mahayana Buddhism further indicates that his interest in Zen and Mahayana, as detailed in chapter 7, is not accidental but is a direct result of introducing a doctrine of spiritually oriented social activities into a religious system where salvation has heretofore been regarded as the result of individual moral effort. However, when action to end the social problems which inhibit others attaining *nibbāna* is also regarded as part of one's own spiritual work for attaining personal salvation, it follows that those welfare-minded activities also contribute towards other people's spiritual salvation. In other words, salvation is no longer something attained wholly by private effort in isolation from others. *Nibbānic* salvation now becomes a more social phenomenon where one person's benevolent assistance may positively contribute to another person's spiritual enlightenment.

As already noted in the previous chapter, the Mahayana-like character of Buddhadāsa's thought also derives from his universalizing the doctrine of salvation from suffering by ending the monk-lay distinction. As Rupp notes, Mahayana has always been

> a more comprehensive path. From its inception laymen as well as monks have been more integral to its program than in the typical Theravada position. And the *bodhisattva* ideal articulates explicitly an active concern with the destiny of all beings, a concern which only remains implicit when the [Theravada] ideal of the *arahant* is dominant.[57]

The Mahayana-like tendencies in Buddhadāsa's notion of spiritual practice as incorporating social welfare activities are further demonstrated by his emphasis on the *bodhisattva* rather than the *arahant* as the Buddhist spiritual ideal. The Theravada saint or *arahant* is honoured for his personal attainment of salvation. On the other hand, the Mahayana saint or *bodhisattva* is honoured because of his or her compassionate vow not to enter ultimate *nirvāṇa* until every sentient being has also reached that exalted condition. In Mahayana teachings a *bodhisattva*, unlike an *arahant*, is regarded as having the ability to positively assist others to attain *nirvāṇa*. Buddhadāsa says,

> We should consider the kind of individual who is called the "blessed *bodhisattva*." That is, a person who sacrifices the benefit or personal happiness which he should get himself, in order to help others to pass beyond suffering . . . . In Mahayana there is a tenet which holds that the blessed *bodhisattva* should accept a moral principle with the gist that, "We will strive to help every last one of those who have fallen into suffering before we will permit ourselves to enter the blessed *nirvāṇa*." This is the highest ideal of helping others or of aiding one's fellow man who is in need of both physical and mental sustenance, a situation which is a complicated social problem at the present time.(T)[58]

However, this should not be taken as meaning that Buddhadāsa has completely abandoned the *arahant* ideal, for there is a sense in which the *arahant* and the *bodhisattva* are compatible notions. While in popular Mahayana cults it is believed that faith in *bodhisattvas* is sufficient to elicit their saving grace, as was seen in chapter 7, Buddhadāsạ explicitly rejects such notions. For Buddhadāsa, a *bodhisattva* is an *arahant* who teaches, guides, and actively assists others along the path to salvation but who, unlike popular Mahayana saints, does not possess the ability to walk along that path on his or her disciple's behalf. Buddhadāsa's *bodhisattva* is therefore a development of rather than a denial of the Theravada ideal of the *arahant*. Once again the change represented by Buddhadāsa's reinterpretation is a matter of refocusing or re-emphasizing notions rather than of the outright rejection of traditional Theravada doctrines.

## SUMMARY

While moral education is central to Buddhadāsa's solution for social problems, it has its effect through people actually practising *chit wang* and lessening the power of self-centredness in their lives. The selflessness of acting with *chit wang* is regarded as solving social problems in two ways. Firstly, by reducing self-centredness through the practice of *chit wang* the divisiveness and greed behind so many problems of poverty and oppression will be ameliorated. And secondly, the welfare-minded practice of aiding those in need, while lessening personal self-centredness, also concretely helps the victims of injustice and poverty overcome the social barriers which prevent them from following the path to end suffering. *Chit wang* or ending self-centredness is therefore the pivot both of Buddhadāsa's interpretation of the Theravada doctrine of liberation and of his social thought. *Chit wang* not only has subjective benefits in leading the practitioner towards salvation but it also has objective social benefits in promoting the realization of *nibbāna* as a social goal.

The dissolution of the distinction between personal and social activities, and of the difference between subjective and objective results, manifests in the structure of Buddhadāsa's system of thought his overriding concern to make the material world as much a domain of spiritual activity as the inner recesses of the contemplative's mind. In the following quote Jayawardene[59] summarizes well the traditional Theravada view of salvation to which Buddhadāsa is opposed:

> Suffering (*dukkha*) is man's own creation. It is not a quality of the external world, nor is it the effect of the external world upon one's self. Man can therefore eliminate suffering by his own efforts . . . . suffering arises when our desire is in conflict with the phenomena that surround us. We can, however, change our desires, and the Buddha recommended this way.[60]

In contrast, for Buddhadāsa the suffering of oppression and social turmoil born of greed is a quality of the external world. And what is more, human beings can change the phenomena that surround them in order to end or at least alleviate suffering by action inspired by Dhamma and performed with *chit wang*. Instead of ending suffering by adjusting our desires to the world, Buddhadāsa maintains that suffering can at least in part be ended by adjusting the world to our desires for spiritual and material well-being.

Were Buddhadāsa, like most Thai monks, to retain the traditional division between clerical and lay Buddhism rather than attempting to create an integrated, comprehensive religion of individual salvation, he would have few difficulties in bringing notions of economic development and modernization into Buddhism. But he effectively excises that traditional lay-social aspect of Buddhism in attempting to interpret the Buddhist doctrine of salvation anew from first principles. Consequently, wanting his interpretation to function as a guide for productive and beneficial social action, he must integrate a traditionally world-renouncing doctrine of salvation with active world involvement. At the theoretical level he must show both that the world and *nibbāna* are not in contradiction and that sociality or involvement with others for the purposes of social development is necessarily related to and in harmony with personal spirituality. As seen above, Buddhadāsa argues for both of these positions. However, his arguments require further development, not because of any specific theoretical lapse but rather because of the tension between his promotion of a socially involved doctrine of salvation and his own traditional and conservative segregation of the monk from worldly activity. At the same time as presenting a systematic reinterpretation of Buddhist doctrine which effectively abolishes the distinction between religious and world-involved activity, he maintains that the Sangha, and here he includes himself, should not engage in social welfare activities. The ideal that emerges from Buddhadāsa's thought is not that of a renunciate *arahant* monk but of a world-involved *bodhisattva*-like layperson who simultaneously works for personal salvation and social welfare by following the practice of *chit wang*. What role the monk plays in his reformed view of Buddhism is, however, unclear.

Buddhadāsa propagates an alternative Thai Buddhist ideology, but it is more an ideology of a spiritually independent and socially active layperson than of the monastic isolation that he himself practices. The place of the monk and of the Sangha in his ideology of spiritual activism is problematic. Anan Senakhan's and Bunmi Methangkun's criticisms that Buddhadāsa seeks to destroy the

Sangha by sending monks out to till the fields, while overstated, do have some substance. Buddhadāsa's ideas have significant implications for the interpretation of the doctrine as well as for the institution of Buddhism in Thailand. However, in striving one-pointedly for both doctrinal consistency and contemporary relevance he tends to overlook the practical issue of Buddhism's institutional role in Thai society. And in the absence of a practical orientation to the realities of institutional Buddhism's place in Thailand, the overall success of Buddhadāsa's attempt to develop an interpretation of the doctrine with direct contemporary relevance can only be regarded as an incomplete and unfinished project.

[illegible] of [illegible] monks [illegible] the [illegible] to [illegible] some [illegible] Buddha [illegible] has [illegible] [illegible] of the [illegible] as well as [illegible] [illegible] of Buddhism in Thailand. [illegible] documents [illegible] of contemporary [illegible] [illegible] of the [illegible] [illegible] And in the [illegible] of [illegible] and [illegible] [illegible] with the [illegible] only [illegible] [illegible] and intellectual project.

# 9 BUDDHADĀSA'S POLITICAL WRITINGS

IN ADDITION to presenting a social doctrine of spiritually-based activism, Buddhadāsa has also commented upon and criticized political matters. However, his views cannot be categorized as following the pattern of any existing political ideology, nor as supporting the programs of any Thai political party or movement. Buddhadāsa's statements on politics are always general and he avoids making remarks on specific political debates and current controversies. He is more concerned with setting out what he regards as correct Buddhist principles for the operation of politics rather than with acting as a Buddhist critic of political events.

Fundamental to Buddhadāsa's conception of politics is the principle that all political doctrines and political activity should be judged against a spiritual criterion. For Buddhadāsa, any political form is good and of benefit if it encourages the populace to reach towards *nibbāna* by uprooting self-centeredness and establishing social and individual peace. What might be considered the traditional goals of political activity, such as promoting the production of wealth or attaining socioeconomic equity and justice, are by no means unimportant in Buddhadāsa's view of politics but are not regarded as having intrinsic value in themselves. Rather, for Buddhadāsa the production of material wealth and the promotion of social equity only have value inasmuch as their attainment permits or encourages the populace to further their spiritual interests. In other words, what are usually taken as ends in traditional political thought are regarded as means by Buddhadāsa—means towards the attainment of a final spiritual end which he calls *dhammocracy*[1] or the rule of Dhamma in the world. Buddhadāsa consequently takes a utilitarian approach to the traditional political ideologies and systems, because he regards none as having any inherent value apart from their capacity to promote Dhamma in the world. This political utilitarianism is shown most clearly when Buddhadāsa says, "When there is *dhammocracy* it could be a dictatorship, a democracy or whatever."(T)[2]

## BUDDHADĀSA ON CAPITALISM AND COMMUNISM

Buddhadāsa's lack of commitment to any existing political ideology is further shown by his equally vehement criticisms of the principles and operation of both capitalism and communism. As already noted in chapter 8, Buddhadāsa has expressed particular concern about the poverty, oppression, and exploitation which prevent people from following the path to *nibbāna*:

> When the country is made up of individuals who are destitute and desperately poor and the farmers are poor, starving, and weak how can the nation be secure? They, the pillars of the nation, will be rotten and worn away.(T)[3]

In stark contrast to many politically conservative Thais, Buddhadāsa maintains that it is not communism per se which is a threat to Thailand but rather the exploitation and oppression which lead impoverished people towards communism and violent revolution:

> We are experiencing the problem that these evil-minded capitalists are sucking the blood of humanity to such an extent that the poor must rise up to fight and destroy their enemy, flooding the world with blood. (T)[4]

Buddhadāsa regards the fundamental threat to Thailand's national security as lying not in communism but in exploitative capitalism.

However, he does not regard capitalist exploitation itself to be the ultimate source of political problems. Buddhadāsa maintains that exploitation has its roots in the ignorance, delusion, and attachment which are the causes of all suffering. Because of the dominance of a materialist mentality, that is, of a deluded attachment to material wealth, Buddhadāsa says that capitalists have used the potentially beneficial social and technological developments associated with industrialization and mechanization to greedily hoard wealth. The systematic greed of capitalists has as a consequence created social conflicts between the impoverished workers and the wealthy capitalist employers. But Buddhadāsa also considers the communist ideal of workers and peasants overthrowing the capitalists as being informed by the same materialist greed which led to the original exploitation. In other words, he regards the workers as being caught in the same traps of delusion and attachment as their capitalist employers.

Buddhadāsa's views on communism are neither wholly supportive nor wholly critical. Because of its materialist doctrines he does regard communism as being fundamentally incompatible with Buddhism:

> Communism cannot be the same as Buddhism. The main point which should be noted is that the principles of Buddhism do not teach that we should acquire anything as being ours. (T)[5]

That is, he regards the communist ideal of state ownership or ownership of the social wealth by the collectivity of the working class as being just another more general form of self-centred greed. But having said this, Buddhadāsa still says of communism, "Yet it still is good; it has benefit for the world if it helps us to build up peace for the world." (T)[6] Insofar as communism ends the greed-based exploitation of the capitalists, which is at the root of the worker-capitalist conflict, it brings peace into the world and so from a Buddhist perspective should be regarded as good.

As already seen, Buddhadāsa characterizes peace as the main distinguishing feature of *nibbāna*. He regards peace as the prime social goal. The absence of peace, that is, *wun-wai* or confusion and disorder, is seen as arising from delusion, attachment, and from craving after material things. Peace, on the other hand, is described as the characteristic of *chit wang*, a mind freed from attachment and the self-centred delusions of "I"–"mine." Therefore, according to Buddhadāsa, when self-centredness is ended peace arises, both internally and externally, for he maintains that social conflict and disorder can be traced to the same self-centredness and material greed which produce inner, mental confusion. Buddhadāsa consequently uses the presence or absence of peace, defined as the absence of confusion or conflict, as his main criterion for determining whether the character of a society is either *dhammic*, i.e. spiritual, or materialist.

The practical question this then raises is, how is social peace to be attained? According to traditional interpretations of Theravada doctrine, social peace is realized if all individuals are peaceful in themselves. However, Buddhadāsa provides a more developed analysis of the origins of peace and disorder. While criticizing the anti-capitalist workers and labour leaders for being as materialist as their capitalist opponents, he also acknowledges that the former's materialism is conditioned by the self-centred greed of the capitalists, and that worker-capitalist conflicts are primarily caused by the latter and not by the former. For Buddhadāsa, peace is not only attained through inner, moral and meditative practice but also by combining this with morally guided social action directed towards ending the power of certain exploitative and self-centred sections of society. Peace is attained by both inner and outer action, not by either alone. It is for this reason that, as noted in the previous chapter, he criticizes both those Buddhists who eschew politics because it is "dirty" (because they do not act in the world) as well as the communists (because they act only in the world without a moral base). However, Buddhadāsa does not go beyond this analysis to suggest a concrete political program to overcome social conflicts. His solution to political conflict is moral and educational, to introduce Buddhist moral principles into political activity, rather than to undertake any specific ideologically aligned intervention in politics as such.

## BUDDHADĀSA'S CRITICISMS OF POLITICS

Buddhadāsa uses his interpretative theory of *phasa khon–phasa tham* to distinguish between what he considers to be the correct interpretations of social and political concepts and their popular, but erroneous, definitions. He says that politics without morality becomes corrupt and factionalized as self-centredness dominates minds and actions and causes confusion and turmoil. In contrast, in *phasa tham*, "Politics is [defined as] performing duties so that the world exists happily."(T)[7] That is, politics is "arranging or acting so that the many, many people who live [in this world] truly live together in peace and happiness."(T)[8] By "happiness" Buddhadāsa means more than simple material pleasures. The happiness politics should promote is *dhammic*: "Dhamma which is politics will make the world pass beyond *kilesa*, harmfulness, evil and the self-centredness of 'I'–'mine.'"(T)[9]

As a consequence of his proposition that political activity should be morally informed, Buddhadāsa maintains that the party politics and political factionalism characteristic of Western democracies are outside his definition of politics, and are in fact a manifestation of immorality: "When there is no morality politics necessarily splits into parties and factions."(T)[10] For Buddhadāsa, politics is an activity which should not only promote harmony but which should also proceed harmoniously itself; otherwise it is "dirty politics," or not a truly beneficial form of politics. This is Buddhadāsa's criterion for judging the appropriateness or beneficial character of political activity, i.e. good political activity is peaceful in itself and in its results. Buddhadāsa's opposition to the conflict inherent in the party politics of traditional democratic forms of government is, however, as much a Thai disdain of *wun-wai* or confusion as it is a Buddhist dislike of disturbing the peace. As Morell and Samudavanija note,

> Participant politics requires confrontation, open conflict, discussion, argument; these have been disdained in Thai culture in preference for a passive stance on political issues, a stance which is dignified and basically non-committal.[11]

Buddhadāsa is not convinced that liberal democracy based on the party system is necessarily the best political form:

> Liberal democracy opens the way for full freedom but doesn't clearly define what freedom is. Then people's *kilesa* snatch the opportunity to be free according to the power of those *kilesa*. (T)[12]

He suggests that an emphasis on political or social freedom without a corresponding degree of moral insight on the part of the populace can only mean freedom for *kilesa* to dominate social and political life. He emphasizes this when he says, "But it [democracy] is extremely dangerous, because if the common person is not yet good it will immediately turn the whole of this world into a hell." (T)[13]

Liberal democracy fails in Buddhadāsa's judgement because it does not lead to social conditions which promote morality or the attainment of *nibbāna*. In place of liberal democracy Buddhadāsa proposes an alternative form of government which he calls a "dictatorial style of *dhammic* socialism." Buddhadāsa considers socialism to be "more moral than other systems" (T)[14] because it restricts individuals' ability to accumulate material wealth, thus putting a check on the dangerous power of *kilesa* and of material attachment. He also values socialism because of its emphasis on cooperative rather than competitive social activities. Buddhadāsa's proposed "*dhammic* socialism" is a form which does not simply aim to provide each person with the necessities of survival. Rather, it has as a higher goal the provision of social circumstances which enable each person to strive for *nibbāna* and, according to Buddhadāsa, such a spiritual form of socialism should proceed in a centralized, dictatorial manner.

Two justifications are provided for a dictatorial rather than liberal democratic form of *dhammic* socialism: the respective examples of the Buddha and of the first Buddhist emperor, Asoka. Buddhadāsa maintains that "The Buddha himself had the principle or ideal of socialism but his method of working was dictatorial." (T)[15] That is, the cooperative way of life of the Sangha, or those striving for *nibbāna*, was the Buddha's "socialism," but in laying down the details of the Noble Eightfold Path and the practices of the *vinaya* in elaborate detail the Buddha was also acting "dictatorially," in saying strictly how *nibbāna* was to be striven for. However, Buddhadāsa's model Buddhist polity is more specifically based on the historical tradition dating from Asoka's North Indian empire some two hundred years after the Buddha's death, for he primarily refers to the traditional notion of the Buddhist monarch. In arguing for a dictatorial style of Buddhist socialism, Buddhadāsa refers to the *dasarājadhamma*, the ten traditional qualities of a Buddhist king,[16] saying that they still have relevance in the modern world: "*dasarājadhamma* . . . is the socialism which has the greatest benefit—a sovereign abiding by the *dasarājadhamma*." (T)[17] But rather than having a king, Buddhadāsa implies that there should be a dictator with these attributes, for he says that the best and quickest way to attain spiritually beneficial social development is by having a dictator controlling a *dhammic* socialist state:

> This [*dhammic* socialism] is not a system which should be abandoned and it is not the absolute monarchy which is so hated. Perhaps this system will be able to remedy the world's problems better than other systems. (T)[18]

While Buddhadāsa calls for a centralized form of government under a Buddhist dictator, it is clear that for him this is only a second best approach given that the Thai monarch no longer has legislative power. He in fact appears to have few objections to the now abolished institution of the absolute monarchy:

> If the King fulfilled his duties like that [according to the *dasarāja-dhamma*] there would be no problems, because the king did not think, "This [national wealth] is mine." He thought only that it was society's, which is why the people give power to the king. (T)[19]

The traditional character of Buddhadāsa's views can here be gauged by the striking similarity between the above statement and an inscription of the fourteenth-century king of Sukhothai, Lithai, who praised himself saying,

> This king rules by observing the ten kingly precepts [*dasarāja-dhamma*]. He has pity on all his subjects. If he sees rice belonging to others he does not covet it and if he sees the wealth of others he does not become indignant.[20]

Buddhadāsa's support for the institution of the absolute monarchy should be seen in the context of the important historical influence of King Mongkut on his ideas and practice, a matter which has already been discussed in chapter 2. As absolute monarch, Mongkut not only reformed the structure of the Thai Sangha by establishing the Thammayut Order but also began the process of national modernization which was so vigorously taken up by his son and heir, King Chulalongkorn. It must be remembered that senior members of the Thai royalty had a significant impact on the Thai Sangha in the first decades of the twentieth century. For example, Chulalongkorn's half brother, Vajirañāṇa (Thai: Wachirayan) was abbot of Wat Bowonniwet in Bangkok, the main Thammayut monastery, from 1892 and supreme patriarch of the Thai Sangha from 1910 to 1921, when he had a lasting impact on Buddhist scholarship and the reform of the Sangha. The Thai absolute monarchy under Rama IV and Rama V thus in many ways had a modernizing impact on the country and there is no doubt that it is this historical ideal which Buddhadāsa has in mind when he calls for a return of the monarchy.

Buddhadāsa's pronouncements on what he calls the "dictatorial form of *dhammic* socialism" are his most specific comments on contemporary Thai politics. These ideas were developed and first published in the turbulent period of 1973–1976 when political polarization in the country was heightened and overflowed into a polarization of the Sangha between rightist and left-aligned monks. This politicization of the Sangha was perceived by many, including Buddhadāsa, as threatening Buddhism's role as a symbol of national unity. Somboon Suksamran has described the left-wing groups of monks as espousing causes which could only be realized through political action, "such as campaigning for the underprivileged, Buddhism or nationalism."[21] On the other hand, the more conservative sections of the politicized monks undertook political action in response to what they perceived as threats to their personal status, privilege, and position because of the populist activities and demands of the leftist monks. Politicization of the Sangha in the mid-1970s thus revealed within the order the same tensions which had become apparent in the broader Thai society.

In this confused and potentially dangerous situation, Buddhadāsa, having no specific alignment with either the political right or the left, intervened by publishing his ideas on dictatorial Buddhist socialism, which he apparently hoped might be taken up as a midway position by the opposed political factions in the Sangha as a means of quelling the divisive disputes. Rather than directly face the political issues involved, Buddhadāsa's solution relied upon a return to the established tradition of maintaining strict separation between the monkhood and social and political affairs. Buddhadāsa opposed the view that monks should be politically or socially active. While this explicit conservatism sits uneasily with his calls for the abolition of the traditional distinctions between the world-involved and renunciate forms of Buddhism, it appears that the crisis within the Sangha was so great that Buddhadāsa felt it could only be overcome by returning to traditional practices. Rather than seeking a resolution by openly debating the issues, which would most likely have led to the development of serious splits within the Sangha, Buddhadāsa's call for monks to refrain from becoming involved in social issues was an attempt to cut off the means for the expression of dissent within the Sangha. That is, he viewed the conflict within the Sangha as essentially irresolvable, because of the danger of the Sangha suffering perhaps permanent damage from the expression of factional interests. As a consequence, he sought to prevent the peace-disturbing expression of either rightist or leftist views at the source. Somboon Suksamran comments on Buddhadāsa's intervention as follows:

> Between 1973 and 1976 when ideological conflict was immensely intensified Buddhadāsa published his formulations of Dhamma socialism (*dhammikasangkhomniyom*), a very complex and closely knit set of Buddhist ideas. It was intended to provide a Buddhist compromise between secular left- and right-wing ideologies. Though

> his ideas were exploited by both left- and right-wing political monks to suit their goals, essentially he had a conservative viewpoint which emphasised the duties and responsibilities of individuals to their religion, government, nation and their fellows.[22]

Despite his progressive and modernist reforms of doctrine and his promotion of a notion of Buddhist social involvement, as a result of the publication of his views on dictatorial socialism, Buddhadāsa came to be seen by some in Thailand today as a political conservative. He offers arguments which support strong, autocratic political control of the country rather than a government democratically elected by the Thai populace. Indeed, this ill-fitting political conservatism draws criticism from those who otherwise support Buddhadāsa's general reformist program. Sulak Sivaraksa comments:

> I think a weak point of Buddhadāsa lies in this matter of "dictator," because dictators never possess Dhamma, and it's like this everywhere because we abandon ourselves to having dictators. Even the abbots at almost every temple are dictators, including Buddhadāsa as well. (T)[23]

Like many of Buddhadāsa's supporters among progressive Thai Buddhists, Sulak is a strong proponent of the democratic processes of government who finds it difficult to accept Buddhadāsa's pronouncements on the desirability of a dictatorial form of Buddhist government. Puey Ungphakorn, a prominent social scientist, echoes the thoughts and feelings of many progressive Thais when he says he sees the bases of a "good modern society" as being efficiency, freedom, justice, and kindness.[24] This contrasts with Buddhadāsa's emphasis on responsibility over freedom, which leads to his relatively poor regard for the notion of liberal democratic government in which he says moral responsibility, the basis of Buddhist practice (*sīla*), is often thrown overboard in an unthinking championing of individualistic freedom.

When considering Buddhadāsa's political conservatism and his criticisms of liberal democracy it is necessary to bear in mind that doctrinal Buddhism provides a weak basis for democratic principles. It is true that in the Buddha's time there were two competing types of government in North India, which can respectively be called republican and monarchical. One of the most commonly mentioned "republics" in the Pali canon is the Vajji region with its capital at Vesali, while Magadha with its capital at Rajagriha was a powerful monarchy. However, it should be noted that the term, "republic" is rather loosely applied to such states as Vajji, which Ling says would be better called aristocratic oligarchies, because the governments of such states were composed only of leading men of the *kśatriya* or warrior caste. However, as Ling notes, because of the expansion of the monarchies and internal feuding amongst the various republics there was a "trend towards an increase in the size and power of the monarchies at the expense of the republics."[25] Indeed, as a result of these forces all the republics had collapsed within a few years of the Buddha's demise.

Rajavaramuni notes that the Buddha laid down principles for guiding the governance of both the republics and monarchies of his day. That is, the Buddha did not support one system of government over the other, but rather tried to ensure that the moral and religious welfare of the people was guaranteed whatever the political system. (T)[26] Buddhadāsa's comprehensive notion of *dhammocracy* and his political pragmatism therefore have well-established precedents in the Buddha's treatment of the political divisions of his time. Nevertheless, Rajavaramuni also observes that the Buddha thought the monarchical system of government would dominate in the long term. On this point Ling comments that

> Social stability appears to have been recognised by the Buddha as a necessary condition for the success of social and moral reconstruction. In the existing situation in North India in the fifth century B.C. the surest guarantee of social stability appeared to be in the direction of a strong and benevolent monarchy.[27]

Thus Buddhist teachings are by no means antithetical to democratic forms of government but neither are they strongly supportive. And given the extensive references to the *cakkavattin* (universal monarch) and to the royal qualities of the *dasarājadhamma* in the Theravada canon, rather than to democratic ideals and virtues, Buddhadāsa's conservatism and the unease of democrats such as Sulak Sivaraksa are both understandable. Buddhadāsa's support for a strong, centralized, even dictatorial form of government appears to be based on a concern for maintaining the peace and social order he regards as being the foundation of the collective moral order of Thai society. Buddhadāsa's political conservatism is the main source of dissatisfaction with his work and ideas among progressive Buddhists, many of whom support a more explicitly democratic formulation of Buddhism. But while at odds with many of his modernist supporters, Buddhadāsa's views are at this point uncharacteristically in accord with those of the majority of Thai citizens, who acquiesce in or support strong centralized regimes. Morell and Samudavanija observe:

> Although many intellectuals and some royalists would prefer otherwise, the remainder of society considers military rule, or at least long-term military tutelage, as both legitimate and reasonable, and certainly important for the stability and order with which it is associated.[28]

## TENSIONS BETWEEN BUDDHADĀSA'S DOCTRINAL REFORMS AND HIS POLITICAL CONSERVATISM

While there are both scriptural and cultural-historical precedents for Buddhadāsa's political conservatism, there is nevertheless a pronounced discontinuity between his work on politics and the remainder of his teachings. In developing his general reinterpretations of Buddhist teachings Buddhadāsa has followed the method of returning to doctrinal fundamentals as expressed in the first sections of the *Suttapiṭaka*, that is, the *Dīgha Nikāya*, *Majjhima Nikāya*, *Aṅguttara Nikāya,* and *Saṁyutta Nikāya*. His reinterpretations have been based on a selective reading of the Buddhist scriptures, concentrating on doctrinal texts and effectively ignoring historical, popular, and non-doctrinal sections of the *Suttapiṭaka* such as the

*Jātakas* and the *Petavatthu*, which contain teachings more aligned with traditional popular Buddhism than with his clerical doctrinalism. However, these otherwise neglected texts, in particular the *Jātakas* or stories of the Buddha's previous incarnations, come to the fore significantly in Buddhadāsa's political writings. For example, the *dasarājadhamma* or ten qualities of a righteous monarch, which Buddhadāsa cites in support of his notion of an ideal political leader, are drawn from the *Jātaka* tales and not from the doctrinal core of the early sections of the *Suttapiṭaka*. That is, Buddhadāsa's use of the Buddhist scriptures in his political writings is inconsistent with the methodological approach taken in the remainder of his reformist work. This creates a discursive discontinuity between his explicitly political and general doctrinal writings. Furthermore, this suggests that these two areas of his work operate under quite different constraints and according to different assumptions. The dissatisfaction of many of Buddhadāsa's lay supporters with his politically conservative views is a consequence of this fundamental dissonance between his political and non-political writings.

The reason for the discontinuity between Buddhadāsa's political and non-political work lies in the tension between his conceptual integration of the spiritual and mundane levels of human activity and the ongoing practical separation of these two levels in his own life and in his treatment of the role of the Sangha in modern Thailand. Political activity is necessarily and irredeemably practical and world-involved, and, given that Buddhadāsa has failed to resolve the dilemmas raised by clerical involvement in the mundane world, his treatment of political activity remains cut off and distanced from his other writings, in the same way that he has distanced himself and the Sangha from active world-involvement. For example, Buddhadāsa's opposition to the participant politics of liberal democratic forms of government is consistent with his own decision over fifty years ago to retreat from the confusion and *wun-wai* of involvement in the political hierarchy of the Sangha in a personal search for insight and peace.

However, the concrete tensions underlying contemporary political conflicts, both in lay society and within the Sangha, appear to have introduced a further, external source of contradiction into

Buddhadasa's work. While the logic of his modernist views inevitably leads him towards the abolition of traditional distinctions in the teaching and practice of Thai Buddhism, this abolition also has the potential of undermining the structure of institutional Buddhism in Thailand. Buddhadāsa clearly does not want the Sangha to collapse, and perhaps it was only the events of 1973–1976 which made it clear to him that institutional Buddhism in Thailand was in fact threatened with being torn apart by the same tensions which he had been trying to resolve in his own work of reform and reinterpretation. However, Buddhadāsa has never acknowledged the potentially subversive implications of his work. Perhaps he does not see them, or perhaps he wishes to ignore them. Wherever the truth lies, it is clear that his response to the political and religious crisis of the 1970s in his book on Dhammic Socialism was an ad hoc reaction designed to preserve the Sangha at all costs, even at the cost of creating inconsistencies in his own work and in his reformist program.

The pragmatic character of Buddhadāsa's approach to politics is further indicated by a softening of his criticisms of liberal democracy in the years since 1976, when a return to relative social and political stability has been accompanied by a gradual liberalization in Thai society. Buddhadāsa's more recent political comments in fact contradict some of his statements made in the mid-1970s. At a talk given in 1982 to commemorate the fiftieth anniversary of Suan Mokh, Buddhadāsa gave the following reasons why it was fitting for him, a monk, to talk about democracy, a political matter:

1. Because democracy was born in Thailand together with Suan Mokh; they were both born in the same year (1932), although Suan Mokh is one month older . . . .
2. Buddhism has in it the spirit of democracy. Buddhist principles, especially in the governance of the Sangha, have in them the spirit or concept of democracy . . . .
3. We [as human beings] by nature have the characteristic of democracy in us . . . . That is, we are all "friends" of suffering, birth, ageing, illness, and death. We all have *kilesa* in us in the same way and suffer the same problems . . . . the

idea of democracy exists in every person by the principles of nature. (T)[29]

The above seem the words of a totally different Buddhadāsa from the one who eight years earlier in 1974 called for dictatorial *dhammic* socialism to remedy the confusing state of Thai society. Indeed, the very title of the book the above remarks are taken from, *Democratic Dawning* (*Fa sang thang prachathipatai* ฟ้าสางทางประชาธิปไตย), stands in stark contrast to the tenor of his work on dictatorship. But while in recent years Buddhadāsa has increasingly supported the liberal democratic pattern he was earlier so critical of, the change is not in fact so dramatic. He still maintains strong support for the notion of dictator or dictatorship (*phadetkan*– เผด็จการ), but is careful to redefine what he means by this:

> The word "dictator" denotes acting resolutely . . . . If it has Dhamma then a dictatorship is resolute and correct. Dictatorship is only a tool, a method that is resolute and decisive . . . . If it is used in a correct way it is good but if it is used wrongly it is bad. (T)[30]

This returns us to Buddhadāsa's politically pragmatic notion of *dhammocracy*, wherein all political systems are seen simply as tools or methods for obtaining "the rule of Dhamma in the world," and have no inherent value in themselves. Buddhadāsa goes on to say that people have criticized his use of the notion of dictator

> because they only know the tyrannical (*thorarat* – ทรราช) destructive dictators and regard it, dictatorship, as a system of political ideals. But I say it isn't. The word "dictatorship" does not denote a political system but a tool which can be used for anything. (T)[31]

Yet despite these recent qualifications of his criticism of democracy and support for dictatorship, insofar as he maintains an essentially suprapolitical stance by calling all political systems tools which are good or bad according to the moral character of the participants or leaders, Buddhadāsa is still in political terms a conservative. This is because he is, as shown in 1974, prepared to abandon democratic principles if, in his opinion, the practice of democracy leads to too great a degree of social confusion. However, the democratic idealists among his progressive lay supporters cannot accept this suprapolitical *dhammic* pragmatism and, like Sulak, part ways with Buddhadāsa at this point.

But while Buddhadāsa can be criticized for the contradictions introduced into his thought by his political and practical conservatism, it is necessary to remember that as a member of the Thai clergy there are limits to what it is possible to say and advocate given the alignment of the Sangha hierarchy with the state and the strictly enforced conservatism of the Thai monkhood. In addition, because of the strongly orthopractic character of Thai Buddhism and, in particular, the significant orthopractic basis of spiritual authority, if Buddhadāsa were to challenge the traditional role and practices of the monk he would also risk losing the repute and esteem needed to authorize his doctrinal reforms. This is because in order to authorize doctrinal changes he must remain strictly orthopractic, even if the new interpretations thereby developed imply a questioning or criticism of the orthopractic tradition itself. Given the severely limited scope for practical innovation in the Thai Sangha, Buddhadāsa in fact has no choice but to take a conservative stand and oppose Sangha involvement in political affairs if he wishes his doctrinal reforms to be considered as legitimate interpretations of the Dhamma. So long as he wishes his interpretations of Buddhism to be considered within the context of Thai Theravada Buddhism, and not as the work of an isolated, unauthorized eccentric or maverick external to that tradition, he can do nothing but abide by or acquiesce in the narrowly defined, non-political and non-involved role laid down for monks.

The contradiction between Buddhadāsa's theoretical integration of the worlds of social action and Dhamma and his own isolationist personal practice and conservative political views is therefore forced upon him as a monk of the official Thai Sangha. While Buddhadāsa does appear to personally support the traditional isolation of the monk from active social involvement, he could not have decided otherwise and still have remained a recognized and respected interpreter of official Buddhism, even if he did have more radical personal views. The contradiction in Buddhadāsa's work is in fact inherent in the institutional character of Thai Buddhism and could only be overcome either by an unprecedented reform in clerical practices or by a schismatic dissociation from the authority and controls of the official church. Buddhadāsa is uninterested in either of these radical alternatives and so the contradictions between his life and work and between his political and non-political thought, in the final analysis, remain irresolvable.

Because he has in practice withdrawn from active world-involvement and because he does not want to engage in confrontational politics, Buddhadāsa's suggestions for the realization of his ideas of a Buddhist polity and social order avoid directly facing or threatening the power and authority of the Sangha hierarchy or the Thai state. As a consequence, his suggestions remain unrealistic and idealist, even if morally laudable. Nevertheless, in order to appreciate the total system of Buddhadāsa's work it is necessary to consider his suggested means of realizing Buddhist ideals in the social world as he himself presents them. By way of completing this study of Buddhadāsa's thought and work, his views on the power of religion to effect social transformation are considered below in the final section.

## RELIGION—BUDDHADĀSA'S SOLUTION FOR SOCIAL ILLS

Buddhadāsa considers the ultimate solution of social and political problems to lie in the development and application of morally informed knowledge or wisdom. For example, he regards both his spiritual and his social thought as providing an alternative approach to the social reforms suggested by communists, a spiritual Buddhist way to attain peace. He maintains that communism only arises as a popular ideology when religion has decayed, and so restrengthening religion must be at the root of ending both the capitalist-caused social problems which communism addresses, as well as the perceived threat of communism itself:

> Communism will only arise when religion loses its power . . . Whenever religion loses its power it no longer has influence over the minds of human beings and then people will of necessity become so selfish that they consider no other person. And those who endure this oppression and exploitation then must rise up to fight it. (T)[32]

Buddhadāsa maintains that religion decays primarily because of misinterpretations of doctrine which, in turn, lead to the growth and spread of materialism:

> Whenever people think that mental matters are less important than material concerns, communism will arise. If religion still has the correct teaching people will necessarily feel that mental things are more important than the material.(T)[33]

When religious doctrines are misinterpreted in the modern context, religion becomes irrelevant to contemporary life and people are forced to look elsewhere, to materialist doctrines, in order to find answers to their current problems. Buddhadāsa's *phasa tham* interpretations are therefore as important to his social doctrine as they are to his reinterpretations of Buddhist philosophy. He regards his *phasa tham* interpretations as revealing the true relevance of Buddhist teachings to modern life. He also considers these reinterpretations to provide the means to prevent people leaving Buddhism for materialism or communism because of disenchantment with the religion's conservatism and contemporary irrelevance. For example, Buddhadāsa regards his *phasa tham* interpretation of "birth" or "life" as the arising of self-centredness, and his emphasis on salvation here and now, as being correct views which, if widely understood, would prevent people becoming interested in communism:

> Our community of Buddhists is still too fatuously concerned with the next world, after death. In fact Buddhism doesn't fatuously place its hopes in the next world but is instead a system of correctly fighting *kilesa* here and now; with being able to completely eradicate thoughts and actions dangerous to humanity here and now for us to see [the results] in this life. (T)[34]

Buddhadāsa does not limit his criticisms of the failings of contemporary religion to Buddhism, and he sees similar misinterpretations in other religions as also promoting the capitalist materialism which produces the social ills of poverty and exploitation in contemporary society and the communist reaction to these ills. He regards all religions as sharing a common *phasa tham* essence, the eradication of self-centredness and the reattainment of *chit wang*, and he sees all religions as having a vital role in solving the world's problems. He says,

> That which is called *nibbāna* is the result of holding to religion, to every religion. According to their preferences other religions do not call it *nibbāna* but the result of practising that religion in reality is that which we call *nibbāna*. (T)[35]

Buddhadāsa maintains that religions should realize their common nature and work collectively and cooperatively in fighting their common enemies. Rapprochement between religious traditions is consequently a central element of his program to better the world:

> Looking on other religions as enemies is the height of stupidity; it is the greatest misunderstanding and the greatest danger to humanity. There is nothing in any religion that need make it an enemy of another religion. That is, if we look at the heart of the thing called religion we will feel that every religion wants to eradicate the feeling called "I"–"mine," or strong self-centredness. That is the core of every religion. (T)[36]

At the supramundane level of *phasa tham* Buddhadāsa says that there are no differences between religions and that we only "separate out Buddhist, Christian, Moslem because we have not attained to the truth." (T)[37] By saying that every religion is at core the same Buddhadāsa not only attempts to build bridges between religions but also presents a justification for the importation of ideas from other religions into Buddhism. The extent of Mahayana and Zen influence upon Buddhadāsa's ideas has already been analyzed in chapter 7, but there has also been input from Christianity. Perhaps the most important influence from Christianity is the notion of God. Buddhadāsa says:

> The classification of religions into two groups, atheistic and theistic, is a very shallow classification and does not touch the real essence or meaning of religion.[38]

He attempts to breach the theistic-atheistic distinction by claiming that, despite popular opinion to the contrary, Buddhism does in fact have a God, arriving at this conclusion via a very Buddhistic reduction of the Christian notion of divinity to Dhamma, or the law of nature. Buddhadāsa gives Dhamma a fourfold theistic interpretation as follows:

1. Nature, or the entire natural system of the cosmos.
2. The laws of nature.
3. Activity in accordance with the laws of nature, i.e. moral action.
4. The results attained from abiding by the laws of nature.[39]

This definition is then used to argue that all of nature is what other religions mean by "God's body," the laws of nature are "God's mind," abiding by the laws of nature is to follow the desires or commands of God, and the result of such moral action is a gift or offering from God.[40] But Buddhadāsa does not only link Buddhism and Christianity doctrinally via the concept of God; he makes a much broader claim that Buddhists

> can accept the passages of Christianity [i.e. the Bible], if they are allowed to interpret the language of Dhamma (*phasa tham*) in the Bible in their own terms.[41]

These views, however, have not been well received by some other Buddhists, particularly in Sri Lanka. An author identified only as "A. de S." says of Buddhadāsa's book *Christianity and Buddhism*,

> this book is an apology for Christianity and a subtle attempt to convert the Buddhists of Thailand . . . . The Office of Christian Education in Bangkok, from which the book comes, has chosen its propagandist and propaganda unwisely and erroneously, for the venerable *bhikkhu's* words will be like seeds cast on stony ground.[42]

Another Sri Lankan, Amarasiri Weerarame, criticizes the theory of *phasa tham* upon which Buddhadāsa bases his rapprochement with Christianity as "so much bluff." "There is no such thing as a common Dhamma language serving as a common denominator to all religions."[43] Weerarame makes the realistic comment that:

> By trying to interpret away Christianity to fit into the thought and concepts of Buddhism he does violence to both Buddhism and Christianity.[44]

Weerarame concludes that Buddhadāsa "is advocating a new brand of religion which is neither Christian nor Buddhist. It cannot be accepted by either party."[45] On this issue Buddhadāsa also has critics in Thailand. Sulak Sivaraksa's accusation is that "He always looks at things from a good perspective. In particular, he sees other religions and other cultures through rose-coloured glasses."[46](T) That is, Sulak criticizes the universalist character of Buddhadāsa's views of other religions which diminish the specific Thai character of Buddhism which many progressive Buddhists, like Sulak, see as a bulwark against foreign cultural influence in Thailand.

But at least some Christians view Buddhadāsa's theories positively. Swearer, an academic and a Christian, says:

> Among the Thai Buddhists with whom I have talked it is generally agreed that Buddhadāsa is the most important as well as the most controversial spokesman for Buddhism in Thailand today. He is praised for his profundity in expounding the Dhamma but at the same time is criticized because his erudition exceeds the understanding of the ordinary man. Others are unhappy with the originality of his

thought asserting he does not expose the scriptures, especially the *Abhidhamma* . . . . Buddhadāsa stands alone as one of the most creative, profound and stimulating thinkers I have discovered in the Buddhist Sangha.[47]

Sulak Sivaraksa retorts, however, that when considered seriously,

> There is no way that Christians can accept Buddhadāsa's rendering of the notion of "God." That Thai Christians do accept it is because it is beneficial for them to do so and because they are the minority in Thailand. (T)[48]

That is, Sulak maintains Buddhadāsa is in effect providing a Buddhist legitimation for a foreign, non-Thai religious form.

However, contrary to the Sri Lankans' claims, Buddhadāsa is not in fact interested in opening the way for Buddhists to convert to Christianity. On the contrary, his emphasis on the common unity of all religions is meant to reinforce each person's commitment to his own religion.

> It is because of ignorance of the language of *Dhamma* that one abandons one's own religion and embraces another. If one really understands the meaning of one's own religion in the language of *Dhamma*, one will love his own religion just as one loves one's own life.[49]

Indeed, Buddhadāsa regards his *phasa tham* interpretations as actively preventing Thai Buddhists becoming Christian, saying that the superstitious accretions to Buddhism tend to make Thai Buddhists despise "their own religion; consequently they embrace Christianity, which is comparatively new to them and has no such superstitious practices."[50] Through appreciating his or her own religion in terms of *phasa tham* he wants each person to know that which is the highest and most profound teaching of that religion. And it is through an in-depth appreciation of one's own religion that Buddhadāsa considers materialism and communism will be fought and defeated:

> Let each person have his own religion, enter into his own religion and then vigorously confront communism. Don't stupidly think that the coming of communism would end Buddhism. Buddhism is not in such a poor state, it is not so weak . . . . Buddhism must be like a mountain. When communism collides with that mountain it must die. We have and keep to the Dhamma which is the heart of religion. It must resist communism. (T)[51]

This attitude differs markedly from that which has been put forward by Anan Senakhan, Kittiwuttho Bhikkhu, and other religious conservatives, namely that communism is a great threat to Buddhism. Fighting communism has been argued as vital to national security because, given the belief that Buddhism underpins both the nation and the monarchy, the anti-religious stance of communism is regarded by conservatives as threatening the whole fabric of Thai society. Morell and Samudavanija note that the traditional accusation of various Thai governments' counter-insurgency propaganda was that "When the communists control a village they will force all the monks to leave the temple and thereby destroy the village's religious life."[52] Buddhadāsa disagrees. Firstly, he sees the primary social problem in Thailand as exploitation—communism is simply a response to the self-centred and greedy hoarding of wealth by capitalists. Secondly, he thinks that communism is only seen as a viable response to exploitation when the religious response is either misinterpreted or dismissed as irrelevant because of misinterpretation. Buddhadāsa considers all forms of materialism to be threats to social well-being and to peace, and does not regard either capitalism or communism as being a better political form. And rather than attacking communism directly, Buddhadāsa proposes that the truth of religions should first be more widely revealed and that a form of *dhammic* or religious socialism should be built upon that universal spiritual truth. By this approach Buddhadāsa maintains that the materialism of both capitalism and communism are attacked simultaneously, in a spiritual and radical rather than merely symptomatic way.

Buddhadāsa is conscious of presenting a social theory which is neither capitalist nor communist and explicitly states that Buddhism "doesn't agree with capitalism . . . . It isn't communism . . . . Buddhism is consequently neither strongly rightist nor strongly leftist."(T)[53] He also says:

> Buddhism is neither materialism nor idealism but a state of correctness between both; or to put it another way it is both kinds in proper proportion. (T)[54]

And Buddhadāsa would like to see Buddhism rather than capitalism or communism as both the religious and social ideology of Thailand. "If the majority of Thais were true Buddhists they would not prefer any ideology other than Buddhism."(T)[55] And in these few words Buddhadāsa reveals the nexus of social and religious motivations behind his work, and the reason for his qualified popularity among progressive Thai Buddhists. He desires a return to the "True Buddhism" as a means of ensuring that the religion not only remains the most important Thai institution but also becomes a catalyst for the progressive transformation of Thai society.

# 10

# CONCLUSION: BUDDHADĀSA BHIKKHU— THERAVADA BUDDHISM'S CONSERVATIVE RADICAL

IN 1990, Sulak Sivaraksa edited a collection of articles on Buddhadāsa's life and work called *Radical Conservatism*, a title that placed slightly greater emphasis on Buddhadāsa's connection to Theravada tradition than on his radical rethinking of Thai Buddhist orthodoxy. Buddhadāsa was both a radical and a conservative, trenchantly criticizing long-accepted views on Buddhist teaching in Thailand by claiming that his position was based on spiritual orthodoxy. Whether one places more emphasis on Buddhadāsa's radical critiq ues or his more conservative continuities with Thai Theravada tradition may in the end amount to little more than quibbling. Both his radicalness and his conservativism are equally essential components of his religious life and his thought. However, in this summary reflection on Buddhadāsa, the man and the thinker, I lean more towards seeing him as a radical at heart. Amidst the entrenched conservativism of the Theravada Sangha in Thailand, only a committed radical could have envisioned a complete reform of the teachings of his country's dominant religion, and spent all his adult life striving to realize that vision.

While Buddhadāsa is a theoretician and his contribution to Theravada Buddhism lies in the realm of doctrinal interpretation, a simply philosophical analysis of his work would nevertheless fail to capture the full import of his intellectual impact. As discussed in the introduction, because of the key role of institutional Buddhism in Thai political, social, and cultural life, the doctrinal aspects of the religion must also be viewed in terms of their extra-religious impact in the secular domain. Similarly, when analyzing contemporary teachings on Buddhism it is as important to investigate the possible social sources of ideas and interpretations as it is to seek out theoretical precedents within the Buddhist tradition itself. In the introduction I also argued that a social and philosophical analysis of Buddhadāsa's thorough review of Theravada teachings should be undertaken with an attitude of sympathetic engagement. That is, Buddhadāsa's work should always be treated sympathetically by acknowledging the specific intellectual and sociocultural contexts which he has worked within and drawn upon. At the same time, however, one should not refrain from engaging Buddhadāsa and making explicit the contradictions and limitations of his presentations of Theravada Buddhist thought.

These above methodological principles are necessary components of any analysis of Buddhadāsa's work which does not oversimplify his contribution to Buddhist scholarship. And for this same reason, when attempting to present an overall evaluation of Buddhadāsa's contribution to Buddhism it is also necessary to avoid overly simplified judgements. It simply is not possible to summarize the results of Buddhadāsa's fifty years of intellectual work in one or two pithy, easily digested statements. Rather, to be true to the man and to his monumental opus one must make multiple evaluations of the various themes which characterize his writings and which set his work apart from both traditional and most contemporary Theravada Buddhist scholarship in Thailand.

Traditionally Buddhism has taught that salvation from suffering is attained by detachment from the world of impermanence, which it was assumed was beyond the power of individual human beings to change or better. In the face of the vagaries of nature and his fellow man the Buddha sought a permanent transcendent reality which could provide human beings with an unshakable spiritual refuge. In contrast to this traditional view of the world, the thought of progressive, modernist Thai Buddhists is informed by the belief that the natural and social worlds can be transformed for the better and that human suffering can be ameliorated through the exercise of human will coupled with technological and political power. In his systematic reinterpretation of Theravada Buddhism, Buddhadāsa has attempted to develop a comprehensive view of human well-being in which neither transcendent *nibbāna* nor active world-involvement is either denied or given exclusive emphasis. He has attempted to subsume the polar opposites of "this world" and the "next world" into a unity which, he hopes, will retain all the truth and saving power of the Buddha's spiritual message while also affirming the material saving power afforded humanity through scientific knowledge and technological skill. In terms of the traditional role divisions of Theravada Buddhism, Buddhadāsa has attempted to integrate the renunciate's hope for salvation with the layperson's hopes for well-being and fulfilment in this world here and now.

It cannot be over-emphasized that in attempting this integration of the spiritual and mundane, Buddhadāsa has embarked on a theoretical enterprise which is without precedent in the history of Theravada Buddhism in Thailand. His goal has been to theoretically reconstruct the entirety of Theravada thought in accord with reinterpreted doctrinal principles. In this effort he has displayed an unparalleled intellectual ruthlessness, being prepared to reject and denounce any views or interpretations which contradict his radical presentation of doctrine, even if those views are contained in time-hallowed commentaries or the scriptures of the *Tipiṭaka* themselves. The consistency and scale of his work in themselves give his work intellectual significance and stature in Thailand. Not content to reform only a few details of Buddhist teaching, Buddhadāsa has instead persistently mounted a radical attack on traditional interpretations of the doctrinal fundamentals of the religion.

To a philosopher and student of religion Buddhadāsa's grand program of innovative reform is at once inspiring and challenging. Not only has he set about instilling vitality into the long-stagnant intellectual environment of Theravada Buddhism in Thailand, but he has also undertaken this task systematically and thoroughly. Buddhadāsa inspires intellectual respect because his work incorporates both a grand vision of the total reform of an intellectual tradition and a scholarly concern for the detailed realization of that vision. Neither a scholastic pedant nor a remote and abstract theoretician, Buddhadāsa manifests in his work a rare integration of intellectual abilities.

Furthermore, the vision which has motivated Buddhadāsa throughout his life is one which is of universal concern in the modern world: the integration of the society- and world-transforming power of contemporary science and technology with the notions of human value expounded in religious ethics. Buddhadāsa inspires respect not only because of the compelling intellectual power of his complete restructuring of Theravada doctrine but also because of his keen awareness of contemporary religious and social issues. While his concern is with the place of Thai Buddhism in the modern world, the issues he deals with are not unique to Thailand or to Buddhism. Despite the differences in theoretical and terminological details, any Western thinker likewise concerned about human and religious values in the age of science cannot but feel sympathy for the ideal to which Buddhadāsa has devoted his life.

More specifically, Buddhadāsa has made major contributions to Theravada Buddhism at three different levels. At the level of Buddhist theory and doctrine he has presented a consistent demythologized view of the religion's teachings. By incorporating notions of scientific rationalism and by re-emphasizing the implicit rationalism of doctrinal Buddhism, Buddhadāsa has presented a radically simplified view of Buddhist teachings which systematically eschews metaphysical accounts of phenomena, whether physical or mental. At a more implicit level his rationalist account of Buddhism has changed the emphasis of the religion, focusing not on the transcendent or the metaphysical "other world" but on the immediacy of life here and now. Without devaluing the pivotal place and significance of *nibbāna* in Buddhist thought, Buddhadāsa has related that condition of ultimate salvation to activity in the social world. Provided it is informed by moral principles and practised with *chit wang*, material activity oriented towards the progressive development of the social, economic and political orders is thereby given religious value, being viewed as part and parcel of the human quest for salvation from suffering.

Buddhadāsa's third major contribution to Theravada Buddhism has been at the level of practice. With moral activity in the social world being defined as part of the Buddhist religious quest, Buddhadāsa has provided a justification for providing the layperson with access to the core of Buddhist teachings and practices which are concerned with the attainment of *nibbāna*. No longer excluded from the inner sanctum of Buddhist teaching or practice, in Buddhadāsa's system the layperson is given spiritual rights and potentials equal to those of the monk.

But while giving due weight to the intellectual significance of Buddhadāsa's work, one cannot overlook the limitations of his system. There are numerous theoretical tensions in his work. For example, the pivotal interpretative theory of *phasa khon–phasa tham* is poorly argued for and its application is described in a vague and highly ambiguous manner. In addition, Buddhadāsa denies the authority of the *Abhidhammapiṭaka*, which provides the most definitive canonical source of the conceptual distinctions which underpin his own two-language theory. There are also numerous places in Buddhadāsa's books, such as in discussions of rebirth, heaven, and hell, where the interpretations developed with the *phasa tham–phasa khon* theory come precariously close to a denial of the Buddha's own statements recorded in the core scriptures of the *Suttapiṭaka*. Because of his strong rationalist approach, Buddhadāsa is prepared to reject sections of the scriptures which contradict or conflict with his strictly doctrinal interpretations.

However, he also explicitly values the Buddha's recorded words in the *Suttapiṭaka* as a singularly authoritative source of interpretations of the Dhamma. Despite this emphasis on the Buddha's own statements, Buddhadāsa nevertheless does not acknowledge or resolve the tensions which arise when his own interpretations contradict what the Buddha himself is reported as having said. For example, in places, the Buddha explicitly describes rebirth and post-death states of being, which Buddhadāsa states are irrelevant to Buddhist spiritual practice. There are also omissions and inaccuracies in Buddhadāsa's use of other textual materials. His misinterpretations of Zen notions and the managed use of Zen texts to support his own reformed Theravada views are one of the clearest examples of the inaccuracies in the details of Buddhadāsa's work.

But while his reinterpretations are flawed in many places by weak or unsupported arguments, by unacknowledged omissions from cited sources, and by the failure to detail the contradictions involved in his views, I do not regard these problems of detail to themselves invalidate or undermine Buddhadāsa's entire enterprise. Many of the logical or theoretical difficulties result from an inadequate elaboration of notions and arguments or from insufficiently detailed analyses. In several places I have shown that Buddhadāsa's position can often be vindicated by a clearer and more detailed presentation of the arguments. The work of the Buddhist scholar Phra Rajavaramuni has been referred to on several occasions to indicate that many of the flaws in Buddhadāsa's work are not insuperable but can often be corrected by a more subtle and careful appreciation of the theoretical issues.

In reinterpreting Buddhist doctrine, Buddhadāsa has always had the intention of effecting a practical reform in Thai Buddhism. However, it does not appear likely that his views will obtain the degree of general support necessary to effect significant religious reform in the immediate future. Of greatest importance to Buddhadāsa's long-term success in this regard is his recognition and acceptance outside of the small group of the Thai middle class and educated elite who constitute his main audience. However, it must be noted that while his work is of indisputable theoretical importance, Buddhadāsa's views are not popular amongst the broad mass of the Thai populace. A clerical follower of Buddhadāsa, *Phra* Pracha Pasannathammo, gives the following lament:

> But the leaders of society, whether of the secular or religious spheres, have barely been influenced by these intellectual waves [of Buddhadāsa's work] in all these fifty years that have passed [since Buddhadāsa's mission began]. Even though each day people get to know more and more about both Suan Mokh and Buddhadāsa, when we take stock of the actual situation we cannot say that Buddhadāsa's thought has any serious influence on Thai society.(T)[1]

It is often argued that the erudite and complex nature of his thought and the novelty of his prose style make Buddhadāsa inaccessible to the average Thai Buddhist. Somboon Suksamran says

> He [Buddhadāsa] has a considerable body of published work, but his level of thought is such as to limit its circulation to intellectuals. Though widely respected in Thailand as a saintly man who has divorced himself from the mundane concerns of Sangha administrators, he is not essentially a political figure and does not command a political following.[2]

However, it is not only his language and style which cut him off from the majority of Thais. The very character of Buddhadāsa's views, which are highly critical of many traditional and still widely-accepted aspects of Thai Buddhism, prevent those views becoming widely popularized. Niels Mulder describes Buddhadāsa and similar reformers as

> . . . propagating the Buddhist path as a solution for all worldly problems, the idea being that, if the Thai say they are Buddhists, they had better be true Buddhists and organise their personal lives and society accordingly. This perspective is of course highly utopian and very much in contradiction with the meaningful structure of domesticated Thai existence.[3]

Religious reformers such as Buddhadāsa are by and large a tiny minority regarded as irritating rather than enlightening by the vast majority of Thais who also call themselves Buddhist.

In a sense Buddhadāsa is an ideologue without an effective social mouthpiece. He is not popular among peasants or workers or in the halls of power but only among a small group of like-minded intellectuals who, by and large, are disenfranchised from the actual decision-making processes of Thai politics and who stand in uneasy relation to the rest of Thai society. Modern journalists, scientists, students, authors, intellectuals, and social critics do not yet appear to have found a place of general acceptance or acknowledged relevance in the changing Thai social system, and Sulak Sivaraksa realistically observes that

> So long as those who govern the country still possess the power of

> carrying out *coups d'etat*, such as began in 1932, and so long as they still govern the land solely by military force they will not consider it important to listen to intellectuals.(T)[4]

The general rejection of Buddhadāsa's ideas even by many sympathetic Buddhists, and particularly by those highly placed in Thai society, is exemplified by the outcome of Buddhadāsa's debate with Kukrit Pramoj (discussed in chapter 5) over the com-patibility of *chit wang* and social development. Commenting on this debate Mulder concludes:

> Buddhadāsa maintained that *santosa* and *śunyatā* are noble and constructive attitudes that are fully compatible with the requirements of modern life, but was never able to convince the pragmatist M.R. Kukrit, and for all practical purposes it would appear that Thai policy makers and administrators will decide about the acceptable contents of Buddhism in Thailand.[5]

The disenfranchisement of Buddhadāsa's main audience among critical, modernist Buddhists from the exercise of real power in Thai society is indicated by their, and Buddhadāsa's, emphasis on a lay rather than a clerical or institutional form of Buddhism. To reform or modernize institutional Buddhism would be to confront and oppose its alignment with the state, and neither Buddhadāsa nor his supporters at present have either the power or the united will to overturn that relation. As such, religious and politico-cultural frustrations are released in marginal or peripheral developments, like the increasing emphasis on lay Buddhism and Buddhadāsa's own work, which do not affect the entrenched political or religious hierarchies.

Because of the entrenched conservatism of the Thai Sangha, significant changes in Buddhist practice and teaching are only possible outside the official religious hierarchy. As a consequence, the most dynamic areas of Thai Buddhism are those least subject to the control of central Sangha authorities, whether amongst the laity, in new heterodox organizations of the Sangha (e.g. Phothirak's establishment of a *de facto* third *nikai* or sect in Thailand), or in isolation from the Bangkok Sangha authorities, as in the forests of southern Thailand. In aiming to reform Thai Buddhism, Buddhadāsa first disengaged himself from the immediate authority and influence of the Sangha hierarchy by retreating into solitary contemplation in the forest. But, nevertheless, he neither disrobed nor split with the official Buddhist church, remaining, at least in name, within that church. This disengagement from the conservative authorities amounted to an admission that, in Mulder's words, any reformist activities he might have attempted in Bangkok would "never stand a chance to clean up the cobwebs of complacency and traditionalism that prevail in the higher levels of the Sangha hierarchy."[6]

Buddhadāsa's return to his remote home town of Chaiya in 1932 was a trade-off, a withdrawal from attempts at changing the Sangha from within in exchange for the freedom to innovate in areas outside the immediate jurisdiction of that hierarchy. In practice, this has meant an emphasis in his work on Buddhism for laypeople, for the lay practice of Buddhism offered, and still offers, the greatest scope for change and adjustment to contemporary conditions of any section of Thai Buddhism. While removing himself from direct involvement with and opposition to the official hierarchy has granted Buddhadāsa a high degree of intellectual freedom, it has not been without the cost of limiting the extent of practical reforms his ideas are capable of effecting. By having chosen an extra-institutional role for himself, Buddhadāsa is thereby limited to an extra-institutional impact. In terms of the institutional alignments of clerical and political authority in the Thai Sangha and government Buddhadāsa's retreat from formal clerical associations to establish his own distinct following and centre of study in the remote south of the country has in fact functioned to siphon religious discontent away from the conservatively intransigent official clerical hierarchy. Buddhadāsa's failure to consider or directly deal with the entrenched power of the conservative Sangha constrains him to act within the limits defined by that hierarchy and introduces into his teachings the fundamental practical contradictions discussed in chapters 8 and 9.

Official Buddhism may more and more become a shell, a residue of magic, superstition, and animism for some, a symbol of political and religious power for others. And correspondingly, the religious meaning of the Buddha's message of salvation may increasingly be found outside rather than inside the Sangha—among laymen and laywomen rather than among monks. But unless and until the shell of institutional practice and ritual is in fact changed, modernizing and reforming Buddhist trends such as initiated by Buddhadāsa will have little impact on religious or social policy, or on state decision making. As such, Buddhadāsa's relative fame and restricted popularity but ultimate impotence remain as a symbol of the divisions and unresolved tensions in Thai society caused by recent economic and sociocultural change. For Buddhadāsa to seriously assist in resolving those tensions and to fulfil the promise of his desire to concretely reform and modernize Buddhism would require him to move out of the realm of theory and step fully into the realm of action which he espouses but refrains from entering.

However, it is unjust to judge the practical or social importance of Buddhadāsa's work by its short term failure to effect significant religious reform. Buddhadāsa's reinterpretation of Buddhism is built upon a modernist view of human existence which has yet to penetrate throughout Thai society. More than 70 percent of the Thai population are still rice farmers, most receiving no more than primary education and continuing to live in traditional village-based communities. If the process of modernization continues in Thailand, if education levels increase and scientific methods of agriculture and industrial production become more and more the norm, and, perhaps more importantly, if the population shift to the cities and towns does not slacken, then in the coming decades social conditions may be created in Thailand which favour a more general acceptance of Buddhadāsa's social and religious vision. After all, as argued in chapter 2, Buddhadāsa's views were influenced by the beginnings of social modernization in Thailand in the nineteenth and early twentieth centuries. If it is the case that the widespread acceptance of modernist religious views is dependent upon social and cultural modernization, then Buddhadāsa's teachings could only be expected to grow in popularity if the proportion of Thais participating in the non-traditional sectors of Thai society continues to grow.

However, by this I am not predicting a necessarily bright future for Buddhadāsa's views in the coming decades, although his work may well attain general popularity by the beginning of the twenty-first century. There are counter-indications to the assumption that social modernism leads to religious modernism and rationalism. While the response to social change by a minority of Thais, like Buddhadāsa and his supporters, has been to seek a firm basis for life by reaffirming the verities of the doctrinal core of Buddhism, others have turned to popular animistic religious forms for support and solace. As Mulder observes,

> Animistic expressions of religion are very much on the increase, with more and more magically gifted monks, amulets and holy water, the veneration of potent images and shrines, and the practice of pure esotericism and magic to ensure good luck and supernatural blessings.[7]

In this context monks are not so much regarded as representatives or expounders of the Dhamma as they are manipulators and mediators of a sacred magic which is regarded as ensuring protection and well-being. Even among many secular Thais there is a tendency to follow the ritualistic practice of religion rather than to be aligned with the modernism expressed by Buddhadāsa. This is because even though they may be uninterested in finding meaning in religion, these secular Thais take the public practice of ritual as simply the way things are done and see more benefit in conforming to such officially sanctioned ritualism than in causing antagonism or ill feeling by explicitly denying it, as does Buddhadāsa.

But whatever the future social conditions in Thailand, there are, nevertheless, internal tensions in Buddhadāsa's reinterpreted system which may limit the further impact of his views. These tensions are not related to the errors, omissions, and other theoretical flaws already mentioned above. Rather, they occur at a deeper structural level of his work, arising at the points where his ideas impinge on the social and practical domains. Most apparent here is the tension between Buddhadāsa's theoretical abolition of the distinctions between monks and laypeople but his highly conservative personal practice, which is based upon a retention of those traditional role divisions. There is also the further contradiction between his promotion of the notion of the right of all people, whether laypersons or monks, to seek ultimate salvation through their own efforts, and his staunch belief that individual political rights should be forsaken in order to guarantee social harmony under a dictator. Furthermore, not only does his own life provide no model of actually living the Dhamma in the social world but his conservative spiritual practice serves to reinforce the traditional idea that spiritual practice requires a literal renunciation of the world.

The contradiction between Buddhadāsa's theoretical radicalism and his conservative practice manifests itself in many ways, all of which raise doubts about the ability of his system to successfully fulfil his stated intention of making Buddhism relevant to the lives of contemporary people. The tensions between theory and practice tend to alienate some of the very people Buddhadāsa has said he is most concerned to reach—the progressive, modernist, and educated Thai laypeople. For example, Buddhadāsa's criticisms of liberal democratic forms of government and his tacit support for the political status quo in Thailand are at odds with the democratic ideals of most progressive Thais. While having effectively isolated himself from the mundane concerns of Sangha administrators, Buddhadāsa is nevertheless not perceived as standing for a politically independent monkhood. His explicit support for authoritarian government tends to alienate a significant number of those who otherwise wholeheartedly support his modernizing enterprise.

However, the structural contradictions in Buddhadāsa's work do not have only a sociological significance. They also raise the question of whether Theravada Buddhist doctrine is in principle capable of being consistently reinterpreted in terms of a modernist world view. Nevertheless, I do not believe that Buddhadāsa's personal inability to effect the sweeping reforms he foreshadowed early in his career should be taken as indicating that Theravada is incapable of adjusting its role and outlook in order to become an effective moral and religious voice in modern Thai society. At the level of doctrine Buddhadāsa has forcefully demonstrated that precisely the opposite is the case. Rather than being an other-worldly religion which deflects human interests away from the realities of concrete social existence, Buddhadāsa has shown that Theravada is in fact a highly adaptable system, with vast theoretical resources for reform and for development in new directions. By abolishing the religious distinction between the monk and the layperson Buddhadāsa has also abolished the doctrinal basis for the traditional pyramidal structure of religio-moral authority in the Thai Sangha. This structure of religious authority is founded upon the traditional notion that only a spiritual elite has access to the truth of *nibbāna*. In contrast, Buddhadāsa maintains that *nibbāna* is universally accessible because it is simply the deepening and development of the mind's natural condition of *chit wang*. The notion of *chit wang* thus lays the foundation for a Buddhist ideology in which all people are regarded as equals, all possessing the moral qualities necessary to be autonomous, responsible individuals. Buddhadāsa's reinterpreted version of Thai Buddhism belies any stereotypical claim that Theravada is an inherently world-negating and elitist religion. One should not make the mistake of equating the scope and potential of such a complex theoretical system as Theravada Buddhism with its interpretation and practice in any particular period or place.

The contradictions of Buddhadāsa's reinterpretations are not at root theoretical but result from the impact of the conservative political and religious context in which he has worked. Given the conservative political situation in Thailand and the strength of entrenched views of the sociocultural significance of the Sangha, the structural contradictions between Buddhadāsa's radical theory and conservative practice are all but unavoidable. As already noted above, the contradictions associated with Buddhadāsa's conservative religious practice and support for the traditional asocial role of the monk derive from his having avoided either direct criticism of or interaction with the Sangha hierarchy. To overcome this contradiction would necessitate a direct confrontation with the Sangha hierarchy. But as also previously noted, the Sangha is universally regarded as a holy institution and to attack or criticize it too vehemently is considered inauspicious, sacrilegious, and highly dangerous, because of the potentiality of unleashing uncontrollable social disorder and confusion or *wunwai*.

Because of the practical limitations of the tradition within which he has worked, Buddhadāsa's thought may represent as radical a reform of institutional Thai Buddhism as is presently possible. The contradiction between his radical thought and conservative practice is after all forced upon him by the orthopraxy of Theravada Buddhism in which interpretations of doctrine are authorized more by the interpreter's strictness in practice than by his or her intellectual acumen or theoretical arguments. For Thai Buddhism to be more fully reformed and for the tension between theory and practice to be resolved may well require a second-generation follower of Buddhadasa to literally emerge from the "forest" into the social world. If Buddhadāsa's teachings do gain increasing acceptance in the future their role may be as a platform or base for further reform. However, it does not seem possible for Buddhadāsa himself to complete the reforms which he has foreshadowed and discussed.

There is in fact only one theoretical stumbling block to the further modernization and reform of Theravada Buddhism, namely, the scripturally sanctioned importance of the role of the renunciate monk, and the definition of the monk's spiritual status as being determined by his degree of detachment from the social world. As already discussed at length in the concluding chapters, despite his radical theoretical innovations in most other areas of Theravada teaching, even Buddhadāsa has not been able to loosen this theoretical knot. The role of the lay Buddhist has been expanded to the point where for some of the more educated laypeople monks are almost an irrelevance. However, for political reasons it is not possible at the present time to expand the role of the monk into the social realm. Attempts are being made in this direction but barriers nevertheless remain. I suggest that the barriers preventing monks from participating in social life more fully are more political than religious or scriptural. For as Buddhadāsa himself has noted, the Buddhist virtues of *mettā* and *karuṇā*, i.e. loving-kindness and compassion, can be interpreted as implying the need to actively assist others to end suffering. Theravada possesses the ingredients necessary to devise a Buddhist theory of clerical social involvement and social action. However, it appears that doctrinal potential has not been realized because of the pressure to maintain the traditionally constituted Sangha hierarchy as the idealogical religious basis of political power in Thailand.

Because of the historical relations between the monarchy, the Thai state, and the Sangha, and because of the long history of political instability since 1932, there is a general reticence to attempt any radical reform which might upset the delicate religious-ideological-political balance in Thailand. More concretely, however, the conservative political forces in Thailand have considerable power and deal strongly with those who attempt to alter the triangular relations of Sangha-king-state upon which their own positions and influence depend. During the 1973–1976 period of civilian government, when many in the Sangha did become involved in social issues, those clerics who supported social reforms such as land reform, labour union rights, housing for the poor and so on, were scapegoated and denounced as communists. With the reestablishment of military rule in 1976 there was a forced return to the traditional clerical role of non-involvement.

Thus while Buddhadāsa's work is without doubt the most important progressive religio-theoretical development in recent Thai history, its full impact and implications have yet to be realized. For Buddhadāsa's religious vision to be fulfilled requires two things. Firstly, there is a need to develop a clear analysis of the role and place of the monk in contemporary Thai society. But more importantly, social and political conditions in Thailand must also change. The realization of Buddhadāsa's ideas in Thai social life would require the existence of an educated audience which has enough social and political power to restructure social relations according to their modernist Buddhist ideals. But whether the proportion of more educated, progressive Thais will in fact increase, and whether they will succeed in obtaining real social and political power, cannot be predicted at this point. Credit must be given to Buddhadāsa for his monumental theoretical work in which he has planted the seeds of an alternative form of Buddhism and a vision of an alternative Thai society. Whether the full potentiality of those seeds is able to develop will depend upon the future course of political and cultural events in Thailand.

# EPILOGUE: BUDDHADĀSA BHIKKHU—HIS LAST DAYS AND HIS LEGACY

## THE PASSING OF BUDDHADĀSA BHIKKHU

BUDDHADĀSA BHIKKHU[1] passed away just after 11.00 A.M. on 8 July 1993 at his forest monastery of Suan Mokh or Wat Than Nam Lai in Suratthani Province, southern Thailand. However, many of his lay and clerical followers believe that the revered monk in fact passed away several weeks before his physical death, soon after he suffered a severe stroke on the morning of 25 May 1993, and that only intensive medical intervention delayed his inevitable passing. In the weeks between late May and early July 1993 the medical treatment provided to the comatose Buddhadāsa and debate on the issue of the right to die became foci of public debate in Thailand. The intensity of feelings generated can be gauged from comments made by one of Buddhadāsa's Western clerical followers, Santikaro Bhikkhu, who described the efforts to keep Buddhadāsa alive after his stroke as "a tragedy of a confused, commercialised, unnatural, and overly politicised medical system."[2]

Buddhadāsa Bhikkhu proved to be almost as great an object of controversy in his passing as he had been while in command of his faculties. As I trace the events from the onset of Buddhadāsa's final illness to his cremation on 28 September 1993, I record the efforts of the revered monk and his devout followers to ensure that the manner of his death and the disposal of his physical remains accorded with the principles that he had espoused and lived by during the more than sixty years he had been an ordained monk.

## BUDDHADĀSA'S FINAL ILLNESS—SUAN MOKH AND SURATTHANI

The Thai press reported that in the weeks before his fatal stroke Buddhadāsa had become tired of living with failing health and often remarked that his period of useful time in this life had passed. *Matichon Weekly* reported that since the end of the *phansa* rains retreat the previous year, Buddhadāsa's discourses had increasingly dealt with the topic of *nibbāna*.[3] A female lay follower, Lamon Khemnak, reported to the magazine *Chiwit Tong Su* that on the day before his stroke Buddhadāsa had said to her,

> The Lord Buddha attained *nibbāna* when he was 80. I'm already 87. I don't know why I'm still alive. It's not good to live longer than the Buddha[4] . . . . My eyes are really blurred. The doctor says that blood vessels in my brain are constricted.[5]

On 25 May 1993 Buddhadāsa woke at his usual rising time of 4.00 A.M. and for a few minutes he wrote notes for a discourse to be given on his eighty-seventh birthday in a couple of days' time. But he told his attendant that he felt ill and returned to bed.[6] A couple of hours later Buddhadāsa told the abbot of Suan Mokh, Phra Khru Palat Silawat (commonly known as Achan Pho Chantasaro), that he was afraid his "old ailment was coming back." Not long afterwards he said, "I can't say anything. My tongue is getting hard." Buddhadāsa's speech became increasingly indistinct in the following period, but he continued making an effort to talk. *Matichon Weekly* reported his final words before he became unconscious as follows:

> His final words that could be understood were a recounting of the *Nibbāna Sutta*, '*na pathavi na apo na tejo na vayo* . . . [no earth, no water, no fire, no wind . . . ].'[7] He repeated this again and again. In addition he also said, 'I don't feel that it's me (*mai rusuek pen tua ku*),'

'[There is] no gain and no loss (*mai buak mai lop*),' 'Peace (*santiphap*),' 'Well being (*santisuk*).'[8]

Buddhadāsa then fell into a coma from which he never regained full consciousness. The supervising doctor at Suan Mokh diagnosed a stroke and recommended that Buddhadāsa be taken to Suratthani Hospital for a CAT scan. At the hospital it was determined that he had suffered bleeding in the left hemisphere of the brain and he was admitted to the intensive care unit and placed on a saline drip. Buddhadāsa's condition gradually worsened on that day, with bronchial congestion and increasing weakness on the right side of his body.

On 27 May Buddhadāsa was placed on an artificial respirator after the intervention of a doctor from Bangkok. Buddhadāsa's followers became concerned about the quality of treatment he was receiving after this intervention, as before his final illness Buddhadāsa had indicated that when he became severely ill and the time of his passing approached he did not want to be attached to any life-prolonging medical equipment. In the event, he remained attached to a respirator from 27 May to his death on 8 July. Later on the afternoon of 27 May, a group of seventeen of his close associates and relatives led by the abbot of Wat Chonprathan Rangsarit, Phra Panyananda Bhikkhu, decided that it would be appropriate to bring the comatose Buddhadāsa back to Suan Mokh, to accord with his often stated wish to die there. He was brought back to Suan Mokh at 5.00 P.M. on that day and put to bed in his own room. From Buddhadāsa's unconscious condition when he returned, his closest followers believed that "he had already passed away."

## KING BHUMIPOL'S CONCERN AND THE MOVE TO SIRIRAJ HOSPITAL

Over the years Buddhadāsa's declining health had been an object of concern to King Bhumipol Adulyadej. Santikaro reports that after Buddhadāsa suffered a heart attack in October 1991 the king requested the revered monk, "Don't let the body cease just yet; please remain to teach the Thai people a while longer."[9] At that time the king also ordered first-class medical care to be made available to Buddhadāsa. King Bhumipol had been particularly concerned by the reports of Buddhadāsa's stroke, and at his request a Royal Thai Air Force plane was prepared at the Suratthani air base to take Buddhadāsa to Bangkok for treatment at Siriraj Hospital.

On 28 May a group of more than twenty of Buddhadāsa's clerical and lay followers headed by Phra Panyananda reviewed the medical prognosis on Buddhadāsa's condition and considered King Bhumipol's offer of assistance. In particular, the meeting discussed a Bangkok neurologist's proposal that Buddhadāsa be transferred to Siriraj Hospital. A majority, but not all, of this group agreed to let the neurologist and his superiors take Buddhadāsa to Bangkok for treatment. This decision was taken after the neurologist assured the group that Buddhadāsa's condition could improve if he were given the proper treatment. The doctor argued that Buddhadāsa's condition was treatable, taking the fact that he had responded to touch and squeezed the hand of Phra Panyananda as indications that he might be able to regain consciousness. The Siriraj doctor also promised the group that Buddhadāsa's treatment would not involve surgery and that if his condition deteriorated severely he would be brought back in time to die at Suan Mokh as he had wished. Buddhadāsa was transferred to Siriraj Hospital on 29 May.

Buddhadāsa had maintained that Buddhism teaches not to unnecessarily prolong life, and that when it becomes clear that death is inevitable "nature should be the doctor."[10] However, Buddhadāsa's illness polarized thought on how his condition should be treated. Many of his clerical and lay supporters believed that Buddhadāsa was on the point of death and intensive medical intervention was pointless and would only delay the inevitable. But some doctors at Siriraj Hospital believed that Buddhadāsa could respond to treatment and regain consciousness if administered with the latest medical technology. The heated public dispute over Buddhadāsa's treatment led to calls in the Thai press for legal and ethical consideration of the issues surrounding the right to die, "so that the conflicts such as those that occurred in the case of Buddhadāsa are brought to an end" (p.17).

Dr. Prawet Wasi, a prominent lay follower of Buddhadāsa and an eminent physician, added a philosophical element to the debate. Three weeks before Buddhadāsa's physical death, Dr. Prawet wrote that "Buddhadāsa 'died' long ago," meaning that he had died to all attachments to this life and to "I" and "mine" (Thai: *ku*, *khong ku*).[11] In arguing that Buddhadāsa should be taken off life support equipment and allowed to die naturally, Dr. Prawet cited a poem by Buddhadāsa titled "Buddhadāsa Will Not Die" (*Phutthathat chak mai tai*)[12] that indicated the revered monk had no fear of acknowledging his mortality. Dr. Prawet also noted that it is his personal policy as a medical doctor not to unnecessarily "prolong death," saying,

> In a society that is irrationally afraid of death they will use various technological methods to prolong death. On precisely this point one group uses a completely opposite term, they call it 'prolonging life' . . . . (p. 10)

Despite earlier promises that Buddhadāsa would not be operated on, a tracheostomy was performed on 27 June and he received the first of several blood transfusions the following day. Buddhadāsa's condition then deteriorated rapidly. In succession, his kidneys failed, a blood vessel burst in his stomach, and his heart began palpitating. A Swan-Ganz Catheter was inserted through a vein in his right wrist, up the arm, and to the heart in order to monitor blood flow and pressure. On 1 July, Buddhadāsa was given a kidney dialysis and another blood transfusion. On the night of 7 July he was diagnosed as having septicemia.

Early on the morning of 8 July 1993 the supervising doctors at Siriraj Hospital agreed that death was imminent and informed his relatives and closest followers. Buddhadāsa was then returned to Suratthani Airport by a Royal Thai Air Force C130 plane, arriving at 10.08 A.M. He arrived at Suan Mokh thirty-five minutes later. At 11.10 A.M. Phra Khru Palat Silawat announced over a loudspeaker that Buddhadāsa had passed away peacefully. After his death Buddhadāsa's Dhamma tapes were played over the loudspeaker at Suan Mokh and in the marketplace at Chaiya, his birthplace, "as if he were still alive."[13] At 12.00 midday on 8 July, Buddhadāsa's will was opened and read at Suan Mokh.

## BUDDHADĀSA'S WILL

On 28 March 1993, just under two months before his fatal stroke, Buddhadāsa had made a will (*phinaikam*) at Suan Mokh in the presence of three male witnesses, including his nephew, Dr. Wichan Phanit, and Chitti Tingsapat, a Privy Councillor.[14] In this document he specified arrangements for the disposal of his remains upon his death. Buddhadāsa indicated that he wanted his funeral to be conducted in accord with the principles by which he had lived. He was concerned to ensure that no elaborate cremation ceremony was performed and that none of the superstitious rituals that he had criticized all his adult life were conducted over his remains.

In his will Buddhadāsa specified that before cremation his body should be kept in a tightly closed coffin which should not be opened for viewing and that there should be no sprinkling of holy water nor any ceremonial recitation of prayers (*suat mon*) over his body. He also requested that after cremation his ashes should be divided into three portions and scattered at three locations: in the sea at Chong Ang Thong, off the northern islands of the Ang Thong Peninsula in Suratthani Province; on the waters at the source of the Tapi River on Khao Sok Mountain in Suratthani's Phanom District; and at Khao Prasong Mountain in Tha Chana District of Suratthani.

Wanaprat says that Buddhadāsa wanted his ashes to be dispersed because "he did not want anyone to keep anything [of his remains] except the Dhamma that he had taught throughout his life."[15] In an interview with *Siam Rath Weekly,* Phra Khru Palat Silawat surmised that Buddhadāsa wanted some of his ashes spread at Khao Prasong because his mother's and father's remains were interred there, and that mountain can be seen in the distance from Suan Mokh.[16] As for the other two locations, Phra Silawat noted that they are places that many people travel to visit and spreading Buddhadāsa's ashes at the source of the Tapi River, for example, would be as if,

> he wanted the Dhamma and his teachings to spread out like the flowing [Tapi] river that passes by so many places over the whole region of what was once the greatness of the Kingdom of Srivijaya, which was a centre of religion, art and culture.

On the evening of 8 July, in accord with his stated wishes, Buddhadāsa's body was interred in a wooden coffin and placed in a newly constructed building behind the Sala Dhammaghosana building at Suan Mokh. At this simple ceremony Phra Panyananda said, "From this moment forward Buddhadāsa will live in all our hearts, may we all continue to perform our duty [to the Dhamma] in his place" (p. 11). Phra Panyananda went on to explain that Buddhadāsa did not want Pali incantations chanted over his body because, "the people who listen [to Pali] can't understand it. The person who chants doesn't translate the meaning for us to hear. He [Buddhadāsa] wanted to reform the way we make merit."

Soon after Buddhadāsa's death, it was announced publicly that his funeral would take place on 27 May 1994, which would have been his eighty-eighth birthday, and that the cremation would be broadcast live on national TV. But Buddhadāsa's funeral was in fact brought forward to 28 September 1993. Phra Silawat later said that the cremation was brought forward to comply with Buddhadāsa's wishes that his funeral be simple and because in the two months after his death almost a hundred thousand people had visited Suan Mokh to pay their respects to Buddhadāsa's remains. Phra Silawat stated that if he had waited until May 1994 to conduct the cremation the expected crush of people would have caused severe logistical problems for Suan Mokh.

September 28 was "Paying Respects to Than Achan [Buddhadāsa] Day" (*Wan tham wat than achan*), a day when Buddhadāsa's followers traditionally visited Suan Mokh to pay their respects. After Buddhadāsa's death the name of this day was changed to "Visiting

Suan Mokh Day" (*Wan yiam suan mok*). While the cremation had not been pre-announced, many followers and admirers of Buddhadasa were present, including Phra Panyananda, Dr. Prawet Wasi, Major-General Chamlong Srimuang, and then Prime Minister Chuan Leekpai. Phra Panyananda was the first to light the funeral pyre and Wanaprat reports that during the cremation a tape that Buddhadāsa had pre-recorded for the occasion was played over loudspeakers.[17] On this tape Buddhadāsa admonished those present not be remiss in their spiritual practice, adding that he had once been like all those who were at that moment sitting in front of the blazing funeral pyre, and that one day everyone will certainly be as he is now. A policeman stood guard over the remains during the night as the ashes cooled in order to prevent theft.

## BUDDHADĀSA BHIKKHU'S LEGACY FOR THAI BUDDHISTS

In speaking to the *Nation Weekly* after Buddhadāsa's death, Dr. Prawet Wasi said, "Buddhadāsa's teachings are something that will never die. They are eternal and lasting, and so that is the same thing as Buddhadāsa still being alive."[18] But writing several years before Buddhadāsa's death, Louis Gabaude maintained that, compared with traditional interpretations of the religion, Buddhadāsa's demythologized Buddhism has two major deficiencies.[19] Firstly, it does not satisfy the need for consolation that many people seek from religion, and secondly, the excision of the supernatural aspects of Buddhism could cut Buddhadāsa's interpretation of the religion off from its popular roots. Gabaude concluded:

> If Buddhadāsa was teaching just for an elite like he [said he] did in the [nineteen] forties, there would be no problem. He has his elite of followers. Let it be. The problem arises when this elite pretends to change popular and general Buddhist habits in Thailand. (p. 226)

Between Prawet's eulogy of hope and Gabaude's qualified appraisal of the likely future influence of Buddhadāsa's ideas in Thailand, how are we to assess the intellectual legacy of the man?

I think this is best done if we consider separately Buddhadāsa's significance for his supporters among the Thai intelligentsia, and the relationship between Buddhadāsa's rationalized Buddhism and the traditional forms of religious belief and practice in Thailand. The disparity between Prawet's and Gabaude's comments reflects the inevitable difference in viewpoint that will exist between an enthusiastic supporter of reformed Buddhism in Thailand and an external observer of the manifold forms of that religion.

## BUDDHADĀSA AND THAI BUDDHIST IDENTITY IN THE ERA OF GLOBALIZATION

Buddhadāsa's legacy is not limited to his reforms of Buddhist doctrine. In Thailand Buddhadāsa's intellectual legacy extends beyond religion and his ideas have had an impact on Thai intellectual culture as a whole, contributing to a growing spirit of reform in many areas of Thai social life including politics and the economy. Since the 1970s, Buddhadāsa has been especially influential in what Jim Taylor calls "counterhegemonic" political movements in Thailand.[20] That is, pro-democratic and antimilitary groups that support political decentralization and the empowerment of marginalized sections of Thai society. On this point, Santikaro observes,

> Achan Buddhadāsa has always been one of the main guides and inspirations [of reform-minded Thais]. Even former students who spent time in the forest with the CPT [Communist Party of Thailand] testify to this.[21]

Buddhadāsa has been an important influence on the Thai environmental movement. The clerical activist Phra Prachak Khuttachitto has been one of the most prominent figures in this movement in recent years. Taylor observes,

> Phutthathat has been an immense influence on many clerical and secular Buddhist activists in the past three decades, including Prajak,

> especially in his notion of a grassroots "socialism" (*sangkhomniyom*) inherent in the teachings of the Buddha. . . . Essential to this philosophy is the need for living a simple and moderate life in harmony with nature. This conflicts radically with the Western notions of modernisation, social and economic achievement, and individual and national progress embedded in capitalist development theories.[22]

In reviewing my 1989 book, *Buddhism, Legitimation and Conflict*, Suwanna Satha-Anand criticized my proposition that Buddhadāsa has provided ideological support for the development of Thai capitalism.[23] However, Suwanna mistakes the anti-capitalist content of Buddhadāsa's writings for the effect that his life work has had upon social and political discourse in Thailand. While it is true that Buddhadāsa's work does not in itself support the materialistic values of capitalism, some Thais have indeed interpreted his rationalist account of Buddhism as supporting modernization and capitalist development in Thailand. Some revisionist interpreters, such as Chokechai Sutthawet, read Buddhadāsa as providing a Buddhist basis for the rationalization of the Thai bureaucracy, polity, and economy, conditions that they regard as important requirements for the further development of Thailand's capitalist economy.[24]

Chokechai in particular has extended Buddhadāsa's religious reforms into a broad-based critique and "radical reform" of traditional Thai values in order to develop a Thai Buddhist basis for the country's integration into the global economy and culture. While Chokechai's views are not representative of the majority of Buddhadāsa's followers, they do show how the reverend monk's ideas were taken up in the 1990s and why Buddhadāsa is likely to have a lasting impact on Thai intellectual life.

Chokechai begins his consideration of Buddhadāsa's ideas by asserting that Thais should emulate the struggle for "rationality" in the history of Western culture, especially in uprooting irrationality from religion. He compares Buddhadāsa to John Calvin, who, he says, "released people from the yoke of the Catholic distortion [of Christianity] . . . and permitted people to approach God directly without needing the intercession of a priest" (p. 34). Chokechai presents a strong version of the Weberian thesis that posits an historical relationship between Protestantism and the rise of capitalism, saying that the Protestant reformation in Northern and Central Europe "(unintentionally!) helped the capitalist style of economy develop and grow quickly" (p. 34).

Chokechai maintains that Buddhism is a highly rational religion, as evidenced by the Buddha's directives in the *Kalama Sutta*,[25] but adds that many Thais are still steeped in religious irrationality. He attributes this irrationality to Phya Lithai's medieval text, the *Traiphum Phra Ruang*,[26] making the unfavorable comparison that Lithai was compiling the "irrational" *Traiphum* at the same time that European thinkers were reforming their own religion in the light of reason.

Reflecting on Buddhadāsa's intellectual impact in Thailand, Chokechai states that his legacy is a "method of radical reform" (*withi kan patirup yang thueng rak ngao*) that can be applied to any context, and which has the capacity to effect significant change in Thai society and culture. According to Chokechai, the effectiveness of Buddhadāsa's method of radical reform depends only on the extent to which it is applied in practice:

> It has been said that [Protestant] Christianity in Europe gave capitalist development there a special difference from capitalism in other regions of the world. But whether Buddhadāsa's rationalist reform of Buddhism will have an impact on economic, political, social and cultural development and on conservation of the environment in Thai society depends on the extent to which Thai people or Buddhists practise the principles of religion and religious ethics in their everyday life and work. (p. 35)

Chokechai adds that those people who apply this rational understanding of Buddhism in their everyday life and strive to improve Thai society "are the hope of Thai society!" (p. 35, emphasis in original). He characterizes the reason espoused by those he calls "the hope of Thai society" in the following ways. Firstly, rationality denotes "self-realization and self-understanding, broad critical insight [*wichan yang ropkhop*], the capacity to anticipate events and . . . to free oneself from habit." Secondly, Chokechai maintains that reason is not only a property of Western culture, but is a fundamental characteristic of the true core (*kaen thae*) of Buddhism that Buddhadāsa revealed to be "a function of Thai indigenous knowledge [*phum panya*]." He says, "we should divest ourselves of attachment [to the idea] that reason is a property of Westerners but not of Easterners." And thirdly, Chokechai believes that the rationality which Buddhadāsa revealed to lie at the core of Thai Buddhist culture is the same reason that has driven historical advances in Western societies and which is at the root of the process of globalization (*lokaphiwat*) in which, Chokechai maintains, the divisions between East and West are being replaced by a unified global culture.

To summarize, Chokechai identifies reason as the key feature of the emerging global economic and cultural culture. And he locates this reason, which is capable of effecting economic, political, social, and cultural transformation, as existing in the core of Thai Buddhist culture. Following this argument, it is therefore possible for Thailand to participate in the global culture of reason on an equal footing with the West. In other words, it is possible for Thailand to move forward from its own Buddhist cultural roots and embrace the global culture of reason while still remaining characteristically Thai. In Chokechai's hands Buddhadāsa's ideas are used, on the one hand, to support Thai cultural irredentism and nationalism and, on the other hand, to support Thailand's integration into the global economic and cultural order. Significantly, in this account Thailand's "globalization" is not only considered possible without the loss of Thai cultural identity but is also represented as a return to the purportedly rational roots of Thai Buddhist culture.

The double-edged thrust of Chokechai's account, simultaneously looking inward to Thailand's past and outward to the modern global economic order, derives from the twofold movement of Buddhadāsa's thought. This twofold movement involves opening up to the powerful world of ideas outside Thailand while at the same time reaffirming the fundamental place of Buddhism and Buddhist identity in Thailand. One of Buddhadāsa's most important legacies to Thai Buddhists is that he has provided an intellectual framework that simultaneously affords the security of affirming the lasting value of Thailand's cultural past while challenging his compatriots to face the outside world head on.

## BUDDHADĀSA AND POLITICAL DISSENT IN THAILAND

Still, Chokechai's rosy views on the impact of globalization on Thailand are not shared by all of Buddhadāsa's followers, and Santikaro Bhikkhu believes that Chokechai has "wandered quite far from Achan Buddhadāsa's message." Presenting an analysis similar to that developed by Taylor and Suwanna, Santikaro says,

> *Tan Ajarn* [Buddhadāsa] never argued for the integration of Thailand into the global economy. Rather, his criticisms of materialism, consumerism, and capitalism—as well as Marxism—should lead thoughtful readers to think of getting disentangled from the global economy . . . . *Tan Ajarn* is highly critical of the capitalist project and the unbridled individualism and selfishness it has fostered.

The conflicting pro- and anti-capitalist readings of Buddhadāsa show that it is not possible to characterize his intellectual impact in Thailand in terms of a single, neatly definable political position.

Taylor states that the "activist theological orientation" of Buddhadāsa's supporters in Thailand as "decisively counterhegemonic," but this describes only one thrust of this activist Buddhist ideology, namely, grassroots environmental activism.[27] Buddhadāsa was consistently counterhegemonic, to use Taylor's term, but there were numerous sites of political opposition in Thailand in the 1990s, not all of whose interests coincided. One tendency amongst the counterhegemonic groups that look to Buddhadāsa is indeed anti-centrist and pro-local, and supports the interests of the uneducated poor against the interests of the political and economic centre. But another tendency is pro-democratic and antimilitary, and supports the interests of the educated professional and commercial Thai middle class, which is now increasingly a part of the political and economic centre of the country that stands in opposition to the urban and rural poor. There is thus a significant disjuncture in the political usages to which Buddhadāsa's ideas are now applied in Thailand, a disjucture which has developed in parallel with shifts in the site and nature of political opposition in Thailand in recent decades.

In the 1970s and early 1980s key sites of opposition to state authority were among the educated middle classes who struggled against entrenched bureaucratic and military power. At that time sections of the middle classes turned to Buddhadāsa for a Buddhist basis for democracy and the rationalization of Thai social and economic life. Chokechai represents a recent development of this middle class appreciation of Buddhadāsa. However, with recent rapid economic growth and a widening income gap between rich and poor, sites of political opposition have arisen among the urban and rural poor, and Buddhadāsa's ideas have also been appropriated by representatives of these marginalized groups and by the Thai environmental movement in order to support anti-capitalist grass-roots activism. In this context, the increasingly wealthy middle class is now more and more a part of the Thai economic and political establishment that stands in opposition to the poor majority of the Thai population. Indeed, some members of the middle class who support the earlier, rationalist, anti-military forms of activism based on Buddhadāsa's ideas are now likely to be among the capitalists opposed by the NGOs and grass-root activists who also look to Buddhadāsa for inspiration.

## BUDDHADĀSA AND TRADITIONAL BUDDHISM

But Buddhadāsa is not only popular among those Thais who see themselves as being opposed to the political and economic establishment. He has also achieved prominence among many apolitical Thais who remain attached to the traditional forms of Buddhism that Buddhadāsa criticized. There is an apparent contradiction here. For even though Buddhadāsa was radically opposed to the religion that many Thais still seek security in, he has nevertheless achieved the status of a Buddhist intellectual guru among those who follow the traditional forms of Buddhism. This was evidenced by the intensive press and media coverage of his final illness.

How is it that Buddhadāsa has become so popular in Thailand? There appear to be at least two reasons. Firstly, the influence of Buddhadāsa's rationalized Buddhism has now spread to sections of Thai society outside the educated middle class, his most important early audience. The already-noted concern of King Bhumipol for Buddhadāsa's health in 1991 and 1993 indicates that his ideas now receive a degree of official approval and support in Thailand.[28] But it is also true that as Buddhadāsa's reputation as a revered monk has spread he has been incorporated within the traditional patterns of religious belief still adhered to by many Thai Buddhists. The name and fame of Buddhadāsa are now known much more widely than his ideas, and he has become increasingly popular because many traditional Thai Buddhists regard him the same way they regard other revered monks, as a source of sacral supernatural power, *saksit.*

## BUDDHADĀSA AND THE THAI MONARCHY

On page 226 of this book I say that by de-emphasizing *kamma* and the related notion of merit in his teachings Buddhadāsa has undermined Theravada Buddhism's historical function of legitimating the monarchy and centralist political institutions in Thailand. However, in the 1990s the legitimating relationship between Buddhism and other important Thai institutions such as the state and the monarchy has changed and my comment, written over a decade ago, now needs to be revised. King Bhumipol's interventions in 1991 and again in 1993 to afford medical treatment to Buddhadāsa, who less than twenty years previously had been accused of being a communist who undermined Thailand's national institutions, bespeaks the extent of the ideological shift that has taken place.[29]

King Bhumipol's concern for Buddhadāsa's health and his 1991 request for Buddhadāsa to "remain to teach the Thai people a while longer" suggest a repositioning of the monarchy relative to the traditional *kammic* account of Buddhism. In this account the monarch's right to rule was legitimized by the notion that Thai kings possessed great personal merit or *bun* and so were the most deserving person to rule the country. Buddhadāsa criticized the notion of merit on which this traditional political legitimating ideology was constructed, replacing it with the notion that those in power earned the right to rule by demonstrating ethical conviction and moral rectitude in their personal conduct.

King Bhumipol's interventions suggest that the rationalist form of Buddhism propounded by Buddhadāsa has "arrived," in the sense of being incorporated within the state-supported ideological construction of Thai Buddhism. This does not mean, however, that the traditional *kammic* interpretation has been rejected. The older interpretation of Buddhism remains as part of the ideological panoply of Thai Buddhism. But it has been moved aside from its former central and dominating position, now sharing the ideological stage with rationalist Buddhism.

In analyzing discourses and practices concerning sexuality in Thailand, Rosalind Morris cites Eve Sedgwick as noting that issues of sexual definition in contemporary societies are not structured by one model superseding another, but rather by the "unrationalised co-existence" of different and often conflicting models.[30] Morris then remarks, "The present appears to be one of those times in Thailand when different and mutually irreconcilable systems cohabit in a single social field." I think Sedgwick's and Morris's insight can be extended to the domain of religion in Thailand. That is, Thai religious culture in the 1990s is characterized by the coexistence of multiple conflicting trends. In the mid-1990s it is difficult to maintain that the forms of Buddhism adhered to by any particular socioeconomic stratum of Thai society—working class, middle class, aristocracy—are integrated or united by a single discourse or set of ritual practices. Indeed, Buddhism at several levels of contemporary Thai society appears riven by contradictory trends and it may be that efforts to discover general patterns that characterize "working class," "middle class," or "royal" forms of Thai Buddhism in the 1990s are misguided.

Peter Vandergeest has made a similar point in his study of Buddhism in southern Thailand in the nineteenth and early twentieth centuries. He writes,

> Religious practices in Songkhla were an assembly of rituals, practices, and meanings which cannot be identified primarily with any single tradition in a totalising manner. Rather, they were structured by the social context of the nineteenth century in Songkhla . . . . Cultural practices are best understood as the historical outcome of a multiplicity of practices with diverse origins in specific historical contexts which, for heuristic purposes, can be seen in terms of different interpretive domains (Buddhism, folk-Brahmanism, and so on).[31]

Thus, while Buddhadāsa's rationalized Buddhism may have "arrived" in terms of being increasingly accepted by many of those in authority in Thailand, the older *kammic* form of the religion has not "departed" from the scene. Furthermore, it is no longer possible to say, as I have in this book and elsewhere, that Buddhadāsa's main Thai audience is found among a certain socioeconomic group. Buddhadāsa now has followers and supporters among all strata of Thai society. In seeking to explain Buddhadāsa's influence in the 1990s we need a more sophisticated analysis that is more aware of context and attuned to the nuances of "time and place" that may lead an individual of any stratum of Thai society to adhere to one or other form of Buddhism.

## BUDDHADĀSA, THE THAI WORKING CLASS AND THE NORMATIVIZATION OF RATIONALIST MONKS

The extent to which Buddhadāsa's influence is spreading among Thai blue collar workers, for example, can be gauged from the wide coverage of his illness and death given in publications oriented at this market. The 17 July 1993 issue of the weekly magazine *Chiwit Tong Su* (in life you have to fight) devoted nine pages and its cover to documenting Buddhadāsa's life. Writing in *The Nation*, Nithinand Yorsaengrat has stated that *Chiwit Tong Su* entertains "the working class with information and stories that are relevant to the lives of local people in community villages and rent-houses," adding that it is a middlebrow magazine, "lighter, more colourful and more sensational than high-class magazines, but higher in quality than the bottom-end throw-aways."[32] Nithinand quoted the magazine's editor, Santi Savetvimol, as saying "Most of our readers are common people or underprivileged people who never give up on life." *Chiwit Tong Su* entitled its article on Buddhadāsa, "A Great Warrior Monk of the Army of Dhamma" (*phra yot nak-rop haeng kong-thap tham*).

The coverage of *Chiwit Tong Su* focused on Buddhadāsa the man rather than the thinker, and reflected what Grant Olson has called the normativization of rationalist monks such as Buddhadāsa.[33] Olson notes that Buddhadāsa's scholarly importance exists "within a small and limited, albeit growing, circle" and that there are many Thais who, despite Buddhadāsa's intellectual accomplishments, still insist on viewing him "within the bounds of more traditional types of devotion." According to Olson, such people are unlikely to have read Buddhadāsa's works and may only have heard of his growing reputation and related "holiness." Buddhadāsa was well aware of the tendencies for popular monks such as himself to be normativized within the traditional patterns of Thai supernatural beliefs. The injunctions he included in his "will" can be seen as an attempt to prevent the development of a supernatural cult around him or his remains after his death.

Other Thai publications have also focused on Buddhadāsa's reputed *saksit* status. One popularly oriented commemorative publication issued after Buddhadāsa's death was entitled, "The *Arahant*, Buddhadāsa Bhikkhu" and included the following as part of its dedication:

> This book has been prepared with pure intentions in order to honour and remember Phra Dhammakosacarya (Buddhadāsa Bhikkhu), [who is viewed as] an *arahant* in the hearts of Thai Buddhists.[34]

The title of a commemorative article in the *Nation Weekly*, "Buddhadāsa, A Monk Enlightened Throughout Eternity" (*Phutthathat phra phu tuen trap niran*), also implied that Buddhadāsa had attained enlightenment and was an *arahant*.[35] And writing of Buddhadāsa's cremation in the periodical *Mahatsachan* (miraculous), which reports on supernatural aspects of Buddhism, the journalist Wanaprat referred to the reverend monk as a *nakbun* (saint, holy man), a term more commonly associated with *saksit* figures than scholar monks.[36] Wanaprat also used the designation *luang pu* (revered grandfather) to refer to Buddhadāsa. *Luang pu* is a common colloquial title for senior monks often regarded as having spiritual authority and sacral power. Buddhadāsa's close followers rarely if ever use this designation, preferring to refer to him by the titles *than achan* (respected teacher) or *mahāthera* (great elder).

In this context, Olson relates an anecdote that shows how many Thai Buddhists regard Buddhadāsa and indicates the way in which even critics of traditional religious beliefs and practices can be appropriated within the very system they oppose. Olson writes that when visiting Suan Mokh in 1982 three soldiers had spoken to Buddhadāsa before his own turn came to talk with the monk. Buddhadāsa laughed as he later told Olson that the three soldiers,

> had driven all the way down to Suan Mokh from the Northeast and had arrived quite drunk. They requested that he [Buddhadāsa] blow in their ears for good luck and protection. He told them that he did not know how to do this (*rao tham mai pen*) and sent them to talk with another monk up the hill (who would tell them about the problems of drinking and smoking and encourage them to quit).

Santikaro Bhikkhu observes that, despite Buddhadāsa's best efforts, he has won a place within the pantheon of Thai holy or *saksit* monks, with all the connotations of supernatural power that attach to such an identification. Santikaro relates that he first realized that many Thai people viewed Buddhadāsa as a supernatural figure

> when I saw, while riding on a public bus in Bangkok, a street merchant hawking posters of *Ajarn* Mun,[37] *Luang Por* Wat Paak Naam,[38] Jesus Christ, some teen idols, and *Tan Ajarn* [Buddhadāsa]. He [Buddhadāsa] quietly chuckled, almost embarrassed, when I told him of this.

On page 265 of this book I write,

> Buddhadāsa is an ideologue without an effective social mouthpiece. He is not popular among peasants or workers or in the halls of power but only among a small group of like-minded intellectuals who, by and large, are disenfranchised from the actual decision-making processes of Thai politics and who stand in uneasy relation to the rest of Thai society.

These comments are now patently inaccurate. For one thing, and as Santikaro Bhikkhu quite rightly observes, Phra Panyananda has been a very effective "mouthpiece" for Buddhadāsa for decades, and that Phra Phayom Kanlayano and a large number of other monks and laypeople have taken his ideas throughout the country. As Donald Swearer reports, the prominent social critic Sulak Sivaraksa has been especially important in promoting Buddhadāsa's ideas as an ideology of political resistance in Thailand.[39] Santikaro notes that Sulak interested many students in Buddhism during the 1970s and that some of these activists subsequently took Buddhadāsa's ideas to the Thai countryside through their involvement in NGOs and rural development activities.

Much has changed in Thailand in the past decade, notably the economic boom and the political rise of the middle class. And together with these changes we see the growing importance of rationalist formulations of Buddhism and their coexistence and interaction with traditional forms of Buddhism. The end point of these changes cannot be easily predicted. It is safe to say, however, that Buddhadāsa's influence in Thailand will last well into the twenty-first century.

## BUDDHADĀSA'S LEGACY FOR WESTERN STUDENTS OF THAI BUDDHISM

In considering Buddhadāsa's legacy we should not forget that his popularity extends beyond the borders of his own society. More has been written about him by Western students of Thai Buddhism than any other recent or contemporary religious figure in Thailand.[40] However, I am not aware of any studies that have reflected on Buddhadāsa's popularity among Westerners and I wish to briefly consider why this Thai Buddhist philosopher monk should occupy such a prominent place in Western discourse about contemporary Thai Buddhism.

We need to look to more than a desire to record and account for Buddhadāsa's importance for Thai Buddhists to explain his popularity among Western students of Thailand. Intellectual values from our own culture are also at play in leading us to give prominence to Buddhadāsa. I suggest that Buddhadāsa is so often written about by Western students of Thai Buddhism because his ideas often come close to the views of rationally minded and scientifically educated Westerners. When we read or hear *kammic* accounts of Buddhism we may understand them intellectually but they remain culturally alien to own our intellectual world. We approach *kammic* accounts of Buddhism as anthropologists, students of that Western discipline which specializes in apprehending what is culturally "foreign" and "other." But when we, as Westerners, read Buddhadāsa we often have the experience of being with a kindred mind and we can appreciate and applaud his radical consistency in demythologizing Buddhism. Buddhadāsa is a Thai thinker whose work Westerners can not only describe anthropologically but also engage intellectually.

Western intellectuals enjoy the *frisson* of debate and our culture thrives on the challenge of confronting new ideas. Reading Buddhadāsa one feels the excitement of approaching a radical thinker. Furthermore, Buddhadāsa exemplifies the Western intellectual value of critique. He adopts a critical attitude to the sources of his tradition and, like a Western philosopher, conceives of his religion in terms of rationally explicable principles. What is more, we in the West value innovation and individuality. It is part of our tradition to lend support to the underdog who struggles against the entrenched positions of privilege and we admire those who take risks in achieving something new and different. Buddhadāsa manifested all these qualities that Westerners admire and for this reason he is an attractive figure for many Western students of Thailand.

Paradoxically, while many Thais regard Buddhadāsa's ideas and writings to be difficult to comprehend, many Western students of Buddhism find his explanations of Buddhist principles to be more accessible than traditional Thai accounts. This indicates the extent to which Buddhadāsa operated within a non-traditional intellectual framework having many affinities with Western discourses on religion. The Western discursive features of Buddhadāsa's work simultaneously made his writings dense to many of his compatriots yet lucid for non-Thais. In summarizing Buddhadāsa's innovativeness Gabaude points to the Western tenor of the man's work:

> Buddhadāsa hardly corresponds to any other figure in the Theravada tradition of Commentators. He has not just repeated sets of texts, and he has been creative in two ways: first by picking up 'jewels' from the Scriptures, brief and inspiring formulas such as 'nothing is worth grasping as me and mine'; secondly by proposing to make those 'pearls' change the society and the world. He probably would not be such an original and dangerous figure in a western Christian country where 'theologies' develop regularly. But he fits neither in the mold of monks preaching only on how to go to paradises by donating to the monks nor in that of monks preaching extinction [*nibbāna*] for monks only. This makes him, for some, the saviour; for others, the destroyer of Buddhism in Thailand.[41]

Gabaude's final point above is especially poignant. For it was precisely the radical and individualistic qualities of Buddhadāsa's life devoted to doctrinal reform that Westerners admire which ensured him a controversial position in Thai intellectual and political life.

In seeking to explain Buddhadāsa's popularity in the West we also need to acknowledge that many Western students of Thai

Buddhism applaud Buddhadāsa's demythologization of the religion. Many Westerners are excited by the idea of a rational, non-theistic religion based on practice and insight rather than faith. Buddhadāsa holds out the promise, but not the realization, of such a religion. Gabaude says that Buddhadāsa is popular among "decultured" Thais.[42] That is, those who are "no more bent towards 'consolation' and ritual security." Gabaude could equally be describing many Western students of Buddhadāsa. Most of us are "decultured" in the late twentieth century. The attitude that Gabaude describes is, after all, close to the heart of what is now called the "postmodern condition" of our society.[43]

In Buddhadāsa's work we find the affirmation of key intellectual values from our own culture and it is possible to read his life as a Southeast Asian instance of the "grand narrative" of the European Enlightenment: the hope for historical triumph of reason over unreason. In this context, Louis Gabaude's previously noted observations about the contradictions between Buddhadāsa's views and traditional Thai Buddhist beliefs and practices are especially relevant. They remind us, firstly, not to equate Buddhadāsa with Thai Buddhism and, secondly, not to unquestioningly adopt the rationality that Buddhadāsa championed as a totalizing explanatory principle in our own studies, perhaps leading us to mistakenly characterize rationalized Buddhism as inherently "progressive" and *kammic* Buddhism as necessarily "backward." For example, I have remarked elsewhere that attitudes to lay sexuality in the *kammic* tradition of Thai Buddhism are often more liberal and accepting of human diversity than among interpreters who work within the framework of rationalized formulations of Buddhism.[44]

## A PERSONAL CONCLUSION

Upon meeting Buddhadāsa one had the experience of encountering a remarkably reasonable person with valuable things to say about living happily and well amid the confusion and disarray of the twentieth century. Kasem Atchalai, writing in the *Arai Ko Dai* ("whatever") column of the *Nation Weekly*, concluded his recollection of an interview with Buddhadāsa, saying, "I remember that after the interview that day I was in a good mood (*arom di*) the whole rest of the day."[45] My own experience concurs with that of Kasem. My own short time with Buddhadāsa in 1983, and my many meetings with his ideas through his books and Dhamma talks on cassette tape, have also had the effect of leaving me in a good mood. I like to think that Buddhadāsa's legacy to us, Thai and *farang*, is not only his philosophy and his erudition but that he left us with a better frame of mind towards ourselves and others than before we encountered him and his work.

# APPENDIX: THE HISTORY AND TEACHINGS OF THERAVADA BUDDHISM

THE HISTORICAL founder of Buddhism was Siddhattha Gotama,[1] a prince born into the ruling Sakya clan of a small kingdom in the Himalayan foothills some two and half thousand years ago. By Buddhists Siddhattha Gotama is sometimes referred to as Sakyamuni, "Sage of the Sakyas," or as Gotama Buddha. The term "Buddha" in fact denotes any person who has attained complete spiritual enlightenment and is not an epithet restricted to the Gotama Buddha, although as the historical founder of the religion he is most commonly referred to simply as the Buddha or "the enlightened one." In the Theravada Buddhist scriptures, the *Tipiṭaka*, he is most commonly referred to as the Tathāgata, the "thus gone," which in Thailand is usually taken to mean the one who has attained the Buddhist spiritual perfection of *nibbāna*. According to tradition, at the age of twenty-nine several pivotal events deeply disturbed Siddhattha Gotama, leading him to renounce his life of royal ease as well as his wife and infant son in order to search for spiritual liberation. He tried but rejected as ineffective the Brahmanical and Yogic spiritual systems then existing in ancient India and after six years of following ascetic practices attained full enlightenment near the present Indian town of Bodhgaya after an effort of supreme concentration. He soon developed a following of fellow renunciates who became the forerunners of the present Buddhist monkhood or Sangha, literally "the community." After his enlightenment, the

Buddha lived to teach his message of liberation from suffering for a further forty-five years and it is from the teachings he then gave that the principles and scriptures of Buddhism are reputed to have come.

After the Buddha's death (c. 543 B.C.),[2] a council of his followers met and formalized his teachings, but for several centuries Buddhism remained a purely oral tradition. The texts accepted as canonical by the Theravada[3] sect now predominant in Thailand were not written down until the first century B.C. when the Ceylonese Buddhist king Vaṭṭagāmini had them inscribed on palm-leaf manuscripts. In opposition to the Sanskrit-speaking Brahmin priests of his time whose religion and teachings he rejected, the Tathāgata used a North Indian vernacular related to Sanskrit as the medium for propagating his teachings. This language is thought to have been close to what is now called Pali, which became the classical language of the Theravada scriptures. The use of Pali distinguishes the Theravada or "Southern School"[4] of Buddhism from the Mahayana[5] or "Northern Schools"[6] whose scriptures are recorded in Sanskrit as well as several national languages such as Tibetan, Chinese, Vietnamese, Mongolian, Korean, and Japanese. Schisms based on points of doctrine had appeared in the Buddhist clergy or Sangha within a couple of centuries of the Buddha's death and it was at a Buddhist council in India around 250 B.C. that the forerunners of the two major surviving schools of Buddhism, Theravada and Mahayana, formally split. Because Pali is traditionally considered to be the language of the Buddha, the followers of Theravada Buddhism in Sri Lanka, Burma, Thailand, Laos, and Cambodia regard themselves as the bearers of the older and purer form of Buddhism.

Buddhism had almost completely disappeared from its Indian motherland by the Middle Ages whence Ceylon, whose Sinhalese king had become Buddhist around 200 B.C., became the centre of the living Theravada tradition. And so when the Thai kings formally adopted Theravada Buddhism in the Sukhothai period some seven hundred years ago it was to Ceylon that they turned for authoritative instruction and definitive versions of the Pali scriptures, which are collectively called the *Tipiṭaka*. *Tipiṭaka* literally means "three baskets," denoting the three wicker containers originally used for storing the main divisions of the palm-leaf manuscripts. The three *piṭaka* or divisions of the Pali Buddhist canon are:

1. *Vinayapiṭaka*—discourses and discussions attributed to the Buddha emphasizing matters of practice and discipline which are collectively called the *vinaya.*
2. *Suttapiṭaka* or *Suttantapiṭaka*—discourses by the Buddha plus discussions about the doctrine, which is in general called the Dhamma.
3. *Abhidhammapiṭaka*—a philosophical development of some of the key ideas of the doctrine or Dhamma.

Traditionally Theravada Buddhism has been organized as a national church of monks arranged under a monarch who, as upholder of the faith, was also ultimate arbiter of clerical disputes and ultimate enforcer of clerical discipline. However, because of the culturally and politically disruptive effects of European imperialism in the other Theravada countries (Sri Lanka, Burma, Laos, Cambodia), this traditional structure is today retained only in Thailand. The Buddhist church itself consists of renunciate monks and the lay persons whose alms and donations support them. However, Theravadin monks are not in any sense priests interceding with divinities on behalf of the laity but are practioners and teachers of the doctrine who in theory have decided to strive for salvation more intensely by strictly following monastic discipline.

## CENTRAL TENETS OF BUDDHIST DOCTRINE

At the level of doctrine and teaching the most important concept in Theravada Buddhism is that of Dhamma. Dhamma is an extremely broad notion which while denoting the notion of doctrine also implies correct practice aimed at attaining salvation. The Thai Buddhist scholar Sunthorn Na Rangsi gives the following fourfold definition of Dhamma:

> 1. *dharma* as nature or natural phenomena, 2. *dharma* as condition or natural law, 3. *dharma* as doctrine as taught and formulated and 4. *dharma* as the quality of right or righteousness.[7]

Dhamma primarily denotes the order of the cosmos, both natural and moral, which patterns all of existence and whose fundamental truth the Buddha realized upon his enlightenment. The Buddha's insight and teachings are regarded as being informed by this cosmic-ethical order and so the doctrine of salvation is also called Dhamma. The editors of the *Pali English Dictionary* provide the following as one gloss on the term Dhamma:

> That which the Buddha preached, the *dhamma* . . . was the order of law of the universe, immanent, eternal, uncreated, not as interpreted by him only, much less invented or decreed by him, but intelligible to a mind of his range.[8]

And insofar as one abides by the Buddha's teachings one also abides by Dhamma and so the notion of righteousness is also integral to that of Dhamma.

At the level of soteriology Buddhism focuses on the truth grasped by the Buddha that human existence is inherently unsatisfactory, incomplete, and inadequate. This is called the truth of suffering, *dukkha*, or the universality of suffering. The Buddha's saving message was that not only is there a cause of suffering but there is also a way to end it, and suffering can be totally extinguished through moral and meditative practice. The cessation of suffering is called *nirodha*, while its complete extinction, even down to its causes, is called *nibbāna*, a term originally associated with extinguishing or putting out a flame. In Buddhist doctrine *nibbāna* is metaphorically interpreted as denoting the extinction of the flames of passion, lust, and delusion regarded as prime causes of suffering. This doctrinal core is usually expressed as the "Four Noble Truths" or *ariyasacca*:

| | |
|---|---|
| *Dukkha* | There is suffering. |
| *Samudaya* | There is a cause of suffering. |

| | |
|---|---|
| *Nirodha* | There is an end to suffering. |
| *Magga* | There is a path to the ending of suffering. |

Suffering or *dukkha* is theoretically linked with the process of rebirth through successive lives and the goal of Buddhism is to attain freedom from the turmoils of repeated births and deaths or *saṁsāra*. The problem of how to end *dukkha* is often expressed in terms of ending the process of rebirth which is, so to speak, the matrix within which suffering inheres. The cessation of suffering thus has both a psychological and a cosmological aspect, involving both the end of the mental state of *dukkha* and of the process of rebirth.

The Buddha proclaimed that the ultimate cause of suffering is *avijjā* or ignorance of reality. The reality of which most people remain ignorant is regarded as having three characteristics or *tilakkhaṇa*, namely, that all things are impermanent, *anicca*, are without an essence, *anattā*, and are inherently related to suffering, *dukkha*. According to the Buddha, everything is in flux and so nothing in the world is permanent or capable of providing either a secure physical or mental refuge. He taught that in ignorance of this reality people delude themselves that the physical and mental objects of desire can provide satisfaction. However, because those objects are impermanent and so pass away, such deluded desires or cravings are left unsatisfied, causing suffering. That is, ignorance leads to the delusion that what is in fact impermanent and inessential can provide lasting satisfaction. This delusion then breeds desire or craving for the impermanent things of the world whose evanescence is then the immediate cause of suffering.

Ignorance is also regarded as causing rebirth because it infects action with delusion so that it falls under the sway of the impersonal law of cause and effect called the law of *kamma*. Specifically *kamma* denotes an action performed with desire or intentionality, that is, with the desire to attain a particular object or goal. As Sunthorn Na Rangsi notes, for any action to be classed as *kamma* it

> must always be associated with the mental state of volition *(cetanā)*. Just an action without volition is not called *karma* in the Buddhist sense of the word, since such an action is not liable to yield any moral

> consequence to the performer. In the strict sense of the Buddhist doctrine of *karma*, it is volition itself which is called *karma*.[9]

At the psychological level, the law of *kamma* states that every intentional action bears an experiential fruit commensurate to the moral quality of the intention. While often simplistically expressed in Thai in the maxim, *tham di dai di, tham chua dai chua* or "Do good get good, do bad get bad," at the theoretical level this doctrine denotes the proposition that every intentional action performed in ignorance is a cause of future suffering. Buddhism isolates the cause of rebirth, and so of suffering, as lying in the necessary reactive working out of past intentional actions performed in ignorance. Because not every action has its reaction or *vipāka* effected within the scope of a single lifetime, Buddhist doctrine postulates the reality of rebirth, as permitting as yet "unripened" *vipāka* to be effected.

## BUDDHIST PRACTICE

At the level of moral practice Buddhism aims to reduce suffering through exerting self-control and self-restraint on cravings, which are the immediate cause of suffering. This system of self-restraint constitutes the Buddhist moral code, of which there are two general sets, a more basic set for the layperson and a much more elaborate codification of two hundred and twenty-seven rules, the *paṭimokkha*, for the ordained monk. Traditionally, Buddhist practice also distinguishes between two levels of spiritual endeavour, the lay or mundane path called *lokiyadhamma*, and the ascetic or supramundane path called *lokuttaradhamma*. The mundane path consists essentially of moral practices and, while regarded as reducing suffering, it nevertheless still leads to the production of the "substratum of rebirth," *paṭisandhicitta*, and does not lead to complete salvation from suffering or from rebirth. That is, it does not result in the attainment of *nibbāna*. The supramundane path, on the other hand, incorporates meditative practices regarded as leading to the complete cessation of rebirth and thus of suffering.

While the practice of morality reduces suffering it does not end it, for so long as there is ignorance there will be the delusion which is the basis of craving. Ignorance is dispelled by the attainment of insight into reality or enlightenment born of meditation. The final key to salvation from suffering is therefore wisdom, *paññā*, or insight into the truths of permanence and non-essentiality. The Buddha taught that when it is seen that everything one craves must necessarily pass away and leave one suffering in loss, such things will no longer be desired, and in ceasing to desire, the proximate cause of suffering is also destroyed.

Meditation is the pinnacle of Buddhist practice, standing atop a system of practices called the "Noble Eightfold Path" or *ariyamagga*, whose eight "limbs" are also rungs on the ladder leading to salvation. The eight limbs of the Noble Path are:

| | |
|---|---|
| *sammādiṭṭhi* | right view |
| *sammāsaṅkappa* | right intention |
| *sammāvācā* | right speech |
| *sammākammanta* | right action |
| *sammāājīva* | right livelihood |
| *sammāvāyāma* | right effort |
| *sammāsati* | right mindfulness |
| *sammāsamādhi* | right concentration or meditation |

*Samādhi*, the eighth limb, is often taken as denoting meditation in general, which in Theravada Buddhism is systematized in an elaborate range of practices. However, there are two basic types of meditation. The first, concentration meditation or *samādhi*, aims to develop calmness and one-pointedness of mind, while the second type, insight meditation or *vipassanā*, aims to use that mental power to delve into the mind and penetrate to a realization of the true nature of all things as *anicca, dukkha,* and *anattā*. One who has attained such saving insight is called an *arahant*, a "worthy one." With the ending of craving no further *kamma* is created but this does not necessarily mean that all action ceases, for Buddhism recognizes a form of liberated activity, *kiriyā*, freed of craving and so also barren of rebirth-causing and suffering-causing results.

*Nibbāna*, salvation, is the complete freedom from suffering which comes from insight into reality. Two conditions of *nibbāna* are recognized. The first, *sa-upādisesanibbāna*, is when as yet unreacted results of past actions continue to sustain the aggregates of individual human existence and is a form of salvation attainable while alive. However, the second form, *anupādisesanibbāna* or *parinibbāna*, is a post-death condition. *Nibbāna* has sometimes been interpreted as equivalent to annihilation and utter extinction into nothingness, seeing as there is no essence or soul to remain after death. However, at least in Thailand this is not the case and *nibbāna* is not regarded as total extinction. Rather, it is seen as the extinction of craving and the other factors that lead to suffering. *Nibbāna* is the attainment of a qualitatively different mode of existing in which all delusions about the self and about the objects of desire are extinguished.

## THERAVADA BUDDHISM IN THAILAND

Because of a too-scriptural and too-philosophical approach, many Western students of Buddhism have in the past portrayed the religion as other-worldly and disparaging of everyday mundane life. However, a fuller reading of the scriptures and a closer, anthropological view of the way Theravada Buddhism is in fact practised and understood by its Southeast Asian adherents reveals it as having had an integral relation to social and political life from the earliest times. However, while it is important to realize that Buddhism is and always has been a sociopolitical force, it is also necessary to appreciate that historically there has been a disparity between the *nibbānic* doctrine of salvation outlined in the previous pages and the popular religion of most Thai Buddhists. Traditionally, it has only been the monks and recluses, and often only some of them, who have aimed directly for *nibbāna*. Terwiel describes the common religious outlook in the Thai countryside as follows:

> No farmer aspires to reach *nibbāna*. This exalted state is reserved for the Buddha and the *arahants*. Whilst *nibbāna* certainly may be equated, in the eyes of the farmers, with a feeling of eternal bliss, no normal person can aspire to reach such a state of perfection.[10]

The religion of the layperson is instead oriented towards the accumulation of *kammic* merit through the performance of good deeds, and this merit, or the beneficial results of well-intentioned actions, is regarded as facilitating a happier rebirth. To quote Terwiel again, "Thai farmers do not aspire to escape rebirth; instead they wish to be born in better circumstances."[11]

Popularly, *kammic* merit, or in Thai *bun* (บุญ), and its opposite of demerit or *bap* (บาป), are regarded as being produced by previous moral or immoral actions. *Bun* and *bap* cannot cancel each other out but each has its own independent consequences determining the physical, mental, and social differences between individuals. To be a man or a woman, whole or deformed, healthy or ill, lord or peasant, wealthy or poor, have all traditionally been regarded as results of one's *kammic* inheritance. Nevertheless, merit or *bun* is not solely an individual thing but can be shared by others in specific ritualized merit-making or *tham bun* (ทำบุญ) ceremonies. For example, a ritual pouring of water at the end of a religious ceremony in a temple is regarded as transferring all or part of the merit generated by the ceremony to "all sentient beings" or to specifically designated people, often the recently dead. And when a man is ordained into the Sangha the sponsors of the ordination are also considered to participate in the merit thereby generated.

Spiro proposes that at least two kinds of Theravada Buddhism should be distinguished:[12] "*nibbanic* Buddhism," which is concerned with ultimate salvation through escaping from the cycle of suffering regulated by the law of *kamma*, and "kammatic Buddhism," which seeks a better rebirth by using the law of *kamma* to acquire merit. In many ways this division corresponds to the distinction found in the commentaries between the *lokiya* or mundane path and the *lokuttara* path described above, but many monks follow a kammatic rather than a *nibbanic* form of Buddhism and some lay people follow the *nibbanic* form of the religion. To avoid confusing these religious forms with religious roles it is better to think of *nibbanic* Buddhism as strict doctrinal Buddhism, as found in the primers of Buddhist philosophy and among more literate and intellectual Buddhists, and to regard kammatic Buddhism as the actual popular religion of most Thais, whether layperson or monk. It should be noted that there is an important difference between Spiro's anthropological concept of kammatic Buddhism and the doctrinal notion of *lokiyadhamma* mentioned above. In the actual popular religion, i.e. kammatic Buddhism, good *kamma* or merit is commonly regarded as itself capable of leading to *nibbāna. Nibbāna* is not seen as a liberation from the net of *kamma* but as resulting from the accumulation of vast amounts of merit, and is regarded as a sort of super-heaven. This is quite different from and actually doctrinally inconsistent with the strict interpretation of *lokiyadhamma* as promoting well-being but not of itself leading to salvation. Strictly speaking, even good actions, if performed in ignorance, lead to suffering because of attachment to their beneficial results which, like all other things, are impermanent. In doctrinal or *nibbanic* Buddhism all *kammic* accumulations, both meritorious and demeritorious, therefore have to be extinguished before complete *nibbāna* can be attained.

Popular Thai religion is also characterized by the worship of Brahmanical or Hindu-derived deities such as Indra and Vishnu, as well as by belief in magic and the power of both good and evil spirits. The rites of Buddhism are often regarded animistically as being capable of affording protection from evil influences rather than as aspects of a path seeking salvation through wisdom. Terwiel notes this magical element of Thai Buddhism:

> Monks who chant Pali texts, who meditate or who preach emanate protective power . . . . the greater the store of beneficial *kamma* a monk possesses, the stronger the power he generates. The monk who follows his precepts and who performs meritorious activities can be seen as a source of protective, beneficial power.[13]

Because of the complexity of the actual phenomenon of religion in Thailand there has been considerable academic debate over whether the discernible animist, Brahmanical, and Buddhist elements form one integrated system or represent distinct and distinguishable strands. Kirsch maintains that animism and Buddhism are integrated in neither theory nor practice. He sees animism standing "in symbolic opposition to that which Buddhism values most highly: asceticism, self-control and predictability."[14] At the level of religious practice he says that,

> In contrast to the respect accorded Buddhist and folk Brahman features [of Thai religion] . . . considerable ambivalence is expressed about the entire animist domain . . . . most animist practitioners have little respect among their fellows. There are clearly deep-seated cleavages between animist elements and Buddhism and folk Brahmanism.[15]

While I would agree with Kirsch if by Buddhism he means *nibbanic* or strictly doctrinal Buddhism, I do not agree that anthropologically speaking there are any deep-seated cleavages between what is traditionally taken as Buddhism and animist beliefs and practices. Kirsch's view of Buddhism above is particularly doctrinal and abstract, and, while an observer knowledgeable in doctrinal Buddhism can distinguish the animist from the Buddhist elements of Thai religious practice, most accounts of the actual forms of popular Buddhism show that many Buddhist doctrines are in fact ignored or misinterpreted. I agree with Spiro when he says that while Theravada Buddhism is the overarching religious system in Thailand, Burma, and Sri Lanka, "many of its doctrines are only rarely internalized by the members of these societies because they are either ignored or rejected by the faithful."[16] Terwiel concurs, saying that,

> Although the Sangha and Buddhism pervade religious life in the villages, this does not necessarily mean that the villager accepts the philosophical tenets of Buddhism or adheres to its soteriology. The Buddhist concepts are often interpreted in such a way that they are in accordance with magico-animist presuppositions.[17]

An example of how Buddhist doctrine is popularly reinterpreted has already been described in the above case of *nibbāna* being regarded as resulting from good *kamma*.

But whatever anthropological explanation of Thai Buddhism one favours, a clear appreciation of the explicit doctrinal inconsistency but practical integration of the various elements constituting Thai religion is nevertheless important if the reformist teachings of monks like Buddhadāsa are to be correctly understood. For Buddhadāsa, "reforming Buddhism" means instituting a doctrinally consistent religion, and as such, Kirsch's comments do describe well the tension between the popular religion and Buddhadāsa's reformed modernist system. However, Spiro's and Terwiel's conclusions of the overall integrity of Thai religion at the popular level are also relevant, especially in analyzing the character of the critical responses of religious traditionalists to the form of Buddhism that Buddhadāsa teaches.

# GLOSSARY OF THAI AND PALI TERMS

Arranged in English alphabetical order

*Abhidhammapiṭaka.* The predominantly philosophical and analytical final section of the *Tipiṭaka.*

*Achan, acharn,* or *ajarn* (Thai). Honorific term for a graduate or honored teacher or lecturer. Used for both monks and laypeople.

*Ākāsānañcāyatana.* The realm of boundless space, the first absorption or *jhāna* of the immaterial sphere, *arūpajjhāna.*

*Anupādisesanibbāna. Nibbāna* without the factors of existence remaining. The ultimate form of *nibbāna* traditionally regarded as being attained after death.

*Anusaya.* An inherent, latent unwholesome proclivity; the underlying cause of explicit *kilesa.*

*Arahant.* An enlightened person who has fully attained *nibbāna*; see *ariyapuggala.*

*Ariya.* A spiritually enlightened person.

*Ariyamagga.* The "noble path" or "noble eightfold path" of Buddhist practice, i.e. *sammādiṭṭhi, sammāsaṅkappa, sammāvācā, sammākammanta, sammāājīva, sammāvāyāma, sammāsati, sammāsamādhi.*

*Ariyapuggala.* "Noble individuals," those who have attained or are in the process of attaining enlightenment, i.e. *sotapañña, sakadāgāmi, anāgāmi, arahant.*

*Ariyasacca.* The "four noble truths" realized by the Buddha and forming the basis of Buddhist doctrine, i.e. 1. There is suffering, 2. There is a cause of suffering, 3. There is an end to suffering, 4. There is a path to the attainment of the ending of suffering.

*Ariyasāvaka.* A "noble follower," a disciple of the Buddha.

*Arūpajjhāna.* The four meditative absorptions or *jhānas* of the immaterial spheres, i.e. *ākāsānañcāyatana, viññaṇañcāyatana, ākiñcaññāyatana, nevasaññānāsaññāyatana.*

*Āsava.* Deep-seated moral defilements. See also *kilesa.*

*Attā.* Self, used to denote the notion of a permanent self or soul. A doctrine which is denied by Buddhist doctrine.

*Avijjā.* Ignorance.

*Bhavacakka.* The "cycle of becoming," an alternative term for *paṭiccasamuppāda.*

*Bhavaṅga.* A subliminal level of consciousness regarded as important in the process of rebirth.

*Bhikkhu.* A Theravadin monk, a member of the Buddhist Sangha.

*Bhikkhunī.* A Theravadin nun.

*Bodhipakkhiyadhamma.* The thirty-seven requisites or items pertaining to enlightenment.

*Bodhisatta.* The Theravada notion of a being destined to attain complete salvation or Buddhahood, c.f. *bodhisattva.*

*Bodhisattva* (Sanskrit). A Mahayana Buddhist saint who vows not to enter into complete *nirvāṇa* until all other sentient beings have likewise been saved; c.f. *bodhisatta.*

*Brahmacariya.* The holy life of a renunciate, usually equated with celibacy.

*Cakkavattin.* Universal monarch, the Buddhist ideal of a king who rules in accord with the Dhamma.

*Cakravartin* (Sanskrit). See *cakkavattin.*

*Cetāsika.* A general term for the mental categories such as *vedanā, saṅkhāra,* and *saññā*, which are characteristic of a mind suffused by craving and ignorance.

*Chit wang* (Thai). Literally: "voided-mind," "emptied-mind" or "freed-mind." Used by Buddhadasa as the Thai rendering of *suññata.*

*Dasarājadhamma.* The ten qualities of a righteous Buddhist monarch.

*Devatā.* A celestial being.

*Dhamma.* The natural order of the cosmos, the doctrine of salvation realized by the Buddha and based upon that natural order, and righteous activities in accord with that doctrine and the order of the cosmos.

*Dhammādhiṭṭhāna*. Exposition of Buddhist doctrine in terms of elements or factors, Dhammas. Distinguished from *puggalā dhiṭṭhāna* (q.v.) or exposition of the doctrine in terms of individuals or persons constituted by those elements.

*Dhātu*. A constitutive element.

*Dukkha*. Suffering; one of the three characteristics of existence or *tilakkhana*.

*Farang* (Thai). A Westerner.

*Iddhi*. Psychic power.

*Jāti*. Birth or rebirth.

*Jhāna*. A trance or "absorption" induced by concentration meditation or *samādhi*.

*Kamma*. Intentional or volitional actions which accrue moral reactions or *vipāka* to the performer.

*Karma* (Sanskrit). See *kamma*.

*Khandha*. One of the five aggregates or elements which constitute human existence, i.e. 1: *rūpa*–materiality; 2: *vedanā* –feeling, 3: *saññā*–perception, 4: *saṅkhāra*–mental factors associated with desire, 5: *viññaṇa*–consciousness.

*Kilesa*. A mental defilement or impurity which leads to suffering.

*Kusala*. Morally wholesome or profitable.

*Lokadhamma*. The worldly conditions of the ordinary person or *puthujjana*.

*Lokiya.* Mundane, worldly; associated with the realm of attachment, craving and suffering.

*Lokiyadhamma.* The spiritual path of practices for the world-involved layperson.

*Lokuttara.* Supramundane, transcendent; associated with *nibbāna* or the path leading to the attainment of *nibbāna.*

*Lokuttaradhamma.* Traditionally the spiritual path of the renunciate monk.

Mahānikai (Thai). Literally, "The Great Division (Sect)," the older and larger of the two official orders of Theravada Buddhism in Thailand.

Mahāyāna. "The Great Vehicle," a generic term for the "Northern Schools" of Buddhism found in China, Vietnam, Japan, Korea, Tibet, and Mongolia.

*Moha.* Delusion.

*Nāma.* Mentality; a generic term for the four immaterial *khandhas* of *vedanā* (feeling), *saññā* (perception), *saṅkhāra* (combining mental factors) and *viññāṇa* (consciousness).

*Nāmarūpa.* Human individuality or individual existence as impermanent and inessential and composed of the five *khandhas*, or of *nāma* and *rūpa*, i.e. mentality and physicality.

*Nevasaññānasaññāyatana.* The sphere of neither perception nor non-perception, the fourth absorption or *jhāna* of the immaterial sphere, *arūpajjhāna.*

*Nibbāna.* Salvation, the complete and permanent extinction of suffering.

*Nikai* (Thai). An order of Theravada Buddhism; see Mahānikai, Thammayut.

*Nikāya*. A subdivision of the Theravada canon, e.g. *Dīgha-nikāya, Majjhima-nikāya*, etc.

*Nirvāṇa* (Sanskrit). See *nibbāna*.

*Opapātika*. Spontaneously born beings.

*Paccekabuddha*. One who attains enlightenment but does not teach or proclaim his realization to the world; c.f. *sammāsambuddha*.

*Paññā*. Wisdom; liberating insight into reality.

*Paramatthasacca*. Absolute truth, founded on transcendent insight into eternal truth, *sacca*.

*Pariyattidhamma*. The doctrines and scriptures of Buddhism; that *dhamma* which is to be learned as opposed to being practised.

*Paṭiccasamuppāda*. The doctrine of dependent origination, explaining the causal relations between ignorance and craving, and the arising of suffering and of rebirth.

*Paṭimokha*. The clerical code of conduct for Theravadin monks.

*Paṭisandhiviññāṇa*. Rebirth-linking consciousness; the link between the end of one life and the beginning of the next.

*Parinibbāna*. Absolute salvation, freedom from suffering.

*Phansa* (Thai). The annual three-month rainy season retreat during which monks remain based at one monastery, the "Buddhist lent."

*Phasa khon–phasa tham* (Thai). Literally "human language"–"Dhamma language," Buddhadāsa's theory of scriptural interpretation.

*Phikkhu* (Thai). The Thai term for *bhikkhu* (q.v.).

*Phra* (Thai). An honorific used before the name of a monk, a Thai term used to mean Buddhist monk.

*Piṭaka*. One of the three main divisions the Theravada scriptures, i.e., *Vinayapiṭaka, Suttapiṭaka, and Abhidhammapiṭaka.*

*Puggalādhiṭṭhāna*. Exposition of the Buddhist doctrine in terms of persons or individuals, cf. *dhammādhiṭṭhāna*.

*Puthujjana*. A "worldling," an ordinary person.

*Rūpa*. Materiality; the *khandha* or aggregate of human existence which confers form and substantiality; c.f. *nāma*.

*Sacca*. Truth.

*Sakadāgāmi*. An enlightened person who will be reborn as a human being just one more time.

*Samādhi*. Concentration meditation.

*Sammā*. Right, correct; righteous.

*Sammāājīva*. Right livelihood.

*Sammādiṭṭhi*. Right belief.

*Sammākammanta*. Right bodily action.

*Sammāsamādhi*. Right concentration.

*Sammāsambuddha.* A universal Buddha who not only attains enlightenment but also proclaims a message of salvation to the world; c.f. *paccekabuddha.*

*Sammāsaṅkappa.* Right thought.

*Sammāsati.* Right mindfulness.

*Sammatisacca.* Conventional truth; truth according to the common conventions of language use.

*Sammāvācā.* Right effort.

*Saṁsāra.* The cycle of rebirth and suffering caused by ignorance and craving.

*Saṅgha.* The Buddhist monkhood; the order of renunciate Buddhist monks.

*Saṅkhāra.* A mental formation resulting from volitional or *kamma*-causing actions which is the immediate cause of rebirth and of *vipāka.*

*Saññāvedayitanirodha.* Extinction of feeling and perception; the temporary suspension of all mental activity following immediately upon the attainment of the eighth *jhāna* or *nevasaññānasaññāyatanā.*

*Sāsanā.* The dispensation of the Buddha; Buddhist teaching; a term used to denote Buddhism as a religion.

*Sassatādiṭṭhi.* The heterodox doctrine that there is an eternal self or *atta.*

*Sa-upādisesanibbāna. Nibbāna* with the factors of existence remaining; traditionally regarded as *nibbāna* attained while still alive; c.f. *anupadisesanibbāna.*

*Sīla.* Ethics, good conduct.

*Sotāpanna.* A "stream enterer;" one who is in the process of attaining *nibbāna.*

*Sukkhavipassaka.* One who follows the path of *nibbāna* via the practice of insight meditation or *vipassanā.*

*Suññatā.* Void, emptiness, a state free from ignorance, craving, and suffering.

*Śunyatā* (Sanskrit). The Sanskrit equivalent of *suññatā.*

*Sutta.* The second main division of the Theravada scriptures composed mainly of expository discourses by the Buddha and his close disciples.

*Suttanta, Suttantapiṭaka.* Another name for the *Suttapiṭaka.*

*Taṇhā.* Craving.

*Tathāgatā.* An epithet of the Buddha.

Thammayut (Thai). Literally, "Those adhering strongly to the Dhamma," one of the two official orders of Theravada Buddhism in Thailand.

Theravāda. The "doctrine of the elders," the "Southern School" of Buddhism predominant in Thailand.

*Thūparāhapuggala.* Literally, "stupa-deserving," an honoured or venerated person considered worthy of having a pilgrimage stupa erected over their bodily remains.

*Tilakkhaṇa.* The three characteristics of existence, i.e. *anicca* (impermanence), *dukkha* (suffering), and *anattā* (non-self).

*Tipiṭaka.* The canonical Theravada scriptures, incorporating the *Vinayapiṭaka, Suttapiṭaka,* and the *Abidhammapiṭaka.*

*Traibhūmikathā.* A fourteenth-century Thai text on Buddhist cosmology.

*Trai Phum Phra Ruang* (Thai). See *Traibhūmikathā.*

*Upacāra.* "Access concentration," a basic level of *samādhi* regarded as sufficient for the practice of *vipassanā.*

*Upādāna.* Attachment, clinging.

*Upekkha.* Equanimity.

*Vaṭṭasaṁsāra.* The cycle of rebirth and suffering; c.f. *saṁsāra.*

*Vicāra.* Discursive thinking.

*Vinaya.* The code of monastic discipline, as laid down in the *Vinayapiṭaka.*

*Vinayapiṭaka.* Section of the canonical Theravada scriptures dealing with the codes of monastic discipline or *vinaya.*

*viññāṇa.* Consciousness.

*viññāṇañcāyatana.* The sphere of boundless consciousness, second of the four absorptions of the immaterial sphere, *arūpajjhāna.*

*vipāka.* The reactive out-working of accumulated *kamma.*

*vipassanā.* Insight meditation, a form of meditation aiming for liberating insight into reality.

*vitakka.* Thought conception, rational thought.

# NOTES

## NOTE ON TRANSLITERATION AND REFERENCING

1. Pali is a language closely related to Sanskrit, probably being a vernacular in Northern India soon after the time of the historical Buddha. While Pali is the classical language of the Theravada scriptures, some authors tend to give Theravada terms in their equivalent Sanskrit forms. This custom is artificial and has no theoretical justification other than indicating an assumed greater stature of Sanskrit, the classical language of Hinduism and of Mahayana Buddhism in India.

2. Thailand uses the Buddhist calendar, dating from the Buddha's death in 543 B.C. The year A.D. 1988 is in the Buddhist Era (B.E.) the year 2531.

3. *Lem/kho/na.*

## INTRODUCTION

1. Buddhadāsa is the Pali spelling of the name. In Thai Buddhadāsa is called Phutthathat (พุทธทาส) or in full Phra Phutthathat Phikkhu. Both of the Thai terms *phra* (พระ) and *phikkhu* (ภิกขุ, Pali: *Bhikkhu*) are used to denote a Buddhist monk and are variously used as honorifics in combination with a monk's actual name.

2. The information detailed in this section has been culled from the following books:

Chit Phibanthaen, *Chiwit lae ngan khong Phutthathat phikkhu* (ชิต ภิบาลแทน, *ชีวิตและงานของพุทธทาสภิกขุ*, 2520). (Bangkok: Sinlapabanakan, 1977).

Pracha Pasannathammo, *Lau wai muea wai sonthaya—Atachiwa-prawat khong than Phutthathat* (พระประชา ปสนนธมโม, *เล่าไว้เมื่อวัยสนธยา – อัตชีวประวัติของท่านพุทธทาส*, 2525). (Bangkok: Komon Khimthong Foundation, 1982).

Ratchananthamuni, *Phutthathat khue khrai, than tham arai* (พระราชนันทมุนี, *พุทธทาสคือใคร, ท่านทำอะไร*, 2525). (Nonthaburi, Thailand: Rongrian Phuttha-tham Wat Chonprathan Rangsarit, 1982).

Arun Wetsuwan อรุณ เวชสุวรรณ,

a. *Suan Mok daen sa-ngop* (*สวนโมกข์แดนสงบ*, 2524). (Bangkok: Phrae Phithaya, 1981).

b. *Suan Mok, mueang Chaiya lae Phutthathat phikkhu* (*สวนโมกข์, เมืองไชยาและพุทธทาสภิกขุ*, 2524). (Bangkok: Phrae Phithaya, 1981).

3. The education of monks in Thailand is systematized into various grades, each having nationally supervised examinations. There are three basic grades for new ordinees and novices starting at Tham III or Naktham III (นักธรรม) and finishing at Naktham I. There are then seven grades of Pali studies for fully ordained monks starting at Parian III (เปรียญ) and finishing at Parian IX.

4. *Pariyattidhamma*—the doctrines and the scriptures; that Dhamma which is to be learned as opposed to being practised.

5. Cited by Dusadi Angsumethangkun, "Than Phutthathat kap kan patirup satsana" in Khana kammakan satsana phuea kan phattana (ed.), *Phutthathat kap khon run mai* (ดุษฎี อังสุเมธางกูร, "ท่านพุทธทาสกับการปฏิรูปศาสนา" ใน คณะกรรมการศาสนาเพื่อการพัฒนา (บก.), *พุทธทาสกับคนรุ่นใหม่*, 2526), (Bangkok: Komon Khimthong Foundation, 1983), 247.

6. Chit Phibanthaen, *Chiwit lae ngan*, 39–40.

7. Ibid., 48.

8. Ibid., 11.

9. Ibid., 114.

10. Ibid., 103–104.

11. In Thai the address was titled, "Phukhao withi phutthatham sing thi khwang kan mai hai khon khao pai su phutthatham" (ภูเขาวิธีพุทธธรรม สิ่งที่ขวางกั้นไม่ให้คนเข้าไปสู่พุทธธรรม) cited by Ratchananthamuni, 26.

12. Sulak Sivaraksa, *Khanchong song phra* (*คันฉ่องส่องพระ*, 2522), Bangkok: Laisue Thai, (1979), 233.

13. Sulak Sivaraksa, introduction to Donald Swearer, *Bhikkhu Buddhadāsa and the Buddhist Reformation in Thailand* (Colombo, Sri Lanka: Ecumenical Institute for Study and Dialogue, n.d.), 2.

14. Mahachulalongkorn is the university for monks from the Mahanikai Order. Mahamakut is the corresponding institution run by the Thammayut sect, admitting monks and novices from both sects.

## CHAPTER 1
## THE SOCIAL AND THEORETICAL CONTEXTS OF BUDDHADĀSA'S WORK

1. Thomas A. Kirsch, "Modernizing Implications of Nineteenth Century Reforms of the Thai Sangha," in Bardwell L. Smith (ed.), *Religion and Legitimation of Power in Thailand, Laos and Burma* (Chambersburg, Penn.: 1978, Anima Books), 53.

2. Frits Staal, *Exploring Mysticism* (London: Penguin Books, 1975), 72.

3. Ibid., 163–164.

4. Sunthorn Na Rangsi, *The Buddhist Concept of Karma and Rebirth* (Bangkok: Mahamakut Rajavidyalaya Press, 1976), 83.

5. Ibid., 82–83.

6. Barend Jan Terwiel, "Religion in Rural Central Thailand," Ph.D. thesis, Australian National University, Canberra, submitted 1971, 164.

7. Robert Lawson Slater, *Paradox and Nibbana* (Chicago: University of Chicago Press, 1951), 60.

8. *Brahmacariya*, "the pure or holy life," a term denoting the renunciate life of the monk.

9. *Cinta Sutta, Papata Vagga, Saṁyutta Nikāya*, vol. 19/verses 1726–7/pp. 441–42.

10. *Agañña Sutta, Dīgha Nikāya*, vol. 11/verses 51–72/pp. 61–75.

11. Cited by S. J. Tambiah, *World Conqueror and World Renouncer* (Cambridge: Cambridge University Press, 1976), 13.

12. Ibid.

13. *Mahāparinibbāna Sutta, Dīgha Nikāya*, vol. 10/verse 135/p. 116

14. *Paccekabuddha*: a person who attains enlightenment but who, unlike the Buddha or *Sammāsambuddha*, does not teach a message of salvation to the world.

15. *Cakkavatti Sutta, Dīgha Nikāya*, vol. 11 /verses 33–50/pp. 43–60.

16. Niels Mulder, *Everyday Life in Thailand* (Bangkok: Duang Kamol, 1979), 140.

17. Somboon Suksamran, *Buddhism and Politics in Thailand* (Singapore: Institute of Southeast Asian Studies, 1982), 40.

18. Dhani Nivat Krommun Bidyalabh, H.H. Prince, *A History of Buddhism in Siam*, (Bangkok: Siam Society, 1965), 23.

19. Somboon, *Buddhism and Politics in Thailand*, 40.

20. Puey Ungphakorn, "The Role of Ethics and Religion in National Development," in *Visakha Pujā* (Bangkok: Buddhist Association of Thailand, 1974), 116.

## CHAPTER 2
## THE SOURCES OF BUDDHADĀSA'S INNOVATIVE VIEWS

1. Cited by Chit Phibanthaen, *Chiwit lae ngan*, 42.

2. Buddhadāsa, *Thalaengkan Suan Mok 50 pi* (*แถลงการณ์สวนโมกข์ 50 ปี*, 2525), (Bangkok: Sukhaphap Chai, 1982), 6–7.

3. John W. Butt, "Thai Kingship and Religious Reform," in Bardwell L. Smith (ed.), *Religion and Legitimation of Power in Thailand, Laos and Burma* (Chambersburg, Penn.: Anima Books, 1978), 47.

4. Kirsch, "Modernizing Implications," 58.

5. The *Tibhūmikathā*, or in Thai the *Traiphum phra rueang*, was composed in the fourteenth century A.D. by Li Thai, a king of the early Thai kingdom of Sukhothai. The *Traiphum* has historically been one of the most important Buddhist texts in Thailand, its elaborate cosmological descriptions being taken as the official account of the various levels of Buddhist hells and heavens attained as a result of individuals' different qualitative and quantitative accumulations of merit and demerit. The *Traiphum* was the central Buddhist commentarial text in old Siam because it was regarded as relating the empirical character of Thai society to ultimate Buddhist reality.

6. Kirsch, "Modernizing Implications," 59.

7. Balkrishna Govind Gokhale, "Anagarika Dhammapala: Toward Modernity Through Tradition in Ceylon," in Bardwell L. Smith (ed.), *Contributions to Asian Studies, Vol. 4: Tradition and Change in Theravada Buddhism* (Leiden, The Netherlands: E. J. Brill, 1973), 39.

8. Heinz Bechert, "Contradictions in Sinhalese Buddhism," in Bardwell L. Smith (ed.), *Contributions to Asian Studies, Vol. 4: Tradition and Change in Theravada Buddhism* (Leiden, The Netherlands: E. J. Brill, 1973), 8.

9. Buddhadāsa, *Buddhism in 15 Minutes*, trans. H. G. Grether, (Bangkok: Suriyaban, n.d.), 18.

10. K. N. Jayatilleke "Buddhism and the Scientific Revolution" in *Buddhism and Science*, no editor given (Kandy, Sri Lanka: Buddhist Publication Society, 1980), 2–3.

11. Robert F. Spencer, "The Relation of Buddhism to Modern Science," in *Buddhism and Science*, no editor given (Kandy Sri Lanka: Buddhist Publication Society, 1980), 12.

12. The *Kālamā Sutta* is also called the *Kesaputta Sutta* and is found in the *Tikanipāta* of the *Aṅguttara Nikāya*, vol. 20/verse 505/pp. 179–184.

13. Ananda Bhikkhu, *Theravada and Zen* (Colombo, Ceylon: Gunasena & Co., 1962), 3–31.

14. *Kālamā Sutta*, see note (12) above.

15. Buddhadāsa, *Buddha-dhamma for Students*, trans. Ariyananda Bhikkhu (Bangkok: Sublime Life Mission, 1982), 16.

16. Ibid., 15.

17. Buddhadāsa, *Buddhism in 15 Minutes*, 19.

18. David Wilson, *Politics in Thailand* (Ithaca, N.Y.: Cornell University Press, 1962), 60–67.

19. Daniel Wit, *Thailand—Another Vietnam?* (New York: Charles Scribner's Sons, 1968), 103.

20. Chao Asok (trans.), "Setthasat choeng phut" in *Khwam lomleo khong setthasat samai mai phro mai sonchai setthasat choeng phut* (ชาวอโศก "เศรษฐศาสตร์เชิงพุทธ" ใน *ความล้มเหลวของเศรษฐศาสตร์สมัยใหม่ เพราะไม่สนใจเศรษฐศาสตร์เชิงพุทธ,* 2525)," (Bangkok: Thammasanti Foundation, 1982), being a partial translation of and commentary upon E. F. Schumacher's *Small is Beautiful.*

21. Wisit Wangwinyu, "Than phutthathat kap setthasat chao phut" in Khana Kammakan Satsana Phuea Kan Phatthana (ed.), *Phutthathat kap khon run mai* (วิศิษฐ์ วังวิญญู, "ท่านพุทธทาสกับเศรษฐศาสตร์ชาวพุทธ" ใน คณะกรรมการศาสนาเพื่อการพัฒนา (บก.), *พุทธทาสกับคนรุ่นใหม่,* 2526). (Bangkok: Komon Khimthong Foundation, 1983), 24ff.

22. Ben Anderson, "Withdrawal Symptoms: Social and Cultural Aspects of the 6 October Coup," in *Bulletin of Concerned Asian Scholars*, vol. 9, no. 3, July–Sept. 1977, 13.

23. On 14 October 1973 the regime of Thanom Kittikhachon was toppled after several days of student-led rioting in Bangkok. The period from October 1973 until October 1976 saw a brief, turbulent liberalization of Thai society under a series of popularly elected governments. Military rule was reestablished by a violent coup in October 1976.

24. Seri Phongphit, "Thamma kap kan mueang: Than Phutthathat kap sangkhom Thai" in *Than Phutthathat nai thatsana khong nak wichakan* (เสรี พงศ์พิศ, "ธรรมะกับการเมือง ท่านพุทธทาสกับสังคมไทย," ใน *ท่านพุทธทาสในทัศนะของนักวิชาการ,* 2525), (Bangkok: Khana Kammakan Satsana Phuea Kan Phatthana, 1982), 33.

25. Pracha Pasannathammo, *"Than Phutthathat kap patiwat watthanatham,"* in *Si nak khit ruam samai* (พระประชา ปสนนธมโม, "ท่านพุทธทาสกับปฏิวัติวัฒนธรรม" ใน *สี่นักคิดร่วมสมัย* 2526) (Bangkok: Thianwan, 1983), 1–61.

26. Ibid., 50.

27. Field Marshal Plaek Phibunsongkhram was the military ruler of Thailand in the 1950s.

28. Pracha Pasannathammo, op. cit., 50–51.

29. Cited by Chit Phibanthaen, *Chiwit lae ngan,* 103.

30. Ibid., 114.

31. Buddhadāsa, *Thalaengkan Suan Mok 50 pi*, 2.

32. Siddhi Butr-Indr, *The Social Philosophy of Buddhism* (Bangkok: Mahamakut Buddhist University Press, 1979), 67.

33. George Rupp, "The Relationship between Nirvarna and Samsara," *Philosophy East and West*, vol. 21, 1971, 67.

34. Donald K. Swearer, *Bhikkhu Buddhadāsa and the Buddhist Reformation in Thailand*, 5.

35. This is how Pun chose to translate the name of his group, the Khana Phoeiphrae Withi Kan Damnoen Chiwit An Prasoet (คณะเผยแพร่วิธีการดำเนินชีวิตอันประเสริฐ), literally "Society for Propagating the Method for Leading One's Life Perfectly."

36. Pun Chongprasoet (ed.), *Wiwatha rawang M.R. Kukrit Pramoj kap Than Phutthathat nai rueang chit wang* (ปุ่น จงประเสริฐ (บก.) *วิวาทะระหว่าง ม.ร.ว. คึกฤทธิ์ ปราโมช กับ ท่านพุทธทาสภิกขุ ในเรื่องจิตว่าง*, 2518) (Samut Prakan Thailand: Ongkan Fuenfu Phra Phutthasatsana, 1975), 24.

37. Siddhi, *Social Philosophy*, 39.

38. Pun Chongprasoet (ed.), *Tamra du phiksu* (*ตำราดูภิกษุ*, 2525) (Bangkok: Thammabucha, 1982), 1.

39. Araya Nikonthai (อารยะ นิกรไทย) is a pseudonym which literally means "the civilized Thai populace." This assumed name was obviously intended to imply that the views contained in the article are held by all "civilized" (read "modernistic") Thais.

40. This is a reference to the 1932 revolution which abolished the absolute monarchy of King Prajadhipok (Rama VII) and established the then Siam as a constitutional monarchy.

41. Araya Nikonthai, "Phutthasatsana champen samrap khon Thai rue" cited in Arun Wetsuwan in *Suan Mok, mueang Chaiya lae Phutthathat phikkhu,* 3rd printing (อารยะ นิกรไทย, "พุทธศาสนาจำเป็นสำหรับคนไทยหรือ" อ้างใน อรุณ เวชสุวรรณ) *สวนโมกข์ เมืองไชยา และพุทธทาสภิกขุ,* 2524), (Bangkok: Phrae Phithaya, 1981), 294. *N.B.* The fact that this quote by Araya Nikonthai is contained in a biography of Buddhadāsa suggests that the author was either a

supporter of Buddhadāsa or someone who holds similar views. It is unlikely that Buddhadāsa himself was the author as he usually signs his name to his own works.

42. John Laurier Van Esterik, "Cultural Interpretation of Canonical Paradox—Lay Meditation in a Central Thai Village," Ph.D. thesis, University of Illinois at Urbana-Champaign, University Microfilm International, Ann Arbor, Michigan, 1977, 172.

43. This pronouncement occurs in the *Dhammadinna Sutta, Saṁyutta Nikāya*, vol. 19/verses 1625–6/pp. 404–405.

44. *Saccadhamma* denotes "the truth of the doctrine of Dhamma" or "the true teachings."

45. Frontispiece to *Than Phutthathat nai thatsana khong nak wichakan* (*ท่านพุทธทาสในทัศนะของนักวิชาการ*, 2525) (Bangkok: Khana Kammakan Satsana Phuea Kan Phatthana, 1982).

## CHAPTER 3
## *PHASA KHON–PHASA THAM*: BUDDHADĀSA'S METHOD OF SCRIPTURAL INTERPRETATION

1. Literally *phasa khon* means "the language of people" or "human language," that is, the everyday speech of human beings. "Dhamma language" is the direct translation of the term *phasa tham*.

2. Buddhadāsa, *Two Kinds of Language*, trans. Ariyananda Bhikkhu, (Bangkok: n.p., 1974), 1.

3. Buddhadāsa, *Mai khaochai satsana phro mai ru phasa tham (ไม่เข้าใจศาสนาเพราะไม่รู้ภาษาธรรม)* (Samut Prakan, Thailand: Ongkan Fuenfu Phra Phutthasatsana, n.d.), 1.

4. Buddhadāsa, *Two Kinds of Language*, 3.

5. Ibid.

6. Cited by Chit Phibanthaen, *Chiwit lae ngan*, 102.

7. Araya Nikonthai, 295–296.

8. *Visuddhimagga*, XIII, 6.

9. Ibid., VII, 7.

10. *Vibhaṅga Sutta*, cited at *Visuddhimagga*, XI, 123.

11. Buddhadāsa, *Barom tham* (*บรมธรรม*, 2525), (Bangkok: Sukhaphapchai, 1982), 4.

12. Ibid., 4–5.

13. Buddhadāsa, *Kharawat tham* (*ฆราวาสธรรม*, 2525), (Bangkok: Thammabucha, 1982), 111.

14. Buddhadāsa, *Buddha-dhamma for Students*, 61.

15. Ibid.

16. *Puggala Sutta, Khuddaka Nikāya*, vol. 25/verse 198/170–1.

17. *Cittajhāyī Sutta, Khuddaka Nikāya*, vol. 25/verse 199/p. 172.

18. Anan Senakhan (ed.), *Khamson diarathi* (อนันต์ เสนาขันธ์, *คำสอนเดียรถีย์,* 2522) (Bangkok: Ongkan Phithak Phutthasatsana Aphitham Foundation, 1979), 43.

19. Ibid.

20. Ariyananda Bhikkhu, *Psychology and Religious Symbolism* (Bangkok: Sublime Life Mission, n.d.), 10.

21. Buddhadāsa, "Upasak haeng kan phoeiphrae tham" in Pun Chongprasoet (ed.), *Arai thuk arai phit* ("อุปสรรคแห่งการเผยแพร่ธรรม" ใน ปุ่น จงประเสริฐ (บก.) *อะไรถูก อะไรผิด,* 2525) (Bangkok: Ongkan Fuenfu Phra Phutthasatsana, 1982), 61.

22. Ibid., 56.

23. Buddhadāsa, *Kharawat tham*, 138.

24. Buddhadāsa, *Khamson phu buat (คำสอนผู้บวช, 2524)*, (Bangkok: Thammabucha, 1981), 18.

25. Buddhadāsa, "Upasak haeng kan phoeiphrae tham," 56.

26. Buddhadāsa, *Kharawat tham*, 138.

27. Pali Text Society, *Dīgha Nikāya*, II, 41.

28. (Venerable Phra Achan Maha) Boowa Nyanasampanno, *The Venerable Phra Acharn Mun Bhuridatta Thera – Meditation Master*, trans. Siri Buddhasukh, (Udon Thani, Thailand: Wat Pa Barn Tard, 1982), 4.

29. Buddhadāsa, *Buddha-dhamma for Students*, 24.

30. *Mahāparinibbāna Sutta, Dīgha Nikāya*, vol. 10/verse 113/p. 102.

31. The *Netti-Pakaraṇa* is attributed to Mahakaccana, an immediate disciple of the Buddha. It is not regarded as canonical by the Sinhalese and is not part of the Thai *Tipiṭaka* but is included in the Burmese canon.

32. George D. Bond, "The *Netti-Pakaraṇa*: A Theravada Method of Interpretation," in Somaratna Balasooriya (ed.), *Buddhist Studies in Honour of Walpola Rahula* (London: Gordon Fraser, 1980), 20.

33. Ibid., 19.

34. Ibid., 22.

35. Ibid.

36. Worldling or *puthujjana* denotes a person who is caught up in desires for the things of the material world.

37. For Buddhadāsa "world" in *phasa tham* denotes a mental state and not a plane of existence.

38. Buddhadāsa, *Nipphan* (*นิพพาน*, 2524) (Bangkok: Thammabucha, 1981), 136–137.

39. Buddhadāsa, *Osaretapphatham* (*โอสาเรตัพพธรรม*, 2525) (Chaiya, Thailand: Thammathan Foundation, 1982), 55.

40. Buddhadāsa, *Tekitcakam* (*เตกิจจกรรม*, 2519) (Chaiya, Thailand: Thammathan Foundation, 1976), 297.

41. The term *sammatisacca* first occurs in the *Kathavathu* of the *Abhidhammapiṭaka*, vol. 37/verse 1062/p. 422. The first occurrence of the term *paramattha* is in the same place, vol. 37/verses 1–190/pp. 1–83. The terms *puggalādhiṭṭhāna desanā* (*desanā*: teaching, instruction, exposition) and *dhammādhiṭṭhāna desanā* are not found in the *Tipiṭaka*, first occurring in a commentary on the *Abhidhammapiṭaka*, the *Paṭisambhidhamagga Atthakathā*.

42. Ratchaworamuni, *Phutthatham* (ราชวรมุนี, *พุทธธรรม*, 2525), (Bangkok: Thammasathan, Chulalongkorn University, 1982).

43. In a private correspondence Phra Ratchaworamuni has indicated to the author that he has read little of Buddhadāsa's work. Nevertheless, he has also indicated that he does share many of Buddhadāsa's views.

44. Ratchaworamuni, *Phutthatham*, 55.

45. The distinction between *sammatisacca* and *paramatthasacca* made in the *Kathāvatthu* of the *Abhidhammapiṭaka* (see footnote 41 above) is based on an analysis of the comments made by the nun Vajira.

46. *Vajirā Sutta, Saṁyutta Nikāya*, vol. 15/verse 554/p. 167.

47. Ratchaworamuni, *Phutthatham*, 56.

48. *Poṭṭhapāda Sutta, Dīgha Nikāya*, vol. 9/verse 312/p. 281.

49. Buddhadāsa, *Christianity and Buddhism*, no translator given, 2nd ed. (Bangkok: Sublime Life Mission, 1977), 8.

50. Ibid., 15.

51. Ibid.

52. Ibid.

53. Cited in Pun Chongprasoet (ed.), *Wiwatha rawang than Phutthathat phikkhu kap M.R. Kukrit Pramoj nai rueang chit wang*, 29.

54. Ibid.

55. Winai Siwakun (วินัย ศิวกุล) is a trained economist working in the Department of the Budget. He teaches *Abhidhamma* at the Aphitham Munnithi (อภิธรรมมูลนิธิ) or Abhidhamma Foundation at Wat Pho in Bangkok. In particular, he teaches about the relationship between the Brahmanical aspects of Thai Buddhism and *Abhidhamma*. He is also head of the Ongkan Phithak Phra Phutthasatsana (องค์การพิทักษ์พระพุทธศาสนา) or

The Society for the Protection of Buddhism, a conservative, traditionalist organization.

56. Winai Siwakun, *"Phasa Phutthathat"* in Anan Senakhan (ed.), *Khamson diarathi* (วินัย ศิวกุล, "ภาษาพุทธทาส" ใน อนันต์ เสนาขันธ์ (บก.), *คำสอนเดียรถีย์,* 2522) (Bangkok: Ongkan Phithak Phutthasatsana Aphitham Foundation, 1979), 104.

57. Cited by Anan Senakhan, in *Khamson diarathi*, 23.

58. Anan Senakhan (clerical name Phra Chayanantho Bhikkhu) was formerly a policeman in the Division of Crime Suppression and was active in an anti-corruption campaign within the police force. However, his criticisms of high-ranking officers and politicians forced him to become a monk for reasons of personal safety in 1975 after a number of threats were made against him. While a monk he became a strong supporter of the Aphitham Foundation at Wat Pho or Wat Phra Chetuphon, and maintained his critical penchant by attacking progressive monks like Buddhadāsa, who he regarded as undermining Buddhist traditions. He disrobed in early 1983 in order to participate in the campaign for the general election but was arrested in April that year on the charge of *lèse majesté* after a controversial public address on the monarchy. He was convicted of that charge and served two three-year prison terms.

## CHAPTER 4
## BUDDHADĀSA ON REBIRTH AND *PAṬICCASAMUPPĀDA*

1. Buddhadāsa, "Upasak haeng kan phoeiphrae tham," 82.
2. Ibid.
3. Ibid., 82–83.
4. Suchip Punyanuphap, *Phra traipidok samrap prachachon* (สุชีพ ปุญญานุภาพ, *พระไตรปิฎกสำหรับประชาชน,* 2525) (Bangkok: Mahamakut Buddhist University Press, 1982).
5. *Kinti Sutta, Majjhima Nikāya*, vol. 14/verses 42–50/pp. 31–36.
6. Suchip Punyanuphap, 461n.
7. The thirty-seven *bodhipakkhiyadhamma* are: the four *satipaṭṭhāna*, the four *sammappadhāna*, the four *iddhipāda*, the five *indriya*, the five *bala*, the *bojjhanga*, and the eight *magga*.
8. *Mahaparinibbana Sutta*, *Dīgha Nikāya*, vol. 10/verse 107/p. 99.
9. Buddhadāsa, *Aphitham khue arai* (*อภิธรรมคืออะไร,* 2517) (Bangkok: Thammabucha, 1974), 9.
10. Ibid., 110.

11. Buddhadāsa, *Tekitcakam*, 294.

12. Four types of *ariyapuggala* are traditionally recognized: *sotāpanna, sakadāgami, anāgāmi*, and *arahant*.

13. Buddhadāsa gives as his reference vol. 20/verse 580/p. 370 in the Pali edition of the *Tipiṭaka* published by Mahamakut Buddhist University Press. This corresponds to the *Assa Sutta* no. 1 in the Thai language edition, found at vol. 20/verse 580/p. 278.

14. Cited by Bunmi Methangkun in *To than Phutthathat rueang chit wang, lem* 1 (*โต้ท่านพุทธทาสเรื่องจิตว่าง - เล่ม 1*, 2522) (Bangkok: Ongkan Phithak Phutthasatsana Aphitham Foundation, 1979), 33–34.

15. Buddhadāsa, *Aphitham khue srai*, 4.

16. In the Introduction to her edited version of the *Abhidhammatthasaṅgaha* Mrs. Rhys Davids dates the text's composition by its reputed author, Aniruddha, to between the eighth and twelfth centuries A.D.

17. Rhys Davids, *Compendium of Philosophy* (London: Pali Text Society, 1972), 8.

18. These details are taken from a citation of Buddhadāsa's book *Aphitham khue arai (อภิธรรมคืออะไร)* in Bunmi Methangkun, *To than Phutthathat rueang chit wang, lem* 1, 11.

19. Kenneth Wells, *Thai Buddhism, Its Rites and Activities* (Bangkok: Suriyaban Publishers, 1975), 225.

20. Winai Siwakun, *Chit chai khue arai* (*จิตใจคืออะไร*, 2525) (Bangkok: Aphitham Foundation, 1982), 3.

21. Buddhadāsa, *Phi mi ching rue mai (ผีมีจริงหรือไม่*, 2522), (Samut Prakan, Thailand: Ongkan Fuenfu Phra Phutthasatsana, 1979), 10.

22. Ibid., 4–5.

23. Buddhadāsa, *Another Kind of Birth*, trans. R. B. (Bangkok: n.p., 1974), 3.

24. In a related discussion Bunmi Methangkun cites an *Abhidhamma* commentary as providing the following elemental analysis of matter: One bean seed or *dhannamasa* is equivalent to seven lice or *uka*, one *uka* is equal to seven louse eggs or *likkha*, one *likkha* is equal to thirty-six bits of chariot dust or *ratharenū*, one *ratharenū* is equal to thirty-six *tajjari* (?), one *tajjari* is equal to thirty-six atoms or *aṇu* and one *aṇu* is regarded as being made up of thirty-six ultimate atoms or *paramāṇu*. One *paramāṇu* is thus equivalent to 1/82,301,184 of a bean seed. Bunmi then says that *opapātika* are made up of a translucent form of *paramanu*. Cited in Bunmi Methangkun, *To than Phutthathat rueang avijja lae phi-sang thewada, lem 2* (*โต้ท่านพุทธทาสเรื่องอวิชชาและผีสางเทวดา เล่ม 2*, 2523) (Bangkok: Aphitham Foundation, 1980), 27.

25. Anan Senakhan, *Khamson diarathi*, 61.

26. Buddhadāsa, *Patitchasamupapat chak phra ot* (*ปฏิจจสมุปบาทจากพระโอษฐ์*, 2524) (Chaiya, Thailand: Thammathan Foundation, 1981), 77.

27. Ibid., 78.

28. Sunthorn, *Buddhist Concept of Karma,* 86.

29. Buddhadāsa, *Patitchasamupapat chak phra ot*, 95.

30. Buddhism lists six senses: sight, hearing, taste, smell, touch and mind. As Sunthorn Na Rangsi notes, "Buddhism regards the mind or consciousness as the sixth sense which has mental states or mental phenomena as its objects of contact" (Sunthorn, 61).

31. The Pali term *jāti* (Thai: *chat*) literally denotes "birth," but is generally used in the sense of "rebirth." *Jāti* can also be rendered into English as "life" in the sense of "past life," "future life," etc.

32. *Visuddhimagga*, XVII, 287.

33. Sunthorn, *Buddhist Concept of Karma,* 191.

34. Ibid., xi.

35. *Potaliya Sutta, Majjhima Nikāya*, vol. 13/verse 54/pp. 39–40.

36. *Siṅgālaka Sutta, Dīgha Nikāya*, vol. 11/verse 174/p. 139.

37. *Visuddhimagga*, XVI, 33.

38. Buddhadāsa, "Upasak haeng kan phoeiphrae tham," 57.

39. Buddhadāsa, *Patitchasamupapat chak phra ot*, 74.

40. Ibid., 66.

41. *Ñaṇakathā, Khuddaka Nikāya*, vol. 31/verse 98/p. 39.

42. Buddhadāsa, *Another Kind of Birth,* 1.

43. Ibid.

44. Ibid., 4–5.

45. Buddhadāsa, "Upasak haeng kan phoeiphrae tham," 60.

46. Buddhadāsa, *Khwam suk thi thae mi yu tae nai ngan* (*ความสุขที่แท้มีอยู่แต่ในงาน*, 2521) (Bangkok: Thammabucha, 1978), 157.

47. Ibid.

48. Ibid., 7.

49. *Visuddhimagga*, XVII, 2.

50. Buddhadāsa, *Duang ta thi hen tham* (*ดวงตาที่เห็นธรรม*, 2511) (Bangkok: Thammabucha, 1968), 9.

51. Buddhadāsa, *Two Kinds of Language*, 15.

52. Anan Senakhan, *Khamson diarathi*, 40.

53. Bunmi Methangkun, *To than Phutthathat rueang chit wang, lem 1.* 57.

54. Bunmi Methangkun, "Phiksu phu thamlai phutthasatsana" (ภิกษุผู้ทำลายพุทธศาสนา) in Anan Senakhan (ed.), *Khamson diarathi*, 92.

55. Buddhadāsa, *Another Kind of Birth,* 19.

56. *Poṭṭhapāda Sutta, Dīgha Nikāya,* vol. 9/verse 292/p. 270.

57. Ibid.

58. *Pāyāsirājañña Sutta, Dīgha Nikāya,* vol. 10/verses 301–330/ pp. 234–260.

59. Mulder, *Everyday Life in Thailand,* 146.

60. Ibid.

61. Bunmi Methangkun, "Phiksu Phu Thamlai Phutthasatsana," 94.

62. Bunmi, *To than Phutthathat rueang chit wang, lem 1,* 48.

63. Ibid., 96.

64. Trevor Ling, *The Buddha – Buddhist Civilisation in India and Ceylon* (London: Temple Smith, 1973), 74.

65. Ibid., 70.

66. David Gosling, "The Scientific and Religious Beliefs of Thai Scientists and Their Inter-relationship," in *Southeast Asian Journal of Social Science,* vol. 4, no. 1, 1975, 10.

67. Ibid., 11.

## CHAPTER 5
## *CHIT WANG* ("FREED MIND") AND THE ABOLITION OF THE MONK-LAY DISTINCTION

1. In the Thai language version of the *Suttapiṭaka* (*Phra traipidok phasa thai chabap luang*) *suññatā* is systematically translated as *wang,* or more commonly as the abstract noun *khwam wang,* "voidness." The specific term *chit wang* has been coined by Buddhadāsa and is unique to his writings and the writings of his followers. While used technically to denote "void," the Thai term *wang* also has the sense of "to be devoid of" or "to be free of." It is also used to denote "being free" in the sense of not being busy, the term *wela wang* meaning literally "free time." The term *chit wang* thus literally means "void mind," but because of the particular thrust of Buddhadāsa's use of the term this literal translation is misleading. I prefer the terms "voided-mind" or "freed-mind," which more accurately catch the sense of Buddhadāsa's term, denoting a mind which is voided of or freed from moral impurities. *Chit wang* most definitely does not mean an "empty mind" in the sense of a mental vacuum or void.

2. *Suñña,* "void," is the adjectival form, while the term *suññatā* is an abstract noun, i.e., "voidness." The Sanskrit equivalents are *śunya* and *śunyatā.*

3. Pali Text Society, *Pali English Dictionary*, T. W. Rhys Davids & William Stede (eds), (London: Luzac & Co. Ltd., 1976), 717.

4. *Mogharāja Māṇavakapañhā Niddesa, Khuddaka Nikāya*, vol. 30 verse 505/p. 197.

5. Buddhadāsa, *Duang ta thi hen tham*, 14.

6. Thai possesses an elaborate pronoun system in which the use of first, second, and third person pronouns varies depending on the relative statuses of the speakers or persons spoken about. The first person pronoun *ku* (กู) is used either derogatorily, as when expressing anger or disgust, or as an intimate form among close friends or relatives. Here Buddhadāsa is using *ku* in its first, derogatory sense, to emphasize the delusory and false nature of the belief in the existence of a self. Had he wished to emphasize the notion of intimacy Buddhadāsa would have chosen a much less ambiguously intimate first person pronoun such as *chan* (ฉัน). The English translation of *tua ku–khong ku* as "I"–"mine," while being the closest possible rendering, fails to catch the emphatic sense of disapproval associated with Buddhadāsa's vernacular Thai rendering of the Pali term *attā*.

7. Buddhadāsa, *Another Kind of Birth*, 15.

8. Buddhadāsa, *Khwam suk thi thae*, 134–135.

9. Ibid., 138.

10. As noted previously, I disagree with the translation of *wang* as "empty" or "emptiness" because this misleadingly implies that *chit wang* is a state of mental vacuity. However, where others have used the term "empty" in translating Buddhadāsa's work, as here, I retain the term for the sake of faithfulness to the cited text.

11. Buddhadāsa, *Another Kind of Birth*, 6.

12. Ibid., 6–7.

13. Buddhadāsa., *Withi fuek samathi wipatsana, lem 1* (วิธีฝึกสมาธิวิปัสสนา *เล่ม 1*), (Bangkok: Phutthasatsana, n.d.), 78.

14. Buddhadāsa, *Chutmai khong kan sueksa* (*จุดหมายของการศึกษา, 2522*) (Bangkok: Thammabucha, 1979), 83.

15. Buddhadāsa, *Thalaengkan Suan Mok 50 pi*, 29.

16. Sunthorn, *Buddhist Concept of Karma*, 68.

17. Buddhadāsa, *Buddha-dhamma for Students*, 64.

18. Buddhadāsa, *Khwam suk thi thae*, 37.

19. Traditionally ten *kilesa* or defilements are enumerated: (1) *lobha*–greed, (2) *dosa*–hatred, (3) *moha*–delusion, (4) *māna*–conceit, (5) *diṭṭhi*–false views, (6) *vicikicchā*–scepticism and doubt, (7) *thina*–mental torpor,

(8) *uddhacca*–mental restlessness, (9) *ahirika*–shamelessness, (10) *anottappa* –a lack of a conscience or moral dread.

20. Buddhadāsa, *Withi fuek samathi wipatsana, lem 1*, 85.

21. Bunmi Methangkun, *To than Phutthathat rueang chit wang, lem 1*, p. 68.

22. Traditionally seven *anusaya* or *anusayakilesa* are listed: (I) *kāma-rāga*–sensuous greed, (2) *paṭigha*–grudge, (3) *diṭṭhi*–false views, (4) *vicikicchā*–skepticism and doubt, (5) *māna*–conceit, (6) *bhava-rāga*–craving for continued existence, (7) *avijjā*–ignorance.

23. *Visuddhimagga*, XXII, 83.

24. Ibid., XXII, 60.

25. Buddhadāsa, *Nipphan phon samai pai laeo rue*? (*นิพพานพ้นสมัยไปแล้วหรือ*, 2508) (Samut Prakan, Thailand: Ongkan Fuenfu Phra Phutthasatsana, 1965), 7. N.B. Buddhadāsa makes it clear in this text that he does not take the term *sakadāgāmi* to denote a person who is literally reborn once more before attaining *nibbāna*. Rather he takes the term as meaning an enlightened person whose remaining *kamma* forces him to return once more to the deluded mental condition of an ordinary person.

26. Buddhadāsa, *Another Kind of Birth*, 8.

27. Anan, *Khamson diarathi*, 41.

28. Buddhadāsa, *Nipphan*, 46.

29. Ibid., 28.

30. Nyanatiloka, *Buddhist Dictionary – Manual of Buddhist Terms and Doctrines*, 4th ed., Nyanaponika (rev.) (Kandy Sri Lanka: Buddhist Publication Society, 1980), 128–129.

31. Ibid., 129.

32. Chinda Chandrkaew, *Nibbana – The Ultimate Truth of Buddhism* (Bangkok: Mahachulalongkorn Buddhist University Press, 1982), 70.

33. Buddhadāsa, *Handbook for Mankind*, trans. Buddhanigama (Bangkok: Sublime Life Mission, 1980), 77.

34. *Dhātu Sutta, Khuddaka Nikāya*, vol. 25/verse 222/192.

35. Buddhadāsa, *Withi fuek samathi wipatsana, lem 1*, 79.

36. Buddhadāsa, *Nipphan*, 25.

37. Buddhadāsa, *Nipphan nok khamphi aphitham* (*นิพพานนอกคำภีร์อภิธรรม*) (Samut Prakan, Thailand: Ongkan Fuenfu Phra Phutthasatsana, n.d.), 14.

38. Slater, *Paradox and Nibbana*, 62.

39. Jane Bunnag, "The Role of the Buddhist Monk in Central Thai Society," in *Visakha Puja*, Buddhist Association of Thailand, Bangkok, 2513 (1970), 48.

40. Kukrit Pramoj, "Khwam hen bang ton khong M.R. Kukrit Pramoj" ("ความเห็นบางตอนของ ม.ร.ว. คึกฤทธิ์ ปราโมช"), in Pun Chongprasoet (ed.), *Arai thuk arai phit*, 2–3.

41. Buddhadāsa, *Buddha-dhamma for Students*, 39

42. Buddhadāsa, *Nipphan nok khamphi aphitham*, 9.

43. Buddhadāsa, *Khwam suk thi thae*, 3.

44. Buddhadāsa, *Buat sam duean* (บวชสามเดือน, 2525) (Bangkok: Thammabucha, 1928), 3.

45. Ibid., 2.

46. Ibid., 5.

47. Ibid.

48. Buddhadāsa, *Kharawat tham*, 123.

49. Ibid., 41.

50. Ibid., 4.

51. Ibid., 49.

52. Bunmi Methangkun, "Phiksu phu thamlai phutthasatsana," 94.

53. Kittiwuttho Bhikkhu, "Rueang chit wang nok phra traipidok mi khwam samkhan nai patchuban mak" ("เรื่องจิตว่างนอกพระไตรปิฎกมีความสำคัญในปัจจุบันมาก"), in Pun Chongprasoet (ed.), *Arai thuk arai phit*, 126–130.

54. *Dhammadinna Sutta, Saṁyutta Nikāya*, vol. 19/verses 1625–1626/pp. 404–405.

55. Buddhadāsa, "Upasak haeng kan phoeiphrae tham," 49.

56. Ibid., 46.

57. *Catukka Nipāta, Aṅguttara Nikāya*, vol. 21/verse 192/p. 180.

58. *Lokavipatti Sutta, Aṅguttara Nikāya*, vol. 23/verse 96/p. 123.

59. *Dhammasaṅgani, Abhidammapiṭaka*, vol. 34/verse 706/p. 248 and vol. 34/verse 911/p. 315.

60. *Poṭṭhapāda Sutta, Dīgha Nikāya*, vol. 9/verse 279/p. 254.

61. Siddhi, *Social Philosophy*, 77.

62. Buddhadāsa, *Nipphan nok khamphi aphitham*, 6.

## CHAPTER 6
## THE PRACTICE OF *CHIT WANG*

1. Melford E. Spiro, *Buddhism and Society* (London: George Allen & Unwin Ltd., 1971), 50.

2. Boowa Nyanasampanno, 60n.

3. Buddhadāsa, *Buddha-dhamma for Students*, 47.

4. Spiro, *Buddhism and Society*, 51.

5. Buddhadāsa, *Handbook for Mankind*, 70.
6. Spiro, *Buddhism and Society*, 51n.
7. Buddhadāsa, *Handbook for Mankind*, 70.
8. Ibid., 73.
9. Nyanatiloka, 83.
10. *Cūlasuññatā Sutta*, *Majjhima Nikāya*, vol. 14/verse 334/pp. 180–181.
11. *Pañcala Sutta, Aṅguttara Nikāya*, vol. 14/verse 246/p. 362.
12. *Cūlasuññatā Sutta*, *Majjhima Nikāya*, vol. 14/verse 341/p. 183.
13. Spiro, *Buddhism and Society*, 51.
14. Ibid., 52.
15. Buddhadāsa, *Buddha-dhamma for Students*, 19.
16. Ibid., 20.
17. Buddhadāsa, *Withi fuek samathi wipatsana, lem 1*, 48–49.
18. Buddhadāsa, *Handbook for Mankind*, 84.
19. Ibid., 87.
20. Ibid., 70–71.
21. Ibid., 77.
22. Ibid., 85.
23. Kukrit Pramoj, 7.
24. Ibid., 2.
25. Soma Thera, *Words Leading to Disenchantment* (Kandy, Sri Lanka: Buddhist Publication Society, 1978), 4.
26. Buddhadāsa, *Chit praphatson, chit doem thae, chit wang – Muean kan rue yang rai* (*จิตประภัสสร จิตเดิมแท้ จิตว่าง – เหมือนกันหรืออย่างไร*, 2517) (Bangkok: Thammabucha, 1974), 22.
27. Cited in Pun Chongprasoet, *Wiwatha rawang M.R. Kukrit Pramoj kap than Phutthathat*, 52.
28. *Subha Sutta, Majjhima Nikāya*, vol. 13/verse 711/492.
29. Cited in Pun Chongprasoet, *Wiwatha rawang M.R. Kukrit Pramoj kap than Phutthathat*, 52.
30. Buddhadāsa, "Upasak haeng kan phoeiphrae tham," 19.
31. Kukrit Pramoj, 4.
32. This may be a reference to Buddhadāsa's involvement in the Thammathan Foundation established in Chaiya, Southern Thailand, by Buddhadāsa together with his brother Dhammadāsa for the purpose of propagating their views on Buddhism. Kukrit may also be referring here to the more openly political involvement of the monk Kittiwuttho with right-wing movements in the 1973–1976 period.
33. Kukrit Pramoj, 5.

34. Buddhadāsa, *Kharawat tham*, 55.
35. Ibid., 61–62.
36. Ibid., 119.
37. Ibid., 124.
38. Ibid., 124–125.
39. Ibid., 128.
40. Tambiah, *World Conqueror and World Renouncer*, 414.
41. Buddhadāsa, *Two Kinds of Language*, 10.
42. Buddhadāsa, *Khwam suk thi thae*, 40.
43. Ibid., 6.
44. Buddhadāsa, "Upasak haeng kan phoeiphrae tham," 18.
45. Buddhadāsa, *Khwam suk thi thae*, 40.
46. Buddhadāsa, "Upasak haeng kan phoeiphrae tham," 55.
47. Buddhadāsa, *Barom tham*, 88–89.
48. Buddhadāsa, *Kan ngan khue tua khwam kao na* (การงานคือตัวความก้าวหน้า, 2521.) (Bangkok: Thammabucha, 1982), 3.
49. Ibid., 5.
50. Buddhadāsa, *Two Kinds of Language*, 19.
51. Buddhadāsa, *Khwam suk thi thae*, 41

## CHAPTER 7
## *CHIT WANG* AND ZEN

1. John Blofeld (trans.), *The Zen Teachings of Huang Po – On the Transmission of Mind* (New York: Grove Press, 1958), 8.
2. The Chinese term which Blofeld translates as "One Mind" has almost as many renderings into English as there have been translators of Zen texts. Wang Muo-lam, translator of *The Sutra of Wei Lang* (*or Hui Neng*) (Westport Conn., 1973) says the original Chinese term denotes "Self-nature" but nevertheless chooses to render it by "Essence of Mind." Suzuki, on the other hand, drawing on the Japanese tradition, variously uses the terms "Mind" or "No-mind."
3. Daisetz Teitaro Suzuki, *The Zen Doctrine of No-Mind – The Significance of the Sutra of Hui-Neng (Wei-Lang)* (London: Rider & Co., 1949), 23.
4. Kittiwuttho, 128–130.
5. Buddhadāsa, *Khwam suk thi thae*, 33.
6. Buddhadāsa, *Buddha-dhamma for Students,* 68.
7. Ibid.

8. Buddhadāsa, *Khwam suk thi thae,* 33.

9. Buddhadāsa (trans.), *Khamson khong Huang Po* (คำสอนของฮวงโป, 2520) Bangkok: Thammabucha, 1977), 1.

10. Buddhadāsa, *Chit Praphatson,* 13.

11. Buddhadāsa, *Chao phut thi di yom pen chao khrit thi di* (ชาวพุทธที่ดียอมเป็นชาวคริสต์ที่ดี, 2523) (Bangkok: Thammabucha, 1980), 13.

12. The most important Zen texts translated into Thai by Buddhadāsa are:

(i) The *Zen Teachings of Huang Po – On the Transmission of Mind,* John Blofeld (trans.), (New York: Grove Press, 1958). Translated as *Khamson Khong Huang Po* (คำสอนของฮวงโป, 2520) (Bangkok: Thammabucha, 1977);

(ii) The *Sutra of Wei Lang* (or *Hui Neng*), Wang Mou-lam (trans.), Christmas Humphries (ed.), (Westport, Conn.: n.p., 1973). Translated as *Sut Khong Wei Lang* (สูตรของเวยหล่าง, 2520) (Bangkok: Thammabucha, 1977).

As is common in Thailand today most translations into Thai are from English originals or English versions of texts.

13. Buddhadāsa, *Khamson khong Huang Po,* 1.

14. Daisetz Teitaro Suzuki, *Zen and Japanese Buddhism* (Tokyo: Japan Travel Bureau, 1958), 19–20.

15. Blofeld, 78n.

16. Buddhadāsa, *Khwam suk thi thae,* 36.

17. *Avijjā Sutta, Aṅguttara Nikāya,* vol. 24/verse 61/p. 103.

18. The "food" of lacking control of the senses is in turn lacking the mindfulness called *satisampajanna,* whose "food" is given as not being mentally clever or ingenious. The "food" or source of a lack of mental cleverness is lacking faith or *saddha,* whose "food" is not listening to the true teaching or *saccadhamma,* whose "food" is not meeting with a person established in truth, a *sappurisa.*

19. Chandrkaew, 50.

20. Boowa Nyanasampanno, 115.

21. Blofeld, 109–110n.

22. Buddhadāsa, *Chit praphatson,* 12.

23. Buddhadāsa, *Osaretapphatham,* 226.

24. Walpola Rahula, "Zen and the Taming of the Bull," in Walpola Rahula (ed.), *Zen and the Taming of the Bull – Towards the Re-definition of Buddhist Thought* (London: Gordon Fraser, 1978), 16–17.

25. Blofeld, 110n.

26. Thich Nhat Hanh, *The Miracle of Being Awake,* trans. Mobi Quynh Hoa, ed. Jim Forest, (Bangkok: Sathirakoses-Nagapradipa Foundation, 1976), 36.

27. Buddhadāsa, *Nipphan phon samai pai laeo rue,* 10.

28. Buddhadāsa, *Khamson khong Huang Po,* 3.

29. Ibid., 6.

30. Ibid., 3.

31. (*Bhikkhu*) Ananda, 24.

32. Suzuki, *The Zen Doctrine of No-Mind,* 53.

33. Blofeld, 39n.

34. Ibid., Section 37 of "Wan Ling Record of the Zen Master Huang Po."

35. Suzuki, *Zen and Japanese Buddhism,* 33.

36. Anan, *Khamson diarathi,* 67.

37. Buddhadāsa, *Nai wattasongsan mi nipphan* (ในวัฏสงสารมีนิพพาน, 2524) (Bangkok: Thammabucha, 1981), 10.

38. Ibid., 7.

39. Ratchaworamuni, *Phutthatham,* 43.

40. Ibid.

41. James W. Boyd, "The Theravada View of Saṁsāra," in Somaratna Balasooriya (ed.), *Buddhist Studies in Honour of Walpola Rahula* (London: Gordon Fraser, 1980), 32.

42. The title of one of Buddhadāsa's pamphlets is *In Vaṭṭasaṁsāra There Is Nibbana.* See footnote no. 37 above.

43. Blofeld, 44n.

44. Rupp, "Nirvāṇa and Saṁsāra," 57.

45. Ibid., 63.

46. Ibid.

47. Thich Nhat Hanh, 17.

48. The Thai translator was a monk, Phra Pracha Pasannathammo, the Thai title being *Patihan haeng kan tuen yu samoe – Khumue fuek samathi samrap khon num sao thi patibatkan nai sangkhom,* first printing (ปาฏิหาริย์แห่งการตื่นอยู่เสมอ-คู่มือฝึกสมาธิสำหรับคนหนุ่มสาวที่ปฏิบัติการในสังคม, 2518) (Bangkok: Komon Khimthong Foundation, 1975).

49. Nilchawee Sivaraksa is the wife of author and Buddhadāsa supporter, Sulak Sivaraksa.

50. Introduction to Thich Nhat Hanh, 10.

51. Ibid., 23.

52. Ibid.

53. Ibid., 24.

## CHAPTER 8
## BUDDHADĀSA ON MODERNIZATION AND DEVELOPMENT

1. In the *Patthana* of the *Abhidhammapiṭaka* causality or the conditional dependence of all phenomena is analyzed into twenty-four different types of conditionality or *paccaya*.

2. Buddhadāsa, *Nipphan*, 19.

3. Ibid., 20.

4. Buddhadāsa, *Hak khomunit khao ma phutthasatsana ko yang yu dai* (*หากคอมมูนิสต์เข้ามาพุทธศาสนาก็ยังอยู่ได้*, 2517) (Samut Prakan: Ongkan Fuenfu Phra Phuttasasana, 1974), 101.

5. Buddhadāsa, *Barom tham*, 74.

6. Buddhadāsa, *Thamma kap lok cha pai duai kan dai rue mai* (*ธรรมะกับโลกจะไปด้วยกันได้หรือไม่*, 2521) (Bangkok: Thammabucha, 1978), 12.

7. Buddhadāsa, *Barom tham*, 84–85.

8. Ibid., 82.

9. Buddhadāsa, *Thamma kap lok*, 9.

10. Buddhadāsa, *Barom tham*, 75–76.

11. Chandrkaew, 33.

12. Buddhadāsa, *Chutmai khong kan sueksa*.

13. Morell and Samudavanija, *Political Conflict*, 30.

14. Buddhadāsa, *Barom tham*, 102.

15. Buddhadāsa, *Hak khomunit khao ma*, 29–30.

16. Buddhadāsa, *Barom tham*, 98.

17. Ibid., 99.

18. Wit, 57.

19. Barbara Watson Andaya, "Statecraft in the Reign of Lu Thai of Sukhodaya," in Bardwell L. Smith (ed.), *Religion and the Legitimation of Power in Thailand, Laos and Burma* (Chambersburg, Penn.: Anima Books, 1978), 4.

20. Tambiah, *World Conqueror and World Renouncer*, 431.

21. Buddhadāsa, *Thammik sangkhomniyom baep phadetkan rue sangkhomniyom tam lak haeng satsana thuk sastana* (*ธัมมิกสังคมนิยมแบบเผด็จการ หรือ สังคมนิยมตามหลักแห่งศาสนาทุกศาสนา*, 2517) (Bangkok: Thammabucha, 1974), 3.

22. Buddhadāsa, *Kharawat tham*, 43.

23. Buddhadāsa, *Christianity and Buddhism*, 16.

24. Ibid., *Chutmai khong kan sueksa*, 9.

25. Ibid. 8–9.

26. Buddhadāsa, "Exchanging Dhamma While Fighting," *Visakha Puja*, Buddhist Association of Thailand, Bangkok, 2513 (1970), 33.

27. Buddhadāsa, *Thamma kap kok*, 5–6.

28. Buddhadāsa, *Thamma nai thana latthi kan mueang* (ธรรมะในฐานะลัทธิการเมือง, 2521) (Bangkok: Thammabucha, 1978), 2.

29. Morell and Samudavanija, *Political Conflict*, 25.

30. Somboon, *Buddhism and Politics in Thailand,* 1.

31. Khana Kammakan Sasana Phuea Kan Phatthana, *Phutthathat kap khon run mai* (พุทธทาสกับคนรุ่นใหม่ 2526) (Bangkok: Komon Khimthong Foundation, 1983), 12–13

32. Buddhadāsa, *Barom tham*, 45.

33. *Vajirañāṇa,* Prince, *Autobiography: The Life of Prince-Patriarch Vajirañāṇa of Siam,* 1860–1921, Craig J. Reynolds (trans.) (Athens, Ohio: Ohio University Press, 1979), xxxvii.

34. Buddhadāsa, *Barom tham*, 4.

35. From an interview with Buddhadāsa reproduced in Sulak Sivaraksa, *Khanchong song phra*, 225.

36. Cited in Donald K. Swearer, "Some Observations on New Directions in Thai Buddhism," in *Visakha Puja*, Buddhist Association of Thailand, Bangkok, 2513 (1970), 56.

37. Bruce F. Morgan, "Vocation of Monk and Layman: Signs of Change in Thai Buddhist Ethics," in Bardwell L. Smith (ed.), *Contributions to Asian Studies, Vol. 4, Tradition and Change in Theravada Buddhism: Essays on Ceylon and Thailand in the 19th and 20th Centuries* (Leiden: E. J. Brill, 1973), 72.

38. Ibid., 70.

39. Ibid.

40. *Visuddhimagga*, IX, 93.

41. Ibid., IX, 94.

42. Boowa Nyanasampanno, 110.

43. Wit, 57–58.

44. *Loka Sutta, Khuddaka Nikāya,* vol. 25/verse 263/266.

45. Rahula, *History of Buddhism in Ceylon,* 193.

46. Ibid. 194.

47. Siddhi, *Social Philosophy*, 118.

48. Buddhadāsa, *Nipphan*, 80.

49. Buddhadāsa, *Hak khomunit khao ma*, 26–27.

50. Ibid., 27.

51. Ibid., *Ba bun–ba sawan* (บ้าบุญ-บ้าสวรรค์, 2518) (Samut Prakan: Ongkan Fuenfu Phra Phutthasatsana, 1975), 6.

52. Buddhadāsa, *Buddha-dhamma for Students*, 44
53. Buddhadāsa, *Hak khomunit khao ma*, 33.
54. Charles R. Keyes, "The Power of Merit," in *Visakha Puja*, Buddhist Association of Thailand, Bangkok, 2516 (1973), 98.
55. Ibid., 100.
56. See appendix for a discussion of participatory merit.
57. Rupp, "Nirvāna and Saṁsāra," 64
58. Buddhadāsa, *Hak khomunit khao ma*, 30.
59. Julius R. Jayawardene was formerly the president of Sri Lanka. The quote here is taken from a lecture given when he was finance minister of the then Ceylon.
60. Julius R. Jayawardene, *Buddhism and Marxism*, Pamphlet of the text of the Tenth Anniversary Lecture to the Ceylon University Brotherhood, Colombo, Ceylon, 6th March 1950, 4.

## CHAPTER 9
## BUDDHADĀSA'S POLITICAL WRITINGS

1. I translate the Thai term *thammathipatai* (ธรรมาธิปไตย) as *dhammocracy*. However, it should be noted that the Thai word is derived from a much older Pali term, *dhammādhipateyya*, which literally denotes "the dominating influence of *dhamma*."
2. Buddhadāsa, *Barom tham*, 53.
3. Buddhadāsa, *Kharawat tham*, 6.
4. Buddhadāsa, *Thamma kap lok*, 7.
5. Buddhadāsa, "*Upasak haeng kan phoeiphrae tham*," 28.
6. Buddhadāsa, *Chao phut thi di yom pen khrit thi di*, 26.
7. Buddhadāsa, *Thammik sangkhomniyom baep phadetkan*, 5.
8. Buddhadāsa, *Thamma kap kan mueang* (ธรรมะกับการเมือง, 2522) (Chaiya, Thailand: Thammathan Foundation, 1979), 6.
9. Buddhadāsa, *Thammik sangkhomniyom baep phadetkan*, 14.
10. Buddhadāsa, *Chutmai khong kan sueksa*, 6
11. Morell and Samudavanija, *Political Conflict*, 28.
12. Buddhadāsa, *Thammik sangkhomniyom baep phadetkan*, 18.
13. Buddhadāsa, *Thamma kap lok*, 17.
14. Buddhadāsa, *Thammik sangkhomniyom baep phadetkan*, 7.
15. Ibid., 39.
16. The *dasarāajadhamma* or ten qualities of the royal *dhamma* are: (1) *dhāna*—almsgiving, (2) *sīla*—to be moral and not under the influence

of *kilesa*, (3) *parijjāga*—renouncing bad aspects of one's personality, such as self–centredness, (4) *ājjava*—honesty and integrity, (5) *maddava* —gentleness, (6) *tapa*—exercise of self–control, (7) *akodha*—not to be angered, (8) *avihiṁsa*—not causing difficulties or problems for others, (9) *khanti*—patience and forbearance, (10) *avirodha*—to be free from suspicion by not violating social norms.

17. Buddhadāsa, *Thammik sangkhomniyom baep phadetkan*, 49.

18. Ibid., 53.

19. Ibid., 37.

20. Cited in Trevor Ling, *Buddhism, Imperialism and War – Burma and Thailand in Modern History* (London: George Allen & Unwin Ltd, 1979), 20.

21. Somboon, *Buddhism and Politics in Thailand*, 7.

22. Ibid., 91–92.

23. Quoted in Khana Kammakan Sasana Phuea Kan Phatthana, *Phutthathat kap khon run mai*, 56.

24. Puey Ungphakorn, 116.

25. Ling, *The Buddha – Buddhist Civilisation in India and Ceylon*, 50.

26. Ratchaworamuni, *Phutthasatsana kap sangkhom thai* (*พุทธศาสนากับสังคมไทย*, 2526) (Bangkok: Komon Khimthong Foundation, 1983), 22ff.

27. Ling, *The Buddha – Buddhist Civilisation in India and Ceylon*, 140.

28. Morell and Samudavanija, *Political Conflict*, 57–58.

29. Buddhadāsa, *Fa sang thang prachathipatai* (ฟ้าสางทางประชาธิปไตย, 2528) (Bangkok: Thammabucha, 1985), 2–3.

30. Ibid., 7.

31. Ibid., 36.

32. Buddhadāsa, *"Upasak haeng kan phoeiphrae tham,"* 22.

33. Ibid., 23.

34. Ibid., 26–27.

35. Buddhadāsa, *Osaretapphatham*, 217.

36. Buddhadāsa, *"Upasak haeng kan phoeiphrae tham,"* 24–25.

37. Buddhadāsa, *Mai mi satsana* (ไม่มีศาสนา, 2517) (Bangkok: Thammabucha, 1974), 5.

38. Buddhadāsa, *Christianity and Buddhism*, 7.

39. Buddhadāsa, *Thamma nai thana latthi kan mueang*, 3–4.

40. Ibid., 8ff.

41. Buddhadāsa, *Christianity and Buddhism*, 7.

42. A. de S. (no other name given), "Buddhist Monk's Apology for Christianity," in *World Buddhism* (Ceylon), May 1969 (B.E. 2513), reprinted in (Bhikkhu) Sivlibodhi (ed.), *Buddhadāsa: Appearance and Reality* (Bangkok: Sublime Life Mission, 1971), 1–3.

43. Amarasiri Weerarame, "Monk's Interpretation of Christianity," in *World Buddhism* (Ceylon), September 1969 (B.E. 2513), reprinted in (Bhikkhu) Sivlibodhi (ed.), *Buddhadāsa: Appearance and Reality* (Bangkok: Sublime Life Mission, 1971), 33.

44. Ibid., 35–36.

45. Ibid., 36.

46. Cited in Khana Kammakan Satsana Phuea Kan Phatthana, *Phutthathat kap khon run mai*, 57.

47. Swearer, *Bhikkhu Buddhadāsa and the Buddhist Reformation in Thailand*, 6.

48. Cited in Khana Kammakan Satsana Phuea Kan Phatthana, *Phutthathat kap khon run mai*, 57.

49. Buddhadāsa, *Christianity and Buddhism*, 6.

50. Ibid., 22.

51. Buddhadāsa, *Mai mi satsana*, 27.

52. Morell and Samudavanija, *Political Conflict*, 229.

53. Buddhadāsa, *Hak khomunit khao ma*, 109.

54. Buddhadāsa, *Thammik sangkhomniyom baep phadetkan*, 11.

55. Buddhadāsa, *Hak khomunit khao ma*, 110.

## CHAPTER 10
## CONCLUSION: BUDDHADĀSA BHIKKHU—THERAVADA BUDDHISM'S CONSERVATIVE RADICAL

1. Pracha Pasannathammo, *Si nak khit ruam samai*, 3–4.

2. Somboon, *Buddhism and Politics in Thailand*, 91n.

3. Mulder, *Everyday Life in Thailand*, 54.

4. Sulak Sivaraksa, *Phutthathatsana phuea kan sangsan sangkhom mai* (*พุทธทัศนะเพื่อการสร้างสรรค์สังคมใหม่*, 2526) (Bangkok: Thianwan, 1983), 3.

5. Mulder, "Buddhism, National Identity and Modernity in Contemporary Thailand," in *Journal of Social Sciences – Chiangmai University*, vol. 2, no. 2, September 1978, 40.

6. Ibid., 37.

7. Ibid., 44.

## EPILOGUE

This epilogue was originally published in the *Journal of the Siam Society*, 1994, vol. 2, pp. 103–114. I wish to thank Phra Santikaro Bhikkhu (Suan Mokh), Craig Reynolds (Australian National University), Louis Gabaude (Ecole Française d'Extrême Orient & Chiang Mai), Grant Olson (Northern Illinois University) and Rosalind Morris (Columbia University) for their valuable comments on earlier versions of this paper.

1. This section has been compiled from details provided by *Phra* Santikaro Bhikkhu (personal correspondence) and reports in the following Thai language sources:

*Arahan Phutthathat phikkhu* (The *arahant,* Buddhadāsa Bhikkhu). Bangkok: N. N. Printing, 2536 (1993).

"Prathip tham song sawang klang chai sayam – 87 pi Phutthathat phikkhu" (The lamp of *dhamma* shines brightly in the heart of Siam – the 87 years of Buddhadāsa Bhikkhu), Santi Butrchai, *Nation Weekly (Sut-sapda)*, 1 (52), 4–10 June 1993 (2536), 8–9.

"Thammanusati chak kan aphat khong than Phutthathat mahathera" (Reflections on the *dhamma* from the illness of *Mahāthera* Buddhadāsa), Dr. Prawet Wasi, *Matichon Weekly (Sut-sapda)*, 13 (669), 18 June 1993 (2536), 8–11.

"Korani aphat khong than Phutthathat kap sitthi thi cha tai" (Buddhadāsa's illness and the right to die), Phongnarin Ulit, *Siam Rath Weekly (Sapda-wichan)*, 40 (3), 20–26 June 1993 (2536), 16–17.

"Rai-ngan phiset – 87 pi anitchang Phutthathat amata thammakhot" (Special report – the passing after 87 years of Buddhadāsa, immortal expounder of the Dhamma), *Matichon Weekly (Sut-sapda)*, 13 (673), 16 July 1993 (2536), 75–76.

"Phra yot nak-rop haeng kong-thap tham" (A great warrior monk of the army of Dhamma), *Chiwit Tong Su*, 1 (34), 17–23 July 1993 (2536), 2ff.

"Moradok tham chak Suan Mok, Phutthathat chak yu pai mai mi tai, rai-ngan phak-sanam doi kong bannathikan" (The *dhammic* legacy from Suan Mokh, Buddhadāsa will live on, never to die, field report by the editorial board), *Siam Rath Weekly (Sapda-wichan)*, 40 (7), 18–24 July 1993 (2536), 10–11.

"Phinaikam than Phutthathat" (Buddhadāsa's will), *Nation Weekly (Sut-sapda)*, 2 (58), 16–22 July 1993 (2536), 40.

"Phutthathat phra phu tuen trap niran" (Buddhadāsa, enlightened throughout eternity), *Nation Weekly (Sut-sapda)*, 2 (69), 1–7 October 1993 (2536), 9–11.

2. Santikaro Bhikkhu, "Buddhadāsa Bhikkhu—A Remembrance," *Crossroads—An Interdisciplinary Journal of Southeast Asian Studies* 8 (1), 1993, 125. Phra Santikaro was one of three monks who stayed with Buddhadāsa throughout his hospitalization at Siriraj Hospital in Bangkok. He kept a detailed diary during this time and is planning to write a book on the events surrounding the passing of Buddhadāsa.

3. *Matichon Weekly,* 16 July 1993, p. 75.

4. Phra Santikaro (personal correspondence, 1994) reports that Buddhadāsa had been saying that it was *bap* (Pali: *papa,* "sin") to outlive the Buddha since before his eightieth birthday.

5. *Chiwit tong su,* 17–23 July 1993, p.4.

6. Phra Santikaro reports that as Buddhadāsa returned to bed he handed his keys over to his attendant, saying "I don't want to die holding these keys *[mai yak tai kha kunchae]*." Phra Santikaro interprets these comments as meaning that "monks are supposed to be without possessions and homeless, and to die with a set of keys on you . . . he did not feel was appropriate. And many of us consider that that was where he was saying, 'Well, this is it, folks.'" (Quotation from a taped interview with Phra Santikaro Bhikkhu by Grant A. Olson at Wat Buddhadharma, Hinsdale, Chicago, 2 September 1993).

7. This denotes the absence of the elements of material existence in *nibbāna.*

8. *Matichon Weekly,* 16 July 1993, p. 75. The anonymous author of the publication *Arahan Phutthathat phikkhu* (The *arahant,* Buddhadāsa Bhikkhu) (1993 [2536]: 9) reports that Buddhadāsa's final words were, "*Mai rusuek pen tua ku mai mi buak mai mi lop santiphap santisuk nipphan,*" and were uttered in a delirium (*phoe*) on 31 May when Buddhadāsa was receiving intensive care at Siriraj Hospital. However, this contradicts other reports that Buddhadāsa was in a coma from 25 May.

9. Santikaro Bhikkhu, "Buddhadāsa Bhikkhu—A Remembrance," 125.

10. *Siam Rath Weekly,* 20–26 June 1993, p. 16.

11. *Matichon Weekly,* 18 June 1993, p. 10.

12. *Buddhadāsa Will Not Die*

Buddhadāsa will live on, never to die;
Even though his body will cease, and become deaf to sound.
The body exists, the body passes; of this I am unconcerned;
It is but a thing that passes through time.

Buddhadāsa will remain, never to die.
Through good and bad he will remain a companion of the *sāsana*,
As befits his unceasing commitment to serve with his body and mind
The commands of the Buddha.

Buddhadāsa still lives on, never to die,
Unceasingly serving his fellow man and woman
With the Dhamma teachings left behind.
Oh dear friend, can you see what it is that has died?
Buddhadāsa Bhikkhu

(From *Arahan Phutthathat phikkhu* (The *arahant,* Buddhadāsa Bhikkhu), N. N. Printing, Bangkok, 1993 (2536), 3, translated by Peter A. Jackson, with advice from Santikaro Bhikkhu). Santikaro (personal correspondence, 1994) reports that this poem first became public in 1986 around the time of Buddhadāsa's eightieth birthday. Santikaro also notes that the poem has a further three verses in addition to those published at the time of Buddhadāsa's death and provides the following translation:

Even when I die and the body ceases
My voice still echoes in comrades' ears,
Clear and bright, as loud as ever.
Just as if I never died, the Dhamma-body lives on.

Treat me as if I never died,
As though I am with you all as before.
Speak up whatever is on your minds
As if I sit with you helping point out the facts.

Treat me as if I never died,
Then many streams of benefit will accrue.
Don't forget the days we set aside for Dhamma discussion;
Realise the Absolute and stop dying.

13. *Siam Rath Weekly,* 18–24 July 1993, p. 11.

14. Wanaprat, in "Yu kap luang pu, ton 4, pritsana kan dap khan khong luang pu Phutthathat lae wan phao sop," *Mahatsachan* 18 (886), 6 April 1994, 14, reports that before making his final will in March 1993, Buddhadāsa had given Phra Silawat quite different verbal instructions

about how his remains should be disposed of upon his death. According to Wanaprat, Buddhadāsa directed that when he died his body should be bound up in a sitting meditation position with cords binding his body, legs, and arms. Then his body should be lowered into a hollow cavity in part of a building at Suan Mokh called the Sala Thammakhot (Pali: *dhammaghosana*) and the top of cavity should be closed with a cement lid that should not be opened for at least one hundred years. But Phra Silawat replied that he did not dare (*mai kla*) do as Buddhadāsa requested, because he thought that many followers in Thailand and overseas would be strongly critical of this unconventional means of burial. Wanaprat reports that Phra Silawat was so vexed about having to carry out Buddhadāsa's request that he became ill. Because of concern about having to carry out his request, some of Buddhadāsa's followers suggested that he write a will about his funeral to make everything clear. In the end Buddhadāsa opted for a more traditional cremation to avoid difficulties for his followers or possible complications with the authorities about the method of his funeral.

15. Wanaprat, "Yu kap luang pu, ton 4," 37.

16. *Siam Rath Weekly,* 18–24 July 1993, p. 11.

17. Wanaprat, op cit., 37.

18. *Nation Weekly,* 1–7 October 1993, p. 11.

19. Dr. Louis Gabaude is currently a Fellow of the Ecole Française d'Extrême Orient based in Chiang Mai. His doctoral dissertation, *Introduction à l'herméneutique de Buddhadāsa Bhikkhu,* was submitted to the Ecole Française d'Extrême Orient, Paris, in 1980 and was published in 1988 under the title *Une Herméneutique Buddhique Contemporaine de Thaïlande: Buddhadāsa Bhikkhu* (Paris, Publications de l'Ecole Française d'Extrême Orient, vol. 150). Gabaude's comment and following quotation are taken from his article "Thai Society and Buddhadasa: Structural Difficulties," in *Radical Conservatism—Buddhism in the Contemporary World, Articles in Honour of Bhikkhu Buddhadasa's 84th Birthday Anniversary,* ed. Sulak Sivaraksa (Bangkok: Sathirakoses-Nagapradipa Foundation, 1990), 211–229.

20. Jim Taylor, "Social Activism and Resistance on the Thai Frontier: The Case of Phra Prajak Khuttajitto," *Bulletin of Concerned Asian Scholars* 25 (2), 1993, 4.

21. Santikaro Bhikkhu, personal correspondence, 1994. All subsequent unreferenced quotations and comments from Santikaro are from this source.

22. Jim Taylor, op. cit., 4.

23. Suwanna Satha-Anand. Review of *Buddhism, Legitimation and Conflict: The Political Functions of Urban Thai Buddhism,*" *Crossroads — An Interdisciplinary Journal of Southeast Asian Studies* 5 (1) 1990, 107.

24. Chokechai Sutthawet, "Phutthathat kap kan patirup khwam mi het mi phon khong khon thai," *Nation Weekly* 2 (65), 3–9 Sept. 1993, 34–35.

25. See my discussion of the *Kālāma Sutta* in this book, pp. 44–46.

26. For discussion on the historical and contemporary importance of the *Traiphum phra rueang* in Thailand, see Peter Jackson, "Reinterpreting the Traiphuum Phra Ruang: Political Functions of Buddhist Symbolism in Contemporary Thailand," in *Buddhist Trends in Southeast Asia,* ed. Trevor Ling (Singapore: Institute of Southeast Asian Studies, 1993), 64–100, and "Thai Buddhist Identity: Debates on the Traiphum Phra Ruang," in *National Identity and Its Defenders, Thailand 1939–1989,"* ed. Craig J. Reynolds (Chiang Mai: Silkworm Books, 1993), 191–231.

27. Taylor, op. cit., 4.

28. Santikaro Bhikkhu (personal correspondence, 1994) observes that Buddhadāsa increasingly received official recognition with the passage of the years noting, in particular, the visit of Somdet Phra Phutthaghosacan (Jaroen Nanavarathera) of Wat Thepsirin to Suan Mokh on 26 June 1937; the granting of a series of ecclesiastical titles to Buddhadāsa from 1946; Buddhadāsa's appointment as head of Dhamma Propagation for the Southern Region and his being made abbot of the royal sponsored monastery Wat Boromthat Chaiya in 1949; and the awarding of numerous honorary degrees from Thai universities.

29. Santikaro Bhikkhu (personal correspondence, 1994) suggests that Professor Sanya Thammasak, a close disciple of Buddhadāsa for many years and chairman of the Privy Council, has been important in informing King Bhumipol of Buddhadāsa's ideas, having had discussions with the king on topics such as *chit wang*. Grant Olson (personal correspondence) relates an anecdote conveyed to him by Suwanna Satha-Anand: "The king had once mentioned that he was thinking of visiting Suan Mokh. Buddhadāsa supposedly replied in a Zen-like fashion, saying, 'Your Majesty would probably not find anything of interest here. There are only rocks and trees.'"

30. Eve Kosofsky Sedgwick, *Epistemology of the Closet* (Berkeley: University of California Press, 1990), 47, cited in Rosalind Morris, "Three Sexes and Four Sexualities: Redressing the Discourses on Gender and Sexuality in Thailand," *Positions* 2 (1) 1994, 15–43.

31. Peter Vandergeest, "Hierarchy and Power in Pre-National Buddhist States," *Modern Asian Studies*, 27 (4) 1993, 862.

32. *The Nation*, 18 July 1993, p. B10.

33. Grant Olson, "From Buddhadasa Bhikkhu to Phra Debvedi," in *Radical Conservatism—Buddhism in the Contemporary World, Articles in Honour of Bhikkhu Buddhadasa's 84th Birthday Anniversary*, ed. Sulak Sivaraksa (Bangkok:Sathirakoses-Nagapradipa Foundation, 1990), 251–267.

34. *Arahan Phutthathat phikkhu*, 5.

35. *Nation Weekly*, 1–7 October 1993, pp. 9–11.

36. Wanaprat, op. cit., 14.

37. Achan Mun Bhuridatta was a famous northeastern monk renowned for his supernatural experiences while practising meditation in the forest. For a detailed account of Achan Mun's life, see Jim Taylor, *Forest Monks and the Nation-State, An Anthropological and Historical Study in Northeastern Thailand* (Singapore: Institute of Southeast Asian Studies, 1993), 75ff.

38. Luang Pho Wat Pak Nam, or Mongkhonthepmuni (Sot Chanthasaro), was the founder of the Thammakai (Pali: *dhammakāya*) meditation system now made famous by the influential Wat Phra Thammakai. For an account of Luang Pho Wat Pak Nam's life and the Thammakai movement that has grown around his teachings, see Jackson, *Buddhism, Legitimation and Conflict—The Political Functions of Urban Thai Buddhism* (Singapore: Institute of Southeast Asian Studies, 1989), 199ff.

39. Donald K. Swearer, "Sulak Sivaraksa's Buddhist Vision for Renewing Society," *Crossroads—An Interdisciplinary Journal of Southeast Asian Studies* 6 (2) 1991, 17–57.

40. Louis Gabaude has compiled valuable bibliographies of Buddhadāsa's translated works and studies of Buddhadāsa and Suan Mokh. See "Bibliography of Buddhadāsa's Translated Works and Bibliography of Studies Concerning Buddhadāsa and Suan Mokh," arranged by Louis Gabaude, in *Radical Conservatism—Buddhism in the Contemporary World, Articles in Honour of Bhikkhu Buddhadāsa's 84th Birthday Anniversary*, ed. Sulak Sivaraksa (Bangkok: Sathirakoses-Nagapradipa Foundation, 1990), 515–547.

41. Louis Gabaude, "Thai Society and Buddhadasa: Structural Difficulties," in *Radical Conservatism—Buddhism in the Contemporary World, Articles in Honour of Bhikkhu Buddhadasa's 84th Birthday Anniversary*, ed. Sulak Sivaraksa (Bangkok: Sathirakoses-Nagapradipa Foundation, 1990), 226.

42. Ibid., 216.

43. Jean-François Lyotard, *The Postmodern Condition* (1979), trans. Geoff Bennington & Brian Massumi (Manchester: Manchester University Press, 1984).

44. Peter Jackson, "From *Kamma* to Unnatural Vice: Male Homosexuality and Transgenderism in the Thai Buddhist Tradition," in *Queer Dharma: A Buddhist Gay Anthology,* ed. Winston Leyland (San Francisco: Gay Sunshine Press, 1997.

45. *Nation Weekly,* 4–10 June 1993, p. 13.

## APPENDIX

1. Siddhattha Gotama is the Pali spelling of the Buddha's name. In Sanskrit it is written Siddhartha Gautama.

2. Thai Buddhists date the Buddha's death at 543 B.C., the year from which the Thai calendar is reckoned. Other Buddhist traditions and many contemporary scholars, however, place his death as late as 480 B.C.

3. Literally Theravada means "doctrine of the elders," where "elders" refers to the senior members of the Buddhist monkhood or Sangha.

4. The countries where Theravada Buddhism has traditionally been dominant are all located in South and Southeast Asia, i.e. Sri Lanka, Burma, Thailand, Laos, and Cambodia.

5. Mahayana literally means "the great vehicle" (for the transmission of the Buddha's teachings). Mahayanists call Theravada Buddhism Hinayana, "the lesser vehicle," a term Theravadins regard as derogatory.

6. The countries where Mahayan Buddhism is dominant are in the main located in North and Northeast Asia.

7. Sunthorn, *Buddhist Concept of Karma,* v–vi.

8. *Pali English Dictionary*, 336.

9. Sunthorn, *Buddhist Concept of Karma,* 49.

10. Terwiel, *Religion in Rural Central Thailand*, 310.

11. Ibid.

12. Spiro, *Buddhism and Society*, 10ff.

13. Terwiel, *Religion in Rural Central Thailand,* 165–166.

14. Thomas A. Kirsch, "Complexity in the Thai Religious System," in *Journal of Asian Studies*, vol. 36, no. 2, February 1977, 259.

15. Ibid.

16. Spiro, *Buddhism and Society*, 10.

17. Barend Jan Terwiel, *Monks and Magic,* 2nd ed., Curzon Press, London, 1979, 22

# BIBLIOGRAPHY OF ENGLISH LANGUAGE TEXTS


A. de S. (no other name given). "Buddhist Monk's Apology for Christianity." Originally published in *World Buddhism* (Ceylon). May 1969 (B.E. 2513). Reprinted in *Buddhadasa: Appearance and Reality, Being a Review of "Christianity and Buddhism" by Venerable Buddhadasa,* edited by Sivlibodhi Bhikkhu, 1–3. Bangkok: Sublime Life Mission, 1971.

Ananda Bhikkhu. *Theravada and Zen.* Colombo, Ceylon: Gunasena & Co., 1962.

Andaya, Barbara Watson. "Statecraft in the Reign of Lu Thai of Sukhodaya." In *Religion and the Legitimisation of Power in Thailand, Laos and Burma,* edited by Bardwell L. Smith, 2–19. Chambersburg, Penn.: Anima Books, 1978.

Anderson, Ben. "Withdrawal Symptoms: Social and Cultural Aspects of the October 6 Coup." *Bulletin of Concerned Asian Scholars* 9, no. 3 (July–Sept. 1977): 13–30.

Ariyananda Bhikkhu. *Psychology and Religious Symbolism—An Interpretation in Terms of Psychology of Some Familiar Allegories from Buddhist, Hindu and Judaic Scriptures.* Bangkok: Sublime Life Mission, n.d.

Bechert, Heinz. "Contradictions in Sinhalese Buddhism." In *Contributions to Asian Studies, Vol. 4, Tradition and Change in Theravada Buddhism: Essays on Ceylon and Thailand in the 19th and 20th Centuries,* edited by Bardwell L. Smith, 7–17. Leiden, The Netherlands: E. J. Brill, 1973.

Blofeld, John, trans. *The Zen Teachings of Huang Po – On the Transmission of Mind, Being the Teaching of the Zen Master Huang Po as Recorded by the Scholar Pei Hsiu of the T'ang Dynasty.* New York: Grove Press, 1958.

Boowa Nyanasampanno, Venerable. *The Venerable Phra Acharn Mun Bhuridatta Thera – Meditation Master.* Trans. Siri Buddhasukh. Udon Thani, Thailand: Wat Pa Barn Tard, 1982.

Bond, George D. "The *Netti-Pakaraṇa*: A Theravada Method of Interpretation." In *Buddhist Studies in Honour of Walpola Rahula,* edited by Somaratna Balasooriya, 16–28. London: Gordon Fraser, 1980.

Boyd, James W. "The Theravada View of *Saṁsāra.*" In *Buddhist Studies in Honour of Walpola Rahula,* edited by Somaratna Balasooriya, 29–43. London: Gordon Fraser, 1980.

Buddhadasa Bhikkhu. *Another Kind of Birth.* Trans. R. B. (no further details given). Bangkok: n.p., 1974.

———. *Buddha-dhamma for Students.* Trans. Ariyananda Bhikkhu. Bangkok: Sublime Life Mission, 1982.

———. *Buddhism in 15 Minutes.* Trans. H. G. Grether. Bangkok: Suriyaban Publishers, n.d.

———. *Christianity and Buddhism – Sinclair Thompson Memorial Lecture, Fifth Series.* No translator given. 2nd ed. Bangkok: Sublime Life Mission, 1977.

———. "Exchanging *Dhamma* While Fighting," in *Visakha Puja* (Bangkok: Buddhist Association of Thailand), 2513 (1970), 33–47.

———. *Handbook for Mankind.* Trans. Buddhanigama. Bangkok: Sublime Life Mission, 1980.

———. *Two Kinds of Language.* Trans. Ariyananda Bhikkhu. Bangkok: n.p., 1974.

Buddhaghosa. *The Path of Purification—Vissuddhimagga.* Translated by Bhikkhu Nanamoli. 4th ed. Kandy, Sri Lanka: Buddhist Publication Society, 1979.

Bunnag, Jane. "The Role of the Buddhist Monk in Central Thai Society." In *Visakha Puja.* (Bangkok: Buddhist Association of Thailand), 2513 (1970), 48–55.

Butt, John W. "Thai Kingship and Religious Reform." In *Religion and the Legitimation of Power in Thailand, Laos and Burma,* edited by Bardwell L. Smith, 34–51. Chambersburg, Penn.: Anima Books, 1978.

Chinda Chandrkaew. *Nibbāna—The Ultimate Truth of Buddhism.* Bangkok: Mahachulalongkorn Buddhist University Press, 1982.

Dhani Nivat Kromamun Bidyalabh, H.H. Prince. *A History of Buddhism in Siam.* Bangkok: Siam Society, 1965 .

Feyerabend, Paul. *Against Method – Outline of an Anarchistic Theory of Knowledge.* London: Verso, 1978.

Gabaude, Louis. "Thai Society and Buddhadasa: Structural Difficulties." In *Radical Conservatism—Buddhism in the Contemporary World, Articles in Honour of Bhikkhu Buddhadasa's 84th Birthday Anniversary,* edited by Sulak Sivaraksa, 211–229. Bangkok: Sathirakoses-Nagapradipa Foundation, 1990.

———, comp. "Bibliography of Buddhadāsa's Translated Works and Bibliography of Studies Concerning Buddhadāsa and Suan Mokh." In *Radical Conservatism—Buddhism in the Contemporary World, Articles in Honour of Bhikkhu Buddhadāsa's 84th Birthday Anniversary,* edited by Sulak

Sivaraksa, 515–547. Bangkok: Sathirakoses-Nagapradipa Foundation, 1990.

Gokhale, Balkrishna Govind. "Anagarika Dharmapala: Toward Modernity Through Tradition in Ceylon." In *Contributions to Asian Studies, Vol. 4, Tradition and Change in Theravada Buddhism: Essays on Ceylon and Thailand in the 19th and 20th Centuries,* edited by Bardwell L. Smith, 30–39. Leiden, The Netherlands: E. J. Brill, 1973.

Gosling, David. "The Scientific and Religious Beliefs of Thai Scientists and Their Inter-Relationships." *Southeast Asian Journal of Social Science* 4, no. 1 (1975): 1–18.

Jackson, Peter A. *Buddhism, Legitimation and Conflict—The Political Functions of Urban Thai Buddhism.* Singapore: Institute of Southeast Asian Studies, 1989.

———. "Reinterpreting the Traiphuum Phra Ruang: Political Functions of Buddhist Symbolism in Contemporary Thailand." In *Buddhist Trends in Southeast Asia,* edited by Trevor Ling, 64–100. Singapore: Institute of Southeast Asian Studies, 1993.

———. "Thai Buddhist Identity: Debates on the Traiphum Phra Ruang." In *National Identity and Its Defenders, Thailand Today,* edited by Craig J. Reynolds, 155–188. Chiang Mai, Thailand: Silkworm Books, 2002.

———. "From *Kamma* to Unnatural Vice: Male Homosexuality and Transgenderism in the Thai Buddhist Tradition." In *Queer Dharma: A Buddhist Gay Anthology,* edited by Winston Leyland. San Francisco: Gay Sunshine Press, 1997.

Jayalilleke, K. N. "Buddhism and the Scientific Revolution." In *Buddhism and Science – Collected Essays* (no editor given), 1–11. Kandy, Sri Lanka: Buddhist Publication Society, 1980.

Jayawardene, Julius R. *Buddhism and Marxism.* Pamphlet of the text of the Tenth Anniversary Lecture to the Ceylon University Buddhist Brotherhood, Colombo, Ceylon, 6 March 1950.

Keyes, Charles F. "The Power of Merit," in *Visakha Puja* (Bangkok: Buddhist Society of Thailand), 2516 (1973), 95–102.

Kirsch, A. Thomas. "Complexity in the Thai Religious System: An Interpretation." *Journal of Asian Studies* 36, no. 2 (February, 1977): 241–266.

———. "Modernising Implications of Nineteenth Century Reforms in the Thai Sangha." In *Religion and the Legitimation of Power in Thailand, Laos and Burma,* edited by Bardwell L. Smith, 52–65. Chambersburg, Penn.: Anima Books, 1978.

Ling, Trevor. *The Buddha – Buddhist Civilisation in India and Ceylon.* London: Temple Smith, 1973.

———. *Buddhism, Imperialism and War – Burma and Thailand in Modern History.* London: George Allen & Unwin Ltd., 1979.

Lyotard, Jean-François. *The Postmodern Condition* (1979), trans. Geoff Bennington & Brian Massumi. Manchester: Manchester University Press, 1984.

Morell, David and Chai–anan Samudavanija. *Political Conflict in Thailand—Reform, Reaction and Revolution*. Cambridge, Mass.: Oelgeschlager Gunn & Hain, 1981.

Morgan, F. Bruce. "Vocation of Monk and Layman: Signs of Change in Thai Buddhist Ethics." In *Contributions to Asian Studies, Vol. 4, Tradition and Change in Theravada Buddhism: Essays on Ceylon and Thailand in the 19th and 20th Centuries,* edited by Bardwell L. Smith, 68–77. Leiden, The Netherlands: E. J. Brill, 1973.

Morris, Rosalind. "Three Sexes and Four Sexualities: Redressing the Discourses on Gender and Sexuality in Thailand." *Positions* 2 (1) 1994: 15–43.

Mulder, Niels. "Buddhism, National Identity and Modernity in Contemporary Thailand." *Journal of Social Sciences – Chiangmai University* (Thailand) 2, no. 2 (September 1978): 34–47.

———. *Everyday Life in Thailand – An Interpretation*. Bangkok: Duang Kamol Publishers, 1979.

Nithinand Yorsaengrat. 1993. "You Are What You Read," *The Nation*, Sunday, 18 July 1993, p. B10.

Nyanatiloka. *Buddhist Dictionary – Manual of Buddhist Terms and Doctrines.* 4th ed. Nyanaponika (rev.), Kandy, Sri Lanka: Buddhist Publication Society, 1980.

Olson, Grant A. 1990. "From Buddhadasa Bhikkhu to *Phra* Debvedi." In *Radical Conservatism—Buddhism in the Contemporary World, Articles in Honour of Bhikkhu Buddhadasa's 84th Birthday Anniversary*, edited by Sulak Sivaraksa, 251–267. Bangkok: Sathirakoses-Nagapradipa Foundation, 1990.

Puey Ungphakorn. "The Role of Ethics and Religion in National Development." Sinclair Thompson Memorial Lectures, Thailand Theological Seminary, Chiang Mai, 1969, in *Visakha Puja* (Bangkok: Buddhist Association of Thailand), 2517 (1974), 115–124.

Rahula, Walpola. *History of Buddhism in Ceylon – The Anuradhapura Period.* Colombo, Ceylon: Gunasena & Co. Ltd., 1966.

Reynolds, Craig J., trans. *Autobiography: The Life of Prince-Patriarch Vajirañāṇa of Siam, 1860–1921*. Athens, Ohio: Ohio University Press, 1979.

Rhys Davids, Mrs. *Compendium of Philosophy – Translation of the Abhidhammatha-Saṅgaha*. London: Pali Text Society, 1972.

Rhys Davids, T. W. & William Stede, eds. *Pali-English Dictionary*. Pali Text Society. London: Luzac & Co. Ltd., 1966.

Rupp, George. "The Relationship Between *Nirvāṇa* and *Saṁsāra*: An Essay on the Evolution of Buddhist Ethics," *Philosophy East and West* 21 (1971): 55–67.

Santikaro Bhikkhu. "Buddhadasa Bhikkhu—A Remembrance." *Crossroads—An Interdisciplinary Journal of Southeast Asian Studies* 8 (1), 1993: 125–130.

Sedgwick, Eve Kosofsky. *Epistemology of the Closet.* Berkeley: University of California Press, 1990.

Siddhi Butr-Indr. *The Social Philosophy of Buddhism.* Bangkok: Mahamakut Buddhist University Press, 1979.

Slater, Robert Lawson. *Paradox and Nibbāna—A Study of Religious Ultimates with Special Reference to Burmese Buddhism.* Chicago: University of Chicago Press, 1951.

Smith, Bardwell L., ed. *Contributions to Asian Studies, Vol. 4, Tradition and Change in Theravada Buddhism: Essays on Ceylon and Thailand in the 19th and 20th Centuries.* Leiden, The Netherlands: E. J. Brill, 1973.

———, ed. *Religion and the Legitimation of Power in Thailand, Laos and Burma.* Chambersburg, Penn.: Anima Books, 1978.

Soma Thera. *Words Leading to Disenchantment.* Kandy, Sri Lanka: Buddhist Publication Society, 1978.

Somboon Suksamran. *Buddhism and Politics in Thailand – A Study of Socio-Political Change and Political Activism in the Thai Sangha.* Singapore: Institute of South East Asian Studies, 1982.

———. *Political Buddhism in South East Asia – The Role of the Sangha in the Modernisation of Thailand.* London: C. Hurst & Co., 1977.

Spencer, Robert F. "The Relation of Buddhism to Modern Science," in *Buddhism and Science – Collected Essays* (no editor given), 12–16. Kandy, Sri Lanka: Buddhist Publication Society, 1980.

Spiro, Melford E. *Buddhism and Society – A Great Tradition and its Burmese Vicissitudes.* London: George Allen & Unwin Ltd., 1975.

Staal, Frits. *Exploring Mysticism.* London: Penguin Books, 1975.

Sulak Sivaraksa, ed. *Radical Conservatism—Buddhism in the Contemporary World, Articles in Honour of Bhikkhu Buddhadasa's 84th Birthday Anniversary.* Bangkok: Sathirakoses-Nagapradipa Foundation, 1990.

Sunthorn Na–Rangsi. *The Buddhist Concept of Karma and Rebirth.* Bangkok: Mahamakut Rajavidyalaya Press, 1976.

Suwanna Satha-Anand. Review of "Buddhism, Legitimation and Conflict: The Political Functions of Urban Thai Buddhism." *Crossroads—An Interdisciplinary Journal of Southeast Asian Studies* 5 (1) 1990: 105–108.

Suzuki, Daisetz Teitaro. *Zen and Japanese Buddhism.* Tokyo: Japan Travel Bureau, 1958.

———. *The Zen Doctrine of No-Mind – The Significance of the Sutra of Hui-Neng (Wei-Lang).* London: Rider & Co., 1949.

Swearer, Donald K. *Bhikkhu Buddhadasa and the Buddhist Reformation in Thailand.* Pamphlet published by the Ecumenical Institute for Study and Dialogue, Colombo, Sri Lanka. N.p. (c. 1982).

———. "Some Observations on New Directions in Thai Buddhism" *Visakha Puja* (Bangkok: Buddhist Association of Thailand), 2513 (1970), 56–58.

———. "Sulak Sivaraksa's Buddhist Vision for Renewing Society." *Crossroads—An Interdisciplinary Journal of Southeast Asian Studies* 6 (2) 1991: 17–57.

Tambiah, Stanley J. *Buddhism and Spirit Cults in North-East Thailand.* Cambridge: Cambridge University Press, 1970.

———. *World Conqueror and World Renouncer—A Study of Buddhism and Polity in Thailand Against a Historical Background.* Cambridge: Cambridge University Press, 1976.

Taylor, Jim. *Forest Monks and the Nation-State, An Anthropological and Historical Study in Northeastern Thailand.* Singapore: Institute of Southeast Asian Studies, 1993.

———. "Social Activism and Resistance on the Thai Frontier: The Case of *Phra* Prajak Khuttajitto." *Bulletin of Concerned Asian Scholars* 25 (2) 1993: 3–16.

Terwiel, Barend Jan. *Monks and Magic – An Analysis of Religious Ceremonies in Central Thailand.* 2nd ed. London: Curzon Press, 1979.

———. "Religion in Rural Central Thailand—An Analysis of Some Ritual and Beliefs." Ph.D. dissertation, Australian National University, Canberra, 1971.

Thich Nhat Hanh. *The Miracle of Being Awake – A Manual on Meditation for the Use of Young Activists.* Trans. Mobi Quynh Hoa, ed. Jim Forest. Bangkok: Sathirakoses–Nagapradipa Foundation, 2517 (1974).

Van Esterik, John Laurier. "Cultural Interpretation of Canonical Paradox—Lay Meditation in a Central Thai Village." Ph. D. dissertation, University of Illinois at Champaign-Urbana. Ann Arbor, Michigan: University Microfilms International, 1977.

Vandergeest, Peter. "Hierarchy and Power in Pre-National Buddhist States." *Modern Asian Studies* 27 (4) 1993: 843–870.

Wang Mou-lam, trans. *The Sutra of Wei Lang (or Hui Neng).* Ed. Christmas Humphries. Westport, Conn.: n.p., 1973.

Weerarame, Amarasiri. "Monk's Interpretation of Christianity." In *World Buddhism* (Ceylon), September 1969 (B.E. 2513). Reprinted in *Buddhadasa: Appearance and Reality, Being a Review of "Christianity and Buddhism" by Venerable Buddhadasa,* ed. Sivlibodhi Bhikkhu, 31–37. Bangkok: Sublime Life Mission, 1971.

Weeraratne, W. G. *Individual and Society in Buddhism.* Colombo, Sri Lanka: Metro Printers. Ltd., 1977.

Wells, Kenneth E. *Thai Buddhism, Its Rites and Activities.* Bangkok: Suriyaban Publishers, 1975.

Wilson, David. *Politics in Thailand.* Ithaca, New York: Cornell University Press, 1962.

Wit, Daniel. *Thailand – Another Vietnam?* New York: Charles Scribner's Sons, 1968.

# BIBLIOGRAPHY OF THAI LANGUAGE TEXTS

ARRANGED IN THAI ALPHABETICAL ORDER.

## 1. Classical Buddhist Texts and Dictionaries

*พระไตรปิฎกภาษาไทยฉบับหลวง* กรมการศาสนา กระทรวงศึกษาธิการ, กรุงเทพฯ, พ.ศ. 2525
*Phra Traipidok phasa thai chabap luang*. (The official Thai language edition of the *Tipiṭaka*). Department of Religious Affairs, Ministry of Education. 45 vols. Bangkok, 1982.

## 2. Other Texts

กิตฺติวุฑฺโฒ ภิกขุ. "เรื่องจิตว่างนอกพระไตรปิฎก มีความสำคัญในปัจจุบันมาก และเรื่องพระพุทธเจ้าสอนโลกุตตรธรรมนายธรรมทินนะขอเปลี่ยนธรรมใหม่" ใน *อะไรถูก อะไรผิด*, ปุ่น จงประเสริฐ (บก.). 126-130. สมุทรปราการ: องค์การฟื้นฟูพระพุทธศาสนา, พ.ศ. 2525.
Kittiwuttho Phikkhu. "Rueang chit-wang nok phra traipidok mi khwam samkhan nai patchuban mak lae rueang phra phutthachao son lokuttaratham nai thammathinna kho plian thamma mai" ("Concerning *chit-wang* as being outside the [teachings contained in the] *Tipiṭaka*—which has great contemporary importance; and concerning the Buddha's teachings on *lokuttaradhamma* and Dhammadinna's request for that Dhamma to be changed."). From a handbill reprinted in *Arai thuk arai phit* (What is correct and what is wrong), ed. Pun Chongprasoet, 126–130. Samut Prakan: Ongkan Fuenfu Phra Phutthasatsana, 1982.

คณะกรรมการศาสนาเพื่อการพัฒนา (รวบรวม). "ท่านพุทธทาสในทัศนะของนักวิชาการ" มูลนิธิโกมล คีมทอง, กรุงเทพฯ, พ.ศ. 2525.

Khana Kammakan Satsana Phuea Kan Phatthana. (Compiled by The Religious Committee for Development, no individual editor given). *Than Phutthathat nai thatsana khong nak wichakan* (Academics' views on Buddhadāsa). Bangkok: Komon Khimthong Foundation, 1982.

คณะกรรมการศาสนาเพื่อการพัฒนา (รวบรวม). *พุทธทาสกับคนรุ่นใหม่ - เมื่อคนหนุ่มสาวถามถึงรากของความเป็นไทย*, กรุงเทพฯ: มูลนิธิโกมลคีมทอง, พ.ศ. 2526.

Khana Kammakan Satsana Phuea Kan Phatthana. (Compiled by The Religious Committee for Development, no individual editor given). *Phutthathat kap khon run mai – muea khon num sao tham thueng rak khong khwam pen thai* (Buddhadāsa and the new generation – when youth ask about the roots of Thainess). Bangkok: Komon Khimthong Fondation, 1983.

คึกฤทธิ์ ปราโมช, ม.ร.ว. "ความเห็นบางตอนของ ม.ร.ว. คึกฤทธิ์ ปราโมช" ใน *อะไรถูก อะไรผิด*, ปุ่น จงประเสริฐ (บก.). 1-8, สมุทรปราการ: องค์การฟื้นฟูพระพุทธศาสนา,

Kukrit Pramoj, M.R. "Khwam-hen bang ton khong M.R.W. Khukrit Pramot" (Some views of M.R. Kukrit Pramoj). In *Arai thuk arai phit* (What is correct and what is wrong), ed. Pun Chongprasoet, 1–8. Samut Prakan: Ongkan Fuenfu Phra Phutthasatsana. 1982.

ชาวอโศก. *ความล้มเหลวของเศรษฐศาสตร์สมัยใหม่ เพราะไม่สนใจเศรษฐศาสตร์เชิงพุทธ*, กรุงเทพฯ: มูลนิธิธรรมสันติ (พุทธสถาน สันติอโศก), พ.ศ. 2525.

Chao Asok, trans. (nom de plume, lit. "The People of Asok", i.e. the residents of Phothirak's temple complex of Santi-Asok in Bangkok, no individual, translator given). *Khwam lomleo khong setthasat samai mai phro mai sonchai setthasat choeng phut* (The collapse of modern economics because of the lack of interest in Buddhist economics). A partial translation of E. F. Schumacher's *Small is Beautiful*. Bangkok: Thammasanti Foundation (Phutthasathan Santi-Asok), 1982.

โชคชัย สุทธาเวศ. "พุทธทาสกับการปฏิรูป ความมีเหตุผลของคนไทย", *เนชั่นสุดสัปดาห์* 2(65), 3-9 กันยายน พ.ศ. 2536, หน้า 34-35.

Chokechai Sutthawet. "Phutthathat kap kan patirup khwam mi het mi phon khong khon thai "(Buddhadāsa and the reform of the rationality of the Thai people). *Nation Weekly*, (2)65, 3–9 September 1993, 34–35.

ชิต ภิบาลแทน. *ชีวิตและงานของพุทธทาสภิกขุ.* กรุงเทพฯ: ศิลปาบรรณาการ, พ.ศ. 2520.

Chit Phibanthaen. *Chiwit lae ngan khong Phutthathat phikkhu* (The life and work of Buddhadāsa Bhikkhu). Bangkok: Sinlapabanakan, 1977.

ดุษฎี อังสุเมธางกูร. "ท่านพุทธทาสกับการปฏิรูปศาสนา" ใน *พุทธทาสกับคนรุ่นใหม่ - เมื่อคนหนุ่มสาวถามถึงรากของความเป็นไทย,* กรุงเทพฯ: มูลนิธิโกมลคีมทอง, พ.ศ. 2526.

Dusadi Angsumethangkun. "Than Phutthathat kap kan patirup satsana" ("Buddhadāsa and religious reform"). In *Phutthathat kap khon run mai – mua khon num sao tham thung rak khong khwam pen thai* (Buddhadāsa and the new generation – when youth ask about the roots of Thainess), comp. Khana Kammakan Satsana Phuea Kan Phatthana. 242–270. Bangkok: Komon Khimthong Foundation, 1983.

เดช ตุลวรรธนะ, พลตรี. *เรียนพุทธศาสนาอย่างปัญญาชน เล่ม 1, หลัก 8 ประการ ในการศึกษาพุทธศาสนาให้ถึงแก่นแท้,* กรุงเทพฯ: บริษัทไทย ไอ. อี., พ.ศ. 2526.

Det Tunlawatthana, Maj. Gen. *Rian phutthasasana yang panyachon, lem 1, lak 8 prakan nai kan sueksa phutthasatsana hai thueng kaen thae* (Study Buddhism like an intellectual, book 1, Eight principles in studying Buddhism so as to reach the core [teachings]). Bangkok: Borisat Thai I. E., 1983.

บุญมี เมธางกูร. *โต้ท่านพุทธทาสเรื่องจิตว่าง เล่ม 1.* กรุงเทพฯ: องค์การพิทักษ์พุทธศาสนา อภิธรรมมูลนิธิ, พ.ศ. 2522.

Bunmi Methangkun. *To than Phutthathat rueang chit wang, lem I* (Criticisms of Buddhadāsa on the matter of *chit wang*, book 1). Bangkok: Ongkan Phithak Phutthasatsana, Aphitham Foundation, 1979.

_______. *โต้ท่านพุทธทาสเรื่องอวิชชาและผีสางเทวดา เล่ม 2.* กรุงเทพฯ: องค์การพิทักษ์พุทธศาสนา อธิธรรมมูลนิธิ, พ.ศ. 2523.

*To than Phutthathat rueang avitcha lae phi-sang thewada, lem 2* (Criticisms of Buddhadāsa on the matter of spirits and celestial beings, book 2). Bangkok: Ongkan Phithak Phutthasatsana, Aphitham Foundation, 1980.

_______. พ.ศ. 2522. "ภิกษุผู้ทำลายพุทธศาสนา" ใน *คำสอนเดียรถีย์,* อนันต์ เสนาขันธ์ (บก.). กรุงเทพฯ: องค์การพิทักษ์พุทธศาสนา อภิธรรมมูลนิธิ

1979. "Phiksu phu thamlai phutthasatsana" ("The monk who is destroying Buddhism"). In *Khamson diarathi* (Heretical teachings), ed. Anan Senakhan, 90–100. Bangkok: Ongkan Phithak Phutthasasana Aphitham Foundation.

ประชา ปสนฺนธมฺโม, พระ. *ปาฏิหาริย์แห่งการตื่นอยู่เสมอ - คู่มือสำหรับคนหนุ่มสาวที่ปฏิบัติการในสังคม.* พิมพ์ครั้งที่ 6. กรุงเทพฯ: มูลนิธิโกมลคีมทอง, พ.ศ. 2526.

Pracha Pasannathammo, Phra, trans. *Patihan haeng kan tuen yu samoe: Khumue samrap khon num sao thi patibatkan nai sangkhom* (The miracle of perpetual wakefulness – a handbook for the practice of *samādhi* for youth who are active in society). (Translation into Thai of Thich Nhat Hanh, *The Miracle of Being Awake – A Manual on Meditation for the Use of Young Activists*, trans. Mobi Quynh Hoa, ed. Jim Forest. Bangkok: Sathirakoses-Nagapradipa Foundation, (2517) 1974.). 6th printing. Bangkok: Komon Khimthong Foundation, 1983.

_______. *เล่าไว้เมื่อวัยสนธยา อัตชีวประวัติของท่านพุทธทาส.* กรุงเทพฯ: มูลนิธิโกมลคีมทอง, พ.ศ. 2525.

_______. *Lao wai mue wai sonthaya – Atta-chiwaprawat Khong Than Phutthathat* (Reflections from the twilight years—autobiography of Buddhadāsa). Bangkok: Komon Khimthong Foundation, 1985.

_______. *สี่นักคิดร่วมสมัย - ในคลื่นความคิดอันสับสน,* กรุงเทพฯ: สำนักพิมพ์เทียนวรรณ, พ.ศ. 2526.

_______. *Si nakkhit ruamsamai nai khluen khwam khit an sapson* (Four contemporary thinkers—amidst the waves of confused thought). Bangkok: Samnakphim Thianwan, 1983.

ปุ่น จงประเสริฐ (บก.) *ตำราดูภิกษุ พุทธพจน์บางเรื่องอันเกี่ยวกับประพฤติของภิกษุซึ่งพุทธบริษัทควรรู้และเผยแพร่ เพื่อส่งเสริมการปฏิบัติธรรมให้สัมฤทธ์ผล.* กรุงเทพฯ: สำนักหนังสือธรรมบูชา, พ.ศ. 2525.

Pun Chongprasoet, ed. *Tamra du phiksu – Phutthaphot bang rueang an kieo kap praphruet khong phiksu sueng phutthaborisat khuan ru lae phoei phrae phuea songsoem patibat tham hai samritphon* (A textbook for observing monks—comments of the Buddha concerning the behaviour of monks, which Buddhists should know and propagate for promoting the successful practice of the Dhamma). Bangkok: Samnaknangsue Thammabucha, 1982.

———. (บก.) *วิวาทะระหว่าง ม.ร.ว.คึกฤทธิ์ ปราโมช กับ ท่านพุทธทาสภิกขุ ในเรื่องจิตว่าง.* สมุทรปราการ: องค์การฟื้นฟูพระพุทธศาสนา, พ.ศ. 2518.

———, ed. *Wiwatha rawang M.R. Kukrit Pramoj kap than Phutthathat phikkhu nai rueang chit wang* (A debate between M.R. Kukrit Pramoj and the reverend Buddhadāsa Bhikkhu on the matter of *chit wang*). Samut Prakan: Ongkan Fuenfu Phra Phutthasatsana, 1975.

———. (บก.) *อะไรถูก อะไรผิด*. สมุทรปราการ: องค์การฟื้นฟูพระพุทธศาสนา, พ.ศ. 2525.
———, ed. *Arai thuk arai phit* (What is correct and what is wrong). Samut Prakan: Ongkan Fuenfu Phra Phutthasatsana, 1982.

พุทธทาสภิกขุ. *การงานคือตัวความก้าวหน้า*. กรุงเทพฯ: สำนักหนังสือธรรมบูชา, พ.ศ. 2521.
Phutthathat Phikkhu. *Kan ngan khue tua khwam kao na* (Working is progress itself). Bangkok: Samnaknangsue Thammabucha, 1978.

———. *ความสุขแท้มีอยู่แต่ในงาน*. กรุงเทพฯ: สำนักหนังสือธรรมบูชา, พ.ศ. 2521.
———. *Khwam suk thae mi yu tae nai ngan* (True happiness exists only in work). Bangkok: Samnaknangsue Thammabucha, 1978.

———. *คำสอนฮวงโป*. กรุงเทพฯ: สำนักหนังสือธรรมบูชา, พ.ศ. 2520.
———, trans. *Khamson khong Huang Po* (The teachings of Huang Po). (Translation into Thai of John Blofeld, *The Zen Teachings of Huang Po—On the Transmission of Mind*. New York: Grove Press, 1958.). Bangkok: Samnaknangsue Thammabucha, 1977.

———. *คำสอนผู้บวช ภาค 1*. กรุงเทพฯ: สำนักหนังสือธรรมบูชา, พ.ศ. 2524.
———. *Khamson phu buat phak I* (Teachings for the ordained, part 1). Bangkok: Samnaknangsue Thammabucha, 1981.

———. *ฆราวาสธรรม*. กรุงเทพฯ: สำนักหนังสือธรรมบูชา, พ.ศ. 2525.
———. *Kharawat tham* (The layperson's Dhamma). Bangkok: Samnaknangsue Thammabucha, 1982.

———. จิตประภัสสร - จิตเดิมแท้ - จิตว่าง *เหมือนกันหรืออย่างไร?* กรุงเทพฯ: สำนักหนังสือธรรมบูชา, พ.ศ. 2517.
———. *Chit praphatson, chit doem thae, chit wang: Muean kan rue yang rai?* (*Prabhassara*-mind – original-true-mind – freed mind: are they the same?). Bangkok: Samnaknangsue Thammabucha, 1974.

———. *จุดหมายของการศึกษา*. กรุงเทพฯ: สำนักหนังสือธรรมบูชา, พ.ศ. 2522.
———. *Chutmai khong kan sueksa* (The goals of education). Bangkok: Samnaknangsue Thammabucha, 1979.

———. *ชาวพุทธที่ดีย่อมเป็นคริสต์ที่ดี* . กรุงเทพฯ: สำนักหนังสือธรรมบูชา, พ.ศ. 2523.
———. *Chao phut thi di yom pen khrit thi di* (A good Buddhist is naturally a good Christian). Bangkok: Samnaknangsue Thammabucha, 1980.

———. *ดวงตาที่เห็นธรรม.* กรุงเทพฯ: สำนักหนังสือธรรมบูชา, พ.ศ. 2511.

———. *Duangta thi hen tham* (The eye that sees Dhamma). Bangkok: Samnaknangsue Thammabucha, 1968.

———. *เตกิจจกรรม.* ไชยา: ธรรมทานมูลนิธิ, พ.ศ. 2519.

———. *Tekitchaka* (*Tekiccakamma*). Chaiya: Thammathan Foundation, 1976.

———. *แถลงการณ์สวนโมกข์ 50 ปี และกฎบัตรพุทธบริษัท.* กรุงเทพฯ: สำนักพิมพ์สุขภาพใจ, พ.ศ. 2525.

———. *Thalaengkan Suan Mok 50 pi lae kotbat phutthaborisat* (Communique on the fiftieth anniversary of Suan Mokh and Buddhist Charter). Bangkok: Samnakphim Sukkhaphap Chai, 1982.

———. *ธรรมะกับการเมือง.* ไชยา: ธรรมทานมูลนิธิ, พ.ศ. 2522.

———. *Thamma kap kanmueang* (Dhamma and politics). Chaiya: Thammathan Foundation, 1979.

———. *ธรรมะกับโลกจะไปด้วยกันได้หรือไม่?* กรุงเทพฯ: สำนักหนังสือธรรมบูชา, พ.ศ. 2521.

———. *Thamma kap lok cha pai duai kan dai rue mai?* (Can Dhamma and the world get along together?). Bangkok: Samnaknangsue Thammabucha, 1978.

———. *ธรรมะในฐานะลัทธิการเมือง.* กรุงเทพฯ: สำนักหนังสือธรรมบูชา, พ.ศ. 2521.

———. *Thamma nai thana latthi kanmueang* (Dhamma as a political ideology). Bangkok: Samnaknangsue Thammabucha, 1978.

———. *ธรรมปราบผีในตัวข้าราชการและนักการเมือง.* สมุทรปราการ: องค์การฟื้นฟูพระพุทธศาสนา.

———. *Thamma prap phi nai tua kharatchakan lae nak kanmueang* (Dhamma eradicates ghosts in public servants and politicians). Samut Prakan: Ongkan Fuenfu Phra Phutthasatsana, n.d.

———. *ธัมมิกสังคมนิยมแบบเผด็จการหรือสังคมนิยมตามหลักแห่งศาสนาทุกศาสนา.* กรุงเทพฯ: สำนักหนังสือธรรมบูชา, พ.ศ. 2517.

———. *Thammik sangkhomniyom baep phadetkan rue sangkhomniyom tam lak haeng satsana thuk satsana* (A dictatorial style of *dhammic* socialism, or socialism in accord with the principles of every religion). Bangkok: Samnaknangsue Thammabucha, 1974.

———. *นิพพาน*. กรุงเทพฯ: สำนักหนังสือธรรมบูชา, พ.ศ. 2524.
———. *Nipphan* (*Nibbāna*). Bangkok: Samnaknangsue Thammabucha, 1981.

———. *นิพพานนอกคัมภีร์อภิธรรม*. สมุทรปราการ: องค์การฟื้นฟูพระพุทธศาสนา.
———. *Nipphan nok khamphi Aphitham* (*Nibbāna* outside of the *Abhidhamma* scriptures). Samut Prakan: Ongkan Fuenfu Phra Phutthasatsana, n.d.

———. *นิพพานพ้นสมัยไปแล้วหรือ*. สมุทรปราการ: องค์การฟื้นฟูพระพุทธศาสนา, พ.ศ. 2508.
———. *Nipphan phon samai pai rue* (Is *nibbāna* old fashioned?). Samut Prakan: Ongkan Fuenfu Phra Phutthasatsana, 1965.

———. *ในวัฏฏสงสารมีนิพพาน*. กรุงเทพฯ: สำนักหนังสือธรรมบูชา, พ.ศ. 2524.
———. *Nai wattasongsan mi nipphan* (In *vattsaṁsara* there is *nibbāna*). Bangkok: Samnaknangsue Thammabucha, 1981.

———. *บรมธรรม*. กรุงเทพฯ: สำนักพิมพ์สุขภาพใจ, พ.ศ. 2525.
———. *Barom tham* (*Paramadhamma*). Bangkok: Samnakphim Sukhaphap Chai, 1982.

———. *บ้าบุญ--บ้าสวรรค์*. สมุทรปราการ: องค์การฟื้นฟูพระพุทธศาสนา, พ.ศ. 2518.
———. *Ba Bun – Ba Sawan* (*Mad over merit – mad over heaven*). Samut Prakan: Ongkan Fuenfu Phra Phutthasatsana, 1975.

———. *ปฏิจจสมุปบาทจากพระโอษฐ์*. ไชยา: ธรรมทานมูลนิธิ, พ.ศ. 2524.
———. *Patitcasamupapat chak phra ot* (*Paṭiccasamuppāda* in the Buddha's words). Chaiya: Thammathan Foundation, 1981.

———. *ผีมีจริงหรือไม่*. สมุทรปราการ: องค์การฟื้นฟูพระพุทธศาสนา, พ.ศ. 2522.
———. *Phi mi ching rue mai* (Are ghosts real?). Samut Prakan: Ongkan Fuenfu Phra Phutthasatsana, 1979.

———. *ฟ้าสางทางประชาธิปไตย*. กรุงเทพฯ: สำนักหนังสือธรรมบูชา, พ.ศ. 2528.
———. *Fasang thang prachathipatai* (Democratic dawning). Bangkok: Samnaknangsue Thammabucha, 1985.

———. *เมื่อธรรมครองโลก*. ไชยา: ธรรมทานมูลนิธิ, พ.ศ. 2522.
———. *Muea tham khrong lok* (When Dhamma rules the world). Chaiya: Thammathan Foundation, 1979.

———. *ไม่เข้าใจศาสนาเพราะไม่รู้ภาษาธรรม.* สมุทรปราการ: องค์การฟื้นฟูพระพุทธศาสนา.

———. *Mai khaochai satsana phro mai ru phasa tham* (Not understanding religion because of not understanding *phasa tham*). Samut Prakan: Ongkan Fuenfu Phra Phutthasatsana, n.d.

———. พ.ศ. 2517. *ไม่มีศาสนา.* กรุงเทพฯ: สำนักหนังสือธรรมบูชา.

———. *Mai mi satsana* (There is no religion). Bangkok: Samnaknangsue Thammabucha, 1974.

———. *วิธีฝึกสมาธิวิปัสสนา - เล่ม 1.* กรุงเทพฯ: สำนักพิมพ์พุทธศาส์น

———. *Withi fuek samathi-wipatsana, lem I* (The method of practising *samādhi-vipassanā,* Book 1). Bangkok: Samnakphim Phutthasat, n.d.

———. (trans.) *สูตรของเว่ยหล่าง.* กรุงเทพฯ: สำนักหนังสือธรรมบูชา, พ.ศ. 2520.

———, trans. *Sut khong Wei Lang* (The *sutra* of Wei-lang). (Translation into Thai of Wang Mou-lam, trans. *The Sutra of Wei Lang* (or Hui Neng). Ed. Christmas Humphries. Westport, Conn.: n.p., 1973.) Bangkok: Samnaknangsue Thammabucha, 1977.

———. *หากคอมมูนิสต์เข้ามาพุทธศาสนาก็ยังอยู่ได้.* สมุทรปราการ: องค์การฟื้นฟูพระพุทธศาสนา, พ.ศ. 2517.

———. *Hak khomunit khao ma phutthasasana ko yang yu dai* (If Communism comes Buddhism can still survive). Samut Prakan: Ongkan Fuenfu Phra Phutthasatsana, 1974.

———. "อุปสรรคแห่งการเผยแพร่ธรรม" ใน *อะไรถูก อะไรผิด,* ปุ่น จงประเสริฐ (บก.), 8-71, สมุทรปราการ: องค์การฟื้นฟูพระพุทธศาสนา, พ.ศ. 2525.

———. "Upasak haeng kan phoei phrae tham" (Obstacles to propagating Dhamma). In *Arai thuk arai phit* (What is correct and what is wrong), ed. Pun Chongprasoet, 8–71. Samut Prakan: Ongkan Fuenfu Phra Phutthasatsana, 1982.

———. *อภิธรรมคืออะไร.* กรุงเทพฯ: สำนักหนังสือธรรมบูชา, พ.ศ. 2517.

———. *Aphitham khue arai* (What is *Abhidhamma*?). Bangkok: Samnaknangsue Thammabucha, 1974.

———. *โอสาเรตัพพธรรม.* ไชยา: ธรรมทานมูลนิธิ, พ.ศ. 2525.

———. *Osaretapphatham* (*Osaretabbadhamma*). Chaiya: Thammathan Foundation, 1982.

ราชนันทมุนี, พระ. *พุทธทาสคือใคร--ท่านทำอย่างไร.* นนทบุรี: โรงเรียนพุทธธรรม วัดชลประทานรังสฤษฎ์, พ.ศ. 2525.

Ratchananthamuni, *Phra. Phutthathat Khue Khrai – Than Tham Arai* (Who is Buddhadāsa? What has he done?). Nonthaburi: Rongrian Phutthatham, Wat Chonprathan Rangsarit, 1982.

ราชวรมุนี, พระ. *พจนานุกรมพุทธศาสตร์.* กรุงเทพฯ: กรมการศาสนา กระทรวงศึกษาธิการ, พ.ศ. 2519.

Ratchaworamuni, Phra. *Photcananukrom Phutthasat* (A dictionary of Buddhism). Bangkok: Department of Religious Affairs, Ministry of Education, 1976.

———. *พุทธธรรม - มัชเฌนธรรมเทศนา / มัชฌิมาปฏิปทา หรือกฎธรรมชาติและคุณค่าสำหรับชีวิต.* กรุงเทพฯ: ธรรมสถาน จุฬาลงกรณ์มหาวิทยาลัย, พ.ศ. 2525.

———. *Phutthatham Matchenathammathesana Rue Kot Thammachat Lae Khunkha Samrap Chiwit* (Buddha-dhamma – *majjhenadhammadesanā/ majjhimapaṭipadā* or the laws of nature and their value for life). Bangkok: Thammasathan, Chulalongkorn University, 1982.

———. *พุทธศาสนากับสังคมไทย.* กรุงเทพฯ: มูลนิธิโกมลคีมทอง, พ.ศ. 2526.

———. *Phutthasatsana Kap Sangkhom Thai* (Buddhism and Thai society). Bangkok: Komon Khimthong Foundation, 1983.

วนปรัสต์. "อยู่กับหลวงปู่ ตอน 4 : ปริศนาการดับขันท์ของหลวงปู่พุทธทาสและวันเผาศพ", *มหัศจรรย์* 18(886), 6 เมษายน พ.ศ. 2537.

Wanaprat (Pali: Vanapsasta) (Pseud.). "Yu Kap Luang Pu Ton 4, Pritsana Kan dap Khan Khong Luang Pu Phutthathat Lae Wan phao Sop" (Being with the reverend father, the mystery of the Reverend Father Buddhadāsa's death and cremation day), *Mahatsachan* 18(886), 6 April 1994.

วินัย ศิวกุล. *จิตใจคืออะไร.* กรุงเทพฯ: อภิธรรมมูลนิธิ, พ.ศ. 2525.

Winai Siwakun. *Chit-chai Khu Arai* (What is the mind?). Bangkok: Aphitham Foundation, 1982.

———. "ภาษาพุทธทาส" ใน *คำสอนเดียรถีย์.* อนันต์ เสนาขันธ์ (บก.) 101-122. กรุงเทพฯ: องค์การพิทักษ์พุทธศาสนา อภิธรรมมูลนิธิ, พ.ศ. 2522.

———. "Phasa Phutthathat" (Buddhadāsa's Language). in *Khamson Diarathi* (Heretical teachings), Anan Senakhan (ed.). 101–122. Bangkok: Ongkan Phithak Phutthasasana Aphitham Foundation, 1979.

วิศิษฐ์ วังวิญญู. "ท่านพุทธทาสกับเศรษฐศาสตร์ชาวพุทธ" ใน *พุทธทาสกับคนรุ่นใหม่ - เมื่อคนหนุ่มสาวถามถึงรากของความเป็นไทย*, 28-53. กรุงเทพฯ: มูลนิธิโกมลคีมทอง, พ.ศ. 2526.
Wisit Wangwinyu. "Than Phutthathat kap setthasat chao phut" (Buddhadāsa and Buddhist economics). In *Phutthathat kap khon run mai – muea khon num sao tham thung rak khong khwam pen thai* (Buddhadāsa and the new generation – when youth ask about the roots of Thainess), comp. Khana Kammakan Satsana Phuea Kan Phatthana, 28–53. Bangkok: Komon Khimthong Foundation, 1983.

สุลักษณ์ ศิวรักษ์. *คันฉ่องส่องพระ*. กรุงเทพฯ: สำนักพิมพ์ลายสือไทย, พ.ศ. 2522.
Sulak Sivaraksa. *Khanchong song phra* (Reflections on the monkhood). Bangkok: Samnakphim Lai-su Thai, 1979.

————. *พุทธทัศนะเพื่อการสร้างสรรค์สังคมใหม่*. กรุงเทพฯ: สำนักพิมพ์เทียนวรรณ, พ.ศ. 2526.
————. *Phutthathatsana phuea kan sangsan sangkhom mai* (A Buddhist vision for renewing society). Bangkok: Samnakphim Thianwan, 1983.

สุชีพ ปุญญานุภาพ. *พระไตรปิฎกสำหรับประชาชน*. กรุงเทพฯ: สำนักพิมพ์มหามกุฏราชวิทยาลัย, พ.ศ. 2525.
Suchip Panyanuphap. *Phra Traipidok samrap prachachon* (The *Tipiṭaka* for the common man). Bangkok: Mahamakut Buddhist University Press, 1982.

เสรี พงศ์พิศ. "ธรรมกับการเมือง - ท่านพุทธทาสกับสังคมไทย" ใน *ท่านพุทธทาสในทัศนะของนักวิชาการ*, คณะกรรมการศาสนาเพื่อการพัฒนา (รวบรวม). 33-88. กรุงเทพฯ: มูลนิธิโกมลคีมทอง, พ.ศ. 2525.
Seri Phongphit. "Thamma kap kanmueang: Than Phutthathat kap sangkhom thai" (Dhamma and politics: Buddhadāsa and Thai society). In *Than Phutthathat nai thatsana khong nak wichakan* (Buddhadāsa in the view of academics), comp. Khana Kammakan Satsana Phuea Kan Phatthana, 33–88. Bangkok: Komon Khimthong Foundation, 1982.

อนันต์ เสนาขันธ์ (บก.) *คำสอนเดียรถีย์*. กรุงเทพฯ: องค์การพิทักษ์พุทธศาสนา อภิธรรมมูลนิธิ, พ.ศ. 2522.
Anan Senakhan, ed. *Khamson diarathi* (Heretical teachings). Bangkok: Ongkan Phithak Phutthasatsana Aphitham Foundation, 1979.

———. *โพธิรักษ์ - ศาสดามหาภัย.* กรุงเทพฯ: นิวัฒน์ ศรีสถาพร, พ.ศ. 2525.

———. *Phothirak – Satsada Mahaphai* (Bodhiraksa – the highly dangerous prophet). Bangkok: Niwat Sisathaphon, 1982.

อรุณ เวชสุวรรณ. *สวนโมกข์แดนสงบ.* กรุงเทพฯ: สำนักพิมพ์แพร่พิทยา, พ.ศ. 2524.

Arun Wetsuwan. *Suan Mok daen sa-ngop* (Suan Mokh, the peaceful land). Bangkok: Samnakphim Phrae Phithaya, 1981.

———. (บก) *สวนโมกข์ - เมืองไชยาและพุทธทาสภิกขุ.* กรุงเทพฯ: สำนักพิมพ์แพร่พิทยา, พ.ศ. 2524.

———, ed. *Suan Mok – mueang Chaiya lae Phutthathat phikkhu* (Suan Mokh, Chaiya and Buddhadāsa Bhikkhu). 3rd printing. Bangkok: Samnakphim Phrae Phithaya, 1981.

อารยะ นิกรไทย. "พุทธศาสนาจำเป็นสำหรับคนไทยหรือ" *บางกอกรายวัน,* วันที่ 15 มกราคม 2490, พิมพ์ซ้ำใน *สวนโมกข์ - เมืองไชยาและพุทธทาสภิกขุ.* อรุณ เวชสุวรรณ (บก). กรุงเทพฯ: สำนักพิมพ์แพร่พิทยา, พ.ศ. 2524.

Araya Nikonthai. "Phutthasasana champen samrap khon thai rue" (Is Buddhism necessary for Thais?). *Bangkok Raiwan* (Bangkok Daily), 15 January 1947. Reprinted in Arun Wetsuwan, *Suan Mok – mueang Chaiya lae Phutthathat phikkhu* (Suan Mokh, Chaiya and Buddhadāsa Bhikkhu). 3rd printing. Bangkok: Samnakphim Phrae Phithaya, 1981.

# INDEX